Palgrave Studies in Economic History

Series Editor
Kent Deng, London School of Economics, London, UK

Palgrave Studies in Economic History is designed to illuminate and enrich our understanding of economies and economic phenomena of the past. The series covers a vast range of topics including financial history, labour history, development economics, commercialisation, urbanisation, industrialisation, modernisation, globalisation, and changes in world economic orders.

Jorge Álvarez · Svante Prado
Editors

Scandinavia and South America—A Tale of Two Capitalisms

Essays on Comparative Developments in Trade, Industrialisation and Inequality since 1850

palgrave
macmillan

Editors
Jorge Álvarez
Social Sciences Faculty
University of the Republic
Montevideo, Uruguay

Svante Prado
University of Gothenburg
Gothenburg, Sweden

ISSN 2662-6497 ISSN 2662-6500 (electronic)
Palgrave Studies in Economic History
ISBN 978-3-031-09197-1 ISBN 978-3-031-09198-8 (eBook)
https://doi.org/10.1007/978-3-031-09198-8

This Palgrave Macmillan imprint is published by the registered company Springer Nature Switzerland AG
The registered company address is: Gewerbestrasse 11, 6330 Cham, Switzerland

Acknowledgements

This book is the outcome of two projects on comparative development in a historical perspective examining divergence between South America and Scandinavia. The first of these projects was called "Industrialization in the resource-rich periphery: A comparative study of Scandinavia, Australasia and Pampas, 1870–1950". It received financial support from the Swedish Research Council (Vetenskapsrådet). The funding allowed a great deal of exchange between Gothenburg and Montevideo. In this regard, Jorge Álvarez thanks Jan Bohlin and Luis Bértola for their confidence, support and stimulating exchange as project partners, and Gastón Díaz Steinberg for his efficient collaboration at different stages of the project. He also thank the Unit for Economic History at the Department of Economy and Society, University of Gothenburg, for the short research visit he made there in 2017, as well as the Department of Economic History, Institutions and Policy and World Economy of Universitat de Barcelona for the visit he made there in 2018. Jorge would like to acknowledge Alfonso Herranz Loncán and his colleagues for their kindness and hospitality. Furthermore, he would like to thank the Social and Economic History Programme, Social Sciences Faculty, the Sectoral Commission of Scientific Research (CSIC) of the University of the Republic, Uruguay, and the National Agency for Research and Innovation (ANII) for supporting the activities connected with this project.

The second project was called "Poles apart: a long-term perspective on inequality, industrialization and labour market institutions in Brazil and

Sweden". It was originally funded by the Swedish Foundation for International Cooperation in Research and Higher Education (STINT) as well as the Coordenação de Aperfeiçoamento de Pessoal de Nível Superior (CAPES). The aim of the project was to facilitate and support collaboration in education and research between a group of Swedish and Brazilian economic historians. The Brazilian team was headed by Renato Colistete at the Faculdade de Administração e Economia (FEA), Universidade de São Paulo (USP). Svante Prado would like to express his gratitude to Renato for the opportunity to visit USP on several occasions and to Dante Aldrighi (FEA, USP) for his great hospitality and for his intellectual input to the project. The workshop held at FEA, USP in December of 2017 was instrumental in developing the ideas for some of the book chapters that made it into this volume.

As the two projects joined forces to head for a book publication, Svante Prado's work was supported by Bromanska stiftelsen för forskning och företagande, and the visits at Facultad de Ciencias Sociales, Universidad de la República, Montevideo were supported by Partnerprogrammets internationaliseringsstöd at the School of Business, Economics and Law, University of Gothenburg. Svante Prado thanks everyone at the Facultad de Ciencias Sociales for the great care offered to him during his visits to Montevideo. In particular, he would like to acknowledge Cecilia Lara and Luis Bértola for their great hospitality.

Several of the chapters of this volume have been presented at conferences, in Helsinki, Gothenburg, Santiago de Chile, Montevideo, Paris and São Paulo. Some of the chapters were presented in a session titled "Contrasting development paths in Latin America and Scandinavia: What can we learn?" at the World Economic History Congress in Boston, 2018. We would like to thank all the participants at these conferences for their valuable comments. We would also like to acknowledge the anonymous referees who commented on the publishing proposals as well as the series editor Kent Deng, who encouraged us to write the concluding chapter of this volume.

CONTENTS

Notes on Contributors

Álvarez Jorge is Professor of History and Ph.D. in Economic History at the Universidad de la República, Uruguay. He is a Full Professor in the Economic and Social History Programme, Social Sciences Faculty, Universidad de la República. His areas of research include the economic performance of the Uruguayan and Latin American economy from a comparative perspective and the relation between institutions and development in the southern settler economies. He has written and edited three books, several articles and book chapters on the topic.

Bengtsson Erik is Associate Professor of Economic History at Lund University in Sweden. His research interests are mainly the history of economic inequality and living standards, agrarian history, economic policy and the welfare state and political history, with a focus mainly on Sweden but also on some other countries.

Bértola Luis (Ph.D. in Economic History, University of Gothenburg, Sweden, 1990) is Full Professor in the Economic and Social History Programme, Faculty of Social Sciences, Universidad de la República, Uruguay. He has given postgraduate courses and seminars at more than 20 universities around the world. He is a member of the Uruguayan Academy of Sciences. His main research interests and publications are focused on Latin American long-run development in a comparative perspective, with special focus on topics such as technical and structural change, institutions, income distribution, human development and foreign trade. He is the author of *The Economic Development of Latin America since Independence* (Oxford University Press, 2012) together with José Antonio Ocampo.

Bohlin Jan is a retired Associate Professor in Economic History connected to the unit for Economic History at the Department of Economy and Society, the University of Gothenburg, Sweden. His research interests include industrial policy, tariffs and economic growth, migration and business cycles. He has published in international economic history journals such as the *European Review of Economic History*, *Explorations in Economic History*, *Scandinavian Economic History Review* and *Australian Economic History Review*.

Kang Thomas is Lecturer on economic history courses at the São Paulo School of Economics, Fundação Getúlio Vargas (FGV EESP). He holds a master's in economics from the Universidade de São Paulo (2010) and a Ph.D. in economics from the Universidade Federal do Rio Grande do Sul (2019). He was also a visiting scholar at the School of Advanced Study, University of London (2018). He has worked in collaboration with the World Council of Churches (WCC), an international ecumenical organization, as a member of consultative and decision-making bodies since 2007. His main research interests include economic history, political economy of education and development ethics.

Lara Cecilia is a Ph.D. in Economic History at the Universidad de la República, Uruguay. She is Full Professor in the Economic and Social History Programme, Social Sciences Faculty, and in the Economic Institute, Faculty of Economics, both at Universidad de la República. She teaches and researches on issues of economic history, demography, economics and gender. Her research interests cover economic development of the Latin American economy from comparative perspectives, with particular focus on the role of public policies, structural change and labour market. Her work has been published in journals such as *Population Review*, Sociedad y Economía and Desarrollo y Sociedad.

de las Mercedes Menéndez María is a Ph.D. Fellow in Innovation, Economics and Governance for Development at UNU-MERIT (Maastricht, the Netherlands). Her research interests lie in the process of structural change and innovation under green and digital transition. She holds a master's degree in economic history from the University of the Republic (UDELAR) in Uruguay. Before joining the Ph.D. programme,

María de las Mercedes worked as a research assistant at UDELAR on topics related to regional development and economic history in Uruguay.

Molinder Jakob is a researcher in Economic History at Uppsala and Lund Universities. His research interests cover the broad area of historical labour markets in Sweden, with a particular focus on wages and inequality. He has also done research on regional aspects of economic growth and labour market change. He has published work on the Swedish model in the post-World War II period, the development of real wages during Sweden's industrialization, and on the factors explaining the trajectory of strikes during the first half of the twentieth century.

Morgan Marc is a research and teaching fellow in the Department of History, Economics and Society at the University of Geneva, and a research fellow at the World Inequality Lab in the Paris School of Economics. His research interests cover political economy, economic history, macroeconomics, development and public economics. His work is mainly centred on the measurement, history and institutional aspects of economic distribution, on how it relates to the macroeconomy, its development and its politics, with a focus on Europe and Latin America. He also does research on policies for shared and sustainable prosperity.

Nilsson Anders is Professor Emeritus in Economic History at Lund University in Sweden. His research centres on education and the labour market in Sweden in the nineteenth and twentieth centuries, with special emphasis on vocational education and training. He has recently published in the *Scandinavian Economic History Review* and the *Nordic Journal of Educational History*.

Pereira Thales is Adjunct Professor at the São Paulo School of Economics, Getulio Vargas Foundation. After he finished his Ph.D. in Economics at the University of São Paulo, he was a postdoctoral fellow at the London School of Economics (British Academy Newton Fund). His Ph.D. thesis analysed the rise and fall of cotton exports in Brazil during the British Industrial Revolution (1780–1860). The results of this research were published in the *Economic History Review* and the *Journal of Latin American Studies*.

Prado Svante is Associate Professor of Economic History at the University of Gothenburg in Sweden. His research interests include Swedish wages and labour markets in comparative perspectives, international comparisons of labour productivity, the impact of technological changes on the skill composition of workers and Swedish income distribution since 1860.

List of Figures

Chapter 3

Chapter 4

Chapter 5

Chapter 7

Chapter 8

Chapter 9

List of Tables

Chapter 4

Chapter 5

Chapter 6

Chapter 7

Chapter 8

Chapter 9

CHAPTER 1

Introduction: A Tale of Two Capitalisms

Jorge Álvarez and Svante Prado

There are historical similarities as well as conspicuous present-day contrasts between South America and Scandinavia that offer great scope for comparisons. The most remarkable contrast between the two groups relates to long-term economic growth rates and comparable levels of GDP per capita.[1] Whereas the Scandinavian countries aspire to top positions in the income and welfare leagues thanks to a close to unbroken record of 150 years of sustainable progress, the countries of South America have instead experimented with different regimes of convergence and divergence throughout the twentieth century and have struggled to keep up

[1] Strictly speaking, Scandinavia consists of Sweden, Norway and Denmark. Finland has not been considered part of this group in the past, among other reasons, because it does not belong to the Scandinavian language family. Nowadays, it is included in the broad linguistic guise of Scandinavian countries, such as the synonym of Nordic countries (Árnason & Wittrock, 2012). Therefore, in this book, the term Scandinavian countries and Nordic countries will be used interchangeably to refer to the four economies of Sweden, Norway, Denmark and Finland.

J. Álvarez
Social Sciences Faculty, University of the Republic, Montevideo, Uruguay
e-mail: jorge.alvarez@cienciassociales.edu.uy

J. Álvarez and S. Prado (eds.), *Scandinavia and South America—A Tale of Two Capitalisms*, Palgrave Studies in Economic History,
https://doi.org/10.1007/978-3-031-09198-8_1

with the growth rates of the rich countries since the 1990s (Bértola & Ocampo, 2012; Bértola & Porcile, 1998).

Although South America and Scandinavia exhibit significant differences today in income per capita, the gap between the two regions was much smaller two centuries ago, when they performed similar functions in the world economy (Blomstrom & Meller, 1991; Ducoing & Peres-Cajías, 2021). In the second half of the nineteenth century, the two regions specialized in producing and exporting primary goods to the core economies of Western Europe and the US. They hence occupied a peripheral and dependent position vis-à-vis the industrialized countries to which they exported staple goods emanating from the agricultural, forestry, and mining sectors. From the core, the peripheral countries imported manufactured consumer goods, machinery, technology, and capital. Nothing seemed to suggest that the roles of the two peripheral regions would change completely, nevertheless the Scandinavian countries managed to break free from their dependence on exports of raw materials and to develop the production of sophisticated manufactured goods by the early twentieth century.

The overarching objective with this book is to explore ways to increase our understanding of the divergence between South America and Scandinavia. We hope that the book will give us a grasp on why the two groups of countries have set out on such different pathways of industrialization, long-term economic growth, and income distribution. To achieve our objective, we offer, besides this introduction and a final reflection, eight chapters comprising comparisons of at least one country in each region, examining economic development variables highlighted by diverse theoretical approaches.

Two parallel threads run through this volume: The first of these offers multi-country comparisons that compare the so-called settler societies of the Southern Cone, Uruguay, and Argentina, with Scandinavia. These chapters focus on economy-wide growth rates, international trade and inequality in landholdings. In order to add additional leverage, we have also thrown in the settler societies of Australasia, New Zealand, and

S. Prado (✉)
University of Gothenburg, Göteborg, Sweden
e-mail: svante.prado@econhist.gu.se

Australia in these chapters. The second thread offers binary comparisons between Brazil and Sweden that examine productivity in manufacturing, education, inequality, and the nexus between welfare distribution and democracy. Despite representing the major share of the land mass and population in South America, Brazil is often absent from comparative studies invoking South America. True, the role of African slaves sets Brazil apart from the rest of South America, rendering Brazilian history akin to the Caribbean Islands and the US South. Over time, however, Brazil and the rest of the countries in South America became closely intertwined in political and economic developments. We cannot therefore leave Brazil out of the account if we aim to gain a more accurate understanding of the divergence between South America and Scandinavia. This volume constitutes a corrective to this lacuna of studies since it offers four chapters comparing Brazil with Sweden.

Like most predecessors in economic history, our method is empirical, and the evidence we seek to establish is mostly, albeit not exclusively, quantitative. We believe that quantitative measures are particularly useful in long-term comparative social science. Quantitative evidence reveals contrasting developments that warrant further attention. Some of our chapters offer binary comparisons; others rely on some of the countries from each region. Case-oriented, comparative research focuses on a narrow selection of cases with the aim of gaining a deeper understanding of events and processes against the background of context and history. It does not pretend to formulate laws or universal trends; rather, it is an approach that yields a very fertile dialogue between theory and historical evidence (Ragin, 1987).

While none of the chapters have the scope and power of truly multi-country studies, they possess other strengths. First, we can bring institutional details into the narrative to make sense of the quantitative measures that we have established. Second, we can ensure that our quantitative evidence rests on firm ground because the project involves experts on each country's source material. Some of the contributions are based on entirely new research employing data that have until now remained unexplored. Others are based on previous work conducted with primary sources by the members of the project. The originality of our approach lies above all in combining these different sources into a comparative perspective.

1 Regional Characteristics

It is important to discuss the differences between the countries in each of the regions that we compare. Generally, the previous works comparing Scandinavia with the countries in the Southern Cone have concluded that within-region heterogeneity has been relatively modest. They have considered both regions sufficiently homogenous to serve as units for historical comparisons. Scandinavian countries have common features in traditions, cultural habits, religion, institutional structures, and politics (Árnason & Wittrock, 2012; Derry, 1979). Barring Finland, the languages of the Scandinavian countries also resemble each other. Scandinavia has joined the group of so-called developed countries, which implies that their living standards are very high. The South American countries share close cultural, religious, and historical ties as former colonies of the Iberian empires (Spain and Portugal). Historically, there are closer ties among the countries of the Spanish-speaking part of South America; Brazil, it is fair to admit, has a history on its own. A common denominator for South American countries is a development pattern dependent on the production and export of commodities (Bulmer-Thomas, 2003; Thorp, 1998). Today, they have gained the status as middle-income countries.

However, there is a great diversity of realities and trajectories within each of these regions. From 1850 to the present day, Sweden and Finland's political, economic, and social modernization were very different. Another contrast concerns the natural resource endowments of Norway and Denmark, which conditioned their respective development paths (Alestalo & Kuhnle, 1987; Derry, 1979). South America is also very diverse if we consider a group of factors, such as climate, population, and production: the northern part has a tropical climate, whereas the southern one has a temperate climate; there are regions with a predominance of indigenous and mestizo populations, Afro-descendants or natives of European origin; and the predominant type of primary production and the markets to which they are oriented, vary by country (Bértola & Ocampo, 2012; Cardoso & Pérez Brignoli, 1979). In addition to these differentials by country, there is also great regional diversity within each of the countries, with Brazil being the outstanding example.

On balance, we consider the Scandinavian countries a more homogeneous group than the South American countries. We therefore include the four Scandinavian countries in the comparison: Denmark, Sweden, Norway, and Finland. In the case of South America, we have chosen three representative cases covering the Atlantic coast of South America: Argentina, Brazil, and Uruguay. These countries exhibit peculiar characteristics in the South American context. By the late nineteenth century, Argentina and Uruguay had achieved high levels of per capita income. In addition to high living standards, they had by then also achieved low levels of inequality by Latin American standards, good social indicators in terms of education enrolment and healthcare, and advanced social legislation. Brazil, on the other hand, had a much lower GDP per capita in the late nineteenth century. Thereafter, Brazil converged relative to the core until about 1980. But since then the growth rates of Brazil have on average merely been on par with the rich countries, implying stagnation in relative terms. Brazil is also plagued by interpersonal and regional inequalities to a greater extent than the other countries of the Southern Cone.

2 Settler Economies

Argentina, Uruguay, and southern Brazil share a heritage as regions of European settlement in the late nineteenth and early twentieth centuries. They also share the fate of specializing in the production and export of goods typical of temperate climates (Lewis, 1954). In this sense, they share a common experience with other southern hemisphere countries, such as Australia and New Zealand, being economies of new European settlement (Denoon, 1983; Nurske, 1961).

Lloyd et al. (2013) point out that, starting in the second half of the nineteenth century, the settler economies had a similar pattern of development as a result of the dynamic interconnections between the following factors: (i) they all received several waves of immigration from Europe; (ii) their native populations were marginalized and reduced demographically; and (iii) their factor endowment was similar in that they had an abundant supply of land but a scarce supply of labour and capital. These factors combined to spur on the emergence of social institutions designed to develop the economy rather than to oversee and regulate activities that were purely extractive, which was the predominant model in many other former colonies.

During the First Globalization of capitalism the settler economies actively participated in the integration of the world market both as producers and exporters of primary goods and as recipients of Europeans and capital. The technological developments of both the First and the

Second Industrial Revolutions were conducive to the increased participation of the peripheral countries in the Atlantic economy: the railway slashed the costs of transporting voluminous goods from the interior to rivers or the coast; the refrigerator made it possible to ship meat and dairy products across long distances; and the steam engine replaced sail as the prime motive power at sea, which also made it profitable to ship goods with a low value to volume ratio. Endowed with a temperate climate and fertile soils, especially suitable for producing meat, wheat, wool, and other crops, the settler societies could capitalize upon the growing demand from the expanding world market. As a result of this favourable configuration, the settler economies entered a growth trajectory based on exports of primary products. Although these factors favoured exports and growth rates, the Rio de la Plata region slipped into relative decline during the twentieth century. The Scandinavian countries, on the other hand, began their ascent to membership of the group of developed countries.

In order to explore the factors responsible for this remarkable shift in growth trajectories, three chapters in this book compare the development patterns of the four Scandinavian countries, Argentina and Uruguay (known as the Rio de la Plata or Pampas Region), and Australasia (Australia and New Zealand), the typical British settler economies of the Southern Hemisphere. The inclusion of the Australasian settler economies helps to set into sharper relief the slower long-term economic growth of the Rio de la Plata. It also helps to identify the factors responsible for this divergence. This design also has important and fruitful antecedents in the discipline, in particular the studies of Senghaas (1985) and Tylecote and Lingarde (1999), which will be discussed further in Chapter 2.

3 Brazil in South America

The other avenue for research in this volume is the four chapters contrasting Brazil with Sweden. Despite the long pedigree of studies with a focus on South America versus Scandinavia, we believe that the pairing of Brazil and Sweden may seem odd to some readers, so we offer a rather lengthy discussion that aims to justify this design, beginning with some thoughts on the role of Brazil in comparative works generally.

Brazil does not fit entirely with the colonial history of Spanish Latin America (Luna & Klein, 2014). This isolation has meant that Brazil has occupied an uneasy position in overviews of Latin American economic development and has often been excluded from the comparative studies of settler societies discussed previously. We can think of at least three reasons why Brazil is often considered a strange bird. The first, and probably most important, is the history of slavery. Since there was a shortage of domestic labour supply to exploit, in contrast to the Andean part of South America, for example, the Portuguese engaged heavily in the transatlantic slave trade. This engagement resulted in large number of slaves being shipped from Africa to Brazil. The slaves were mostly employed in the sugar plantations of the north-east and to some extent in the rapidly growing production of coffee in the south-east in the nineteenth century. In agriculture, the share of slaves in the labour force was as high as 70% in 1872, whereas slaves made up only 5% of the population at large in 1887, hence right before abolition (Merrick & Grahamn, 1979: 66). The high investments in slaves required to run these plantations led Brazil to specialize for a long time in the production of these cash crops for the world market. The unparalleled importance of slavery set Brazil apart from other countries in South America.

The slavery factor has, moreover, made scholars more likely to compare Brazil with the experience of the US, and in particular the South. This inclination to choose the US as the reference point is not uniquely Brazilian, however; Latin America is more often compared with North America than with Europe (Engerman & Sokoloff, 1997; Fukuyama, 2008). Both regions were colonized by Europeans and were dependent on large-scale immigration. This shared experience of colonization ties North America and Latin America together. Also, the ultimate aim of the independence that the Latin American countries achieved in the nineteenth century was to break free from the colonial shackles. The movement for freedom in Brazil sought to break with absolutism to increase representation in government and influence policymaking regarding for instance taxation. The new leaders in the post-independence era looked with keen eyes on the economic and political developments that were under way in the US and attempted to emulate as far as possible these American achievements (Bértola & Ocampo, 2012).

Even though slavery persisted longer in Brazil than elsewhere—it was abolished in 1888—its influence was rivalled by European immigrants, mostly from southern Europe, who began to pour into Brazil in great numbers in the second half of the nineteenth century, settling particularly in the south-east region. This immigration wave, and others that would follow in the twentieth century, transformed Brazil into a place where people with different cultures coexisted, united by the role Portuguese played as a lingua franca. No one can deny that slavery has continued to leave a deep mark in the socio-political development of Brazil despite the wide time span since the abolition in 1888. Nevertheless, the time is now ripe to consider Brazil a country that notwithstanding its colonial past has had a fair chance to realize the potential of democratization and modern economic growth. As a country that lagged behind the living standards of the developed countries since the mid-nineteenth century, she could also have mustered the benefits of backwardness in her efforts to catch up.

Our attempts to look beyond the slavery inheritance and to focus on the developments of the nineteenth and twentieth centuries challenge the so-called persistence literature, or what Bértola (2011) calls neo-institutional approaches, that has proliferated in recent decades (Acemoglu et al., 2005; North et al., 2000). According to the proponents of these ideas, the fate of Latin America was sealed by the establishment of colonial institutions, among which slavery in Brazil is a telling example. The essence of this type of literature is succinctly distilled by Engerman and Sokoloff (1997: 272), who argued that besides the legally codified inequality associated with slavery, "the greater inequality in wealth contributed to the evolution of institutions that commonly protected the privileges of the elite and restricted opportunities for the broad mass of the population to participate fully in the commercial economy even after the abolition of slavery". If we embrace this view entirely, it would make little sense to compare any former slave society with one that does not share this legacy, at least if our attention is directed at institutional change as an important determinant of economic development. Many of the chapters in this volume support, instead, the view that institutional and political changes during the nineteenth and twentieth centuries have shaped the outcomes of many economic and social variables. The slavery factor should not intrinsically rule out Brazil as a potential counterpart in binary comparisons.

We gather that the second reason why scholars have eschewed Brazil in favour of other countries is merely its size. The borders of Brazil swallow nearly half of the landmass of South America, and adjoin all other countries of South America barring Chile and Ecuador. These massive dimensions might feed into the notion that Brazil is a continent in herself rather than a country suitable for binary comparisons. Even so, Brazilians are not spread across this huge landmass uniformly. Instead, the population has clustered in large urban areas along the Atlantic coast, most prominently in the north-east and south-east. The population density is only 25 people per square kilometre. The vast hinterland is used mostly for pumping resources out of nature to feed the unquenchable appetite of internal and external markets for commodities. There is nothing spectacular in this concentration of people at one end and a vast hinterland used for exploitation at the other. The population distribution in Russia and Australia, two other huge land masses, is similar. Looking at smaller, similarly peripheral countries, the pattern of population density is again similar. In Uruguay, half of the population lives in Montevideo; in Sweden, Norrland, which occupies 60% of the landmass, has a population density of below 5 people per square kilometre. As it happens, the Swedish population density is 25 people per square kilometre, thus the same as in Brazil. Moreover, in our chapters, the target outcomes, such as welfare distribution, education, and productivity, are not conditioned on these geographic and demographic circumstances.

The third reason, which combines the history of slavery with the vast landmass, is the conception of Brazil as being two countries instead of one. The great divide runs through the north-east and the south-east. This bifurcation cuts through all sorts of economic, social, political, and cultural aspects, and the causes of this discontinuity reach back to the colonial past. It is a perennial theme in the Brazilian historiography (Barros, 2011; Leff, 1982; Prado Jr, 1945). In economic terms, the north-east depended from the outset on sugar plantations and large-scale use of African slaves. Slavery then spread to other regions in Brazil, and about 1820, the share of slaves in the population was even higher in some south-east states than in the north-east (Pereira, 2018). The African heritage as well as the asymmetric power relations that were codified by slavery have left indelible marks in the economic development of the north-east. The region has struggled, with little success, to move away from the archaic production structure of the past towards the modernization of industry and service sectors. This failure to spur on structural transformation has left the region behind in all sorts of social indicators, including purchasing power.

The development of the south-east stands in sharp relief against that of the north-east. Coffee production, which was the dominating cash crop grown in the south-east, proved conducive to spillover effects in other sectors (Dean, 1969). The immigration of European workers exceeded the influx of slaves by the 1880s. Early on, the south-east, and in particular the Greater São Paulo region, became the workhorse of the Brazilian economy, thanks in no small degree to massive industrialization (Cano, 1975). As a result of this dynamic, the regional gap expanded during the twentieth century. Although the historical dimension of the divide between these two macro-regions has been over emphasized, owing to the use of faulty evidence of real wages (Pereira, 2020), we must always tread carefully in reference to Brazil as a whole, to the north-east, or to the south-east.

Having said so much about the possible reasons why scholars have shied away from Brazil in comparative studies, we would also like to point out that the growing catalogue of global economic history is filled with odd couples, and for good reasons. The epochal study of Pomeranz (2000) is a duel between China, a giant in landmass and population, and Britain, a North Sea island roughly the size of the Korean peninsula. The Great Divergence debate that this book sparked has also juxtaposed Britain with India, making up most of South Asia in its own right (Parthasarathi, 2011). The intensity of the discussions that followed these publications illustrates that the selection of countries must depend on the research question. Only if the research question requires comparability in the size of the population and the landmass should these parameters be given our due recognition. Otherwise, we are better advised to leave them out of the equation.

4 Scandinavia in the Swedish Mirror

Sweden, our counterpart in Scandinavia, also merits some justification. Among the Scandinavian countries, Sweden has earned a special status in social science research, as a yardstick in research on the welfare state and the evolution of inequality (Esping-Andersen, 1990; Piketty, 2020). We may compare the weight of Sweden in this regard with that of the US, which is often selected as a benchmark in studies of productivity and GDP per capita (Maddison, 2001; van Ark, 1993). Sweden's status as a model for welfare distribution and egalitarianism is of quite recent origin, reaching back to the 1960s and the emergence of the welfare state and the so-called Swedish model. Researchers have called attention to the country's high ambitions in welfare distribution, the universal welfare state, a large public sector and far-reaching levelling of incomes and wealth (Lindbeck, 1997). Although the role of archetype has been bestowed upon Sweden, it must be emphasized that this description of Sweden is a mirror of Scandinavia as a whole. Without meticulous investigation, it is often not possible to convey anything but subtle nuances that differentiate one Scandinavian welfare state from another.

The egalitarian label of Sweden reaches back to the 1970s and 1980s. In the early 1980s, Sweden had a Gini coefficient of about 0.2, which was unparalleled among developed countries (Björklund & Jäntti, 2011). That all-time low point was achieved through a conspicuous income compression that began in earnest in the late 1960s and continued unabated throughout the 1970s. The tendency towards additional compression in the 1970s ran counter to the stagnating or increasing inequality in many other countries (Piketty, 2014). The resulting very low Gini coefficient in the early 1980s conferred on Sweden the status of being egalitarian par excellence. However, it should also be said that at present the egalitarian label sits somewhat uneasily because Sweden has slipped down the ranking of Gini coefficients since its all-time low in the early 1980s. By the mid-2010s Sweden's Gini index had increased to 0.29 and it had been overtaken by 18 countries, including Denmark, Norway, and Finland, all of which had lower Gini indexes than Sweden.[2] We can nevertheless conclude that the Scandinavian countries have similarly low levels of Gini coefficients, which means that regarding inequality and welfare distributions, we see much of Scandinavia in the Swedish mirror.

5 Comparing Sweden with Brazil

Our research questions in fact distil two opposing justifications for comparing Brazil with Sweden. Two of our chapters examine dimensions of inequality. In both cases we have been guided by the principle of poles apart. Inequality is higher and therefore poses a greater challenge in Brazil than in other South American countries. Although declining in recent decades, the Gini index of Brazil stood at 0.53 in the mid-2010s, clearly exceeding the index in other countries in the Southern Cone. As we saw, this is in startling contrast to Sweden, which, despite increasing inequality since the record low in the early 1980s, has a Gini index of 0.29. The convergence in Gini coefficients since the early 1980s masks to some extent the polarization between the two countries that manifested itself during the twentieth century and culminated in 1980. Up

[2] https://data.worldbank.org/indicator/SI.POV.GINI.

to that point, the two countries marched steadfastly in opposite directions to each other along the inequality axis: Sweden joined several other developed countries in the Great Levelling and explored the very frontiers of equality in the 1970s, whereas Brazil, despite being relieved of the burden of slavery in 1888, missed the Great Levelling and explored instead the very frontiers of inequality. These divergent outcomes of the opportunities offered by modern economic growth and democratization provide the backdrop against which our chapters on inequality should be seen.

For the study of productivity, our Sweden to Brazil comparison instead departs from the notion of resemblance. Both countries have, namely, shared the attribute of being particularly dependent on the manufacturing sector. The primary way to grow rich has for most countries been through industrialization (Amsden, 2001). But the share of GDP generated by the goods-producing sector has varied across countries and over time. From a Latin American viewpoint, Brazil distinguishes herself by having developed the greater dependence on manufacturing industries since the early twentieth century (Bértola & Ocampo, 2012; Duran et al., 2017), and from a Scandinavian viewpoint, Sweden depended most on manufacturing industry (Jörberg, 1973).

Both countries have a history of industrialization going back at least to the fourth quarter of the nineteenth century. Although Brazilian industrialization is associated foremost with the state-led development of the post-World War II period, the late nineteenth century also witnessed the rise of textile industries (Haber, 2006; Stein, 1957). True, in contrast to Sweden, Brazil was never swept away entirely by the late nineteenth-century wave of industrialization; its full-blown effort awaited the heyday of import substitution industrialization of the post-World War II decades. The industrialization of Brazil was, and still is, heavily skewed towards the south-east region and especially greater São Paulo. This area is also, colloquially, "the largest Swedish industrial region" thanks to the presence of Swedish multinationals such as ABB, Ericsson, Scania, Telia and Volvo, which all invested massively in the area to make inroads into the Brazilian and South American markets.

While the development strategies drew heavily on manufacturing in both countries, the outcomes were very different. Whereas the manufacturing industry, owing to its size and productivity, has propelled the Swedish economy forward ever since the fourth quarter of the nineteenth century, the Brazilian industry seems to have lost the momentum it gathered in the post-World War II decades (Aldrighi & Colistete, 2015). The manufacturing sector has not been able to reap the benefits of the technologies undergirding the Third Industrial Revolution. As a result of this lacklustre performance, the convergence that seemed to be underway has come to naught since the early 1980s (Lara & Prado, 2022). Considering the twentieth century in sum, we can see that Brazil has made admirable efforts to catch up but has so far lacked the sustained leverage required to qualify as "a developed country". Rather, along with most of South America, Brazil seems to have been caught in the famous middle-income trap (Gill & Kharas, 2007).

In a follow-up chapter, we have examined differences in human capital, one of the probable determinants of the divergence between the two countries (Barro, 2013; Easterlin, 1981). The differences in the supply of well-educated workers of most kinds are stark, and can be traced to the late nineteenth century. Sandberg (1979) described Sweden as an impoverished sophisticate and grounded this description on the well-educated Swedish population. But it is a label that must also be seen against the backdrop of the low GDP per capita level in Sweden. In Sandberg's view, the stock of human capital was wildly disproportionate to the very low Swedish income level in the mid-nineteenth century, and this favourable disproportion helped Sweden achieve very high growth rates thereafter. Recent advances in historical national accounts have challenged the image of Sweden as a very backward country in a European perspective, which also calls for a reinterpretation of the ostensibly high growth rates portrayed by Sandberg (Edvinsson, 2013). But the purport of Sandberg's influential expression pertains. In contrast, Brazil's stock of human capital was curtailed by the large proportion of slaves in the labour force. These differences in the supply of human capital offer a likely explanation why Sweden, and not Brazil, made a head start with industrialization in the late nineteenth century, though the legacy of slavery does not suffice as an explanation for the continuous neglect of investment in education in Brazil throughout the twentieth century.

6 Chapter-Wise Account

This introduction is followed by a review of the various studies comparing Scandinavia and Latin America written by Jorge Alvarez, Luis Bértola, and Jan Bohlin (Chapter 2). A striking component of this review is the rich supply of previous attempts to compare these two regions. Besides highlighting this long-term comparative paradigm in economic history, it also reviews, first, the different analytical tools used to gain insights into the divergence between the two regions. The authors show that this comparative approach has changed over time in response to the emergence of new theories in development economics. Natural resources are seen as crucial in many of these analyses, by determining the fate and composition of exports and by setting the stage for the development of growth and productivity in the domestic economy. Many of the previous accounts stress the nexus between the levels of inequality and the gains made from the exploitation of natural resources.

Chapter 3, by Jorge Alvarez, Luis Bértola, and Jan Bohlin, investigates the nexus between growth trajectories and the capacity to undergo structural change in the Nordic societies, Sweden, Finland, Norway, and Denmark on the one hand, and in the southern settler societies on the other, where South America is represented by Uruguay and Argentina, and Australasia by Australia and New Zealand. Two stylized facts serve as points of departure for this investigation. The first concerns the reversal of fortunes between the Nordic societies and the southern settler societies that took place from the nineteenth century until the present. Whereas the Nordic societies enjoyed a trajectory of sustainable growth and convergence with the core, Argentina and Uruguay slipped into decline relative to the core, and New Zealand and Australia grew at a similar pace to the core. The second stylized fact relates to structural transformation in a broad sense, measured as the degree of industrialization, as the share of manufactured goods in total exports, or as the change in the structure of the manufacturing sector in favour of more dynamic industries. The authors argue that structural change is not simply the corollary of growth; instead, there is a dynamic interplay between these two phenomena, so any obstacle to achieving structural transformation will inevitably thwart growth. Thus, the key to understanding divergence is to identify the factors that hampered structural transformation in the southern settler societies but promoted it in the Nordic societies.

The chapter examines several theoretical approaches in order to identify the factors that promoted or hampered growth. By themselves, none of these theories offers a convincing explanation. The so-called staple theory has exercised a great impact on our thinking about resource endowments and structural transformation. Although it offers several insights into the link between endowments and growth, the problem with it, the authors argue, is that it cannot explain why similar patterns of endowments lead to diverging outcomes. The so-called Tyranny of Distance, which is another concept used to explain divergence, loses its explanatory power once we factor in the role of the transport revolution in the late nineteenth century. As the cost of shipping declined, the importance of distance between producers and consumers diminished. The late nineteenth-century pattern of migration is another possible explanation, resulting in increased supply of labour in the south and decreasing supply in the north. This cannot, however, explain why most of the reversal of fortunes occurred in the twentieth century. Finally, inequality appears to have played an important role. Too much inequality is inimical to growth. Experience shows that equality encourages broad-based participation, which in turn spurs on innovation. The late nineteenth-century globalization boom served to diminish inequality in the Nordic societies and increase it in the southern settler societies, worsening the already high level of inequality in Rio de la Plata attributable to the region's colonial legacy.

Acknowledging the importance so often assigned to foreign trade in shaping the development destiny of peripheral countries relative to the core, Chapter 4 by Jorge Alvarez, Luis Bértola, and Jan Bohlin tackles head-on the relationship between foreign trade and economic growth. It does so by calling on Thirlwall's Law, which postulates that the long-run growth rate of a country is constrained by the balance of payments (Thirlwall, 2011). More formally, it posits that the growth rate of a country equals the ratio between the income elasticities of demand for its exports and imports multiplied by the growth rates in its export markets. In other words, the more a country's composition of exports is tailored towards those products for which demand is increasing, the greater the potential to achieve fast and sustainable growth rates domestically. In the 1870s, Australasia was richer than Scandinavia, whereas the Rio de la Plata region occupied the middle ground. In the following hundred years, Scandinavia caught up with the rich countries, while the Rio de la Plata region fell behind. The chapter illustrates that much of this reversal of fortunes was the outcome of exports performance. In Scandinavia, the composition of exports changed towards a variety of manufactured goods for which there was rising demand in the growing world market. The other peripheral countries, and in particular those in the Rio de la Plata region, were stuck with exports of a few staple goods based on the supply of natural resources, the demand for which declined relatively in the world market.

Obviously, Thirlwall's Law, which conditions economy-wide growth rates exclusively on export performance, cannot explain the underlying fundamentals, namely, which factors account for the changing composition of output over time. A supply-side framework would instead argue that the evolution of productivity for different sectors weighs heavier in the end; the causality runs from the productive capacity to structural transformation and from there to export performance. That a focus on the supply side carries weight is made apparent in Chapter 5, by Cecilia Lara and Svante Prado, which compares levels of labour productivity in manufacturing in Brazil and Sweden. The authors use the industry-of-origin approach to establish a benchmark of comparable levels of output and labour input in 1975. From this benchmark they have extrapolated these comparative levels using time series of labour productivity for both countries from 1912 to 2014. The result bears testament to the struggle Brazil has had in catching up with the productivity levels of the developed countries. In the early twentieth century, the Brazilian level was about 20% of the Swedish. A massive catching up then took place until the early 1980s, but by the early 2010s the level had in fact reverted to the same position as in the early 1910s. Given this dull record, it should come as no great surprise that Brazil has remained a country still largely dependent on exports of staple goods despite a century of industrialization and structural transformation. The result of this chapter also questions the notion that convergence between different countries' productivity levels in manufacturing occurs unconditionally, as was suggested by Rodrik (2013). The catching up of less-developed countries, also at sectoral levels, is conditioned by several factors.

Education, one of those conditional factors, is the focus of Chapter 6 by Thomas Kang and Anders Nilsson. They offer a treatment on differences in human capital between Sweden and Brazil that focuses on the two periods from 1870 to 1910 (extended until 1930 in the case of Brazil) and from 1945 to 1973 against the background of the different responses to international challenges arising during these years. The Swedish lead in education was very wide in 1870 and Brazil caught up slowly and incompletely. In 1970, Brazil had not achieved the level of average years of schooling that Sweden had reached a century earlier. For religious reasons, Sweden had also attained a head start relative to many other countries before 1842, when the Swedish Riksdag decided to introduce primary schools throughout the country. The vicar in each parish held catechetical examinations on a regular basis. These included reading specified religious texts and knowledge of prayers and hymns. The basic training in writing and reading served the need for skills during the early phase of industrialization. During the Second Industrial Revolution, the demand for engineering skills increased. The flurry of new schools and educational practices that sprang up in the second half of the nineteenth century, such as grammar schools and technical schools, served the growing demand for trained technicians and vocational training, as well as providing the basis from which the technical colleges could recruit their students. In Brazil, the response triggered by the growing world economy was increasing exports of staple goods. This specialization did not spur on demand for well-educated workers. Immigrants, mainly from southern Europe, raised the average number of schooling years in Brazil somewhat. They could be considered as unskilled relative to the North European emigrants going to North America, but skilled in comparison with native Brazilians, and certainly skilled in relation to slaves.

In the post-World War II period, demand for trained workers grew in tandem with the growing manufacturing sector. Because supply could not keep up with demand, a solution was urgently required that catered to the need of manufacturing for trained workers. Initially, labour market organizations promoted apprentice-based blue-collar training in both countries. The company-based training programme, however, proved difficult to scale up sufficiently. The Swedish state reacted by creating an extensive school-based system for vocational education, which despite its lower standard served to supply young people with the skills necessary for the tasks at hand in the labour markets. No such reform was properly implemented in Brazil, which the authors explain as a lack of priority given to educational matters. The skill shortage among workers would continue to hamper the industrial development in Brazil until the present day.

The last three empirical Chapters (7–9) examine different dimensions of inequality, one of the socio-economic factors to which scholars have accorded great importance for our understanding of divergence between the Southern and Northern peripheries (Senghaas, 1985). Today, whereas inequality is high in South America, it is low in Scandinavia, and Australasia occupies a middle position. Chapter 7, the first of these inequality studies, written by Jorge Alvarez and María de las Mercedes Menéndez, compares Denmark, New Zealand, and Uruguay. Thanks to favourable conditions for livestock rearing, all three countries thrived in the first era of globalization in the late nineteenth and twentieth century.

This similarity aside, the twentieth century then witnessed growing differences in GDP per capita terms, with Denmark racing ahead and Uruguay falling behind.

The foremost reason for this growth divergence, the authors argue, can be found in the different distributions of land ownership. As a result of the egalitarian ownership structure in Denmark, the income generated from exports spread across people from many social strata. A similar description applies to New Zealand. In Uruguay, on the other hand, land ownership was concentrated in the hands of a few large landowners. This concentration of land ownership entailed a skewed distribution of the incomes from exports of agricultural produce. The chapter illustrates the dynamic interplay between the institutions that govern the structure of landowning and the benefits of exports of agricultural products. If institutions do not promote broad-based participation in the markets for agricultural produce, the rewards from exports will be concentrated in the hands of a few wealthy property owners. The experiences of Denmark, Uruguay, and New Zealand suggest that a very skewed distribution of land has been inimical to economic growth.

Chapter 8 by Jakob Molinder, Thales Pereira, and Svante Prado is devoted to a quest for the historical roots of inequality in Brazil and Sweden. As previously discussed, today these two countries are poles apart in the ranking of inequality levels: Brazil is unequal; Sweden is equal. Should we blame the enduring colonial legacy, or should we focus instead on the twentieth-century trajectory? The chapter focuses on inequality in labour market outcomes from 1830 to 1920, which is a period that stretches as far back as the evidence permits and ends before the great levelling of the twentieth century that swept across the developed countries. The chapter employs the method of welfare ratios; it allows the authors to make a comparison of living standards as well as of inequality. The result shows a sharp divergence in living standards in the 1880s, when the welfare ratios of Swedish workers pulled ahead of those in Brazil. Before the 1880s, the welfare ratios of the two countries were rather equal. The development of GDP per capita was similar to that of welfare ratios, which downplays the role of the inequality forces identified in the epochal works of Lewis (1954) and Kuznets (1955); in other words, real wages trailing GDP per capita do not figure prominently in either Sweden or Brazil from 1830 to 1920.

The chapter then proceeds to compare inequality by earnings differentials across regions, occupations, skills, and sex. The only aspect that differentiated Brazil from Sweden significantly was regional inequality, which was higher in Brazil for the two benchmark years of 1912 and 1920. Across the other inequality measures, differences were quite small. These rather similar records of inequality lead the authors to conclude that most of today's abysmal gap between the two countries is attributable to developments that occurred after 1920. Whereas Sweden excelled in the great levelling of the twentieth century, Brazil seems to have missed it entirely.

Chapter 9, finally, written by Erik Bengtsson and Marc Morgan, examines how democracy affected redistribution through public spending and taxation, comparing Sweden with Brazil. Since both social spending and taxes are inextricably linked to the welfare state, the author's topic has an antecedent in the discussion of democracy and the welfare state; as in for instance Lindert (1994), who argued that the expansion of suffrage to women and lower-income strata increased the pressure for social spending, which would eventually lead to the welfare state in many countries. The authors conjecture that Lindert was right, although they add the disclaimer that the rise of a welfare state requires intellectuals and reformist ideologues as well as a competent and willing bureaucracy.

In Sweden, universal suffrage was applied for the first time in the election of 1921. Before that reform, however, suffrage was extended to male voters in 1909. The chapter marshals several reforms that were carried out between the reform in 1909 and the late 1930s. Democratization led to an incipient rise in welfare spending, which in turn caused some redistribution. The effect of democracy on reforms required to achieve redistribution was far from instantaneous, though. In Sweden, the parliamentary chaos of the 1920s probably delayed the implementation of the reform agenda for redistribution. The formation of a stable coalition in which each party felt they had a stake had to wait until the mid-1930s, and a stream of reforms poured forth thereafter.

Unlike Sweden, in Brazil the democratic reforms were reversible. They swung from oligarchy to expanded suffrage (1891, 1934), to dictatorship, to re-democratization, to dictatorship again, and finally to universal suffrage in 1989. It was not a self-sustained evolution, which is a possible explanation why it took Brazil 100 years to pass the equivalent number of reforms passed in Sweden in 10 years. The bumpy road towards democracy also explains why it is difficult to disentangle the nexus between democracy and redistribution by examining reforms in Brazilian history. The experience does not offer unequivocal support for the hypothesis that democratization entails redistribution. Social spending made great strides between 1964 and 1985 during the military dictatorship, when democratic rights were severely curtailed. The military governments might have used an expanded coverage of social transfers to gain increased political legitimacy and to distribute patronage at the regional and local levels.

Brazil appears to exemplify the functional role of social policy in a context of delayed economic development and highly skewed resource distribution. In contrast to Sweden, democracy in Brazil was not accompanied by an organized social movement with a reformist ideology, neither was it supported by a cooperative bureaucracy or the required political arithmetic to render equalizing reforms possible. The authors conclude that the link between democratization and redistribution is weaker and more complex than Acemoglu and Robinsson (2000) and Lindert (1994) envision. As conveyed by Bismarck's social insurance reforms of the 1880s and by Brazil's ambitious reform agenda during military rule, redistribution can occur without democratization. Rulers have launched welfare programmes to undermine the threat of popular mobilizations and organized labour.

References

Acemoglu, D., & Robinson, J. A. (2000). Why did the west extend the Franchise? Democracy, inequality, and growth in historical perspective. *Quarterly Journal of Economics, 115*(4), 1167–1199. https://doi.org/10.1162/003355300555042

Acemoglu, D., Johnson, S., & Robinson, J. A. (2005). Institutions as a fundamental cause of long-run growth. In P. Aghion & S. N. Durlauf (Eds.), *Handbook of Economic Growth* (Vol. 1A, pp. 385–472). Elsevier.

Aldrighi, D., & Colistete, R. (2015). Industrial growth and structural change: Brazil in a long-run perspective. In W. Naudé, A. Szirmai, & N. Haraguchi (Eds.), *Structural change and industrial development in the BRICS* (pp. 162–198). Oxford University Press.

Alestalo, M., & Kuhnle, S. (1987). The scandinavian route: Economic, social, and political developments in Denmark, Finland, Norway, and Sweden. *International Journal of Sociology, 16*(3/4), 3–38.

Amsden, A. H. (2001). The rise of "the Rest": Challenges to the west from late-industrializing economies. *Oxford University Press*. https://doi.org/10.1093/0195139690.001.0001

Árnason, J. P., & Wittrock, B. (2012). *Nordic path to modernity*. Berghahn Books.

Barro, R. J. (2013). Education and economic growth. *Annales of Economics and Finance, 14*(2), 301–328.

Barros, A. R. (2011). *Desigualdades regionais no Brasil: Natureza, causas, origens e solução*. Elsevier.

Bértola, L. (2011). Institutions and the historical roots of the Latin American divergence. In J. A. Ocampo & J. Ros (Eds.), *The Oxford handbook of Latin American economics* (pp. 26–49). Oxford University Press.

Bértola, L., & Ocampo, J. A. (2012). The economic development of Latin America since independence. *Oxford University Press*. https://doi.org/10.1093/acprof:oso/9780199662135.001.0001

Bértola, L., & Porcile, G. (1998). Argentina, Brazil, Uruguay and the World Economy: An approach to different convergence and divergence regimes. *DT 42. Montevideo: Unidad Multidisciplinaria, Facultad de Ciencias Sociales.*

Björklund, A., & Jäntti, M. (2011). *Inkomstfördelningen i Sverige*. SNS.

Blomström, M., & Meller, P. (1991). *Diverging paths: Comparing a century of Scandinavian and Latin American economic development*. Inter-American Development Bank.

Bulmer-Thomas, V. (2003). *The economic history of Latin America since independence*. Cambridge University Press.

Cano, W. (1975). *Raízes da concentracão industrial em São Paulo*. DIFEL.

Cardoso, C., & Pérez Brignoli, H. (1979). *Historia económica de América Latina (Vol. I y II)*. Crítica.

Dean, W. (1969). The industrialization of São Paulo, 1880–1945. *University of Texas Press*. https://doi.org/10.2307/980623

Denoon, D. (1983). *Settler capitalism: The dynamics of dependent development in the southern hemisphere*. Clarendon University Press.

Derry, T. K. (1979). *A history of Scandinavia*. University of Minnesota Press.

Ducoing, C., & Peres-Cajías, J. (2021). *Natural resources and divergence: A comparison of Andean and Nordic trajectories*. Palgrave Macmillan.

Duran, X., Musacchio, A., & Paolera, G. d. (2017). Industrial growth in South America: Argentina, Brazil, Chile, and Colombia, 1890–2010. In K. H. O'Rourke & J. G. Williamson (Eds.), *The spread of modern industry to the periphery since 1871* (pp. 318–342). Oxford University Press. https://doi.org/10.1093/acprof:oso/9780198753643.003.0013

Easterlin, R. A. (1981). Why isn't the whole world developed? *Journal of Economic History, 41*(1), 1–19.

Edvinsson, R. (2013). New annual estimates of Swedish GDP 1800–2010. *Economic History Review, 66*(4), 1101–1126. https://doi.org/10.1111/1468-0289.12004

Engerman, S. L., & Sokoloff, K. L. (1997). Factor endowments, institutions, and differential paths of growth among New World Economies: A view from

economic historians of the United States. In S. Haber (Ed.), *How Latin America fell behind* (pp. 260–304). Stanford University Press.
Esping-Andersen, G. (1990). *The three worlds of welfare capitalism*. Polity.
Fukuyama, F. (Ed.). (2008). *Falling behind: Explaining the development gap between Latin America and the United States*. Oxford University Press.
Gill, I., & Kharas, H. (2007). *An East Asian renaissance: Ideas for economic growth*. World Bank.
Haber, S. H. (2006). The political economy of industrialization. In V. Bulmer-Thomas, J. Coatsworth, & R. Cortes-Conde (Eds.), *The Cambridge economic history of Latin America* (Vol. Part IV Sectoral Development and Equity, pp. 537–584). Cambridge University Press.
Jörberg, L. (1973). The industrial revolution in the Nordic Countries. In C. M. Cipolla (Ed.), *The Fontana economic history of Europe, Vol. 4 1700–1914* (pp. 375–479). Collins.
Kuznets, S. (1955). Economic growth and income inequality. *American Economic Review, 45*(1), 1–28.
Lara, C., & Prado, S. (2022). *From boom to gloom: Brazilian labor productivity in manufacturing relative to the US, 1912–2019*. Forthcoming in *Economic History Review*.
Leff, N. H. (1982). *Underdevelopment and development in Brazil. Vol 1. Economic structure and change, 1822–1947*. George Allen & Unwin.
Lewis, W. A. (1954). Economic development with unlimited supplies of labour. *Manchester School, 22*(2), 139–191.
Lindbeck, A. (1997). The Swedish experiment. *Journal of Economic Literature, 35*(3), 1273–1319.
Lindert, P. (1994). The rise of social spending, 1880–1930. *Explorations in Economic History, 31*(1), 1–37.
Lingarde, S., & Tylecote, A. (1999). Resource-rich countries' success and failure in technological ascent, 1870–1970: The Nordic countries versus Argentina, Uruguay and Brazil. *Journal of European Economic History, 28*, 77–112.
Lloyd, C., Metzer, J., & Sutch, R. (2013). *Settler economies in World History*. Brill.
Luna, F. V., & Klein, H. S. (2014). The economic and social history of Brazil since 1889. *Cambridge University Press*. https://doi.org/10.1017/CBO9781107337046
Maddison, A. (2001). *The world economy: A millennial perspective*. OECD.
Merrick, T., & Grahamn, D. (1979). *Population and Economic Development in Brazil, 1800 to the Present*. The Johns Hopkins University Press.
North, D. C., Summerhill, W., & Weingast, B. R. (2000). Order, disorder and economic change: Latin America versus North America. In B. B. De Mesquita & H. L. Root (Eds.), *Governing for prosperity* (pp. 17–58). Yale University Press.

Nurske, R. (1961). *Equilibrium and growth in the world economy*. Harvard University Press.

Parthasarathi, P. (2011). *Why Europe grew rich and Asia did not: Global economic divergence*. Cambridge University Press. https://doi.org/10.1017/CBO9780511993398

Pereira, T. A. Z. (2018). Poor man's crop? Slavery in Brazilian cotton regions (1800–1850). *Estudos Econômicus (são Paulo), 48*(4), 623–655. https://doi.org/10.1590/0101-41614843tzp

Pereira, T. A. Z. (2020). The north-south divide: Real wages and welfare in Brazil during the early 20th century. *Journal of Iberian and Latin American Economic History, 38*(March), 185–214. https://doi.org/10.1017/S0212610919000132

Piketty, T. (2014). *Capital in the twenty-first century*. The Belknap Press of Harvard University Press.

Piketty, T. (2020). *Capital and ideology*. Harvard University Press.

Pomeranz, K. (2000). *The great divergence: China, Europe, and the making of the modern world economy*. Princeton University Press.

Prado Jr., C. (1945). *História económica do Brasil*.

Ragin, C. (1987). *The comparative method: Moving beyond qualitative and quantitative methods*. University of California Press.

Rodrik, D. (2013). Unconditional convergence in manufacturing. *Quarterly Journal of Economics, 128*(1), 165–204. https://doi.org/10.1093/qje/qjs047

Sandberg, L. G. (1979). The case of the impoverished sophisticate: Human capital and Swedish economic growth before World War I. *Journal of Economic History, 39*(1), 225–241.

Senghaas, D. (1985). *The European experience: A historical critique of development theory*. Berg.

Stein, S. (1957). The Brazilian cotton manufacture: Textile enterprise in an underdeveloped area, 1850–1950. *Harvard University Press*. https://doi.org/10.4159/harvard.9780674592575

Thirlwall, A. P. (2011). Balance of payments constrained growth models: History and overview. *PSL Quarterly Review, 64*(259), 307–351. https://doi.org/10.1057/9781137023957_2

Thorp, R. (1998). *Progress, poverty and exclusion: An economic history of Latin America in the 20th century*. Inter-American Development Bank.

Tylecote, A., & Lingarde, S. (1999). Resource-rich countries' success and failure in technological ascent, 1870–1970: The Nordic countries versus Argentina, Uruguay and Brazil. *Journal of European Economic History, 28*(1), 77–114.

van Ark, B. (1993). *International comparisons of output and productivity: Manufacturing productivity performance of ten countries from 1950–1990*. Groningen Growth and Development Centre Monograph Series 1.

CHAPTER 2

Scandinavia and South America: A Renewed Tradition of Comparative Studies

Jorge Álvarez, Luis Bértola, and Jan Bohlin

1 Introduction

For many years now, historical comparisons of the economic performance of different countries have loomed large in economic history research programmes. In the second half of the twentieth century, the problems of development and international comparisons were at the centre of theoretical and empirical research in the field of development studies. There were

Present Address:
J. Álvarez (✉) · L. Bértola
Social Sciences Faculty, University of the Republic, Montevideo, Uruguay
e-mail: jorge.alvarez@cienciassociales.edu.uy

L. Bértola
e-mail: luis.bertola@cienciassociales.edu.uy

J. Bohlin
University of Gothenburg, Göteborg, Sweden
e-mail: jan.bohlin@econhist.gu.se

J. Álvarez and S. Prado (eds.), *Scandinavia and South America—A Tale of Two Capitalisms*, Palgrave Studies in Economic History,
https://doi.org/10.1007/978-3-031-09198-8_2

various reasons for this, as decolonization and the creation of new independent nations, the specific problems of Third World countries which were facing increasing income gaps relative to developed countries, and the challenge of the Socialist Block to Western capitalist development.

Development as a historical problem was approached in different ways in the post-Second World War period. There were simple schemes that identified development with economic growth (Solow, 1956); it was seen as a succession of stages that economies had to go through until they achieved the full maturity of their productive structures (Rostow, 1960). There were dual growth models (Kaldor, 1979; Lewis, 1954), as well as approaches that emphasized the role of international and domestic demand in the development of underdeveloped countries (Myrdal, 1959). In this context, Latin American structuralism (Prebisch, 1949; Rodriguez, 2006) made an original contribution in which the predominant linear and Eurocentric vision was abandoned, and this view was subsequently echoed, with different emphases and approaches, by the theory of dependence (Cardoso & Faletto, 1971).

One interesting aspect of that international context is the historical trajectory of a group of countries rich in natural resources and with development patterns that did not completely fit with the theoretical developments mentioned above. One attempt to tackle this problem inspired the analytical approach called staple theory to explain how a naturally resource-rich country can achieve high growth rates and high per capita income if it specializes in producing and exporting primary goods (Mackintosh, 1964). However, not all countries that are rich in natural resources developed the same way. Some managed to successfully change their productive structure, but others that had enjoyed rapid economic growth based on exploiting their natural resources before the First World War, failed to change their productive structure.

In this context, and especially from the 1980s onwards, the divergent long-term development trajectories followed by the Scandinavian countries, as an example of development success, and South America, representing a less successful development process, from the nineteenth century to the present, attracted the interest of the economic historiography (Blomström & Meller, 1991; Senghaas, 1985; Lingarde & Tylecote, 1999, among others). Comparative studies of these regions shed light on the factors involved in the development processes of natural resource-rich countries, both in terms of historical knowledge and of theoretical elaborations. This occurred for two main reasons.

First, the Scandinavian countries and South America had a set of shared characteristics at the dawn of the first globalization of capitalism. Both regions, rich in natural resources, were linked to the world economy as countries specializing in the production and export of raw materials and food. This trade specialization pattern allowed both sets of countries to adapt to the growth of the world economy, driven by the dynamic development of industrial powers. This trajectory was defined by Senghaas (1985), Árnason and Wittrock (2012) and Bertola and Ocampo (2012) as being peripheral and dependent on the growth of the developed economies of Western Europe, especially of Great Britain. Therefore, the peripheral condition of the Scandinavian countries and South America responded, fundamentally, to the position they occupied in the international division of labour, between suppliers of raw materials and food on one hand, and industrialized regions on the other. Thus, the peripheral condition depended to a lesser extent on geographical location or distance from the main markets, and more on the role of the country in the world market. Nevertheless, the Scandinavian countries had exhibited highly integrated trade circuits with Western Europe since before the first globalization era (Derry, 1979). In contrast, South America—and the Australasian countries, as we will see below—had until that time been subject to the "tyranny" of distance (Blainey, 1966). Their opportunity to participate in the world economy appeared only in the last third of the nineteenth century due to falling transport costs.

The second reason is that historical and comparative analysis of development patterns of similar and, at the same time, divergent cases contributed to enrich theoretical elaboration in the fields of economic history and development studies (Senghaas, 1985; Skocpol, 2003; Sumner & Tribe, 2008).

Finally, it should be noted that comparisons between countries rich in natural resources but with divergent development patterns have been influenced in recent years by the natural resource curse debate (Sachs & Warner, 1995). This perspective suggests a negative correlation between resource abundance and economic growth in the long term. However, recent works have emphasized that some resource-based economies, such as the Scandinavian countries and some settler economies, have avoided the curse (Lederman & Maloney, 2007; Ranestad, 2016; Ville & Wicken, 2012).

The main questions that have guided the comparison between the Scandinavian countries and Latin America can be summarized as follows:

why, despite the similarities, including a similar starting point in the nineteenth century, did these regions have divergent trajectories? What explains the fact that some regions rich in natural resources managed to transform their productive structure and develop high-technology sectors, while others remained dependent on the production and export of commodities? Why did the Scandinavian countries manage to overcome their peripheral condition and close the gap with the rich countries, while for South America the gap remained, or even grew?

From a methodological point of view, most of the studies apply systematic case-oriented comparisons. The aim of this kind of comparison is to produce a kind of knowledge that does not involve an attempt to formulate laws or universal trends; rather it is an approach that yields a very fertile dialogue between theory and historical evidence (Skocpol, 2003). As Ragin (1987) states, the qualitative modality of the comparative method contributed to investigate the underlying similarities in the group of cases considered, to analyse the phenomena of interest based on the similarities that have been identified and to formulate a general explanation based on the similarities and differences identified. This method is deductive, because the initial theoretical concepts serve as a guide for examining similarities and differences that have a certain causal importance. It is also inductive, because it enables the researcher to determine which of the similarities and differences are theoretically relevant for analysing the different cases. However, it is not easy to find explicit discussions about the analytic frameworks and methodological strategies that guide the comparative studies on these regions.

The conclusions reached by comparative studies in explaining the divergent trajectories of the Scandinavian and South American regions mainly highlight the importance of a set of domestic transformations (institutional, political, economic, productive and technological) and the interaction with the opportunities and challenges that they had to face in the international arena at critical junctures. In particular, the domestic transformations that took place in the second half of the nineteenth century and the beginning of the twentieth century stand out in the way they conditioned the subsequent development of each region. In short, the main conclusions indicate that divergent development processes are closely linked to the degree of egalitarianism that was consolidated in these societies. The main differences identified have to do with the distribution of wealth and income, and in particular, with the distribution of land ownership—the principal resource in economies specialized in agricultural production—the distribution of political power and the distribution of economic opportunities for broad sectors of the population. The nature of the state and public policies were also key factors. All these factors would have had a positive or negative impact on the relevant processes for development. In particular, they would have conditioned the agricultural modernization process, structural change and industrialization; the transformation of the export basket, the educational levels of the population and the accumulation of human capital; as well as the rates of incorporation of technological change and increased productivity.

Although it is possible to identify both a Scandinavian development path (Árnason & Wittrock, 2012; Derry, 1979; Senghaas, 1985) and South American development path (Bértola & Ocampo, 2012; Cardoso & Faletto, 1971) each region contains diverse realities. Therefore, the most common comparisons usually include the Scandinavian countries—or some of them—and the relatively more developed countries of South America such as Argentina, Uruguay and Chile, as well as the southern region of Brazil (Senghaas, 1985; Lingarde & Tylecote, 1999). Along with Australia, New Zealand and Canada, these South American countries conform to the group of so-called new settler economies in temperate climate zones (Denoon, 1983; Lloyd et al., 2013). The most fruitful comparisons between the Scandinavian countries and those of the Latin America Southern Cone therefore tend to include in the comparative analysis the successful European settler economies of Australasia. More recently, an innovative research project looks at the Andean region of Latin America (Chile, Bolivia and Peru) and the Scandinavian countries, emphasizing some common ground between these regions in the nineteenth century and the differences that explain their long-term divergent trajectories (Ducoing & Peres-Cajías, 2021).

In the next section, we summarize the main contributions of the comparative literature on both regions that has been produced in recent decades (see Table 1). The main aim of this chapter is not to discuss the central conclusions of the literature but to present the grounds on which the main contributions of this book are based.

Table 1 Authors, countries, main topics analysed and period

Author	*Cases*	*Main topics*	*Period*
Senghaas (1985)	Scandinavian countries and Southern settler economies of Australasia (Australia and New Zealand) and South America (Argentina and Uruguay)	Export growth-led, structural changes and industrialization, education, income distribution and economic growth	Nineteenth and twentieth centuries
Lingarde and Tylecote (1999)	Scandinavian countries and Latin America Southern Cone (Argentina, Brazil, Chile and Uruguay)	Technological paradigms and the role of inequality and income distribution	1870–1970
Maloney (2007)	Scandinavia, Latin America and other regions	Technological innovation, education and capacity to absorb new technology and domestic innovation, natural resource abundance and economic growth debate, trade policy	Nineteenth and twentieth centuries
Blomström and Meller (1991)	Scandinavian countries and some South American countries (Colombia, Chile, Ecuador and Uruguay)	Agricultural reforms, income distribution, education, structural changes, commercial and industrial policy, technology, the role of the state, institutions	Twentieth century
Ducoing et al. (2018)	Nordic countries and Andean regions of South America (Chile, Perú, Bolivia)	Trade specialization, export basket, economic growth volatility, the role of natural resources on the development path	Nineteenth and twentieth centuries
Ducoing and Peres-Cajías (2021)	Nordic countries and Andean Regions of South America (Chile, Perú, Bolivia)	Export basket, technology in mining and oil sectors, fiscal policy, state role, population growth, education	Nineteenth and twentieth centuries
Ranestad (2016)	Norway and Chile	Mining sector, education, research centres, technology, innovative environment	1870–1940
Havro and Santiso (2012)	Norway and Chile	Natural resource curse debate, the role of oil and copper, political economy, technology transfer, institutions	ca 1980–2010

(continued)

Table 1 (continued)

Author	*Cases*	*Main topics*	*Period*
Bull (2019)	Scandinavia (with emphasis on Norway) and Latin America	Varieties of capitalism approach, inequality, income distribution	2000–2015

2 South America and Scandinavia in a Comparative Context

One of the best examples of comparative analysis that include Scandinavia and Latin America is the classic book by Senghaas (1985) about European development paths. It contains a fascinating comparison between the Scandinavian countries, some South America economies and the former British settler economies. Senghaas' book is a critique of modernization theories from a comparative historical analysis in which he identifies two possible development paths in the international arena from a world system approach: auto-centric and peripheral development. The former refers to the industrialized countries' development process, in which sustained growth and social development are combined. The second is the typical path followed by countries that fell behind in the world economy and form part of the so-called "Third world".

The emergence of Britain as leader of the world economy in the nineteenth century, and the world market integration that resulted from the First Globalization of capitalism, imposed enormous challenges for countries around the world. Most of them had to face the pressure of peripheralization. In this sense, a key question that is tackled in the book is how peripheral economies can avoid further peripheralization and move towards auto-centric development paths. Senghaas emphasizes two possible development policies in response to peripheralization: associative and dissociative strategies. The first means openly accepting the challenges of the world economy and adapting to the leader—Britain—through the international division of labour. The dissociative strategy attempts to develop the domestic economy by implementing protectionist measures in order to industrialize.

To understand the development paths of European countries, Senghaas elaborated a typology identifying five types of auto-centric development.

One of them—type III—combines a sequence of associative and dissociative development paths. This was the kind of development experienced by the small, agricultural, export-oriented economies of Scandinavia and the so-called European settler societies of Australasia (Australia and New Zealand) and South America (Argentina and Uruguay). In both groups of countries, the export-orientated production of agricultural, forestry and mineral commodities did not lead to the emergence of typical exclave economies but paved the way for a broad-based and well-proportioned opening up of the domestic market. In all these cases, their growth dynamics during the First Globalization era are characterized as exogenously determined and dependent. But the key issue that Senghaas highlights in comparing both groups of countries is to understand why some have succeeded in developing from an agricultural trade specialization into mature capitalist national economies, while others devolved into peripheries of the world economy. In this sense, in the temperate zone of the southern hemisphere, there are divergent experiences of development between Australia and New Zealand, on the one hand, and Argentina and Uruguay, on the other hand.

The central assumption of Senghaas that justifies the comparison between both groups of countries is that, despite facing the same initial world economic conditions, a successful development path cannot be taken for granted. The export economies of Argentina and Uruguay had good export opportunities at the turn of the twentieth century. However, their growth did not have the structural spillover effects that were enjoyed by Australia, New Zealand and, especially, the Scandinavian countries.

Beyond specific differences, Scandinavian countries and European settler societies had similar conditions in the nineteenth century. Mainly, they all enjoyed similar natural resource endowments and a similar insertion in the international market. In this regard, one of the main conclusions of Senghaas is that other factors, beyond their initial conditions, governed the development chances of export economies. A fundamental factor was the prevailing social structure at the beginning of the export growth period; that is, the different institutional and social conditions in which the production of export-orientated agricultural commodities took place.

Therefore, according to Senghaas, the existence of a series of prerequisites was critical as a starting point to move towards an auto-centric development path and to lower the risk of peripheral development. The most important was the extent of inequality. In particular, a land ownership structure that did not impede agricultural modernization, a moderate level of inequality in the distribution of essential resources such as land and mining ownership, and improvements in the income distribution that facilitated saving and investment in productive activities. Additionally, Senghaas emphasized the importance of a high level of education, a stable political framework resulting from increasing democratization of political institutions and the emergence of new social movements. In a nutshell, the development path of a country depends on the initial distribution of resources and on a shift of political power towards new economic groups over the course of the development process. Therefore, income distribution was a critical factor for both the agricultural modernization process, and the consolidation of the domestic market to create demand for manufactured goods.

To a large extent, the historical dynamics that Senghaas compares are based on earlier work and secondary sources that present stylized facts about development patterns. In order to explore these hypotheses in depth, more comparisons based on better empirical evidence and the reconstructions of historical data series are required. Probably one of the best-accomplished examples in the book—albeit based on a set of secondary sources—is the comparison between Denmark and Uruguay, and the contrast with the case of New Zealand. However, as we will see in Chapter 7, this kind of comparison demonstrates how relevant are currently in the field of economic history, based on the historical analysis of the processes of distribution of natural resources and their effects on the distribution of income.

Another fruitful comparison between the Scandinavian countries and the Southern Cone of South America was written by Lingarde and Tylecote (1999). They contrast the development path of both regions focusing on the role of technology. The general theme of this work is the convergence of peripheral countries with the core countries during the one-hundred-year period between 1870 and 1970. The problem identified regards the fact that some countries were more successful than others in achieving this convergence. Tylecote's long wave theory, which places a focus on the technological forces that drove growth, trade and intercountry specialization in different periods, is used by the authors to explain the relative success of some peripheral countries in comparison to others. This allows them to put the focus on two aspects of development. The first is the changing opportunities and challenges that appear over time. The second is the cyclical nature of world developments which oblige countries to respond by "reassessing" their trade relationships; some with more success than others.

They emphasize changing core–periphery relationships with regard to changing underlying technological paradigms. As understood by the authors, these are relationships between high-technology and low-technology countries. During cyclical upswings, peripheral countries find opportunities to engage in the production and export of primary goods, but may overcommit to certain exchange relationships and suffer when their export prices fall (due to world oversupply) or foreign investment cannot be repaid. This can drive countries to try to reposition themselves through import substitution and technological advancement. Low inequality helps in this, through its impact on education, reduction of social distance between workers and managers, and broadening the market for domestically produced goods. Long-wave downturns, where terms of trade turn against the periphery, provide incentives for instituting changes. These windows last for 20–25 years, and the success of countries in this endeavour depends on complex social and institutional factors. If sufficient change is implemented before the wave upswing, countries can successfully move towards the production, and even export, of high-tech goods, and begin importing low-tech goods.

Thus, the goal of Lingarde and Tylecote's (1999) paper is to explain the success or failure of two groups of countries in ascending towards the high-technology core. The first group, the Nordic countries, includes Denmark, Norway, Sweden and Finland. The second is a group of three Latin American countries: Argentina, Brazil and Uruguay. All of these countries were linked to the world economy beginning roughly in the last third of the nineteenth century. They share other characteristics, as well as displaying certain differences, that are highlighted by the authors.

The main shared characteristic is that they were all rich in natural resources and had relatively low population densities. However, only the South American countries were truly "land abundant", in the sense that land was available for settlement by European immigrants. This allowed for subsistence agriculture and mass commodity exports. The Scandinavian countries in fact had mass emigration in the early part of the period under study.

According to Tylecote and Lingarde, the countries in the two groups were also similar in terms of GDP per capita and human capital levels in 1870. In general, the Nordic countries (except Finland) were better off than the Latin American countries in this regard, although intra-country disparities mean that, for example, literacy rates in Argentina's capital, Buenos Aires, were likely as high as those in the Nordic countries, and the same can be said about the Uruguayan case. However, the South American countries seem to have been better off in terms of nutrition levels, with Norway, Sweden and Finland having low average daily calorie intakes and periods of mass starvation. Countries in both groups also needed foreign capital for investment. One of the main differences between the two groups of countries is in inequality levels, both in strictly economic terms (income and wealth), as well as in the distribution of land and political power. The Scandinavian countries had much lower levels of inequality and higher levels of social integration than the South American countries.

The paper describes, mostly narratively, the production, trade and technological performance of these countries during three different periods which are defined by their underlying technologies: steam technology (i.e. steamships and railways), steel and electricity, and Fordist production. In general, the Nordic countries were better able to take advantage of the opportunities offered by changing technologies, and responded with domestic innovation which allowed them to move up the technological ladder. By the 1920s, Denmark, Norway and Sweden had caught up to the core European countries in terms of GDP per capita. This was due to their high performance during the steam technology and steel and electricity phases. Their low inequality levels and high degrees of social cohesion created conditions for their entrepreneurial sectors to respond to the opportunities offered by these technologies. Finland lagged behind the other Nordic countries, but performed well in the Fordist production phase, closing the gap in welfare levels.

The South American group was less successful at this, in large part due to their higher inequality levels, especially in terms of land distribution. Nevertheless, the trajectory of these three countries was not the same. All were able to take advantage of the first wave, inserting themselves into the world economy as primary product exporters. Argentina and Uruguay, however, were not able to take advantage of cyclical downturns in order to modify these trade relationships. Their small domestic markets and relatively high real wages prevented local entrepreneurs from responding to the opportunities offered by new technologies. They simply were not sufficiently remunerative. Thus, their GDP per capita growth stagnated, and they fell behind their European peers. Brazil, on the other hand, responded to international shocks, such as the First World War, through greater levels of import substitution and production of industrial and capital goods for the domestic market. The country's lower real wages and large domestic market meant these shocks were sufficient to provide profitable, although limited, opportunities for economic diversification. Its success was qualified. Although it did launch itself on a technological advancement trajectory, it did not reach core levels of development.

Maloney (2007) also emphasizes the role of technological innovation to understand why Latin America lagged behind developed countries. This paper focuses on development in resource-rich countries. The issue investigated is not the possible existence of a resource curse, but rather why some resource-rich countries were able to successfully develop high-technology sectors, while others were not. The main question asked is why Latin American countries failed to successfully move beyond pure natural resource exploitation into technologically intensive sectors. The author defends the idea that it is not necessarily the industrial sector that is important, but rather, the key is to have sectors that can promote innovation.

Maloney (2007) compares Latin America to a range of countries in other parts of the world. The author uses the term "late modernizing, resource-rich countries", a group which includes Latin American and Scandinavian countries, as well as Canada, Australia and New Zealand. Although the article does not focus specifically on a comparison between Latina America and the Scandinavian countries, a dichotomy between those two regions appears throughout the paper. The author describes a continuum of performance, especially during the import substitution period, with the Latin American countries as the worst-performing, and the Scandinavian countries, especially Sweden, as the best performers.

Two explanations are offered for Latin America's poor performance. First, historically, Latin American countries had lower capacities to absorb new technologies and for domestic innovation. Second, these countries had intense import substitution regimes, which stifled adoption of new technologies. Before entering into each explanation in detail, Maloney offers up a regression analysis relating resource abundance to economic growth. It shows that a negative coefficient on a Latin American dummy variable disappears when variables capturing innovative capacity and trade openness are included, suggesting these are the variables that explain the region's divergent path.

In regard to the first explanation, the author argues that Latin America had "deficient national learning and innovative capacity" in comparison to other countries. This is shown through a discussion of literacy rates and technical education. Latin American countries lagged behind the US, Australia, Canada and Sweden, in part due to the former's high inequality levels. Literacy was important for absorbing new technologies, since these were largely accessible in written form. Latin America also had more limited technical education. While Sweden, for example, already had universities and technical schools in the early nineteenth century, Latin America did not develop these institutions until the end of the century. This can be seen reflected in the number of engineers per capita, which was much higher in the US, Sweden and Australia than in Latin America. It can also be seen in the reliance on immigrants for developing technologically advanced sectors in Latin America. For example, mining in Mexico, industry in Chile and cattle ranching in Argentina were dependent on immigrants for innovation and advancement.

The second explanation for Latin America's failure to move to high-technology production was its more intense import substitution regimes compared to countries in other parts of the world. The main initial impetus for many import substitution programmes, the Great Depression, seems to have affected all the countries studied roughly equally (in terms of reduction in trade and export prices, and rises in unemployment). However, the reactions to this event were quite different, with some countries closing themselves off economically, while others remained much more open. In Latin America, protectionism, as measured by tariffs as a per cent of imports, was higher, and lasted much longer than in Australia, Canada and the Scandinavian countries. The author notes, however, that high tariffs have been blamed for slow growth performance and for lowered innovation in other countries, notably Australia and Canada. The fact is though, that the impacts were worse in Latin America.

An exciting effort to understand the divergent development paths of Latin America and Scandinavian countries is presented in Blomstrom and Meller's (1991) book. However, it is not a comparative economic history in a strict sense. It contains economic histories of four Scandinavian countries—Sweden, Denmark, Norway and Finland—and four medium-sized Latin American cases—Chile, Uruguay, Ecuador and Colombia—that illustrate their divergent paths. The introductory chapter offers some lessons for Latin America that arise from the comparison of the two regions, focusing on six factors in which the historical trajectories of the two regions were different: agriculture, education, natural resources and industrialization, commercial and industrial policy, technology and foreign investment and sociopolitical factors and the role of the state.

Despite large differences in the levels of development between Latin America and Scandinavia today, Blomstrom and Meller (1991) remind us that in the late nineteenth and early twentieth centuries, the countries in the latter region were as underdeveloped as their counterparts in Latin America. Regarding the differences that determined divergent path, they state that in Scandinavia agricultural reforms were carried out early on, as far back as the late eighteenth century (Denmark) up to the early twentieth century (Finland). This allowed for more productive use of the land, development of artisanal (and later industrial) activities linked to agriculture, and a more equal distribution of income, with consequent effects on demand for manufactured goods.

The Scandinavian countries not only extended education early on; the focus placed on science and technical skills served them well in the process of technological advancement. Mass adult education, financed by the state, kept unemployment low and fostered structural change. Latin America's higher education systems are less developed, targeted towards the elite and traditionally have not taken practical and applied approaches.

While Latin America forced industrialization during the import substitution industrialization (ISI) period, attempting to replicate the US input–output matrix from one day to the next, Scandinavian industrialization developed slowly, beginning in the late nineteenth century, and was based on their natural resources. Although small-scale and artisanal at first, they gradually developed modern, competitive industries.

The two regions also differ in terms of commercial and industrial policy. Scandinavia kept tariff barriers low and supported companies in areas where their countries had a comparative advantage, with the state providing infrastructure and incentives for them to prosper. Because their economies were relatively open, they could allow large companies without fear of monopolistic behaviour, since international competition would discipline them and guarantee efficiency. They also allowed inefficient industries to decline, counting on their social security and education systems to help transfer workers to high productivity sectors. Latin America's economies, relatively closed off during the ISI period, suffered from inefficient companies, often propped up by the government in order to preserve employment.

New technology can be adopted through a variety of channels: imports, movement of people, foreign investment, etc. The Scandinavian countries used several methods throughout their history. One factor that made this fruitful for them was their capacity to apply new technologies resulting from their educational achievements. Latin America's relative backwardness in this respect has hindered technological adoption.

The final difference between the two regions that Blomstrom and Meller (1991) highlight is their sociopolitical relations and the role of the state. In Scandinavia, the state played a fundamental role in supporting technological advancement and growth, but in general did not participate directly in the economy. This contrasts, according to the authors, with the Latin American experience, where state involvement in production, finance and even economic planning is common.

More recent comparative research analyses the divergent development paths of Scandinavia and Latin America by considering the natural resource curse debate (Sachs & Warner, 1995). Ducoing et al. (2018) place their research within the debate about the "curse of natural resources". According to this view, there is a negative relationship between the level of natural resources in a country and its economic performance. The problem identified by the authors is that there are countries rich in natural resources which have performed well economically and have transitioned from primary goods exporters to knowledge economies (Lederman & Maloney, 2007; Ranestad, 2018).

They discuss the relative economic performance of six countries, seeking to explain the divergence between two groups of countries: Nordic and Andean. The countries are chosen for two reasons. First, they are all rich in natural resources. Second, the income per capita levels in 1850 were much closer than they are today. In other words the Nordic and Andean countries have diverged over time.

The paper reviews the literature on the development of these countries from the mid-nineteenth century up to 2015 and presents data on their economic performance over time (population, GDP per capita, trade, human capital and taxation). It seeks to delineate some stylized facts that can shed light on the divergence mentioned above and to describe historical processes that explain how natural resources impacted development.

The population data show, essentially, the effects of the delayed demographic transition in the Andean countries (and the different moments when this transition occurs within the group). It is suggested—although it is not discussed in depth—that this could be a major factor in the differing impacts of natural resource abundance. The GDP per capita data show the relative volatility of the Andean countries, as well as the importance of the Great Depression as a break point in the divergence trajectories.

In regard to trade, export baskets were much less diversified for the Andean countries, with consequent volatility and relatively little structural change. Industrialization was limited in these countries. In contrast, in the Nordic countries, industrialization was successful, and involved technological transfers from advanced countries and adaptation to local conditions. This has to do with the Nordic countries' greater literacy rates and education levels, as well as entrepreneurial links to industrial sectors in the advanced economies. In essence, Nordic countries were able to diversify out of natural resources, often into adjacent industries, due in part to social structures and human capital. Andean countries were less successful in this matter, and thus remained dependent on natural resources (and thus were more subject to the "curse").

Tax revenues as a percentage of GDP were similar in all six countries at the beginning of the period, but diverged in the twentieth century. Tax revenues in the Nordic countries rose significantly, while those in the Andean countries remained low. Regarding this variable, the paper does not explicitly identify the connection to natural resources, but the suggestion appears to be that the development of a broader tax base in the Nordic countries may have liberated them from dependence on natural resources.

Ranestad (2016) also puts the focus of the comparative analysis on the Nordic and Andean countries, comparing the mining sectors of Norway and Chile from the First Globalization era up to the Second World War. Ranestad states that the main problem with the resource curse hypothesis is that there are many resource-rich countries that have developed rapidly. Some countries seem to develop not only in spite of, but also because of, their natural resources. Earlier comparisons of Latin America and Scandinavia, to explain differences, focus on "foreign technology, agricultural reforms, political regulations and education". However, the author believes these discussions have remained too general, failing to understand these phenomena in detail. In another book, Ranestad (2018) presents a more in-depth discussion on this issue.

The main idea is that "learning depends on an innovation-friendly institutional and organizational context (Ranestad, 2016: 1)". The paper studies knowledge organizations, such as education, industrial societies and research centres, in Chile and Norway that were tasked with generating technical knowledge for application in those countries' mining sectors. It goes beyond simply looking at the aims of these organizations, and examines how the people that worked in them learned and how they applied knowledge to change and adapt technology.

Chile and Norway are chosen because of their geographical and geological similarities (mountainous, long coastlines, rich mineral resources). Furthermore, similar types of public and private organizations designed to develop knowledge for mining can be found in both countries. These include engineering programmes, technical societies, professionals, consultants, scholarships and industrial exhibitions.

The paper finds differences between Chile and Norway in regard to how intensively mineral ores were utilized, the level of technology in the mining sector and in the linkages formed to other industries. Thus, they make good comparative case studies for answering the question why some resource-rich countries developed rapidly while others stagnated.

Havro and Santiso (2012) compare these same two countries—Norway and Chile—highlighting the role of development policy. However, this text takes a different perspective, in that it views both countries as successful experiences of natural resource-based development. The paper studies Norway, and its oil boom beginning in the mid-twentieth century, and Chile's experience with copper since the 1970s. These countries are chosen in part for their similarities, both are small, open economies that rely heavily on natural resources, and because they are the most cited exceptions to the natural resource curse.

The authors state that the success of Norway and Chile has been due, in large part, to the way that their governments have managed the natural resources and the income that derives from them. In the case of Chile, this assertion may be viewed, at the least, as polemical. In any case, both countries used the revenue generated from natural resource exploitation to pay down debt and to establish sovereign wealth funds. These funds help absorb income during times of high resource prices in order to help insulate the economy from inflation and Dutch disease. They are also used to fund economic stimulus during downturns. Both countries have experienced political pressure to spend greater amounts of natural resource income on development needs, such as education, but have maintained these funds and used them to provide macroeconomic stability. They have also increased tax revenue from other sources so as not to be so dependent on natural resources.

Both countries have also managed to diversify away from the natural resource sector, building linkages to adjacent industries or stimulating other sectors. For example, Norway successfully developed engineering and supply sectors for the oil industry by insisting companies have onshore bases in the country, use domestic workers and source inputs with local content. Chile also tried to encourage technology transfer, in part through the state-owned company Codelco, which manages the country's largest copper mine. The internal policy of this company was to use local content when possible, and it partnered with foreign firms, which gave local engineers exposure to the latest technology. Chile also managed to promote the wine and fruit exporting industries.

The quality of institutions in these countries is also seen as an important factor in their success. According to the authors, both countries historically have had strong bureaucracies and strong checks and balances between different areas of government. This is especially important with regard to management of the natural resource funds and to the implementation of counter-cyclical fiscal policy. Political stability (in the case of Chile, since the end of the dictatorship) has helped, providing an appropriate policymaking climate and relative consensus among interested parties. However, Havro and Santiso (2012) appear to take an optimistic view of the Chilean path when evaluating its results vis à vis those of Norway. The Chilean political economy has systematically ignored inequality as a central problem of the pro-market development model initiated by the military dictatorship and continued by democratic governments until today (Rodríguez, 2017). Thus, exclusion and inequality were the main reasons for the popular mobilizations and social protests in 2019 (Mayol, 2020).

For this reason, other recent works place the focus on the issue of inequality and how the historical management of inequality in the Scandinavian countries can offer lessons for the future development of Latin America. In this sense, Bull (2019) tackles the issue of inequality reduction in developing regions. The paper studies the forces behind inequality reductions in Scandinavia and Latin America. First, the decades-long reduction in inequality in the Scandinavian countries is examined, looking at "structural factors, policy changes and strengthening or weakening of change agents", as is the more recent fall in inequality in Latin America. Bull (2019) uses this background to discuss the possibility of a more sustained, Scandinavian-style reduction in inequality in the latter region. The general conclusion is that it would be quite possible for Latin America to continue reducing inequality through democratization, wage compression, structural transformation and social spending, although there are many obstacles particular to the region which must be tackled.

The author discusses several factors contributing to sustained historical inequality reductions in Scandinavia (roughly from the 1930s to the 1990s). Broad agreement between workers and employers kept wages in the export sector lower than they otherwise would be, ensuring competitiveness. At the same time, wages in the non-tradable sector were raised. This "wage compression" helped the lowest-skilled workers and incentivized investment in the export sectors, reducing inequality while also raising average productivity. This was achieved through institutionalized wage negotiation mechanisms. Social policy promoted high labour market participation, in part through guaranteeing maternal and paternal rights, and subsidizing healthcare and childcare. The expansion of high productivity sectors and labour market participation and the universalist welfare state model generated rapid economic growth and guaranteed broad political support.

Although there is much disparity among countries, the more recent reduction in inequality in Latin America (2003–2013/2015) appears to have been primarily the result of reductions in wage inequality, and not due to an increase in the wage (vs. capital) share, which is very low compared to other regions. In addition, the income of the top 1% appears to have been left untouched. Some of the drivers were increased education and an ageing population (more experienced workers). Increased commodity prices created a demand for services, drawing workers out of low-productivity agriculture and the informal sector and into the not-so-low wage service sector. Another factor was changing tariffs; while tariff reductions in the 1990s tended to increase inequality, their stabilization in the 2000s reversed this trend, and reinforced the supply of better-paying, low-skilled jobs in the service sector. In some countries, emigration also played a role in reducing inequality, as high-skilled workers left, while remittances helped the poorest households. Other factors that contributed to inequality reductions were increases in social transfers and wage policies aimed at increasing the minimum wage (Bertola & Williamson, 2017).

With this background in mind, Bull (2019) discusses the possibility of Scandinavian-style inequality reductions in Latin America, highlighting how several of the phenomena associated with inequality reductions in the former might play out in the latter. They point out that moves towards democratization, with marginalized groups slowly gaining representation, have occurred recently in Latin America, although these groups tend to be more at odds with capitalism than were social and labour movements in Scandinavia. Wage compression, important in Scandinavia, could be achieved in Latin America, but would require institutional mechanisms to limit wages in the export sectors, thus incentivizing investment and promoting structural transformation. Low unionization and high informality rates could be an obstacle in this sense. Guaranteeing a diverse production structure and technological advancement is also important. Latin America exhibits some impediments in this respect, such as commodity dependence, institutional obstacles to efficient investment (clientelism, exclusive institutions) and macroeconomic distortions. However, the author points out that Latin America is not in a worse position than the Scandinavian countries were when they embarked on their inequality reduction paths. For example, a higher percentage of Norway's economy in the 1930s was in primary products compared to Latin America today. Social spending in Latin America, which increased in the first decades of the twenty-first century, tended to be targeted towards the most vulnerable groups. However, the lesson from Scandinavia appears to be the importance of universalist policies which encourage, rather than substitute for, labour market participation. In this sense, Latin America's weak state capacity may present an obstacle.

Finally, the book recently published by Ducoing and Peres-Cajías (2021) represents an up-to-date contribution to the comparison between Latin American and Scandinavian countries. It compares the performance of the Andean region of South America with the Scandinavian countries (with a focus on Norway and Sweden) from multiple perspectives. The book analyses the composition of exports from both regions and their long-term transformation, the technological gap in the mining sectors and the oil industry. Fiscal policies are also examined, considering the relationship of this last item to the exploitation of natural resources and the state's role. It also analyses the performance of each region, taking account of the costs of development in terms of sustainability. To this end, the book presents new data sets and novel historical evidence to explain long-term divergent development patterns. Some interesting conclusions of the work establish that the Andean countries, especially Chile, show a clear re-primarization and strong dependence on a single natural resource whose exploitation did not require extensive knowledge investments. By contrast, Norway combined exports in primary natural resources with a broader base of natural resource-based products and even increased its exports of high-tech manufactured goods (Peres-Cajías et al., 2021). Also, while the Andean countries showed lower fiscal pressure in the long run compared to the Scandinavian countries, taxes on international trade represented the most crucial revenue source until the early 1980s for the first group. On the other hand, besides avoiding fiscal dependence on natural resources, the Scandinavian countries developed a more broad-based tax system, where local taxes eventually represented a significant share of total revenues (Peres-Cajías et al., 2021). Additionally, the performance of the mining sector is a crucial aspect of the divergent trajectories. According to Peres-Cajías and Ranestad (2021), both regions were very similar in industrial structures and geophysical conditions (mineral and metal deposits) during the mid-nineteenth century. However they show an increasing gap in the capability to generate local knowledge and innovation in the mining sector before the Second World War because of the differences in the spread of mass education and the development of engineering programmes. In that sense, Rivero-Cantillano and Llorca-Jaña (2021) emphasized the divergent trajectory of each region in terms of schooling, education and human capital, in addition to an entirely different demographic trajectory (population growth, migration and the timing of the demographic transition).

An alternative way to measure the relative performance of both regions is through genuine saving estimations. Ducoing (2021) shows that the Andean countries performed worse than Scandinavian countries because of their longstanding strong dependence on natural resource exploitation. The investment in physical capital and intangible assets such as human capital and technology may result in higher consumption wages and well-being in the future. However, the author highlights that both the gap and the understanding of this gap between Andean and Scandinavian countries will not be narrowed by focusing solely on income indicators.

3 Lessons from the Literature Review

This brief review of earlier research focused on the Scandinavian countries and Latin America—and most specifically South America—from a comparative perspective sheds light on the relevance and usefulness of this kind of comparative research, mostly in the sense of understanding what structural factors have determined the divergent development path of these regions. Beyond their historical specificities, most of the research discussed assumes the presence of a set of common characteristics, having much to do with their position as natural resource-rich countries. They also highlight that the historical plot that traced the development trajectories of each region depended, to large extent, on the endogenous capacities built by each society, rather than solely on the advantages provided by nature and geography. One of the main lessons that emerge from this accumulated knowledge is that the economic performance and development of both regions were closely linked to the political economy that they set up.

Both regions benefited from the opportunities provided by the first globalization of capitalism as agricultural, export-oriented economies. However, long-term economic growth depended on how each society invested and converted the revenues captured through trade with the world economy into development policies. The authors highlight the role of domestic institutional factors. In the case of the Scandinavian countries, these domestic factors were associated with the formation of more equal social structures, in terms of the distribution of land ownership and income. The construction of institutional environments conducive to technological development in critical sectors, such as primary exports, and for investment in public goods, such as education, was important. These factors laid the foundations for sustained and balanced growth, the consolidation of domestic markets capable of supporting the transformation of the productive structure and the diversification of the export basket itself, incorporating processed goods with high technological content. The Scandinavian social structure helped to prevent the emergence of structural heterogeneity. Facing the same world market conditions, but under different local circumstances, Scandinavia could have become part of the third world and followed a peripheralization path as stated by Senghaas (1985).

Latin America, and specifically South America, presents a diverse panorama of historical experience. Most studies tend to compare the Scandinavian countries with the Southern Cone countries that have had more successful relative development. These countries specialized mainly in the production of agricultural goods typical of a temperate climate. Recent works have incorporated the Andean countries into these comparisons (Ducoing & Peres-Cajías, 2021), focusing on several issues highlighted by earlier research and also emphasizing new topics, for instance, the comparative analysis of the mining sectors, and the link between the fiscal contract and production based on natural resources.

They also examine the role of sustainability in the analysis of the divergent development paths between the two regions. As Bull (2019) highlights, the Scandinavian path of relatively equitable societies can provide lessons for Latin America in reducing structural inequality, beyond the achievements made by this region in the upward phase of the last economic growth cycle.

These studies also show the need to improve the accuracy of data on which the comparative studies are based. In particular, it is necessary to improve historical estimates of income distribution, wages, productivity growth in the agricultural sector during the modernization process of the nineteenth century, international trade, and industrial productivity in the different stages of growth throughout the twentieth century, to mention just a few areas. This research also shows the importance of improving the analysis of the role of the State in promoting development and education and in the construction of welfare states.

Regarding this last point, much can be learned from other comparative studies between the Nordic countries and the settler economies of Australasia, as shown by Davidson (1989), who compares the conformation and evolution of the welfare states of Sweden and New Zealand, and Castles (1994), comparing the welfare states of the Nordic countries and Australia.

Another exciting line of research to incorporate into the comparison between Latin America and Scandinavia is that developed by Ville and Wicken (2012) and Ville et al. (2019), comparing Australia and Norway as successful cases of natural resource-based economies. These countries have achieved modern levels of development and have been able to avoid the natural resource curse, building resource-intensive development strategies. These authors state that Australia and Norway have both developed based on exploitation and exports of natural resources, and they do not fit neatly into more traditional frameworks regarding resource-intensive development. The authors believe that by the twentieth century, natural resource industries had become knowledge-intensive. Countries with sufficient innovation capabilities and institutions were able to continue developing along a natural resource-intensive path.

As described in Chapter 1, the following chapters seek to advance on these lines of work by providing comparisons in each of the dimensions identified by these earlier works as a key to development, but with new historical data series and new methods of analysis.

References

Árnason, J. P., & Wittrock, B. (2012). *Nordic path to modernity*. Berghahn Books.

Bértola, L., & Ocampo, J. A. (2012). *The economic development of Latin America since Independence*. Oxford University Press.

Bertola, L. & Williamson, J. G. (2017). *Has Latin American inequality changed direction? Looking over the rong run*. Springer Open. https://doi.org/10.1007/978-3-319-44621-9

Blainey, G. (1966). *The tyranny of distance: How distance shaped Australia's history*. Sun Books.

Blomström, M. & Meller, P. (1991). *Diverging paths: Comparing a century of Scandinavian and Latin American economic development*. Inter-American Development Bank.

Bull, B. (2019). Is there a "Scandinavian Way" to reduce inequality in Latin America? *Iberoamericana – Nordic Journal of Latin American and Caribbean Studies*, *48*(1), 53–66. https://www.iberoamericana.se/articles/10.16993/iberoamericana.454/

Cardoso, F. H. & Faletto, E. (1971). *Dependencia y desarrollo en América Latina*. Siglo XXI.

Castles, F. G. (1994). Comparing the Australian and Scandinavian welfare states. *Scandinavian Political Studies*, *17*(1), 31–46. Accessed 11 May 2018. https://tidsskrift.dk/scandinavian_political_studies/article/view/32804/31058

Davidson, A. (1989). *Two models of welfare. Theorigins and development of the welfare state in Sweden and New Zealand, 1888–1988*. Uppsala University.

Denoon, D. (1983). *Settler capitalism: The dynamics of dependent development in the Southern Hemisphere*. Clarendon University Press.

Derry, T. K. (1979). *A history of Scandinavia. Norway, Sweden, Denmark, Finland and Iceland*. University of Minnesota Press.

Ducoing, C. (2021). Weak sustainability trends in the Andean and Nordic countries: A historical perspective. In C. Ducoing, & J. Peres-Cajías, J. (Eds.), *Natural resources and divergence. A comparison of Andean and Nordic tajectory* (pp. 257–278). Palgrave Macmillan.

Ducoing, C., & Peres-Cajías, J. (2021). *Natural resources and divergence. A comparison of Andean and Nordic trajectories*. Palgrave Macmillan.

Ducoing, C. et al. (2018). Natural resources curse in the long run? Bolivia, Chile and Peru in the Nordic countries mirror. *Sustainability*, *10*(965). https://doi.org/10.3390/su10040965

Havro, G. B. & Santiso, J. (2012). Rescuing the resource rich: How can international development policy help tame the resource curse? *SSRN Electronic Journal*. Elsevier BV. https://doi.org/10.2139/ssrn.1622687

Kaldor, N. (1979). *Equilibrium theory and growth theory in economic and human welfare: Essays in honour of Tibor Scitovsky*. In M. Baskia (Ed.). New York Academic Press.

Lederman, D. & Maloney, W. F. (2007). *Natural resources neither curse nor destiny*. Stanford University Press and the World Bank.

Lewis, C. (1954). Economic development with unlimited supplies of labour. *The Manchester School of Economic and Social Studies*, *22*, 139–191.

Lingarde, S., & Tylecote, A. (1999). Resource-rich countries' success and failure in technological ascent, 1870–1970: The Nordic countries versus Argentina, Uruguay and Brazil. *Journal of European Economic History*, *28*(1), 77–114.

Lloyd, C., Metzer, J., & Sutch, R. (2013). *Settler economies in world history. Global economic history series*. Brill.

Mackintosh, W. A. (1964). *The economic background of dominion-provincial relations*. McClelland and Stewart.

Maloney, W. F. (2007). Missed oportunities: Innovation and resource-based growth in Latin America. In D. Lederman, & W. F. Maloney (Eds.), *Natural resources. Neither curse nor destiny*. Stanford University Press and the World Bank.

Mayol, A. (2020). Protests and the political and social disruption in Chile in 2019: The crisis of legitimacy of the neoliberal model and a possible political resolution through the agreement on constutitonal change. *Asian Journal of Latin American Studies*, *33*(2).

Myrdal, G. (1959). *Economic theory and underdevelcped regions*. Durkwonh.

Peres-Cajías, J. & Ranestad, K. (2021). Engineers and the knowledge gap between Andean and Nordic countries, 1850–1939. In C. Ducoing, & J. Peres-Cajías (Eds.), *Natural resources and divergence. A comparison of Andean and Nordic trajectory* (pp. 169–218). Palgrave Macmillan.

Peres-Cajías, J., Torregrosa-Hetland, S. & Ducoing, C. (2021). The "fiscal contract" in Andean and Nordic countries, 1850–2010. In C. Ducoing, & J. Peres-Cajías (Eds.), *Natural resources and divergence. A comparison of Andean and Nordic trajectory* (pp. 113–142). Palgrave Macmillan.

Peres-Cajías, J., Badia-Miró, M., Carreras-Marín, A., Navarro, C.. (2021). Globalization and natural resource abundance: Is export diversification possible? A comparison of export composition in Chile and Norway, 1870–2017. In C. Ducoing, & J. Peres-Cajías (Eds.), *Natural desources and Divergence. A comparison of Andean and Nordic trajectory*. Palgrave Macmillan.

Prebisch, R. (1949). El desarrollo de la América Latina y algunos de sus principales problemas., *Relaciones CEPAL*, pp. 296–314.

Ragin, C. (1987). *The comparative method: Moving beyond cualitative and cuantitative methods*. University of California Press.

Ranestad, K. (2016). *The mining sectors in Chile and Norway, ca. 1870–1940: The development of a knowledge gap*. No. 105.

Ranestad, K. (2018). *Knowledge-based growth in natural resource intensive economies. Mining, knowledge development and innovation in Norway 1860–1940.* Palgrave S. Palgrave Macmillan. https://doi.org/10.1007/978-3-319-96412-6

Rivero-Cantillano, R. & Llorca-Jaña, M. (2021). Population, biological welfare and human capital in Norway, Sweden, Bolivia, Chile and Peru during the nineteenth and twentieth Centuries. In C. Ducoing, & J. Peres-Cajías (Eds.), *Natural resources and divergence. A comparison of Andean and Nordic trajectory* (pp. 143–168). Palgrave Macmillan.

Rodríguez, J. (2017). The political economy of income inequality in Chile since 1850. In L. Bértola, & J. G. Williamson (Eds.), *Has Latin American inequality changed direction? Looking over the long run* (pp. 43–64).

Rodriguez, O. (2006). *El estructuralismo latinoamericano.* Siglo XXI Editores y CEPAL.

Rostow, W. W. (1960). *Las etapas del crecimiento económico: Un manifiesto no comunista.* Edited by FCE.

Sachs, J. D. & Warner, A. M. (1995). *Natural resource abundance and economic growth, Working Paper.* National Bureau of Economic Research.

Senghaas, D. (1985). *The European experience: A historical critique of development theory.* K. H. Kimmig.

Skocpol, T. (2003). The promise of comparative historical analysis In J. Mahoney, & D. Rueschemeyer (Eds.), *Comparative historical analysis in the social sciences.* Cambridge University Press.

Solow, R. M. (1956). A contribution to the theory of economic growth. *Quarterly Journal of Economics, 70*(1), 65–94.

Sumner, A., & Tribe, M. (2008). *International development studies theories and methods in research and practice.* SAGE Publications Ltd.

Ville, S., & Wicken, O. (2012). The dynamics of resource-based economic development: Evidence from Australia and Norway. *Industrial and Corporate Change, 22*(5), 1341–1371. https://doi.org/10.1093/icc/dts040

Ville, S., Wicken, O., & Dean, J. (2019). Dynamic paths of innovation in natural resource industries in Australia and Norway since World War Two. *Scandinavian Economic History Review, 67*(1), 90–109. https://doi.org/10.1080/03585522.2018.1530136

CHAPTER 3

Trade Specialization, Industrial Growth and Economic Development in the Nordic and the Southern Settler Societies, 1870–1970

Jorge Álvarez, Luis Bértola, and Jan Bohlin

1 Introduction

The Nordic Societies (NS) and the Southern Settler Societies (SSS) of Latin America (Argentina and Uruguay) and Australasia (Australia and

J. Álvarez (✉) · L. Bértola
Universidad de la República, Montevideo, Uruguay
e-mail: jorge.alvarez@cienciassociales.edu.uy

L. Bértola
e-mail: luis.bertola@cienciassociales.edu.uy

J. Bohlin
University of Gothenburg, Gothenburg, Sweden
e-mail: jan.bohlin@econhist.gu.se

J. Álvarez and S. Prado (eds.), *Scandinavia and South America—A Tale of Two Capitalisms*, Palgrave Studies in Economic History,
https://doi.org/10.1007/978-3-031-09198-8_3

New Zealand) had one thing in common: by the end of the nineteenth century they were peripheral regions of the world economy, led by the industrialized countries. They all exported primary products, such as minerals or other raw materials, crops or foodstuffs. During the period 1870–1913, all these countries faced a dynamic demand for their exports, which significantly influenced the dynamics of the whole economy. The radical changes in the world order during the interwar years, and later during the Golden Age of the post-World War II era, imposed completely new challenges on these economies.

The focus of our attention is two strong stylized facts. First, by 1870, and taking the per capita GDP of the core countries as a reference, the NS countries were, on average, worse off than the SSS. However, during the century 1870–1970, the NS tended to converge with world leaders, while the SSS tended to diverge. The NS forged ahead of Argentina and Uruguay and converged with Australasian countries. The Australasian countries were always better-off than the Latin American, despite showing parallel divergent paths. In short, a process of reversal of fortunes took place, between the Northern and the Southern economies. Second, we can find some correlation between the ranking of the relative movements of these countries' per capita income and their capacity to undergo structural change, either measured by the degree of industrialization, the share of manufactured goods in total exports or changes in the structure of the manufacturing sector in favour of more dynamic branches. In short: relative performance went hand in hand with structural change.

The aim of the chapter is to discuss some possible explanations for these two stylized facts. We will first present these stylized facts in more detail, as far as the scarce available information allows us to do that. We will then discuss different theories that may help explain the relation between the two stylized facts, i.e., economic growth and structural change. Structural change, as Douglas North once remarked, is not an explanation of growth, it is growth. We will therefore discuss some possible fundamental explanations for the success of the NS and the poorer performance of the SSS. In our attempt to explain the better initial conditions of the SSS societies, and the later reversal, we will go through various possible explanations, covering the wide range between resource determinism and political economy approaches.

2 The Stylized Facts

2.1 *Crossing Roads*

By 1870, as shown at the country level in Table 1, and at the regional level in Fig. 1, the Southern Settler Societies had a very privileged position in the world ranking according to per capita GDP. The Australasian economies had a per capita GDP that was 20% above the average of the leading industrial nations. The Rio de la Plata countries did not lag too far behind the industrialized countries' position. On the other hand, the Northern Societies, and particularly Sweden and Finland, showed clearly lower relative positions.

During 1870–1970, these different regions showed quite different relative changes in relation to the industrialized core. Let us remember that the core grew rather rapidly until 1913, that growth slowed down during the interwar years, and that during the Golden Age of Capitalism, around 1950–1970, growth rates were among the highest in history. Against this background, NS went through a process of catching up that continued after the end of our period of study. On the other hand, the SSS showed the opposite trend. Both Australasian countries lost their relative advantage, more so New Zealand than Australia. The Rio de la Plata countries showed a parallel path with Australasia but at lower per capita income. Beyond our period, this divergent trend continued until the present, with some fluctuations.

Table 1 GDP per capita as share of core (average of core countries =100)

	Argentina	*Australia*	*Denmark*	*Finland*	*Norway*	*New Zealand*	*Sweden*	*Uruguay*
1870	57.6	128.5	78.6	44.8	53.6	121.7	52.8	90.6
1913	76.7	104.2	79.1	42.7	56.0	104.1	58.1	61.3
1930	73.8	85.2	96.6	48.2	65.6	89.8	76.7	67.5
1950	68.2	101.4	95.0	58.2	74.3	115.7	92.2	60.2
1970	55.7	91.7	96.8	73.1	76.5	85.4	97.0	38.4

Sources Core countries, Nordic Societies, Latin American Southern Settler Societies, and Australasia: Maddison Project Database (2020) and Bolt and Van Zanden (2020); Uruguay, Bértola (2016); Argentina, Bértola and Ocampo (2012); Sweden, Schön and Krantz (2015); and Norway, Grytten (2015)

Note Core: France, German, United Kingdom, United States

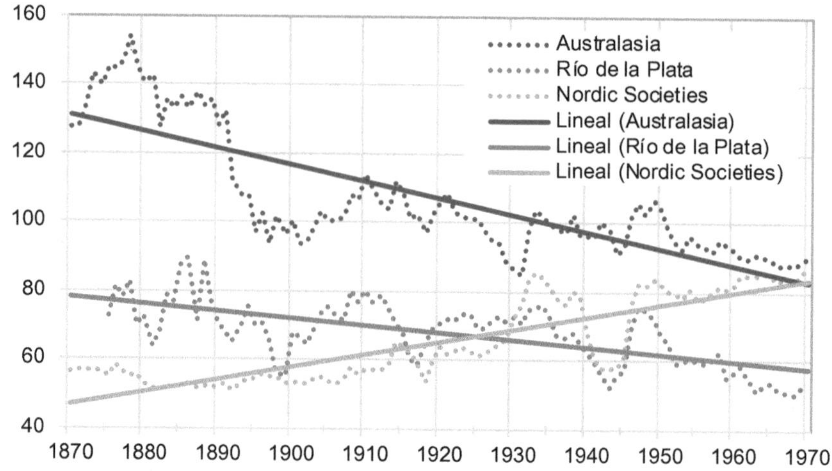

Fig. 1 Per capita GDP of the Nordic Societies, the Latin American Southern Settler Societies, and Australasia, 1870–1970 (*Sources* Based on sources of Table 1. *Note* Core countries as in Table 1 [weighted averages, core countries = 100])

2.2 *Industrialization, Structural Change and Industrial Exports*

One central concern is whether performance is linked to structural change and industrialization. Before we look at arguments and theories, let us look at the facts. As shown in Fig. 2, the three regions show quite different degrees of industrialization. The Nordic countries industrialized at a relatively stable rate, from the 1880s until the early 1960s. War periods and post-war recoveries presented minor disruptions to this steady march. The levels of industrialization of Australasia fluctuated strongly. Industrialization during the last decades of the nineteenth century was followed by de-industrialization, especially during the early 1920s, when these countries faced stagnating demand from the British economy. The late 1920s presented a recovery, but the real industrialization spurt took place in 1930–1960. In any case, the Australasian countries never reached the Nordic levels. The South American cases did not show such fluctuations as the Australasian before WWI, except for the critical decade of the 1870s. Otherwise, these countries showed a slight increase in the manufacturing share. As in the case of Australasia, industrialization accelerated after the 1930s, without ever reaching Nordic levels.

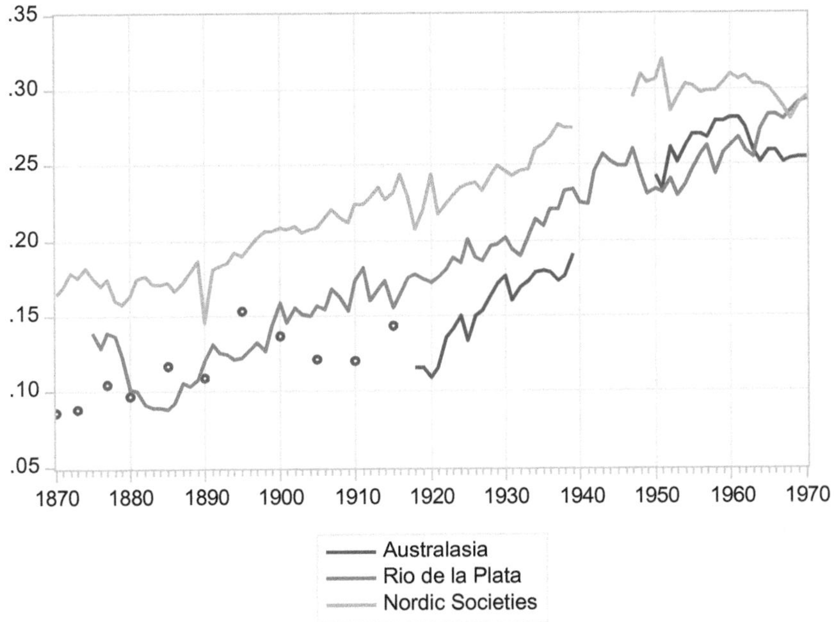

Fig. 2 Manufacturing share of GDP by region, 1870–1970 (*Sources* Sweden, Edvinsson [2014]; Denmark, Hansen [1974]; Norway, Grytten [2015], Nasjonalregnskap 1865–1960, Statistisk Årbok 1972; Finland, Hjerppe [1989]; Argentina, Ferreres [2010], Kosacoff [1993]; Uruguay, Bértola et al. [2014]; Australia, Ville and Withers [2015]; New Zealand, Briggs [2003])

The degree to which these countries could diversify their export baskets reflects the structure of the manufacturing sector. The scarce availability of information for the different countries and the differences in the applied statistical categories make it difficult to compare the structures. We were forced to aggregate the data in very broad groups: the traditional consumer industries, such as foodstuffs, clothing, footwear, beverages and tobacco, the group of industries linked to the forestry industrial complex, building materials and miscellaneous industries, and the more dynamic metal, engineering and chemical industries. Such broad categories obviously conceal important information and differences between countries, but some conclusions can nevertheless be drawn from Table 2.

Table 2 Structure of the manufacturing industry (percentage share of total output of the manufacturing industry) selected countries, ca 1870–1970

Sweden	**1870**	**1900**	**1913**	**1938**	**1970**
Food and drink, textiles and clothing, leather and footwear	36	30	28	24	13
Wood, paper, stone and building material and other industries	27	30	28	25	25
Metal, engineering and chemical industries	36	40	43	51	63
	100	100	100	100	100
Denmark		**1896**	**1913**	**1938**	**1970**
Food and drink, textiles and clothing, leather and footwear	–	60	60	55	34
Wood, paper, stone and building material and other industries	–	24	21	20	30
Metal, engineering and chemical industries	–	16	18	25	36
		100	100	100	100
Norway		**1896**	**1913**	**1938**	**1970**
Food and drink, textiles and clothing, leather and footwear	–	45	40	38	22
Wood, paper, stone and building material and other industries	–	41	34	24	26
Metal, engineering and chemical industries	–	15	27	38	52
		100	100	100	100
Finland	**1860–64**	**1900–04**	**1920–24**	**1935–39**	**1970–73**
Food and drink, textiles and clothing, leather and footwear	41	35	30	28	18
Wood, paper, stone and building material and other industries	26	43	55	51	51
Metal, engineering and chemical industries	33	22	15	21	31
	100	100	100	100	100
Australia			**1910**	**1939/40**	**1970/73**
Food and drink, textiles and clothing, leather and footwear	–	–	43	39	23
Wood, paper, stone and building material and other industries	–	–	29	22	23
Metal, engineering and chemical industries	–	–	27	39	54
			100	100	100

(continued)

Table 2 (continued)

New Zealand	**1873**		**1910**	**1938**	**1960–62**
Food and drink, textiles and clothing, leather and footwear	33	–	39	39	36
Wood, paper, stone and building material and other industries	60	–	43	33	30
Metal, engineering and chemical industries	7	–	18	28	34
	100		100	100	100
Argentina			**1914**	**1935**	**1974**
Food and drink, textiles and clothing, leather and footwear	–	–	61	52	33
Wood, paper, stone and building material and other industries	–	–	25	22	12
Metal, engineering and chemical industries	–	–	14	26	55
			100	100	100
Uruguay			**1930**	**1954**	**1972**
Food and drink, textiles and clothing, leather and footwear	–	–	64	57	60
Wood, paper, stone and building material and other industries	–	–	21	29	15
Metal, engineering and chemical industries	–	–	15	14	25
			100	100	100

Sources Own elaboration based on Australia, Hutchinson (2015: 292, Table 13.1), Boehm (1979: 127, Table 33); New Zealand, Rankin (1992: 13–25, Tables 1–13); Argentina, Vázquez Presedo (1988: 154–175, Tables III-3.8–III.18); Uruguay, Bértola et al. (2014: 53, Tables 4–5); Sweden, Bruttoproduktion, bruttoförädlingsvärde och insatsförbrukning för 9 industribranscher till löpande priser 1800–2000 downloaded from historia.se, based on methods and data presented in Edvinsson (2005); Denmark, Hans Kryger Larsen National Income Accounts downloaded from Larsen, Hans Kryger: Hans Kryger Larsen National Income Accounts, https://sites.google.com/site/danishnaproject/earlier-national-accounts/hans-kryger-larsen-national-income-accounts. Statistisk Årbog various years; Norway Grytten (2015), Nasjonalregnskap 1865–1960, Statistisk Årbok 1972; Finland, Hjerppe (1989, Table 10, p. 78)

Sweden stands out as the country with the deepest transformation, in the sense that here the group containing the metal, engineering and chemical industries was the largest around 1970, while the traditional consumer goods sector was the smallest. The story of Swedish industrial development is well-known. After World War II, Swedish industry was among the international leaders in fields such as the automotive industry, consumer durables, fighter aircraft, capital goods of various kinds, the shipbuilding industry and more (Chapter 5).

Finland stands out for the predominant role of the primarily export-oriented forestry industrial complex in its manufacturing sector, while Denmark stands out among the Nordic countries for the large role of the traditional sector. This reflected the important role of food products in Danish exports. The structural transformation of Norway's manufacturing industry was like that of Sweden, but not as deep, meaning that the traditional sector had a larger share and the modern sector a smaller share than in Sweden.

While the structure of the Australian manufacturing sector also underwent deep transformations, especially in the 1950s and 1960s, it did not reach a similar share of Australian exports or the penetration the Swedes achieved in the world market. The traditional consumer goods sector had a much larger share than in Sweden, more like the other Nordic countries. Despite its similarly narrow domestic market, New Zealand was able to undertake a process of structural change, even if the impact on the export basket was not impressive.

Argentina is a particular case. There, the traditional industries continued to play an important role. Argentina lacked the dynamic forestry industry, but the metal, engineering and chemical industries experienced significant development. Nevertheless, these branches mainly produced goods for the domestic market, with limited impact on exports. Uruguay is the country that underwent the least structural change by far, and the traditional sector continued to dominate. The inward-looking path of industrialization and the narrow domestic market were barriers very difficult to overcome.

In the late nineteenth century, all the countries in our sample were particularly dependent on demand growth from the core industrializing countries, especially Great Britain. The export ratios (exports divided by GDP in current prices) of the three groups of countries tended to increase up to WWI, reaching a level of around 25%. From then onwards, export ratios fluctuated strongly and tended to decline in the SSS. By contrast they remained high and relatively stable in the NS (see Fig. 2, Chapter 4).

Initially, all these countries exported primary and agricultural goods, but the types of commodities they exported differed. The difference in the initial export specialization between the countries is obviously related to the difference in their endowments of natural resources: vast areas of pasture and land in Australasia and Rio de la Plata (and land suited to wheat production in the case of Australia and Argentina) and vast areas of forest land in Sweden, Norway and Finland.

The question is whether these countries were successful in changing the structure of their exports throughout this long period. Tables 3, 4, 5, 6, 7, 8, 9, and 10 give a broad overview of the export composition for the countries in some selected years.

The Rio de la Plata countries overwhelmingly exported agricultural goods. In the case of Uruguay, the main export articles (hides & skin, meat, wool) accounted for 74% of export earnings in 1885. In 1960, the

Table 3 Export composition of Argentina for selected years (percentage shares)

	Hides & skin	*Meat*	*Wheat*	*Wool*	*Other agricultural products*	*Others*
1885	25	5	4	43	9	14
1900	14	6	32	18	15	16
1925	9	19	22	8	23	18
1950	13	11	14	16	9	37
1965	3	22	25	8	14	28

Source Mitchell (1983)

Table 4 Export composition of Uruguay for selected years (percentage shares)

	Hides & skin	*Meat*	*Wool*	*Others*
1885	30	14	29	26
1900	27	26	27	20
1925	15	39	29	16
1950	11	17	60	11
1960	12	24	35	29
1969	12	31	22	36

Source Mitchell (1983)

Table 5 Export composition of Australia for selected years (percentage shares)

	Butter & meat	*Wheat*	*Wool*	*Other products*
1885	2	8	63	27
1900	17	6	54	23
1925	10	21	39	29
1950	8	10	51	31
1970	11	9	16	64

Source Mitchell (1983)

Table 6 Export composition of New Zeeland for selected years (percentage shares)

	Meat, dairy and other agr. prod. incl. fish	*Wool*	*Gold*	*Forestry products*	*Others*
1875	0	61	25	3	11
1900	23	36	11	6	23
1925	50	32	1	2	15
1950	45	41	1	0	13
1970	52	19	0	3	25

Source Mitchell (1983)

Table 7 Export composition of Denmark for selected years (percentage shares)

	Agricultural products and food	*Of which animal products*	*Industrial products*	*Other*
1875	86	49	6	8
1900	89	71	5	6
1925	82	73	17	2
1950	71	53	24	4
1970	29	17	65	6

Source Johansen (1985)

same export items still accounted for 71%. The picture looks similar for Argentina, although Argentinian exports diversified into more types of agricultural goods. In 1885, 86% of Argentinian exports were agricultural goods. The most important export items in order of importance were wool, hides & skin, meat and wheat. In 1972, 72% of exports were still of

Table 8 Export composition of Sweden for selected years (percentage shares)

	Agriculture & fishing	*Timber and other wood products, pulp & paper*	*Mining and metal*	*Other industry*
1875	20	45	24	12
1900	1	53	24	21
1925	1	51	30	18
1950	5	44	41	11
1970	3	25	63	14

Source Petersson (1984)

Table 9 Export composition of Norway for selected years (percentage shares)

	Shipping	*Fish*	*Timber, paper & pulp*	*Other manuf. and mining*	*Other*
1875	45	20	19	10	6
1905	33	16	21	13	17
1925	29	14	24	26	7
1946	47	11	13	20	9
1960	44	7	10	26	13

Source Bjerke (1966)

Table 10 Export composition of Finland for selected years (percentage shares)

	Agriculture	*Forestry products*	*Wood products industry*	*Paper & paper products*	*Textile products*	*Other manu-facturing*	*Other products*
1875	23	15	36	7	12	7	1
1900	18	16	47	11	4	5	0
1925	14	11	44	28	1	3	0
1950	4	15	35	42	1	4	0
1970	4	26	16	39	7	8	0

Source Hjerppe (1989)

agricultural origin, with wheat and meat comprising the most important export articles.

The Australasian countries had a similar export specialization in the late nineteenth century. In the Australian case, dairy products, meat, wheat and wool accounted for 73% of export earnings in 1885. Wool alone accounted for 63%. In 1950, the same products still accounted for 69% of export earnings and wool alone accounted for 51%. However, in contrast to the Rio de la Plata countries, Australia managed to transform the composition of its exports in the post-war period. The relative importance of the traditional export staples diminished, while the share of manufactured goods increased from slightly more than 10% in the early 1950s to around 25% in the late 1960s (McLean, 2013: 197–198).

New Zealand's export specialization in the late nineteenth century was similar to Australia's, with the exception that gold accounted for a sizable share of New Zealand's exports. However, New Zealand did not manage to change its composition of exports in the post-war period to the same extent as Australia did. In 1950, meat, dairy products and wool still accounted for 86% of export earnings. Twenty years later, the share of these commodities in total exports had declined to 71%. Exports of manufactured goods, mainly to Australia, now made up a larger share (Briggs, 2003: 66; Hawke, 1985: 210).

Among the Scandinavian countries, Denmark's export specialization looked more like that of Australasia and the Rio de la Plata countries in the late nineteenth century. Denmark mainly exported bacon and egg and dairy products. In 1875, agricultural and foodstuffs accounted for 86% of total exports. The share was still 86% in 1950, but by 1970 it had declined to 29%. Industrial products increased as a share of Danish exports in the twentieth century from 17% in 1925 to 24% in 1950. By 1970, the share of industrial products had increased further to 65%.

Sweden also started out with a high share of primary goods in its exports. From the 1870s onwards products from forestry played a large role. It started with timber exports. Later, from the 1890s onwards, pulp and paper increasingly replaced timber as major export articles. Forestry and wood products accounted for 45% of Swedish exports in 1875, and the share was roughly the same 75 years later, in 1950. In the post-war period, the importance of pulp, paper and other forestry-based products declined. Their share of total goods exports was 25% in 1970. The export share of products from mining, metal and engineering industries expanded steadily from around 25% in 1900 to around 60% in 1970.

Norway's export specialization is peculiar. As in Sweden, forestry-based products played an important role. Another important export article was fish, which accounted for 15–20% of total export earnings in the late nineteenth century. However, the sector that accounted for most of Norway's export earnings during the entire period from 1870 to 1970 was shipping. In 1875, shipping accounted for roughly 45% of Norway's export earnings. Its share was about the same in 1960. As in the other Scandinavian countries, exports from the manufacturing industries made up an increasingly large share of Norwegian exports. Manufactured products other than wood products, pulp and paper increased from around 10% in the late nineteenth century to around 25% in the 1960s.

Finland had the least diversification in exports of the Nordic countries. From the late nineteenth century until 1970, Finland's exports were heavily dominated by products from the forestry industrial complex. From 1900 until 1970 these products accounted for between 70 and 80%, sometimes even more, of Finnish exports. As in Sweden, the composition of goods in this export category shifted from timber to an increasing proportion of processed goods such as pulp and paper. But unlike Sweden and the other Scandinavian countries, exports of other manufactured goods never gained much importance in this period.

In short:

- The NS significantly reduced the income per capita gap in relation to the world leaders in 1870–1970. On the other hand, the SSS lost relative positions. The Rio de la Plata countries showed a similar trend to Australasia but always showed lower levels.
- The NS showed overall higher levels of industrialization steadily increasing with some minor fluctuations up to the 1960s. Contrastingly, the SSS showed more fluctuating levels of industrialization with low figures up to the 1930s and a spurt afterwards.
- The NS showed a deeper transformation of the industrial structure in favour of more dynamic sectors.
- The three groups of countries showed increasing export ratios up to WWI but the ratios subsequently remained higher and stable in the NS, while they fluctuated strongly and tended to decrease in SSS.
- Finally, despite all the countries initially having very high shares of primary goods in their export baskets, the NS succeeded in transforming the structure of exports in favour of manufactured goods.

These are the stylized facts. In the next section we will discuss some theoretical approaches that give plausible explanations for the links between performance and structural change. Later, we will discuss other theories to explain these developments.

3 Theories About Structural Change and Economic Growth

The relation between economic growth and structural change has been at the centre of many research traditions. The fact that structural change takes place alongside the process of development can hardly be denied. However, there are many discussions about the relation between the two. Very briefly, the question is whether growth can be understood without understanding the dynamics of structural change and whether obstacles to structural change may block growth. Expressed another way, the question is whether structural change must be a policy goal to achieve high growth rates. We cannot aim to present an exhaustive literature review here. We will just mention a few references.

Conventional growth models, such as Solow's, do not care about structural change. Structural change is an outcome of the allocation of resources. Despite this, structural change has been a focus of interest for development economists. This line of research was important at a time when industrialization was seen as the most important economic transformation, and the lack or limits thereof were crucial for the understanding of underdevelopment. Furthermore, this strand of research made clear the difference between growth and development, thus emphasizing the need of holistic approaches to understand development. Paradoxically, one very strong approach was that of Kuznets (1966, 1971), who did not distinguish between growth and development, as he took for granted that growth was tightly linked to structural change and that structural change took place between different sectors associated with different social actors, and hence, to conflicts between them. Growth could not therefore be understood without a political economy approach, in which economic considerations must go hand in hand with a broader approach from the social sciences (Syrquin, 2007).

The structuralist tradition, as represented by Chenery and Syrquin (1975), stressed the existence of some universal patterns of structural change. Different development economists centred their attention on the conditions needed for such structural change to happen, and emphasized that this process took different forms and showed different dynamics in different historical contexts. Moreover, many development theories took into consideration the important role played by asymmetries in the international economy.

The well-known work by Gerschenkron (1962) stressed that followers based their catching-up processes on quite different forces, replicating with differences the pattern of development of the central economies. The Latin American structuralist tradition stressed that the labour and commodity markets worked differently in the centre and the periphery, and the fruits of technical change were distributed in different ways within and between the different world regions. Further, the demand-induced rate of technical change was faster in industrialized countries, where exports showed a higher income elasticity of demand. W.A. Lewis' classical model of unlimited supply of labour (Lewis, 1954) saw development as the growth of a modern high-productivity sector based on cheap labour, until the labour reservoir was absorbed, and real wages started to grow. This approach gave, as a result, an income distribution curve like that of Kuznets.

An already classical work regarding structural change and economic growth is Luigi Pasinetti's (1983). His goal is to study the related structural changes in production and consumption along neo-Ricardian lines, departing from a labour-based value theory, with the focus on technical change and uneven productivity and demand growth in different economic sectors.

More recent approaches from different schools of thought emphasize the role of structural change in development in the context of what we can call centre-periphery contexts. The post-Keynesian tradition, following the works of Kaldor, worked with growth models with endogenous technical change. Technical change is induced by demand expansion, through the Verdoorn law, meaning that countries with different patterns of specialization grow at different rates. Thus, countries with less dynamic patterns of specialization should diverge with respect to others (McCombie & Thirlwall, 1994).

The neo-Schumpeterian tradition, as represented by Perez (1983), Freeman (1987) and Lundvall (1992), focuses on the way different countries take part in the various technological revolutions and can exploit the potentialities of new technological styles. National systems of innovation are the crucial variable in this process. Also along Schumpeterian lines, Saviotti and Pyka (2013) see modern economic growth as the result of three processes: increasing productive efficiency, increasing output variety, and increasing output quality and differentiation.

Endogenous growth theory improves the supply-led neo-classical Solow model through the incorporation of endogenous technological change approached through investment in technical change with increasing returns to scale. The sector producing technology and innovation is critical for the growth process. The existence of differences in the dimension of this sector leads to increasing divergence among world nations' growth rates unless technological spillovers counteract this effect. Local capabilities to take advantage of the technological gap are crucial for catching up (Grossman & Helpman, 1991).

The evolutionary tradition, as represented by Verspagen (1992), presents a continuum of productive sectors in the North and in the South with different technical gaps. He combines supply-side neo-Schumpeterian and evolutionary approaches, with a demand-side post-Keynesian approach, to analyse the movements of the technical gaps. The gap depends on the rate of growth of technical change, due to the expansion of knowledge available to companies, and on the demand-induced technical change in different sectors. Peripheral countries may also take advantage of the technological gaps. As a result, a multiple equilibrium model is proposed. A more descriptive approach in line with Verspagen can be found in Lavopa (2011).

Neo-structuralist approaches, mainly developed at ECLAC, grew out of close interaction with the referred research traditions (Cimoli & Porcile, 2014). Also, along neo-classical lines of research, the role of structural change has been highlighted recently. Most well-known are the works of Hidalgo et al. (2007), who stress that different countries specialize in the production of different kinds of products: while rich countries can produce all kinds of products but are particularly competitive in products that only rich countries export, poor countries are specialized in the production of goods that are exported by poor countries.

4 How Can Differences Be Explained?

We have seen how these three groups of countries showed different performances during the 1870–1970 century and that they also showed related differences in terms of industrialization, structural change and export performance. We have also reviewed different theories that give support for the link between both stylized facts.

What we aim to do next is to explore some possible explanations of why these groups of countries evolved differently, without pretending to test any hypothesis. We just want to present plausible explanations that could form the subject of more ambitious research in the future. First, we need to understand why these countries had such different per capita income levels at the point of departure.

One approach that has been particularly dynamic during recent decades is Thirlwall's Law, a post-Keynesian approach to international growth rate differences, based on the relation between the different countries' productive structure and the resulting income elasticity of demand for exports and imports. As technical change is assumed to be dependent on demand growth, the productive structure determines the pace of productivity growth, under balance of payments equilibrium. Chapter 4 in this volume is exclusively centred in the discussion of Thirlwall's Law, so we will not expand further on this approach here.

4.1 The Levels at the Point of Departure

According to Table 1, the per capita GDP levels at our point of departure were quite different among the different regions. The only countries that do not fit the ranking are Argentina and Denmark, the latter being the only Nordic country with higher per capita income than an SSS (the former). Argentina was also a country with important domestic differences, between the very rich Buenos Aires and *Litoral* provinces, and the poorer so-called *Interior*. The initial differences make the study of the later reversal even more interesting.

How can we explain these very important initial differences? The answer is also of interest because it helps to understand the important per capita income difference between the Rio de la Plata countries and the rest of Latin America. Moreover, the question is also relevant to understanding why Argentina and Uruguay had so much higher per capita incomes than other Latin American countries.

According to Bértola and Ocampo (2012: Ch. 3), at least three factors may explain the difference between Argentina (Buenos Aires and *Litoral*) and Uruguay, on the one hand, and the rest of Latin America, on the other:

(a) the fact that they were relatively marginal and very sparsely populated regions during the colonial period—without mineral resources and without an indigenous population suitable for the extraction of coercive work—meaning that population growth relied mainly on European immigration, which was employed under capitalist relations or established as landowners and tenants;
(b) the relative abundance of natural resources that were in strong demand in Europe, and rising relative prices, especially with the arrival of transatlantic steam ships and the expansion of railways in the region;
(c) the fact that these countries with their temperate climate produced the same kind of products as the core industrialized countries determined that marginal prices were set at the core, and not in the periphery as in the famous Ricardian model. Thus, the rent of the soil was appropriated along the complex production and commercial chain, favouring, at least partially, both landowners and workers of the Río de la Plata region. As many typologies of Latin American development put it, the existence of a large domestic landowning class, despite the concentration of property, made a difference with respect to other countries specialized in the production of minerals, where the concentration of property of income was much higher and often in the hands of foreigners.

Despite the even longer distance to consumer markets, a similar argument can be used to understand the case of Australia and New Zealand. Nonetheless, the income difference between Australasia and the Río de la Plata was huge. To understand that we can add two arguments. On the one side, it is possible to speculate about higher levels of technical, organizational, and social efficiency, reflecting path dependence with respect to the former (and even current) colonial powers. On the other side, we can also consider the availability of mineral resources in Australia and New Zealand (such as gold), which helped to diversify the export basket and increase the availability of natural resources per capita.

By contrast, while the Nordic countries were much closer to foreign markets, their agrarian sectors had been under considerable demographic pressure which eventually led to a very high level of emigration to the New World. We can find some correlation between the level of per capita income and the emigration rates in the 1870s and 1880s: the Danish figures were 20.6 and 39.4; the Norwegian 47.3 and 95.2 and the Swedish 23.5 and 70.1.[1] In 1870–1913, the Nordic countries lost 1.759 million people, i.e., 15% of the population for the year 1890. The Finnish case is different: the low level of emigration may be seen in relation to a less intensive transformation of the traditional agrarian structures. The Finnish migration timing is closer to that of Latin Europe.

4.2 *Staple Theory*

Starting the discussion about how these groups of countries evolved, one possible explanation is the so-called staple theory (STh). This research tradition has stressed the fact that the type of primary endowments available is crucial for the prospects for development and structural change. This is important, because all our countries were primary goods exporters at the start of the process and their export activities provided the dynamic growth impulse, but their natural endowments differed significantly. The STh has for a long time focused on the particular backward and forward linkages inherent in the various export products, and the dynamics of productive and technical change they may imply (Innis, 1930, 1940; Mackintosh, 1939; Watkins, 1963). In contrast to the thesis of resource-curse literature, STh argued that a country specialized in processing natural resources could achieve high growth rates and high levels of per capita income through the rising income derived from exports and its consequent effects on the structure of the domestic economy. One crucial variable is whether staples are suitable for developing dynamic linkage effects. As noted by Schedvin (1990), backward linkages influence the pattern of investment activity, while forward linkages stimulate manufacturing and service industries using the output of the export industry as an input. A second crucial variable, which is interrelated with the previous, involves the distribution of the income from staples generated directly and indirectly. A more even income distribution is a positive stimulus for domestic growth and induces spending and investment in other sectors. This is what Watkins (1963) calls demand linkages.

In Sweden, the commodities that dominated the early export drive came from forestry and iron ore mines (Södersten, 1990). In Denmark, foodstuffs or industrial inputs from agriculture were more important

[1] All figures per thousand mean population, according to Ferenczi and Willcox, quoted by Hatton and Williamson (1994: Table 1.1).

(Hveem, 1990; Jensen et al., 2018). The Finnish economic development rested on forestry products: first sawn timber and later cellulose, wood fibre and paper pulp (Kaukiainen, 2006). The Australasian countries combined mining with agricultural production, with outputs such as gold, wheat, wool and meat. In the 1890s, frozen meat and dairy products became relevant staples because of the introduction of refrigeration technology in overseas transport. Most attention has been paid to the negative impacts of specialization in wool in Australia (Greasley, 2015; Hutchinson, 2015), and New Zealand (McAloon, 2009; Bertram, 2009), as wool provided little direct stimulus for manufacturing (Schedvin, 1990). The same can be said about wool and meat production from extensive livestock rearing in Argentina and Uruguay (Finch, 1981, 2005; Fogarty, 1985). The linkages flowing from the more land-intensive wool production and cattle-raising industries were less significant for regional economies than, for instance, the more capital- and labour-intensive mining industry and dairy farming. Thus, some staples had more linkage effects than others on growth and diversification, reflecting different consequential effects in terms of production and income distribution. Nonetheless, the final demand linkages of small economies, like those of New Zealand and Uruguay, may have proved insufficient to achieve any appreciable diversification (Álvarez, 2014; Hendy & Callaghan, 2013).

In short, the story told by staple theory is that Sweden benefitted from the opportunities opened by the forest and iron industries to advance in the productive chain. However, the STh can hardly explain Denmark's success in relation to the settler economies, even if, in this case, the income distribution effect, that is, demand linkages, could have played a crucial role. Other variables, such as proximity to consumer markets, must be considered. On top of that, it is important to keep in mind that our countries showed quite different outcomes despite similarities in resources.

STh has been developed in new ways by the so-called Product Space Theory (PSTh) (Hidalgo et al., 2007). This approach has an empirical point of departure. It studies the relatedness of different products in terms of networks and identifies the types of product networks that characterize countries with different levels of income. Rich countries export products that are only exported by rich countries. Therefore, the pattern of specialization of the different countries is crucial for their development prospects. This argument obviously has important implications in terms of industrial policy and challenges conventional ideas about comparative advantage.

The empirical finding is rather obvious: less developed countries specialize in products that are peripheral in the product space network and face many obstacles in moving towards the more dynamic sectors at the core of the global network. However, different peripheral products have different potentials; they move in forests with different distances between the trees, according to one analogy. In this case, forestry and iron production have more opportunities to move forward than cattle breeding, for instance.

One clear shortcoming of this theory is that it is not able to explain the radical structural changes produced in many economies, nor identify the underlying forces. The approach is very much empirical and does not aim to provide fundamental explanations of growth, as the neo-institutionalists like to say.

The same argument may be directed at the resource-curse tradition (RC). Many authors have argued that natural resource abundance is not a blessing but a curse. Countries with abundant natural resources are locked in a development path that does not encourage society to invest in knowledge and innovation but to extract rents from the control of these resources, thus inhibiting the development of other economic sectors and diversification. Often, the argument is linked to the Dutch disease explanation, i.e., that successful exports of natural resources lead to currency appreciation, thus favouring imports and damaging the competitiveness of other exports, and slowing down the aggregate growth rate.

There is a particular version of the staple theory, in fact linked to the neo-institutional approach. The argument is that certain crops show increasing returns to scale, thus favouring concentration of property and a development path based on the coercive extraction of labour and very limited human capital building. In this context, the institutional framework tends to reproduce this balance of forces, enriching the elite but hindering development (Engerman & Sokoloff, s. f., 1997).

This latter approach has many shortcomings, especially for our cases. It can hardly be argued that the Argentine problem, for instance, lay with the kind of staples it produced, as they were rather similar to those produced by the Australasian countries, or even the USA and Canada. We must broaden our view to give plausible explanations for the divergent trends we have identified and for the different patterns of structural change.

4.3 *The Tyranny of Distance*

The "tyranny of distance" is an expression used by Blainey (1966) to describe how geographical remoteness shaped the Australian identity and its development path. Similarly, the concept applies to New Zealand. We argue that in the cases of the SSS and the NS, distance played a decisive role in the development processes, but that this role changed over time depending on two key factors: the patterns of trade insertion and the pace of structural change.

Blainey (1966) highlighted two paradoxical features of the relationship between Great Britain and Australasia in the nineteenth century. On the one hand, their close political, economic and cultural connections and, on the other hand, the enormous geographical distance which place Australasia at the antipode of Britain. "Tyranny of distance" also implied that the transport revolution should have an important impact on the economy of the remote countries. This was also the case, if to a lesser extent, for the Southern Latin American countries, which were a marginal region during colonial times because of the lack of precious metals, mining resources or abundant native labour.

The first globalization boom and the transport revolution radically changed the remoteness of Australasia and the River Plate countries from Europe. Distance ceased to be a severe obstacle to the integration and connection of these lands with the world economy. The growing European demand for temperate climate goods (wool, grains, meat, hides, dairy products) triggered the expansion of the agricultural frontier in the SSS, and the four countries significantly increased the amount of formerly unused land that was now used for production. This process was also made possible by the increasing flow of European immigrants and capital to the new lands in search of better living conditions and more profitable opportunities for investment (Álvarez et al., 2007; Denoon, 1983; Lloyd et al., 2013).

The transport revolution and refrigeration further strengthened Australasian economic relations with Britain. Belich (2001) defined this process as re-colonization. Even though Argentina and Uruguay's political and cultural connection with Britain was not as close as Australasia's, both countries formed part of the so-called informal British empire from the first globalization era onwards.

While globalization, i.e., the transport revolution and the integration of factor markets, stimulated SSS development, its impact dwindled in importance at the beginning of the twentieth century, even before the institutional framework of the Belle Époque collapsed. From then onwards, the SSS moved towards a development model based on inward-looking industrialization. Paradoxically, together with changes in relative prices in favour of manufactures, and protectionist policies, distance became an ally of the domestic industry, which in some sectors found some kind of natural protection. However, inward-looking industrialization was unable to benefit from economies of scale and had to apply technologies designed for larger markets. Exports, however, remained mainly concentrated on raw materials and industrial products with relatively low industrial value added. During the 1960s, Argentina, as well as Brazil, started a modest process of industrial exports mainly directed at the regional market.

In the nineteenth century, the NS were fully integrated into the commercial circuits of Northern Europe. Although the first globalization had an impact on agricultural production and the composition of primary exports (the Danish "great transformation" in the late nineteenth century is perhaps the most outstanding example), globalization did not represent such a radical change as in the SSS, at least in terms of commercial insertion in the European market. The distance from the main industrialized markets of Western Europe was not a significant obstacle as industrialization proceeded in Europe and demand for imports from the Nordic region increased.[2] Later in the twentieth century the geographical proximity contributed to a more complex commercial relationship, in which the Nordic region enjoyed the positive effects of economies of scale and agglomeration.

In a nutshell, the first globalization boom implied a weakening of the tyranny of distance, helping to increase the relative price of primary production and access to world markets. Once the Belle Époque came to an end, SSS had to rely on inward-looking industrialization. Distance, together with tariffs and relative prices, became an ally of local industry. However, once world trade recovered momentum after WWII, southern

[2] This does not mean that communications have not been a severe problem. Sweden and Norway had to overcome geographical constraints that limited communications. As Derry (1979) points out, the railway did not enter the northern half of Sweden until 1886, and the network there took another thirty years to complete. In Norway, where the obstacles were still more significant, even in the southern half, Oslo and Bergen had no rail link until 1909. Denmark problems in this respect were much smaller.

industries found themselves badly prepared for international competition and the negative effect of the tyranny of distance was restored. NS faced a quite different situation. Despite the critical interwar period, these countries could smoothly develop their manufacturing sectors and easily overcame the limits of the narrow domestic market through dynamic integration into the wider European market, increasing their economic growth rate at a faster pace than the SSS.

4.4 *Demographic Dynamics and Economic Growth: The Case of Natural Resources*

Historical evidence has shown that, far from the Malthusian approach, economic growth and population growth can reinforce each other. Population growth, even if productivity levels do not improve significantly, may be seen as a sign of progress, as societies are able to feed more people within the same ecological environment. However, it is also well-known that modern economic growth has been a process in which the contribution of population growth to GDP growth has been permanently reduced in favour of the contribution made by per capita GDP growth, i.e., productivity growth.

Regardless of these general trends, the stylized facts of the period show quite different pictures in the Southern and Northern hemispheres. Between 1870 and 1970, the population in the NS doubled, while that of Australasia and the River Plate countries grew 8- and 12-fold, respectively (see Figs. 3 and 4). The main differences in growth rates could be seen in 1870–1930. Growth rates thereafter were significantly reduced.

Population dynamics has two sides: natural growth and migration. All countries went through the first phase of the demographic transition during this period, with some differences in timing. The River Plate showed very high natural growth rates until the beginning of the twentieth century. The most important difference was migration. In 1870–1913, for instance, the contribution of net migration to demographic growth was −38% in NS, while it was +28 and +44% in Australasia and RP, respectively (Table 11). In other words, 29% of the population increase in Australasia and 25% of the increase in the River Plate countries was due to the migratory balance. On the other hand, in 1870–1970, emigration slowed down population growth in the NS by 15%.

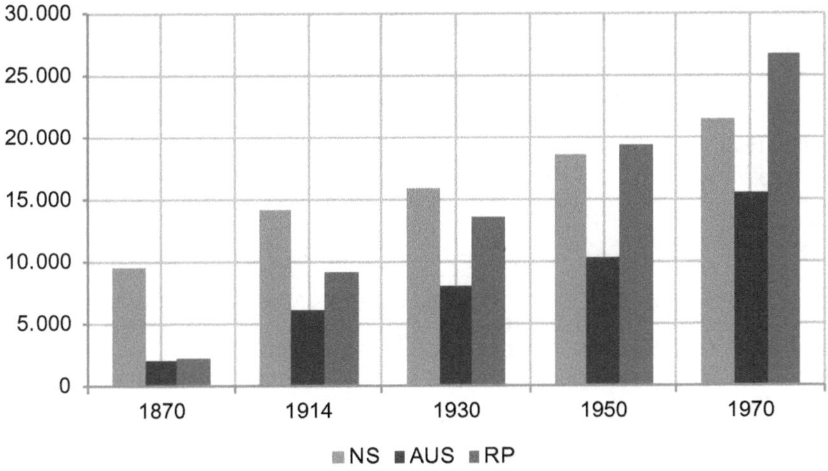

Fig. 3 Population (thousands) (*Sources* NC, Denmark, Hansen [1974]; Finland, OSF [2017]; Sweden, Edvinsson [2014]; Norway, Grytten [2003]; RP, Argentina, Ferreres [2010: Table 2.1]; Uruguay, Bértola [2016]; AUS, Australia, Ville & Withers [2015]; New Zealand, Briggs [2007])

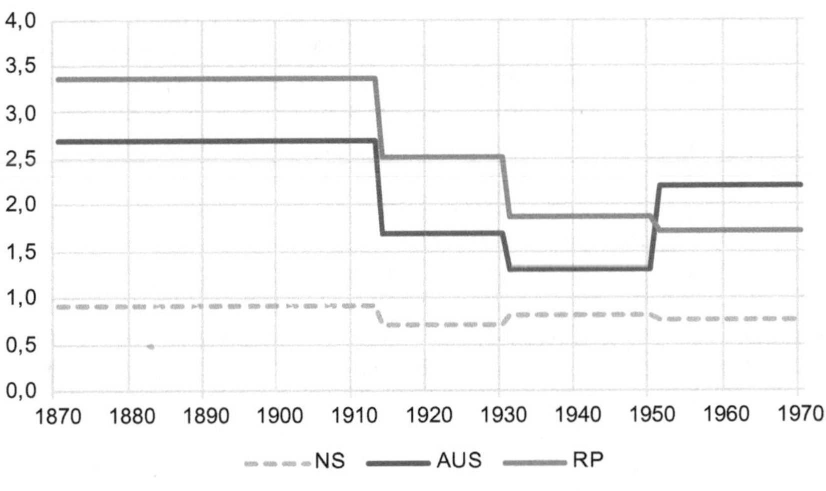

Fig. 4 Population growth rate per year (%), NS, AUS and RP (*Sources* Own estimation based on sources from Fig. 3)

Table 11 Net migration (thousands) and proportion of population increase due to net migration (%)

	NS		*AUS*		*RP*	
1870–1913	−1758	−38	1186	28	3083	44
1914–1930	−215	−12	385	20	1093	25
1931–1950	102	4	437	20	841	15
1951–1970	63	2	1867	35	675	9
1870–1970	−1793	−15	3874	29	5699	25

Sources Norway, Statistics Norway (2018); Australia, ABS (2014); New Zealand, Briggs (2007); Argentina, Ferreres (2010: Table 2.3); Uruguay, 1870–1911, Millot and Bertino (1996), 1910–1949, 1950–1955, Millot et al. (1973), 1962–1972, United Nations (2017)
Note A negative net migration figure means a reduction in the natural rate of increase of the population in the corresponding period. *Source* Denmark and Sweden, Mitchell (2003). Finland, Statistics Finland (2018), net migration estimated as the difference between population growth and natural increase in population for each year

The literature has explained migrations in terms of push and pull factors such as business cycles, labour demand, international wage gaps, the presence of established immigrant communities, etc. (Bohlin & Eurenius, 2010; Hatton & Williamson, 1998).

Our focus here is to examine whether population dynamics may help explain differences in long-run per capita GDP growth. If original differences in per capita income could be at least partly explained by the availability of employed natural resources per capita, it seems that fast population growth in the Southern hemisphere should reduce availability of natural resources per capita (Lloyd et al., 2013) and erode this advantage. Of course, the opposite effect could be seen: population growth expands the domestic market (generating economies of scale) and promotes the transfer of tacit knowledge brought by immigrants, for instance. In the NS, by contrast, while the dominating rural emigration (Lowell, 1987) slowed down economic growth to some extent, it also reduced extreme poverty and increased the land per capita and the capital per capita ratio (Södersten, 1990), and thus led to higher productivity. The changes in availability of agricultural land per capita are clearly presented in Table 12. While a general historical trend is the reduction of this variable, as production and employment diversify, and although differences between the countries still remain in the 1970s, the gap was significantly reduced, except for Australia.

Table 12 Agricultural land per capita (hectares)

	Denmark	*Sweden*	*Australia*	*New Zealand*	*Uruguay*
1870s	1.3	5.3	19	29	36
1910s	1.2	4.7	81	15	14
1930s	0.9	4.4	65	11	9
1950s	0.7	3.8	46	9	7
1970s	0.6	3.4	39	6	6

Sources Population, Table 1. Total agricultural area, Denmark, Johansen (1985); Sweden, Central Bureau of Statistics (1959: 33–34, Table E.2–3) and Central Bureau of Statistics (s. f., several years); Australia, Taylor (1992: 16–21, Table 6–10), for Victoria, Queensland and South Australia, and Vamplew (1987: 73, Table AG 19–27) for New South Wales, Tasmania, Western Australia and Northern Territory, ABS (2018); New Zealand, Briggs (2007); Uruguay, 1871–1914, Álvarez (2014: 121), 1937–1970, Agrarian Census, several years

This factor may help explain the divergent development trends, especially during the last decades of the nineteenth century. However, as we have seen, what really makes the difference is the capacity to diversify the economy and compete internationally with new products based on innovation and technology, and this process, and particularly the NS success, mainly took place during the twentieth century. We must keep searching for other explanations.

4.5 *Inequality and Growth*

The relation between income and wealth inequality, on the one side, and economic growth, on the other, has been widely studied. The Kuznetsian tradition has focused on how growth impacts on inequality. Here, we are interested in the reverse causation: how inequality impacts on growth and may help explain our stylized facts.

In Chapter 2 we referred to this literature, and Chapter 7 studies in more detail some particular cases (Denmark and Uruguay). We can briefly summarize some arguments. There is a strong link between equality and human capital formation, which is crucial for modern economic growth. A less concentrated pattern of land ownership favours the process of innovation and weakens the extraction of rents of privilege. This has an important impact on the development of applied science and technology institutions for the creation of "useful knowledge". In turn, it strengthens the demand for industrial capital goods and inputs, favouring structural change (Álvarez et al., 2011; Jörberg, 1973). In other words, lower inequality levels lead to higher human capital formation and to a wider base for domestic mass consumption, which can be a point of departure for some export industries. A more even distribution of land strengthens the power of the agrarian middle classes and the transition to democratic regimes based on a tight agro-industrial cooperation.

Classical political economy, by contrast, had stressed the positive role of inequality for capital accumulation. The Kuznetsian tradition, as well as the Lewis model, link early development to increasing inequality. Moreover, property rights and wealth inequality were seen as pre-conditions for capital accumulation and for the control of the labour market. The process we want to explain, however, is that of modern economic growth based on productivity growth, innovation and structural change. Thus, we can assume that inequality limits this process.

To simplify the study of our problem, we can identify two different aspects: (i) inequality trends due to relative price movements and (ii) institutional features of these societies, which determine whether a process of convergence may or may not take place.

Price movements. The powerful process of market integration in 1850–1930 led to the already mentioned migration waves, as well as the expansion of the agrarian frontier mainly in order to produce raw materials and foodstuffs in the peripheries to satisfy European demand.

The primary expected outcomes are contradictory distributional processes within the countries of the different hemispheres. Following the rule that market integration increases the relative price of the abundant factor, we can expect that, in labour-abundant NS, the wage/rental ratio should increase, while in land-abundant SSS it should decrease. This means that inequality tends to increase in the SSS and decrease in the NS. This process has been intensively studied and documented (Álvarez, 2013; Bértola et al., 1999; Bohlin & Larsson, 2007; Greasley et al., 2007; Lindert & Williamson, 2003; O'Rourke & Williamson, 1999; Shanahan & Wilson, 2007; Williamson, 1999, 2002). The series reproduced in Fig. 5 confirms this general trend. Nevertheless, it is important to keep in mind that an open agricultural frontier may counteract the upward trend in relative land and rental prices. This is probably why Uruguay showed a drastic fall in this ratio.

Institutional conditions. Another prediction arising from the process of market integration is factor-price convergence. However, this outcome

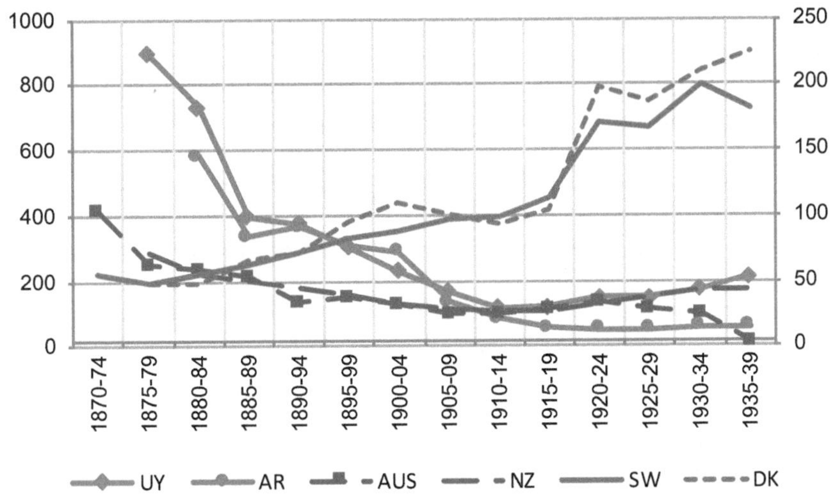

Fig. 5 Trends in the wage/rental ratio, 1870–1940 (*Sources* UY, NZ and DK sources from Fig. 1, Chapter 7; AR and AUS, Williamson [2002: 73–73, Table 3–4], Bohlin & Larsson [2007]. *Note* UY, AR, AUS, NZ: left axis. SW, DK: right axis)

does not seem to hold. Beyond the static resource allocation logic, long-run income growth is determined by productivity growth and technical change. The fruits of technical change are distributed through a combination of market mechanisms and collusive arrangements. While further research is needed to show how a more even income and wealth distribution create better conditions for structural change and productivity growth, it is true that the fruits of productivity growth do not lead to lower market prices but are appropriated by different actors under different power relations. That is why modern economic growth has gone hand in hand with increasing divergence, at least until the end of the nineteenth century. In this sense, Oxley and Greasley have developed Allen's conclusion that a process of convergence in real wages did not even take place within the English-speaking world. Of special interest for us is the idea that Australia's industrial system was very much linked to the declining British system, contrasting with the more dynamic Canadian system that was linked to American manufacturing leadership. The Nordic experience, and the Swedish in particular, was linked to the emerging

German industrial development pattern, with strong linkages between far-sighted capital investment and financial institutions, as pointed out by Gerschenkron.

As family-operated small and medium-size farms predominated in Nordic agriculture, export receipts were widely spread and rewarded a substantial fraction of the population (Alestalo & Kuhnle, 1987; Senghaas, 1985). In the SSS, there were fewer rural holdings than in the NS, so the population share receiving income derived from agricultural exports was also smaller (see Chapter 7). Notwithstanding that, the Australasian countries transitioned from an extensive agricultural system based on large estates to a system of family farms at the end of the nineteenth century, especially in New Zealand (Fairweather, 1985; McAloon, 2009). In contrast, the River Plate countries consolidated an extensive agricultural system and a concentrated land ownership structure which, in turn, contributed to concentrating export receipts. There were no incentives for agricultural modernization and intensification in the River Plate and therefore linkage effects between agriculture and industry were weak. Argentina and Uruguay, however, showed a better distributional pattern than other Latin American countries. This was partly because of the features of their labour markets, dominated by free labour with a significant proportion of European immigrants, and partly because of the agrarian export base, where many owners appropriated export incomes, as compared to the highly concentrated ownership of mineral-exporting economies.

The Kuznetsian paradox. Our argument seems to go against Kuznets' findings that in the early stages, industrialization goes hand in hand with increasing inequality. The Nordic countries were probably no less unequal than other European countries by the end of the nineteenth century. However, during the period in which technological change and industrialization advanced more rapidly and as the process of convergence with the European core progressed, the Nordic countries, and Sweden in particular, experienced a drastic reduction in inequality, first in the 1920s, and later in 1950–1970 (Roine & Waldenström, 2005). The relation between Latin American industrialization and income inequality shows that it is difficult to find a general pattern. Both Argentina and Uruguay, as well as Chile, in a context of inward-looking industrialization, experienced a sharp reduction in inequality. However, real wages and other social benefits could improve as export prices rose and resources were directed towards capital imports favouring industrialization. As the endogenous capabilities were weak, the model stagnated soon after the international price changes. By contrast, other Latin American countries could grow and to some extent converge with leading countries during 1930–1970, following some form of Lewis model, i.e., with increasing inequality due to the large labour reservoir (Bértola, 2018).

In sum, the impact of factor market integration in the late nineteenth and early twentieth centuries led to the reduction of the wage/rental ratio in the South and its increase in the North. The Nordic structure of land ownership, and after the 1890s even that of Australasia, showed lower inequality levels than that of the Río de la Plata, thus providing a more fruitful environment for industrial development and structural change. Even though early industrialization in the Nordic countries favoured a rise in inequality, the trend changed after the 1920s, favouring a more profound transformation of the productive structure. State-led inward-looking industrialization in the Rio de la Plata went hand in hand with an important reduction in inequality, but on weak innovative grounds.

5 In Short

This chapter identified two stylized facts: one with reference to relative per capita GDP growth, and a second concerning structural change. First, during 1870–1970, the NS significantly reduced the income per capita gap in relation to the world leaders, and while the SSS lost its relative standing, the Australasian countries always maintained higher levels than those of the Río de la Plata.

Second, the NS showed overall higher levels of industrialization steadily increasing with some minor fluctuations up to the 1960s, while the SSS showed more fluctuating levels of industrialization with low figures up to the 1930s and a spurt afterwards. The NS showed a deeper transformation of the industrial structure in favour of more dynamic sectors. The three groups of countries showed increasing export ratios up to WWI. Later, a difference appeared: while export coefficients remained high and stable in the NS, they fluctuated strongly and tended to decrease in the SSS. Moreover, despite the fact that all the countries began with very high shares of primary goods in the export basket, the NS succeeded in transforming the structure of exports in favour of manufacturing goods.

These two stylized facts are, in our opinion, linked to each other. In Sect. 3 we reviewed several theoretical approaches that give support to this connection between economic growth and structural change. According to many of these theories, structural change is not just an outcome of growth, but a feature or even a precondition for growth. Limits to structural change will, in the end, hamper growth. With this point of departure, in Sect. 4 we also reviewed various possible explanations for why the NS could converge and go through a process of deep structural change, while the Australasian and even less the Río de la Plata countries, failed to do so.

We first needed to explain why there was an original advantage in per capita income in favour of the SSS. The transport revolution made it economically possible to incorporate idle abundant natural resources that were subject to strong demand in Europe and increasing relative prices. As they were countries of temperate settlement, they produced similar goods to the European economies with which they competed and which were transformed into marginal producers. Domestic landowners could accumulate the rent of the soil. The reason why the Australasian countries achieved higher per capita income than the Rio de la Plata countries can be explained by superior levels of organization and technical capabilities, as well as the existence of mineral products that the Río de la Plata lacked. The agrarian sectors of the Nordic countries were facing significant demographic pressure which, in the end, led to a very high level of emigration to the New World.

We discussed several variations of the Staple Theory. The original version has a supply-side variant that focuses on the forward and backward linkages in production, as well as a demand-side version that focuses on how the surplus of staple production is appropriated and distributed and on the distribution of property implied. New versions, such as the product space approach, were considered, along with the resource-curse literature, which is more pessimistic than the original staple theory regarding the chances for successful development based on natural resources.

We find that this literature makes important contributions to understanding different development paths but by itself is insufficient to explain the stylized facts we want to understand. In history and among these countries we can find many similarities in resources that produce quite different outcomes.

We also discussed the role of distance. The NS were clearly favoured by their proximity to the main markets for primary production, but the first globalization boom implied a weakening of the tyranny of distance, helping to increase the relative price of primary production and easing access to world markets. Once the Belle Époque came to an end, the SSS had to rely on inward-looking industrialization. Distance, together with tariffs and relative prices, became an ally of local industry. However, once world trade recovered momentum after WWII, southern industries found themselves badly prepared for international competition, and the tyranny of distance finally regained its negative impact. Despite the critical interwar period, NS could smoothly develop their manufacturing sectors and easily overcame the limits of the narrow domestic market through a dynamic integration into the wider European market.

Another area of interest is the contradictory demographic movements during the first globalization boom, as millions of people emigrated from the European periphery to the New World. These movements had many consequences: increasing inequality in the SSS and decreasing it in the NS; decreasing pressure on natural resources in the NS and increasing it in the SSS; and transferring tacit knowledge from the North to the South, carried by immigrants. This factor may help explain the divergent development trends, especially during the last decades of the nineteenth century. However, the success of the NS mainly took place during the twentieth century.

Finally, we discussed the role played by differences in inequality levels and patterns of asset distribution. The impact of factor market integration in the late nineteenth and early twentieth centuries led to a reduction in the wage/rental ratio in the South and to its increase in the North. The Nordic structure of land ownership, and after the 1890s even the Australasian structure, reflected lower inequality levels than in the Río de la Plata, thus providing a more fruitful environment for industrial development and structural change. Even if early industrialization in the Nordic countries favoured the rise in inequality, the trend changed after the 1920s, favouring a more profound transformation of the productive structure. State-led inward-looking industrialization in the Rio de la Plata went hand in hand with an important reduction in inequality, but on weak innovative grounds.

It was not the aim of this chapter to test any of the mentioned explanations but to identify them. The next chapter is however intended to test another theory that can help to understand these different development patterns: the post-Keynesian approach known as Thirlwall's Law.

References

ABS. (2014). *Australian historical population statistics*. Retrieved 2 June 2018, from https://www.abs.gov.au/AUSSTATS/abs@.nsf/DetailsPage/3105.0.65.0012014?OpenDocument

ABS. (2018). *Year Book Australia* (1301.0). http://www.abs.gov.au/AUSSTATS/abs@.nsf/second+level+view?ReadForm&prodno=1301.0&viewtitle=Year%20Book%20Australia~1928~Previous~01/01/1928&&tabname=Past%20Future%20Issues&prodno=1301.0&issue=1928&num=&view=&

Alestalo, M., & Kuhnle, S. (1987). The Scandinavian route: Economic, social, and political developments in Denmark, Finland, Norway, and Sweden. *International Journal of Sociology, 16*(3/4), 3–38.

Álvarez, J. (2013). *The evolution of inequality in Australia and the River Plate, 1870–1914. Documento de Trabajo, Programa de Historia Económica y Social* (Vol. 31). Montevideo. https://doi.org/10.2139/ssrn.3962473

Álvarez, J. (2014). *Instituciones, cambio tecnológico y productividad en los sistemas agrarios de Nueva Zelanda y Uruguay. Patrones y trayectorias de largo plazo (1870–2010). Programa de Historia Económica y Social. Tesis de Doctorado.* Universidad de la República. https://hdl.handle.net/20.500.12008/8022

Álvarez, J., Bértola, L., & Porcile, G. (2007). *Primos ricos y empobrecidos: Crecimiento, distribución del ingreso e instituciones en Australia-Nueva Zelanda vs Argentina-Uruguay*. Editorial Fin de Siglo.

Álvarez, J., Bilancini, E., D'Alessandro, S., & Porcile, G. (2011). Agricultural institutions, industrialization and growth: The case of New Zealand and Uruguay in 1870–1940. *Explorations in Economic History, 48*(2), 151–168. https://doi.org/10.1016/j.eeh.2010.05.004

Belich, J. (2001). *Paradise reforged: A history of the New Zealanders from the 1880's to the year 2000*. Penguin Book.

Bertram, G. (2009). The New Zealand economy 1900-2000. In B. Giselle (Ed.), *The new Oxford history of New Zealand* (pp. 537–572). Oxford University Press.

Bértola, L. (2016). *El PBI per capita de Uruguay 1870–2015: Una reconstrucción. Programa de Historia Económica y Social. Documentos de Trabajo* (Vol. 48). Montevideo.

Bértola, L. (2018). Viewed up close nobody is normal: Industrialization and income inequality in Latin America. In *Presidential Session, World Economic History Congress, Boston.*

Bértola, L., Bittencourt, G., Lara, C., & Segantini, M. (2014). *Un balance histórico de la industria uruguaya: Entre el "destino manifiesto" y el voluntarismo* . Montevideo: UdelaR-MIEM/FCS.

Bértola, L., Calicchio, L., Camou, M. M., & Porcile, G. (1999). *Southern Cone real wages compared: A purchasing power parity approach to convergence and divergence trends, 1870–1996. Documento de Trabajo No. 44* (Vol. 44). Unidad Multidisciplinaria. Facultad de Ciencias Sociales.

Bértola, L., & Ocampo, J. A. (2012). *The economic development of Latin America since Independence*. Oxford University Press.

Bjerke, J. (1966). *Langtidslinjer i norsk økonomi 1865–1960*. Statistisk sentralbyrå.

Blainey, G. (1966). *The tyranny of distance: How distance shaped Australia's history*. Sun Books.

Boehm, E. A. (1979). Australia y Argentina en el Periodo de 1914–1933, Comentarios. In Argentina y Australia (Ed.), *Argentina y Australia*. Instituto Torcuato Di Tella.

Bohlin, J., & Eurenius, A.-M. (2010). Why they moved—Emigration from the Swedish countryside to the United States, 1881–1910. *Explorations in Economic History, 4*(47), 533–551. https://doi.org/10.1016/j.eeh.2010.07.001

Bohlin, J., & Larsson, S. (2007). The Swedish wage–rental ratio and its determinants, 1877–1926. *Australian Economic History Review, 47*(1), 49–72. https://doi.org/10.1111/j.1467-8446.2006.00196.x

Bolt, J., & van Zanden, J. L. (2020). *Maddison style estimates of the evolution of the world economy. A new 2020 update* (Maddison-Project Working Paper No. 15). Groningen.

Briggs, P. (2003). *Looking at the numbers: A view of New Zealand's economic history*. NZ Institute of Economic Research.

Briggs, P. (2007). *Looking at the numbers: A view of New Zealand's economic history*. NZ Institute of Economic Research.

Central Bureau of Statistics. (1959). *Historical statistics of Sweden*. Statistiska Centralbyran.

Chenery, H. B., & Syrquin, M. (1975). *Patterns of development 1950–1970*. Oxford University Press.

Cimoli, M., & Porcile, G. (2014). Technology, structural change and BOP-constrained growth: A structuralist toolbox. *Cambridge Journal of Economics, 38*(1), 215–237. https://doi.org/10.1093/cje/bet020

Denoon, D. (1983). *Settler capitalism: The dynamics of dependent development in the Southern Hemisphere*. Clarendon University Press.

Derry, T. K. (1979). *A history of Scandinavia. Norway, Sweden, Denmark, Finland and Iceland*. University of Minnesota Press.

Edvinsson, R. (2005). *Growth, accumulation, crisis: With new macroeconomic data for Sweden*. Almqvist & Wiksell International.

Edvinsson, R. (2014). The gross domestic product for Sweden within ints present borders, 1620–2012. In *House prices, stock returns, national accounts, and the Riksbank balance sheet, 1620–2012* (pp. 101–182). Historical Monetary and Financial Statistics for Sweden.

Engerman, S. L., & Sokoloff, K. L. (s. f.). The evolution of suffrage in the New World: A preliminary examination. In *2001 Cliometrics Conference Meeting*.
Engerman, S. L., & Sokoloff, K. L. (1997). Factor endowments, institutions and differential paths of growth among New World Economies: A view from economic historians of the United States. In S. Haber (Ed.), *How Latin America Fell Behind* (pp. 260–304). Stanford University Press.
Fairweather, J. R. (1985). Land policy and land settlement in New Zealand. An analysis of land policy goals and an evaluation of their effect. *Agricultural Economics Research Unit, Research Report*. Lincoln College.
Ferreres, O. J. (2010). *Dos siglos de economía argentina 1810–2010: Historia argentina en cifras*. El Ateneo, Fundación Norte y Sur.
Finch, H. (1981). *A political economy of Uruguay since 1870*. Palgrave Macmillan. https://doi.org/10.1007/978-1-349-16623-7
Finch, H. (2005). *La economía política del Uruguay contemporáneo, 1870–2000*. Montevideo: Ediciones de la Banda Oriental.
Fogarty, J. (1985). Staples, super-staples and the limits of staple theory: The experiences of Argentina, Australia and Canada compared. In D. C. Platt & G. Di Tella (Eds.), *Argentina, Australia & Canada. Studies in comparative development, 1870–1965* (pp. 19–36). St. Antony's/Macmillan Series.
Freeman, C. (1987). *Technology gaps, international trade and the problems of smaller and less developed economies* (Science Policy Research Unit). Sussex.
Gerschenkron, A. (1962). *Economic backwardness in historical perspective*. Harvard University Press.
Greasley, D. (2015). Industrialising Australia's natural capital. In *The Cambridge economic history of Australia*. Cambridge University Press.
Greasley, D., Inwood, K., & Singleton, J. (2007, March). Factor price and income distribution in less industrialised economies 1870–1939. *Australian Economic History Review, 47*(1). https://doi.org/10.1111/j.1467-8446.2006.00193.x
Grossman, G., & Helpman, E. (1991). *Innovation and growth in the global economy*. MIT Press.
Grytten, O. H. (2003). The gross domestic product for Norway 1830–2003. In Ø. Eitrheim, J. T. Klovland, & J. F. Qvigstad (Eds.), *Historical monetary statistics for Norway 1819–2003* (pp. 241–288). Norges Bank.
Grytten, O. H. (2015). *Gross domestic product by industry 1830–1930* (Norges Bank Working Paper, 19).
Hansen, S. A. (1974). *Økonomisk vækst i Danmark. Bind II: 1914–1970*. Akademisk forlag.
Hatton, T. J., & Williamson, J. G. (1994). International Migration, 1850-1939: An Economic Survey. In T. J. Hatton & J. G. Williamson (Eds.), *Migration and the international labour market*, 1850–1939. Routledge.

Hatton, T. J., & Williamson, J. G. (1998). *The age of mass migration: Causes and economic impact*. Oxford University Press.
Hawke, G. R. (1985). *The making of New Zealand. An economic history*. Cambridge University Press.
Hendy, S., & Callaghan, P. (2013). *Get off the grass: Kickstarting New Zealand's innovation economy*. Auckland University Press.
Hidalgo, C., Klinger, B., Barabasiand, A. L., & Hausmann, R. (2007). The product space conditions the development of nations. *Science, 317*(5837), 482–487. https://doi.org/10.1126/science.1144581
Hjerppe, R. (1989). *The Finnish economy, 1860–1985. Growth and structural change* (B. of Finland, Ed.). Government Printing Centre.
Hutchinson, D. (2015). Manufacturing. *Australian Economic History Review*. Cambridge University Press.
Hveem, H. (1990). Desarrollo de una economía abierta. La transformación de Noruega, 1845–1975. In M. Blomström & P. Meller (Eds.), *Trayectorias divergentes* (pp. 145–174). Editorial Universitaria.
Innis, H. A. (1930). *The fur trade in Canada: An introduction to Canadian economy history*. University of Toronto Press.
Innis, H. A. (1940). *The cod fisheries: The history of an international economy*. University of Toronto Press.
Jensen, P. S., Lampe, M., Sharp, P., Skovsgaard, C. V., Ager, P., Becker, S., ... Simpson, J. (2018). *'Getting to Denmark': The role of elites for development* (No. 125). Recuperado de http://www.ehes.org/EHES_125.pdf
Johansen, H. C. (1985). *Danish historical statistics, 1814–1980*. Gyldendal.
Jörberg, L. (1973). The Industrial revolution in the Nordic countries. In C. Cipolla (Ed.), *The Fontana economic history of Europe* (Vol. 4, 1700–1914, pp. 375–479). Collins.
Kaukiainen, Y. (2006). Foreign trade and transport. In *The road to prosperity. An economic history of Finland*. Suomalaisen Kirjallisuuden Seura.
Kosacoff, B. (1993). *La industria argentina. Un proceso de reestructuración desarticulada* (No. 53).
Kuznets, S. (1966). *Modern economic growth*. Yale University Press.
Kuznets, S. (1971). *Economic growth of nations: Total output and production structure*. Harvard University Press.
Lavopa, A. (2011). *The impact of sectoral heterogeneities in economic growth and catching up: Empirical evidence for Latin American manufacturing industries*. (UNU-MERIT Working Papers).
Lewis, C. (1954). Economic development with unlimited supplies of labour. *The Manchester School of Economic and Social Studies, 22*(2), 139–191.
Lindert, P., & Williamson, J. G. (2003). Does globalization make the world more unequal? In M. D. Bordo, A. M. Taylor, & J. G. Williamson (Eds.),

Globalization in historical perspective (pp. 227–276). University of Chicago Press.
Lloyd, C., Metzer, J., & Sutch, R. (2013). *Settler economies in world history. Global Economic History Series*. Brill.
Lowell, B. L. (1987). *Scandinavian exodus. Demography and social development of 19th-century rural communities*. Westview Press.
Lundvall, B. (1992). *National systems of innovation: Toward a theory of innovation and interactive learning*. Anthem Press.
Mackintosh, W. A. (1939). *The economic background of dominion-provincial relations*. McGlelland & Stewart.
Maddison Project. (2020). *Maddison project database*. https://www.rug.nl/ggdc/historicaldevelopment/maddison/releases/maddison-project-database-2020?lang=en
McAloon, J. The New Zealand economy 1792–1914. In B. Giselle (Ed.), *The new Oxford history of New Zealand* (pp. 197–217). Oxford University Press.
McCombie, J., & Thirlwall, A. P. (1994). *Economic growth and the balance-of-payments constraint*. Palgrave Macmillan. https://doi.org/10.1007/978-1-349-23121-8
McLean, I. W. (2013). *Why Australia prospered: The shifting sources of economic growth*. Princeton University Press.
Millot, J., & Bertino, M. (1996). *Historia económica del Uruguay (1860–1910)*. Fundación de Cultura Universitaria.
Millot, J., Silva, C., & Silva, L. (1973). *El desarrollo industrial del Uruguay. De la crisis de 1929 a la post-guerra de la segunda guerra mundial*. Departamento de Publicaciones de la Universidad de la República.
Mitchell, B. R. (1983). *International historical statistics. The Americas and Australasia*. MacMIllan.
Mitchell, B. R. (2003). *International historical statistics: Europe, 1750–2000* (5th ed.). Palgrave Macmillan.
O'Rourke, K. H., & Williamson, J. G. (1999). *Globalization and history: The evolution of a Nineteenth-Century Atlantic Economy*. MIT.
OSF, O. S. of F. (2017). Annual national accounts.
Pasinetti, L. L. (1983). *Structural change and economic growth: A theoretical essay on the dynamics of the wealth of nations*. Cambridge University Press.
Perez, C. (1983). Structural change and the assimilation of new technologies in the economic and social system. *Futures*, *4*, 357–375.
Petersson, L. (1984). Svensk utrikeshandel 1871–1980. In *Studie i den intraindustriella handelns famväxt*. Lund Economic Studies.
Rankin, K. (1992). Manufacturing output in New Zealand: 1870–1940. In *Conference of the economic history association of Australia and New Zealand, Perth, July 8–10*. Perth.

Roine, J., & Waldenström, D. (2005). *The evolution of top incomes in an egalitarian society: Sweden, 1903–2004* (SSE/EFI Working Paper Series in Economics and Finance).

Saviotti, P. P., & Pyka, A. (2013). The co-evolution of innovation, demand and growth, economics of innovation and new technology. *Economics of Innovation and New Technology, 22*(5), 461–482. https://doi.org/10.1080/10438599.2013.768492

Schedvin, C. B. (1990). Staples and regions of Pax Britannica. *The Economic History Review, 43*(4), 533–559. https://doi.org/10.2307/2596734

Schön, L., & Krantz, O. (2015). *New Swedish historical national accounts since the 16th Century in constant and current prices* (Lund Papers in Economic History No. 140).

Senghaas, D. (1985). *The European experience: A historical critique of development theory.* K.H. Kimmig.

Shanahan, M., & Wilson, J. (2007). Measuring inequality trends in Colonial Australia using factor price ratios: The importance of boundaries. *Australian Economic History Review, 47*(1), 6–21. https://doi.org/10.1111/j.1467-8446.2006.00194.x

Södersten, B. (1990). Cien año de desarrollo económico sueco (1870–1970). In M. Blomström & P. Meller (Eds.), *Trayectorias divergentes* (pp. 29–52). Editorial Universitaria.

Statistics Finland. (2018). OSF, Vital statistics and population in 1749 to 2016. Retrieved 30 May 2018, from http://pxnet2.stat.fi/PXWeb/pxweb/en/StatFin/StatFin__vrm__synt/statfin_synt_pxt_011.px#_ga=2.264090634.703507848.1528129994-57064615.1528129994

Statistics Norway. (2018). Population.

Syrquin, M. (2007). *Kuznets and Pasinetti on the study of structural transformation: Never the twain shall meet?* (ICER Working Papers, ICER).

Taylor, A. (1992). *The value of land in Australia before 1913* (Papers in Economic History No. 19). Canberra.

United Nations. (2017). World population prospects: 2017 Revision. Retrieved 2 June 2018, from https://esa.un.org/unpd/wpp/Download/Standard/Migration/

Vamplew, W. (1987). *Australians, historical statistics.* Fairfax, Syme & Weldon Associates.

Vázquez Presedo, V. (1988). *Estadísticas históricas.* Academia Nacional de Economía.

Verspagen, B. (1992). *Uneven growth between interdependent economies: An evolutionary view on technology gaps, trade and growth.* https://doi.org/10.26481/dis.19921016bv

Ville, S., & Withers, G. (2015). *The Cambridge economic history of Australia* (S. Ville & G. Withers, Eds.). Cambridge University Press.

Watkins, M. H. (1963). A staple theory of economic growth. *The Canadian Journal of Economics and Political Science/Revue Canadienne D'economique Et De Science Politique, 26*(2), 141–158.
Williamson, J. G. (1999). *Land, labor and globalization in the pre-industrial third world* (Working Paper No. 7784).
Williamson, J. G. (2002). Land, labor, and globalization in the third world, 1870–1940. *Journal of Economic History, 62*(1), 55–85.

CHAPTER 4

Foreign Trade and Economic Growth in the Nordic Countries, Australasia and the Rio De La Plata Region, 1870–1970

Jorge Álvarez, Luis Bértola, and Jan Bohlin

1 Introduction

In 1870 Australia was the richest country in the world as measured by GDP per capita, and its Australasian neighbour New Zealand was not far behind.[1] By the same measure Argentina and Uruguay were about level with Germany and France in the 1890s, clearly richer than the Nordic

[1] https://www.rug.nl/ggdc/historicaldevelopment/maddison/releases/maddison-project-database-2020?lang=en.

Present Address:
J. Álvarez (✉) · L. Bértola
Universidad de La República, Montevideo, Uruguay
e-mail: jorge.alvarez@cienciassociales.edu.uy

L. Bértola
e-mail: luis.bertola@cienciassociales.edu.uy

J. Bohlin
University of Gothenburg, Göteborg, Sweden
e-mail: jan.bohlin@econhist.gu.se

J. Álvarez and S. Prado (eds.), *Scandinavia and South America—A Tale of Two Capitalisms*, Palgrave Studies in Economic History,
https://doi.org/10.1007/978-3-031-09198-8_4

countries (Denmark, Sweden Norway and Finland). By 1970 a complete reversal of fortunes had taken place. The Nordic countries had already overtaken Argentina and Uruguay by the inter-war period. And in the 1960s Sweden and Denmark also outstripped the GDP per capita of the Australasian countries.

Why did the Nordic countries grow so much faster than Australia and New Zealand and why did the Rio de la Plata region fall behind so dramatically? A full answer to such a complex question cannot, of course, be given in a short chapter. What we will do here is explore one important aspect, namely the relationship between foreign trade and economic growth. Though dramatically different in many other respects these countries shared one important commonality in the late nineteenth century. In all of them foreign trade played a large role in comparison with the industrial core in North America and Western Europe. They were all initially also dependent on a few staple goods for their export earnings.

Different types of goods differed in price volatility and in long-run growth prospects, since the income elasticity of demand for them differed. Consequently, the evolution of export earnings was also dependent on the extent to which the countries were able to change the composition of their exports to goods with higher income elasticity of demand. In this regard the countries in the sample differed enormously, which had consequences for their growth paths.

When exploring the relationship between foreign trade and economic growth we have found Thirlwall's Law (Thirlwall, 2011a) to be a useful framework. It argues that the long-term growth rate of a country is constrained by the balance of payments. It has mostly been applied to the period after World War II, where it has a good track record in predicting growth rates. In this paper, we will explore to what extent it can shed light on the varying growth experiences in the Nordic countries, Australasia and the Rio de la Plata region over the hundred-year period 1870–1970, or more precisely over the periods 1870–1913 and 1950–1970. Before we do that, we will first present some basic data on GDP growth and exports for these economies in this period.

2 Economic Growth 1870–1970 in the Three Regions

Compound interest is a powerful mechanism. The annual average growth rate in GDP per capita of the Nordic countries between 1870 and 1970 was 2.0%, while it was 1.0% in the Australasian countries (Table 1, Fig. 1). This difference in growth rates made it possible for the Nordic countries to close the gap with the Australasian GDP per capita level in the 1960s (and in the case of Sweden and Denmark even surpass it), even though their GDP per capita level in 1870 was less than half that of Australasia. The long-run growth rate in GDP per capita of the Rio de la Plata countries was slightly higher than Australasia's, but since they started from a level not much above the Nordic countries in 1870, they had fallen hopelessly behind by the post-war period.

Another clear difference between the three regions portrayed in Fig. 1 is the high volatility in growth rates in Australasia and the Rio de la Plata countries compared with the Nordic countries. The three Scandinavian

Table 1 Annual growth rates in GDP and GDP per capita (percentage growth rate of exponential trend)

	GDP			*GDP per capita*		
	1870–1930	*1930–1970*	*1870–1970*	*1870–1930*	*1930–1970*	*1870–1970*
Australasia	**2.9**	**3.9**	**2.9**	**0.6**	**2.1**	**1.0**
Australia	2.8	3.9	2.9	0.6	2.1	1.0
New Zealand	3.2	4.0	3.1	0.8	2.3	1.1
Rio de la Plata	**4.7**	**3.3**	**3.8**	**1.5**	**1.5**	**1.2**
Argentina	5.0	3.3	4.0	1.7	1.5	1.3
Uruguay	3.0	2.8	2.9	0.4	1.6	1.1
Nordic countries	**2.5**	**3.6**	**2.8**	**1.6**	**2.8**	**2.0**
Denmark	2.7	3.2	2.7	1.6	2.3	1.7
Sweden	2.5	3.6	2.8	1.8	2.9	2.2
Norway	2.3	3.7	2.7	1.5	2.8	1.9
Finland	2.4	3.9	2.9	1.3	3.1	2.0

Sources Core countries, Nordic countries, Latin American Southern Settler Societies, and Australasia, Maddison Project Database (2020) and Bolt and Van Zanden (2020). Uruguay, Bértola (2016), Argentina, Bértola and Ocampo (2012), Sweden, Schön and Krantz (2015) and Norway (Grytten, 2015)

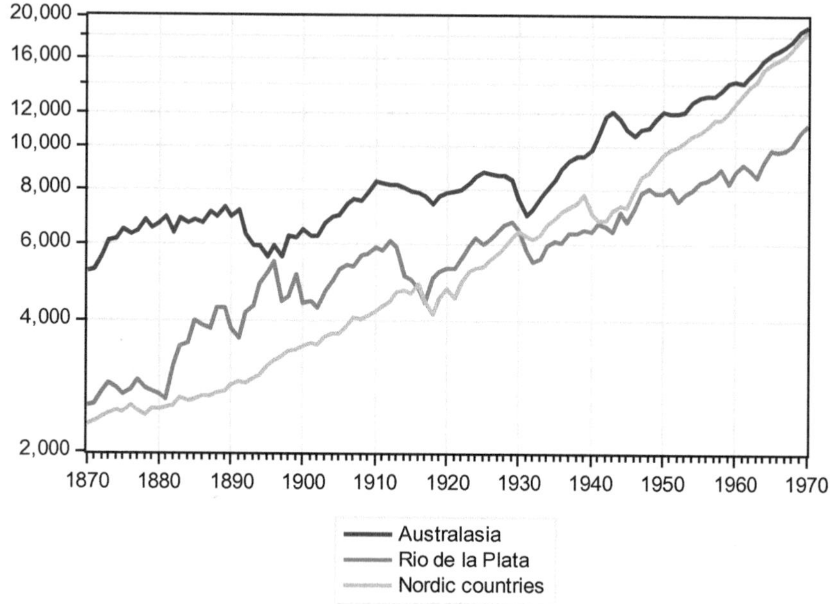

Fig. 1 GDP per capita level in Australasia, the Nordic countries and the Rio de la Plata region 1870–1970 (PPP adjusted 2011 US dollar) (*Source* Based on sources of Table 1)

countries and Finland experienced dents in their growth curves during the two World Wars and to a certain extent during the crises of the early 1920s and 1930s, but otherwise economic growth in the Nordic region was a fairly linear process which accelerated in the 1950–1970 period. In the other two regions growth fluctuated wildly during the first globalization period.

2.1 1870–1930

The purchasing-power-adjusted GDP per capita growth rates did not differ much between the Rio de la Plata region and the Nordic region in the 1870–1930 period, according to the figures presented in Table 1, even though fluctuations in growth rates were much more dramatic in the Rio de la Plata region. After a hectic rise in growth rates in the 1880s a dramatic decline occurred in the early 1890s as the Baring crisis broke out in Argentina, when British investors became increasingly nervous about the Argentinians' ability to service the large debts they had amassed in the previous decades. The flow of foreign capital dried up at the same time as prices for Argentine exports fell. Argentina managed to bounce back from the financial crisis, however. Its debts to British investors were rescheduled, the rates of interest on debts were lowered at the same time as the periods of repayment for the loans were prolonged. Moreover, Argentina effectually devalued its currency by instituting a dual currency system with a gold and a paper peso. The exchange rate for the gold peso was maintained but the paper peso depreciated. This caused import prices to rise for domestic consumers, stimulating production for the home market. At the same time, exports continued to grow at the same pace as in the previous two decades for another twenty years (McLean, 2013: 129–131). Consequently, the Argentine economy resumed its strong growth until World War I. During World War I, the growth rate of the Argentinian economy slowed down even more dramatically. Growth resumed after World War 1, but the Rio de la Plata region was again severely hit by the economic depression in 1929–1932. This proved to be a major turning point for the economic development of Argentina as well as for its neighbouring country, Uruguay. By the 1920s it had already become increasingly obvious that there was an oversupply of agricultural commodities in the international markets (McLean, 2013; Thorp, 1986), which was underlined even more by the depression in the early 1930s followed by the collapse of international trade.

GDP per capita growth rates were much lower in Australasia than in the other two regions in the 1870–1930 period. As in the Rio de la Plata region, growth rates also fluctuated dramatically. For the largest economy in Australasia, Australia, the crises were defining moments for its growth path. The first occurred in the early 1890s. The inflow of foreign capital dried up as British investors became increasingly worried about the Australians' ability to service their loans. The Australian economy bounced back again from the late 1890s but experienced another shock when WWI broke out. After the war, growth resumed in the 1920s, but Australia was hit again by the worldwide depression in the early 1930s, as export earnings plummeted. The combined effects of severe crises and feeble post-crisis recoveries led to anaemic GDP per capita growth rates.

According to Maddison's figures, the GDP per capita level in constant US dollars was only slightly higher in 1930 than in 1890.[2]

Unlike the other two regions there was no major crisis in the Nordic countries in the early 1890s. On the contrary growth accelerated in the period 1890–1913 compared with the period 1870–1890. In Sweden, the largest economy in Scandinavia, strong export growth was now joined by strong growth in home market industries protected by tariffs (Bohlin, 2005; Schön, 2010). Exports from Sweden increasingly came from the manufacturing industry, while they were still heavily dominated by agricultural goods in the case of Denmark and shipping in Norway. Industrial growth in these two countries was not as swift as in Sweden and in the case of Denmark in particular it was more or less exclusively oriented towards the home market. Finland was the most backward in economic structure among the Nordic countries. The country also had the lowest GDP per capita level and did not succeed in narrowing that gap until the 1930s (Jörberg & Krantz, 1973).

2.2 1930–1970

After World War I, the growth rate of the Argentinian economy slowed dramatically. The economic depression in 1929–1932 was a major turning point for the economic development of Argentina as well as for its neighbouring country, Uruguay. The already mentioned oversupply of agricultural commodities in the international markets was underlined even more by the depression in the early 1930s followed by the collapse of international trade. Unlike Australia and New Zealand, the Rio de la Plata countries did not have access to preferential treatment of their exports by the British commonwealth, so they were affected even harder by the collapse in world trade in the 1930s. With the breakdown of international trade, economic activity was directed more towards the home market, with an increasing role for the manufacturing sector and services, while the relative weight of agriculture in the economy declined (Bértola & Ocampo, 2012: ch. 4; Diaz Alejandro, 1970: ch. 2).

Industrial growth was stimulated by relative price movements. It was also stimulated by the collapse of multilateral trade, as both Argentina and Uruguay exported mainly to Great Britain but imported mainly

[2] https://www.rug.nl/ggdc/historicaldevelopment/maddison/releases/maddison-project-database-2020?lang=en.

from the USA. Forced imports from Great Britain meant even worse terms of trade (Gerchunoff & Llach, 2011). Industrialization changed the structure of imports in favour of intermediate goods, energy sources and capital goods, which required steady increases in foreign exchange. Import substitution made a limited contribution as a source of growth, both in Argentina and Uruguay, while domestic demand became the most dynamic source of growth, so the period is better defined as state-led growth (Bértola & Ocampo, 2012: ch. 4). To solve the recurrent foreign exchange crises Argentina tried to reorient industrial production towards the regional market, with some success during WWII, and even more after the war. Additionally, particularly during the 1960s, important efforts were made to attract investment by multinationals, to both solve the foreign exchange shortages and improve productivity and competitiveness. Nevertheless, policy was mainly driven by short-term needs, rather than by a strategic view of development goals (Gerchunoff & Llach, 2011; Schvarzer, 1996), and productivity gains were limited by the acquisition of mature technology and industrial plants dimensioned for larger markets than the regional (Katz & Kosacoff, 1989, 2000).

Economic development in Uruguay was in many respects similar to Argentina's. The export sector of the country was hard hit by the worldwide economic crisis in the 1930s. Uruguay restructured its agrarian sector towards the production of inputs for the local manufacturing industry. During the post-WWII period, in the context of favourable terms of trade, manufacturing grew rapidly thanks to favourable exchange rates and a labour market policy that helped the expansion of the domestic market. However, in contrast to the Argentine case, the very limited domestic market did not attract foreign manufacturing investment and did not constitute a good base for expansion towards the regional market. Domestic demand expansion lost momentum in the mid-1950s and Uruguay became one of the pioneers in demonstrating the limits of this model of industrialization (Bértola, 1990; Schlueter, 2014).

As was the case in Argentina, the 1929–1932 crisis may be seen as a watershed in Australian economic development. The role of the export sector in the Australian economy diminished in the inter-war period, while the manufacturing sector which primarily produced for the domestic market increased its share of the economy. Behind tariff protection and the natural protection offered by transport costs, an industrialization directed towards the home market unfolded (Butlin et al., 2015; Hutchinson, 2015).

As in other countries, economic growth took a hit during WWII. In the post-war period Australian growth increased, even though its GDP per capita growth was slower than in the fast-growing economies of Western Europe and Japan. The industrialization process, which had started in the inter-war period, accelerated in the 1950s and 1960s. The output of the manufacturing sector was now to an increasing extent exported, mainly to the economies of South-east Asia and New Zealand (McLean, 2013: 197–198).

Economic development in New Zealand was in many respects like that in Australia after the crisis in the 1930s. However, New Zealand failed to broaden its export sector into manufacturing in the post-war period.

The economies in the Nordic region were also hit by the crises following World War I and the breakdown of international trade in the 1930s, though not nearly as hard as the other two regions. The economic downturn during World War I as well as the post-war deflation crisis in the early twenties and the depression in the early 1930s appear as mere dents in the long-term growth path of the Nordic economies.

Due to the economic hardship caused by the occupation of Denmark and Norway by Nazi Germany and the wars in Finland, growth in the Nordic region took a hit during World War II. After the war the Nordic countries resumed their growth paths and benefited from strong economic growth in their export markets, mainly Western Europe.

Of the Nordic economies, Denmark was most similar to the Australasian and Rio de la Plata regions in its economic structure and export orientation. Consequently, it was also hard hit by the disintegration of the world market for agricultural products in the 1930s, although not to the same extent as the other two regions. Like other countries, Denmark managed to expand its manufacturing sector, in the inter-war period overwhelmingly for the domestic market, but in the post-war period increasingly also for the export market. Nevertheless a large share of Danish exports consisted of agricultural goods in the post-war period. Since Denmark largely lacked domestic resources for industrialization, it was dependent on imports of inputs and raw materials for its manufacturing industry. The lack of good growth prospects for agricultural exports compared with industrial goods and the instability of incomes due to fluctuations in export prices thus led to recurrent balance-of-payment problems for the Danish economy in this period. Although starting from a lower economic level and with a different export orientation (service exports instead of agricultural goods) Norwegian development was in many respects similar to that of Denmark (Jörberg & Krantz, 1976).

After quite rapid economic growth in the 1930s the Finnish economy was hard hit by wars in 1939–1944. In the 1950s and the 1960s Finland had the fastest growth rate of the Nordic countries, driven by the manufacturing industry, particularly the export-oriented paper and pulp-industries (Jörberg & Krantz, 1976).

The economic downturn during the deflation crisis in the early 1920s was much more severe in Sweden than the crisis in 1929–1932. After recovery from the crisis, the Swedish economy grew strongly in the 1930s. As in other countries, growth was increasingly geared towards the home market, but export growth was also remarkably strong. Before the outbreak of World War II, the share of export in GDP was still around 20%. In the post-war period, the Swedish economy, like its Nordic neighbours, benefited from strong economic growth in its export markets, mainly Western Europe. The fast-growing sectors of the Swedish manufacturing industry increasingly produced for these export markets, while consumer goods industries producing for the home market declined or vanished. This ability to sustain an ongoing structural change was key to the successful development of the Swedish economy in this period (Jörberg & Krantz, 1976; Schön, 2010).

3 GDP and Foreign Trade

In the late nineteenth century, all the countries in our sample were peripheral in the sense that their growth was predicated on economic growth in the core of the world economy, especially the growth in Great Britain. Industrialization and economic growth in the core created demand for primary products supplied by peripheral countries. Consequently, export demand had a big role in the economic development of these countries. With an export ratio (exports divided by GDP in current prices) between 20% and 30% for most of the late nineteenth century (Fig. 2), the role of export demand in these countries was about as high as in the UK and considerably higher than in Germany and France, not to speak of the USA. If we take a population-weighted average of the latter four countries to represent the industrial core of the world at the time, we see (Fig. 2) that the export ratio in our three regions was much higher. In the Nordic countries, this high export ratio was maintained throughout the entire hundred-year period, or even increased in the post-war period.

In the other two regions, the share of export earnings in GDP tended to fall after the worldwide depression in 1929–1933.

The evolution of the export ratio of the countries had everything to do with what they produced and exported. At the start they all mainly exported primary and agricultural goods, but the Nordic countries, particularly Sweden, succeeded in steadily changing and upgrading the composition of their exports towards more manufactured goods. The Rio de la Plata countries, on the other hand, remained stuck with the same type of commodity basket in their exports throughout the entire hundred-year period. After World War II, the Australasian countries managed to diversify their exports away from the primary goods sector to

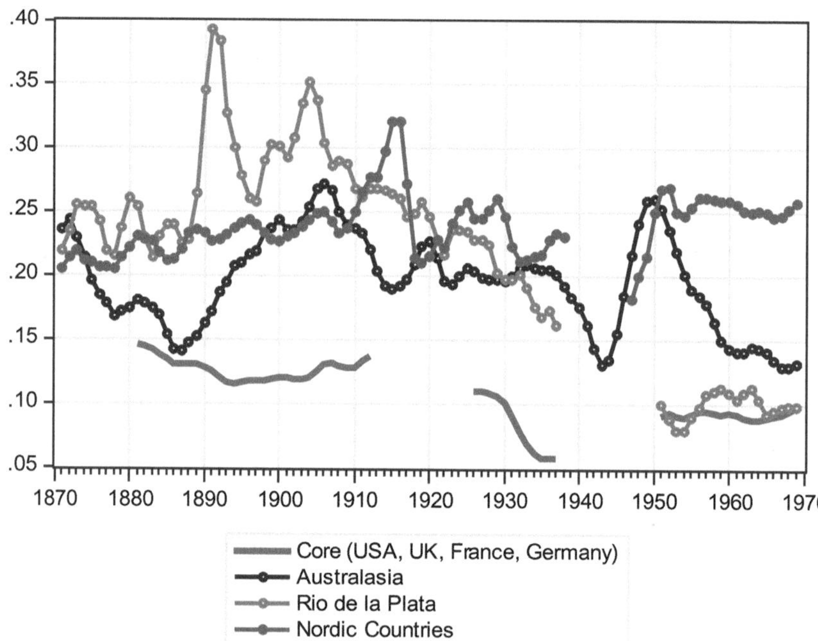

Fig. 2 Export share in three regions and the industrial core, 1870–1970 (*Sources* Core countries, Mitchell [1983, 2003]; other regions, see Appendix. *Note* Centred 3-year moving average)

some degree, but the shift was much less pronounced than in the Nordic countries.[3]

3.1 *Trade Shares and Terms of Trade*

Export earnings and their capacity to finance imports depended on export prices and import prices as well as export volumes. Figure 3 shows how the commodity terms of trade evolved in the three regions. We see that in the late nineteenth century there was an upward trend amid sharp fluctuations for all three regions. The long-run trend for the twentieth century was pretty much stable for all three of them. There is, however, one important difference between the three regions. While the terms of trade were quite stable for the Nordic countries they fluctuated wildly for the Australasian and Rio de la Plata countries. This obviously influenced short-run fluctuations in export earnings for the Southern Countries. Increased export earnings—whether through increased export volumes or favourable prices, which often coincided—stimulated the export sector and indirectly production for the home market as well. The flipside of this was that when terms of trade worsened, the business cycle turned downwards, so that in these regions the trade cycles also translated into cycles of real output (for a long-term study of the Uruguayan case that confirms this, see Bértola & Lanzilotta, 2021). It has been argued that fluctuations in the terms of trade also affect the long-term growth rate of a country negatively, quite irrespective of its long-term trend (Blattman et al., 2007).

We have already seen that the evolution of the export ratio differed between the regions. The growth rate in export ratios may be decomposed into a price and volume component:

$$(p_x - p_y) + (x - y)$$

where p_x = growth rate in export prices, p_y = growth rate in the GDP deflator, x = growth rate in export volumes, y = growth rate in real GDP.

In Table 2 this decomposition of the export share is shown for three periods, 1870–1913, 1913–1938 and 1946–1970. In the 1870–1913 period, the export share increased for all countries in our sample, except

[3] For an overview of the evolution of export specialization in the three regions, see Chapter 3.

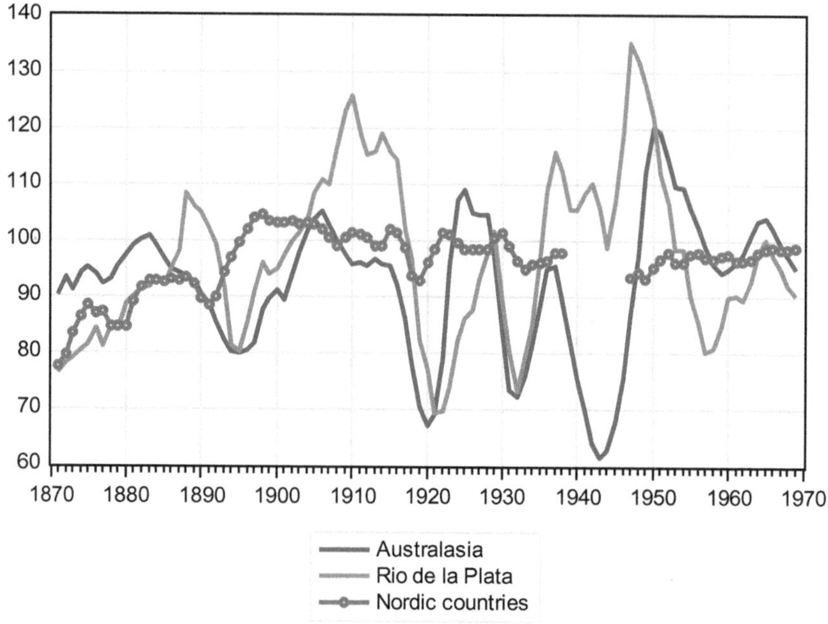

Fig. 3 Commodity terms of trade in three regions (*Sources* see Appendix. *Note* Centred three-year moving average)

Uruguay. In the Nordic countries and Australasia, the increase was caused by a faster increase in the export volume than in real GDP. In Argentina, the increase was caused by export prices rising more or falling less than the GDP deflator while the export volume still increased slightly more than real GDP. Uruguay experienced similar price movements as Argentina but here the export share fell because of a slower growth in the export volume than in real GDP.

In the period 1913–1938, the trend in the export share fell in all countries except New Zealand, where according to our data growth in the export volume was higher than the sluggish growth in GDP, which compensated for adverse price movements. The fall in the export share was most dramatic in the Rio de la Plata region. It was mainly caused by export prices falling relative to the GDP deflator, which was inadequately compensated for by increases in export volumes.

Table 2 Average annual export share growth (percentage growth rate of exponential trend), decomposed into price and volume changes, 1870–1913, 1913–1938 and 1950–1970

	1870–1913			*1913–1938*			*1946–1970*		
	$p_x - p_y$	$x - y$	*Export share*	$p_x - p_y$	$x - y$	*Export share*	$p_x - p_y$	$x - y$	*Export share*
Australasia	**–0.3**	**1.0**	**0.7**	**–1.4**	**1.3**	**0.0**	**–2.7**	**–0.4**	**–3.3**
Australia	–0.4	1.1	0.7	–1.5	1.2	–0.2	–3.2	–0.3	–3.8
New Zealand	0.5	0.3	0.8	–1.2	1.7	0.6	–0.7	–0.6	–1.0
Rio de la Plata	**1.0**	**–0.2**	**1.0**	**–2.5**	**0.3**	**–2.3**	**0.1**	**–1.0**	**–1.0**
Argentina	1.1	–0.1	1.2	-2.8	0.9	-2.0	0.5	–0.9	–0.5
Uruguay	0.8	–1.1	–0.3	–0.6	–3.9	–4.5	–2.6	–1.6	–4.4
Nordic countries	**–0.3**	**0.8**	**0.6**	**–1.7**	**1.2**	**–0.6**	**–2.0**	**3.0**	**0.9**
Denmark	0.1	0.9	1.0	–2.0	1.4	–0.8	–2.3	3.7	1.3
Sweden	–0.6	1.1	0.5	–1.1	–0.4	–1.6	–2.0	2.6	0.4
Norway	–0.5	0.7	0.3	–3.1	1.5	–1.6	–1.8	2.9	1.2
Finland	0.1	0.5	0.6	–1.2	3.5	2.3	–1.8	3.1	1.3

Sources See Appendix

In the post-war period, 1946–1970, export shares increased in the Nordic countries because export volumes grew faster than GDP, which more than compensated for the fact that export prices rose less than the GDP deflator. In the Australasian countries, the export share fell because the increase in export volumes was not high enough to compensate for a fall in export prices relative to the GDP deflator. The export share fell dramatically in Argentina and Uruguay primarily because export prices developed unfavourably compared to the GDP deflator, but also because export volumes grew less than real GDP.

4 The Theory of Balance-Of-Payments-Constrained growth—Thirlwall's Law

In an influential paper from 1989 Paul Krugman (1989) pointed to a strikingly strong empirical correlation between the ratio of income elasticities for exports and imports and long-run growth rates of nations.

Krugman also noted that price elasticities were of minor importance in explaining demand for imports and exports. The same empirical regularity had already been pointed out by Houthakker and Magee (1969) for a group of industrial countries in the 1950s and 1960s and Krugman confirmed it for a group of industrial countries in the 1970s and 1980s. He showed that the data points in a graph with the ratio of export and import income elasticities on the *y*-axis and GDP growth rates on the *x*-axis were scattered around a 45-degree linear trend with an intercept close to zero. He termed the relationship the 45-degree rule. Such a strong empirical regularity calls for explanations. Krugman ruled out "a priori" that income elasticities in exports and income could explain growth rates, since "we all know that differences in growth rates among countries are primarily determined in the rate of growth of total factor productivity" (Krugman, 1989: 1037). He concluded that the long-term and quite striking differences between countries in their income elasticities for imports and exports must be explained by supply-side characteristics, so that growth determines income elasticities in trade and not the other way around. He then proceeded to outline a trade theory in which increasing returns and monopolistic competition play a large part in determining divergences in income elasticities.

Ten years earlier Thirlwall had already pointed to the same correlation between income elasticities in trade and growth rates of countries (Thirlwall, 1979, 1983, 1997, 2011a, 2011b, 2013) but he reversed the causal connection. Thirlwall proceeded from the empirically well-founded assumption that in the long run the value of imports and exports must balance for a country, or else the country would run up unsustainable debts or alternatively pile up foreign assets indefinitely. In other words, in the long term the balance of payments will tend to be zero. This means that the requirement for sustained balance-of-payments equilibrium is that the current values of exports and imports grow at the same rate as expounded in Eq. (1).

$$x + p = m + p^* + e \tag{1}$$

All variables in (1) are expressed in rates of change, where x = volume of exports; p = domestic prices; m = volume of imports; p^* = foreign prices; and e = the exchange rate.

The growth rates in import and export volumes can be expressed by customary export and import demand functions, Eqs. (2) and (3).

$$x = \eta(p - p^* - e) + \varepsilon z \tag{2}$$

$$m = \psi(p + e - p^*) + \pi y \tag{3}$$

where η = the price elasticity of exports, ε = the income elasticity of exports, z = growth of world income, or rather the income of trading partners, Ψ = price elasticity of imports, π = income elasticity of imports and y = growth of domestic income.

By inserting (2) and (3) in (1) we arrive at the balance-of-payments-constrained growth rate, y_B:

$$y_B = \frac{(1 + \eta + \psi)(p - p^* - e) + \varepsilon z}{\pi} \tag{4}$$

The import and export price elasticities are both expected to be negative. In order for them to have a positive impact on domestic growth following increased price competitiveness (e.g. as a result of a depreciation of the exchange rate) the sum of their absolute values has to be larger than unity. This is the so-called Marshall-Lerner condition, which can be found in textbooks on international economics. It has been shown empirically that in the very long run, there is no trend in the commodity terms of trade for most countries (Ocampo & Parra-Lancourt, 2010), although this does not necessarily hold for shorter periods. If there is no long-term trend in the terms of trade and/or the sum of the price elasticities of exports and imports does not deviate much from unity, Eq. (4) reduces to:

$$y_B = \frac{\varepsilon}{\pi} z \tag{5}$$

Or under the same assumptions

$$y_B = \frac{x}{\pi} \tag{5b}$$

Equation (5) expresses Thirlwall's Law, which says that in the long run the growth of a nation is dependent on its export growth divided by the price elasticity of imports. The growth of exports is in turn dependent on non-price competitiveness expressed by the size of the income elasticity of demand for exports.

The balance-of-payments constraint may be temporarily alleviated if there is an inflow of capital which finances imports that are not covered by export receipts, as elaborated by Thirlwall and Hussain (1982) (Thirlwall, 2013: ch. 5). Taking capital inflow into account, Eq. (1) is modified into:

$$\omega(x + p) + (1 - \omega)(c + p) = m + p^* + e \tag{1b}$$

where c = the rate of growth of the volume of capital inflow; ω = the share of nominal imports covered by export receipts. By inserting (2) and (3) into (1b) we arrive at:

$$y = \frac{(1 + \omega\eta + \psi)(p - p^* - e) + \omega\varepsilon z + (1 - \omega)c}{\pi} \tag{4b}$$

The first term in Eq. (4) shows the effects on economic growth resulting from changes in the commodity terms of trade given the price elasticities for exports and imports; the second term expresses how growth among the trading partners affects the growth rate of a nation given the income elasticity of demand for its exports; and the last term expresses the impact on growth resulting from inflow or outflow of capital. If there is no trend in the terms of trade and/or the import and export price elasticities are not large enough to have any impact, Eq. (4b) reduces to:

$$y = \frac{\omega\varepsilon z + (1 - \omega)c}{\pi} \tag{5c}$$

From (5c) it follows that the growth rate of a country is the weighted sum of the growth of exports and real capital inflow divided by the income elasticity of demand for imports. If the growth rate of real capital imports is higher than the export growth rate, the country's growth rate will be enhanced; if it is less or negative (i.e. there is capital outflow) the growth rate will be reduced. Obviously, it would be unsustainable for a country to have a larger growth rate in its real capital inflow than in its growth rate for a long period, since that would continuously increase its foreign debt burden. It is therefore of some interest to examine how the growth rate would be affected if, starting from a deficit in the current account, its share of GDP stays the same. In that case the growth in the inflow of capital must be the same as the growth rate in GDP and we get:

$$y = \frac{\omega x}{\pi - (1 - \omega)} \tag{5d}$$

With reasonable values for the parameters in (5d), it cannot deviate much from the simple Thirlwall rule in (5), which means that the growth of exports divided by the income elasticity of demand for imports drives the GDP growth rate.

So, Thirlwall concluded that growth of exports ultimately drives growth rates. According to him, given the balance-of-payments requirement the growth of a country is constrained by the growth of demand from the rest of the world for its products. As to supply-side factors, Thirlwall pointed out that slow growth imposed by the balance-of-payments constraint in and of itself hampers productivity since there is a well-known empirical correlation between growth and productivity, as shown by the literature concerning Verdoorn's law. Moreover, the balance-of-payments constraint can also influence growth negatively in that it hampers the possibility to import inputs and technologies that stimulate productivity. In his polemic against Krugman, Thirlwall (1991) also stressed that differences in income elasticities for countries' exports to a certain extent are exogenously determined by their endowments of natural resources and the characteristics of goods produced, which are the products of history and independent of the growth of output. To this can be added that certain natural resources lend themselves more to further processing and diversification of output than others (Hausmann et al., 2007), such as the forest-industry complex in Sweden compared with the agricultural commodities exported by the Australasian and Rio de la Plata countries.

Thirlwall's Law has given rise to a voluminous empirical literature. It has been tested and found accurate on different data sets in numerous articles and books (Bértola et al., 2002; López & Cruz, 2015; López & Thirlwall, 2006; Setterfield, 2012; Thirlwall, 2013; Thirlwall & Hussain, 1982). Most of the tests have been done on data for industrialized countries in the late twentieth century, but there are also some empirical results from other parts of the world and for other time periods.

Some authors have interpreted Thirlwall's Law in a different way. For them, income elasticities of demand for exports and imports are seen as a mixed result of demand and supply forces, and, among the latter, particular attention is paid to the national systems of innovation (Bértola & Porcile, 2006; Fagerberg, 1987, 1994). Following Verspagen

(1993), changes in the productivity gap depend on specialization-induced technical change, domestic technological efforts and technological spill-overs. Furthermore, income elasticities of demand also depend on market shares and different institutional aspects affecting foreign trade (tariffs, subventions and more) (Bértola & Porcile, 2006).

In the following two sections we shall explore to what extent Thirlwall's Law can shed some light on the varying growth process in our three groups of countries.

5 Estimation of Import and Export Demand Functions

In order to test whether Thirlwall's Law may explain the path of economic growth of our group of countries we need to estimate the parameters in the export and import demand functions in Eqs. (2) and (3).

In order to obtain estimates of the parameters in the export demand function we have regressed the log of export volume against a constant, the log of export prices divided by foreign prices and the log of GDP in the export markets. For the price variable, we have used indexes of export prices in US dollars divided by a price index for world exports in US dollars.[4] For the income variable, we have calculated a weighted average of the GDP in the export markets, where the countries receiving the exports have been weighted by their shares of the total export value of the exporting country.

The parameters in the import demand function have been analogously estimated by regressing the log of the import volume against a constant, the log of import prices divided by home prices and the log of domestic GDP. For home prices, we have mostly used the GDP deflator for lack of better alternatives. This is not ideal, since arguably the GDP deflator is heavily influenced by prices in the non-tradable sector of the economy. For Sweden, Denmark and Finland we have therefore constructed price indexes that are weighted averages of the deflators of the manufacturing and agricultural sectors. These should arguably better reflect the evolution of prices of goods competing with imports.

Since we are dealing with time-series data, we need to investigate the order of integration of the various variables. The variables are generally

[4] Sources for the data used are given in Appendix.

non-stationary and I(1) variables. In order to use them in level form for estimation, they need to be co-integrated. To estimate import and export demand functions we have used an autoregressive distributed lag (ARDL) model.[5] The use of ARDL models has the advantage that they may also be used to test for a long-run level relationship between the variables. This test, the Bound test, has the advantage that it can be used irrespective of whether the included variables are I(0) or I(1) (Pesaran et al., 2001). In order to choose the number of lags in the ARDL models we have used the Schwarz information criterion. In searching for the appropriate model, the maximum number of lags allowed has been set to 2. If the Schwarz information criterion gives almost identical values for different models, we have generally chosen the simplest one. All estimations have been carried out in Eviews 12.

We have estimated export and import demand functions for the entire period 1870–1970. It might be argued, however, that the parameters are not representative for the entire period. We have therefore also made estimations for the period 1870–1913, usually called the first globalization period (O'Rourke & Williamson, 1999) and the post-war period 1950–1970. We also tried to estimate export and import demand functions for the period 1913–1938 and the inter-war period 1922–1938. These periods were characterized by much turbulence with dramatically increased inflation and increasing trade barriers during WW1; deflation crises in the aftermath of the war; the return to the gold standard in the 1920s; the depression and the following breakdown of the gold standard and shrinking world trade in the 1930s. It therefore proved difficult to obtain reliable estimates. They proved to be very sensitive to the inclusion or exclusion of yearly observations at the beginning or end of the period, and the choice of the order of lags.

For both the 1870–1913 period and the period 1950–1970 as well as for the entire period 1870–1970, the estimated parameters have the expected signs and look reasonable in size. For example, the estimated income elasticities for the period 1950–1970 are mostly similar to those obtained by Houthakker and Magee (1969) for the period 1951–1966 for countries where comparisons can be made. The estimates of income elasticities seem generally more reliable than those for price elasticities, meaning that they exhibit much lower standard deviations. The absolute

[5] The same strategy to estimate export and import demand functions have been advocated by Senhajidi and Montenegro (1998) and Senhadji (1998).

values of the estimated price elasticities are generally lower than income elasticities and are often not statistically significant, according to conventional criteria. Price elasticities are also generally lower or less statistically significant in the post-war period compared to the first globalization period, meaning that the role of price competitiveness had declined.

5.1 *Export and Import Demand Functions, 1870–1970*

Generally, the income elasticities for both exports and imports are statistically significant, while the corresponding price elasticities often are not. For the entire period 1870–1970 the export income elasticities are much higher for the Nordic countries than for the other two regions, while the difference is not so pronounced when it comes to import income elasticities. If we compare the income elasticities for exports between the sub-periods it is also remarkable that these were quite stable over time in the Nordic countries while they declined in the other regions.

5.2 *Export and Import Demand Functions, 1870–1913*

The estimated price and income elasticities for exports are all of the expected signs. Most of them are also statistically significant according to conventional criteria. The income elasticities were in all cases higher in absolute value than the price elasticities. They are also estimated with a higher precision than the corresponding price elasticities, i.e. their standard deviations are lower. The estimated income elasticities for the Nordic countries were generally around 1.5 or slightly higher, while they were slightly higher for the Australasian countries. In the Rio de la Plata region, Argentina stands out with an exceptionally high-income elasticity of demand for exports of around 3. Argentina was able to exploit the growing demand for wheat, wool and other agricultural products by expanding the land area devoted to agricultural production and by rapidly augmenting its labour force through immigration, mainly from southern Europe. Uruguay, on the other hand, lacking an open frontier and having natural resources that were not as good for growing agricultural crops as Argentina, stands out with an exceptionally low export income elasticity of around unity.

As in the case of the export demand function, the income elasticities for imports are estimated with higher precision than the corresponding price elasticities. The latter were in many cases not statistically significant according to conventional criteria. The estimated income elasticities for imports were in all cases except Finland lower than the export income elasticities. The Nordic countries had higher income elasticities for their imports than the other countries in our sample. Uruguay stands out with a low-income elasticity of demand for imports of around 0.7.

5.3 Export and Import Demand Functions, 1950–1970

For the period 1950–1970 all three Scandinavian countries had income demand elasticities for their exports of around 1.5, while that of Finland was slightly lower. These countries succeeded in reorienting their exports towards more manufactured goods, and within this group towards goods for which the income elasticity of demand was higher than for more traditional manufactured goods.

In the other regions, Australia's income elasticity for exports is estimated to be around 1.3, which was clearly lower than in the Scandinavian countries. Australia also managed to reorient its exports towards more manufactured goods, but not to the same extent as in the Nordic region. Argentina and Uruguay as well as New Zealand still mainly exported the same types of goods that dominated their exports in the first globalization period, 1870–1913. This explains the remarkable gap between the income elasticity of demand for their exports and those in the Nordic region. The income elasticity of demand for exports is estimated to be about 0.7 for Argentina and New Zealand. For Uruguay it is even lower, although the estimate is not statistically significant according to conventional criteria.

In the Nordic countries there was not much change in the estimated income elasticities of imports if we compare the late nineteenth century with the period 1950–1970. In the Swedish case the income elasticities of demand for imports and exports were roughly the same, meaning that according to Thirlwall's Law Sweden should grow at the same rate as its trading partners. Denmark and Norway both had income elasticities for imports of around 1.3, which was slightly lower than their corresponding income elasticities for exports. In all Nordic countries price elasticities for imports were markedly lower than their corresponding income elasticities and also estimated with less precision, or of lower significance to use statistical jargon.

As in the case of the Nordic countries our estimated income elasticity of imports did not change much between the late nineteenth century and the post-war period for Australia. It was 1.1 in the first period and 1.2 in the latter. In the case of New Zealand and the Rio de la Plata region the change was more dramatic. In New Zealand it declined from 1.1 to 0.7, while in the Rio de la Plata countries we could not obtain meaningful estimates for the import demand functions in this period. Constrained by lower growth in export earnings the countries in this region were forced to cut down on import growth and rely more on a strategy of import substitution. In the case of Uruguay, the trend in import volume even declined in the 1950–1970 period according to our data, despite sluggish economic growth.

Some interesting points can be made by comparing income elasticities in the 1870–1913 period and in the post-war period. In the first globalization period, income elasticities of exports in the Nordic countries were similar to, or only slightly lower, than in Australasia, with the exception of Denmark which was somewhat higher. As already pointed out Argentina stands out with an exceptionally high elasticity of 3. In the post-war period, the export income elasticities of the Nordic countries remained similar to the 1870–1913 period. The same goes for income elasticities of imports. In Australasia and the Rio de la Plata region, on the other hand, the income elasticities of exports had dropped dramatically. Income elasticities of imports also dropped, except for Australia, but not as much. The limited transformation of the goods composition of exports in the Australasian countries or the total lack of it in the Rio de la Plata countries in the twentieth century is reflected in the decline in estimated export elasticities. Since in the long run the balance-of-payments constraint is binding, this negatively impacted the growth rates of the Australasian and particularly the Rio de la Plata countries. According to Thirlwall's Law, if the growth of exports declines, whether through an unfavourable development of the income elasticity of demand for exports or a low-income growth in export markets, it can be counteracted by a decline in the income elasticity of imports. This happened to a certain extent, both in the Australasian and the Rio de la Plata countries. However, there is a limit to the extent that growth rates can be upheld by an import substitution strategy, especially in relatively small economies. The balance-of-payments constraint forced these countries to lower their import growth, reflected in declining income elasticities of demand, but this also limited the possibility of importing investment goods and other inputs for growth.

6 Predictions of Thirlwall's Law and Economic Growth in Three Regions

The estimated income and price elasticities for imports and exports make it possible to test to what extent Thirlwall's Law predicts actual growth rates for our group of countries in the period 1870–1970. Thirlwall's Law may be tested according to Eqs. 5 or 5b. The former is considered to be a more stringent test, since it is based on predicted growth rates in exports derived from estimated income elasticities of exports and growth rates of GDP in the export markets. Another test that has been seen in the literature is based on a comparison between estimated income elasticities of imports and the elasticities implied by Eq. 5b, given the actual growth rates in exports and GDP.

In Table 5 we have put together data on export and import growth for our countries together with the estimated elasticities from Tables 3 and 4. For the entire period 1870–1970 Thirlwall's Law predicts growth rates quite well for Sweden and Denmark while it overpredicts the growth rate for Norway and markedly so in the case of Finland. In the case of the Australasian countries the predicted growth rates are not wide off the mark, while for the Rio de la Plata countries, on the other hand, the predictions of Thirlwall's Law are far less accurate. Since we have already established that the estimated income elasticities of exports and imports changed over time, particularly for the Australasian and Rio de la Plata countries, it is, however, more interesting to compare actual growth rates with the growth rates predicted by Thirlwall's Law for the two periods 1870–1913 and 1950–1970. For Argentina and Uruguay, it was only possible to obtain meaningful estimates of the required elasticities for the period 1870–1913, so we cannot make the comparison for these countries except for that one period.

If we look at the first globalization period, 1870–1913, we see from Table 5 that Thirlwall's Law in most cases predicts the actual growth rates quite accurately, at least when we consider the weak form of the test, except for Australia, where the predicted growth rates according to Thirlwall's Law are overstated by roughly 25–30%. For most countries, the more stringent test fares slightly worse. In this case the Danish growth rate is also overestimated by roughly 25%. Given that the data underlying the estimates are far from perfect we cannot expect to get any precise concordance between predicted and actual growth rates of exports. Moreover, in this period, the evolution of the terms of trade and

Table 3 Estimates of long-run price and income elasticities for exports in the 1870–1970, 1870–1913 and 1950–1970 periods

Country	*ARDL*[(1)]	*Price el*	*Standard dev. Price el*	*Income el*	*Standard dev. Price el*	*Bound F-stat*[(2)]	*BG F-test, p-value*
1870–1970							
Sweden	1,1,1	–0.67	0.42	1.45***	0.09	3.26	0.32
Denmark	2,1,0	–0.29	0.30	1.60***	0.09	5.24	0.11
Norway	1,0,0	–0.69***	0.15	1.41***	0.04	26	0.15
Finland	1,2,0	–2.32	0.79	2.07***	0.20	4.89	0.03
Australia	1,0,0	–1.71**	0.73	1.00***	0.11	8.13	0.22
New Zealand	1,1,0	-3.31	2.64	1.14***	0.32	6.93	0.16
Argentina	2,1,0	–0.32	1.26	0.60*	0.66	3.02	0.00
Uruguay							
1870–1913							
Sweden	1,2,2	–1.05**	0.41	1.49***	0.09	4.03	0.96
Denmark	1,0,0	–1.08**	0.33	1.92***	0.10	11.34	0.35
Norway	1,0,0	–1.13	0.47	1.38***	0.12	8.7	0.50
Finland	1,0,0	–0.40	0.31	1.57***	0.17	9.30	0.63
Australia	1,0,0	–1.06***	0.15	1.78***	0.05	17.02	0.88
New Zealand	1,1,1	–1.13***	0.20	1.86***	0.06	10.28	0.02
Argentina	1,0,0	–0.95***	0.30	2.99***	0.16	9.11	0.59
Uruguay	1,0,0	–0.44	0.60	1.08***	0.28	4.1	0.95
1950–1970							
Sweden	1,0,0	–1.24*	0.67	1.51***	0.08	21	0.30
Denmark	1,0,0	–0.73***	0.21	1.54***	0.04	38.75	0.13
Norway	1,0,0	–0.07	0.12	1.57***	0.03	44.4	0.12
Finland	1,1,0	–0.29	0.12	1.31***	0.10	33.81	0.72
Australia	1,2,0	0.65	0.55	1.34***	0.20	11.2	0.60
New Zealand	1,1,2	–0.57***	0.17	0.71***	0.07	5.34	0.14
Argentina	2,1,1	–0.28	0.16	0.77***	0.08	23.04	0.30
Uruguay	1,1,0	0.69	0.48	0.53	0.31	4.01	0.91

Sources See Appendix

Note ***, ** and * denote statistical significance at the 1%, 5% and 10% levels, respectively. (1) Number of lags in the independent variable and in the price and quantity variables, respectively. (2) Critical bounds for the *F*-test for I0 and I1 series (lower and upper bounds): 10% significance (2.63, 3.35), 5% significance (3.10, 3.87), 1% significance (4.13, 5.00)

Table 4 Estimates of long-run price and income elasticities for imports in the 1870–1970, 1870–1913 and 1950–1970 periods

Country	*ARDL (1)*	*Price el*	*Stand dev. Price el*	*Income el*	*Stand dev. Price el*	*Bound F-stat (2)*	*BG F-test, p-value*
1870–1970							
Sweden	1,0,1	-1.51**	0.72	0.84***	0.14	7.44	0.10
Denmark	1,0,1	-1.00***	0.13	1.09***	0.02	11.06	0.21
Norway	2,2,2	-0.21***	0.41	0.89***	0.13	4.91	0.60
Finland	1,01	-1.19**	0.56	0.71***	0.21	9.07	0.49
Australia	2,1,1	-0.24	0.19	0.89***	0.04	9.08	0.12
New Zealand	1,1,2	-0.18	0.39	1.08***	0.05	9.14	0.05
Argentina	1,1,2	-0.31	0.48	0.64***	0.09	4.37	0.04
Uruguay	1,1,2	-0.56	0.27	0.56***	0.09	4.13	0.35
1870–1913							
Sweden	1,0,1	-0.35	0.68	1.29***	0.28	4.19	0.26
Denmark	1,0,0	-1.25***	0.39	1.22***	0.10	10.67	0.47
Norway	2,0,1	-1.19***	0.22	1.23***	0.10	6.51	0.71
Finland	1,1,0	-0.05	0.21	1.75***	0.14	11.76	0.27
Australia	2,1,1	-0.01	0.52	1.10***	0.09	5.90	0.55
New Zealand	2,1,2	-0.92	0.61	1.09***	0.11	5.02	0.04
Argentina	1,0,1	-0.51**	0.69	1.03***	0.11	4.67	0.19
Uruguay	2,0,0	-0.67*	0.37	0.66***	0.1	6.21	0.77
1950–1970							
Sweden	1,0,1	0.51	0.58	1.51***	0.09	9.58	0.75
Denmark	1,0,0	-1.11***	0.19	1.32***	0.12	46.2	0.84
Norway	2,2,0	-0.61***	0.12	1.22***	0.05	32.14	0.17
Finland	2,2,0	-0.25	0.19	1.58***	0.05	43.03	0.11
Australia (1946–1970)	1,0,1	0.36	0.61	1.24***	0.41	5,52	0.82
New Zealand (1951–1970)	2,0,1	-0.75***	0.24	0.67***	0.13	8.13	0.69
Argentina	1,0,1	-0.42	0.50	0.32	0. 50	2.27	0.17

Sources See Appendix

Note ***, ** and * denote statistical significance at the 1%, 5% and 10% levels, respectively. (1) Number of lags in the independent variable and in the price and quantity variables, respectively. (2) Critical bounds for the *F*-test for I0 and I1 series (lower and upper bounds): 10% significance (2.63, 3.35), 5% significance (3.10, 3.87), 1% significance (4.13, 5.00)

the price elasticities of imports and exports should also have had some influence on growth rates. Capital inflows and outflows were also substantial for all our countries in this period. They may have had even greater effects on growth rates. Particularly in the case of Argentina and Australia huge capital inflows in the 1870s and 1880s were interrupted by financial and banking crises in the early 1890s, which reversed the tide and led to substantial capital outflows. There have been attempts in the literature to estimate the impact of price movements as well as capital inflows and outflows (Thirlwall & Hussain, 1982). The reasoning is that since Thirlwall's Law is based on a national income accounting identity we should be able to estimate the importance of prices residually if we have good data on capital flows. It is hard to get accurate capital flow data for the entire hundred-year period for the countries in our sample, and we also regard the underlying historical national accounts data and hence the estimated trade elasticities as being too error-prone to make such an attempt.

Among the Nordic countries, Thirlwall's Law predicts growth rates quite successfully for Sweden for the period 1950–1970, and slightly less so for Denmark, while in the case of Norway, growth is overestimated by about 25–30%. For Finland, Thirlwall's Law in its strict form (Eq. 5) underestimates growth by about 20% while in its weak form (Eq. 5b) it comes closer to the actual growth rate. In the case of Australia, the weak form of Thirlwall's Law performs well for the 1950–1970 period, while the more stringent formulation (Eq. 5) overestimates the actual growth rate, apparently because the growth rate in exports is exaggerated when calculated according to the formula in Eq. 5. For New Zealand, Thirlwall's Law overestimates growth rates by about 30% in this period, even though export growth is predicted well. In order for the simple model to predict growth rates with any precision for this country the income elasticity of demand would have had to be around 0.9, while according to our estimate it was roughly 0.7. In other words, New Zealand did not reduce imports and replace them with domestic production to the extent predicted by the simple model of Thirlwall's Law, assuming our estimates of the import income elasticities are nearly correct. Apart from obvious problems with the quality of data underlying our estimates, this indicates that the evolution of the terms of trade was not without importance. In both Australasia and the Rio de la Plata region the evolution of terms of trade was characterized by wild swings, which was not the case in the Nordic countries.

Table 5 Actual growth rates and predictions according to Thirlwall's Law for the periods 1870–1970, 1870–1913 and 1950–1970

	Export income elasticity	*Import income elasticity*	*Export growth*	*GDP growth of export recipients*	*GDP growth*	Y_B *according to Eq. 5*	Y_B *according to Eq. 5b*
1870–1970							
Sweden	1.45	1.09	3.3	2.2	2.8	2.9	3.0
Denmark	1.60	1.10	3.2	2.1	3.0	3.1	2.9
Norway	1.41	0.90	3.4	2.4	2.8	3.8	3.8
Finland	2.07	0.71	3.1	1.9	2.9	5.6	4.4
Australia	1.00	0.89	2.5	2.3	2.6	2.6	2.8
New Zealand	1.14	1.08	3.0	2.1	2.8	2.2	2.8
Argentina	0.6	0.64	2.75	2.2	2.0	4.3	4.0
Uruguay		0.56	0.7	2.8	2.6		1.3
1870–1913							
Sweden	1.49	1.43	3.3	2.1	2.2	2.5	2.3
Denmark	1.92	1.22	3.6	2.1	2.7	3.4	2.9
Norway	1.38	1.23	2.6	2.2	1.9	2.5	2.1
Finland	1.57	1.75	3.14	2.3	2.7	2.0	1.8
Australia	1.57	1.10	3.9	2.2	2.8	3.0	3.6
New Zealand	1.86	1.09	4.1	2.2	3.8	3.7	3.7
Argentina	2.99	1.03	5.7	2.1	5.8	6.1	5.5
Uruguay	1.08	0.66	2.6	2.6	3.7	4.3	3.9
1950–1970							
Sweden	1.51	1.51	6.59	4.3	4.3	4.3	4.4
Denmark	1.54	1.32	6.63	4.2	4.3	4.9	5.0
Norway	1.57	1.22	6.55	4.2	4.2	5.3	5.4
Finland	1.31	1.58	6.75	4.3	4.6	3.6	4.3
Australia	1.34	1.24	5.42	5.5	4.5	6.0	4.4
New Zealand	0.71	0.67	3.39	4.8	3.8	5.0	5.1
Argentina	0.77	NA	3.98	4.7	3.5	-	-

Note Growth rates in GDP and exports are growth rates of exponential trends

7 Summary and Conclusion

In this chapter we compare the economic performance of Australasia (Australia and New Zaland), the Nordic countries (Denmark, Norway, Sweden and Finland) and the Rio de la Plata region (Argentina and Uruguay) in the period 1870–1970. These three regions were all peripheral to the industrial core in the Atlantic economy in the late nineteenth century. In all of them exports played a relatively large role in their economies. Initially they were all also dependent for their exports on a few staple goods, based on their respective resource endowments. In the late nineteenth century there were large differences in the economic wellbeing of these regions as measured by their level of GDP per capita. Australasia, at that time arguably the richest region in the world, was much richer than the Nordic countries, with the Rio de la Plata region in between. One hundred years later, the Nordic countries had caught up with, or in the case of Sweden and Denmark even surpassed, Australasia, while the Rio de la Plata region lagged far behind. We explore this development from the vantage point of the relationship between foreign trade and economic growth.

Besides differences in GDP per capita growth rates, the three regions differed in how their exports evolved. The Nordic countries succeeded in maintaining or even raising their share of exports in GDP, while the export share of the other regions fell in comparison to the level in the late nineteenth century. This was related to the evolution of the commodity composition of exports of the various regions. The Nordic countries, particularly Sweden, managed to diversify their exports in the twentieth century into more and more industrial goods. Australasia did this to a much lesser degree and only in the post-war period, while the Rio de Plata region more or less exclusively exported the same types of agricultural products throughout the entire period. Since demand growth was much slower for agricultural goods than for industrial products, due to lower income elasticity of demand, the share of exports in GDP declined for countries that did not manage to diversify out of the specialization pattern formed in the late nineteenth century. Moreover, primary and agricultural products underwent heavy price fluctuations, which added to the problems of countries heavily reliant on them for their exports. In periods of sharp declines in export prices it was difficult for these countries to finance imports of industrial goods, whose prices were much more stable. Consequently, these countries had recurrent balance-of-payment problems.

Economists from different traditions have established that there is strong positive correlation between the growth rate of a country and the ratio of its export growth divided by its income elasticity of demand for imports. Moreover, it has been established that in the long run the growth of exports of countries is primarily determined by non-price competitiveness as expressed in the income elasticity of demand. We arrive at the same conclusion when estimating export and import demand functions for the seven countries in our sample for the period 1870–1970, as well as for the periods 1870–1913 and 1950–1970. From the reasonable assumption that in the long run the value of exports and imports of countries must balance, and observation of the negligible role of the commodity terms of trade for the long-term growth of exports and imports, Thirlwall derived what has been called Thirlwall's Law. In its strong form the law states that the growth rate of a country is equal to the ratio between the income elasticities of demand for its exports and imports times the growth rate in its export markets. Thirlwall's Law predicts actual growth rates reasonably well for the Nordic countries, particularly Sweden, in all three periods, and also performs reasonably well for Australasia. In the case of the Rio de la Plata region the predicted growth rates come close to the actual rates in the 1870–1913 period, while for the 1950–1970 period it was not possible to obtain the required elasticities to test the model. While this may partly be the result of errors in the dataset, since historical national accounts data are very much error-prone, it also shows that the evolution of the terms of trade and capital flows had a non-negligible influence, especially on the Rio de la Plata and the Australasian regions. Since Thirlwall's Law is essentially based on a national income accounting identity it should be possible, with accurate data and good estimates of the required elasticities, to quantify the respective influences of terms of trade and capital flows on growth rates. However, we have not deemed the data accurate enough for such an endeavour. Nonetheless it goes without saying that for the Australasian and Rio de la Plata regions, the major influence on the growth of exports over the hundred years period was also the evolution of the income elasticity of demand for their export goods.

Can we then conclude that differences in export growth rates are the dominant factor behind the differences in growth rates among the countries in our sample? That would obviously be too rash a conclusion. The observed correlation between export growth divided by the income elasticity of imports can be and has been interpreted in different ways. Broadly speaking we may distinguish between supply-oriented and demand-oriented explanations.

In a supply-oriented theoretical framework it is argued that countries that for various reasons manage to raise their production capacity will also diversify and upgrade the composition of their export goods away from a narrow dependence on a few staple goods and towards more industrial goods.

On the other hand, in the Post-Keynesian tradition it is argued that export growth as an exogenous source of demand governs economic growth. According to this perspective the initial specialization of a country within the worldwide division of labour, largely dependent on its natural resource endowments, can be more or less conducive to the possibility of diversifying its productive forces into other sectors of the economy. It may be argued for example that Sweden's forestry-based industrial complex had more growth potential and also more linkages to other sectors of the economy than the types of agricultural goods that dominated exports in Australasia and the Rio de la Plata region. It may also be argued that the geographical proximity of the Nordic countries to the fast-growing industrial economies of Western Europe was clearly beneficial to them compared with the other two regions. However, among Post-Keynesian economists it is also widely recognized that differing growth rates are not simply a passive reflection of external demand growth. Of importance is the capacity of a country to adapt its productive forces to changing composition of demand in the world market. Otherwise, it would for example be difficult to explain the diverging growth experiences of Australasia and the Rio de la Plata region in the twentieth century. Countries differed not only in their resource endowments but also in their institutional framework, economic and industrial policies, education, etc. The institutional framework is also related to foreign trade policies. No doubt, particularly since the 1930s, tariffs affected commodity trade in different ways in different regions. Their impact was more important in Southern societies, and particularly in those of the Rio de la Plata.

For a more complete understanding of economic growth, comparative research should be deepened in these areas.

Appendix: Sources for Data

Australia: GDP and GDP deflator Butlin et al. (2014), Export and import volumes, http://dfat.gov.au/trade/resources/trade-statistics/Pages/trade-time-series-data.aspx;
Export and import prices, http://dfat.gov.au/trade/resources/trade-statistics/Pages/trade-time-series-data.aspx
(Bambrick, 1970; Butlin et al., 2014; Wilson, 1931).
New Zealand: GDP and GDP deflator: http://www.stats.govt.nz/browse_for_stats/economic_indicators/nationalaccounts/long-term-data-series.aspx, table E1.1
Rankin (1992)
Export and import volumes, export and import prices
http://www.stats.govt.nz/browse_for_stats/economic_indicators/nationalaccounts/long-term-data-series.aspx
Briggs (2003)
Argentina: Ferreres (2010)
Uruguay: GDP and GDP deflator, Bértola (2016)
Exports and imports (nominal and real) Baptista & Bértola (1999) and Bértola (1990).
Moxlad database, http://moxlad-staging.herokuapp.com/home/es
Sweden: GDP nominal and real. Edvinsson (2014)
Exports and imports, nominal Edvinsson (2014)
Export and import price indexes.
1870–1913, own calculations.
1913–1970, Johansson (1967), Edvinsson (2014)
Denmark: GDP nominal and real Hansen (1974)
Exports and imports, current values.
1870 74, Hansen (1974)
1874–1970, Bjerke and Ussing (1958), Johansen (1985)
Export and import prices.
Hansen (1974), Ølgaard (1966: 243), Johansen (1985)
Norway: GDP nominal and real Grytten (2003)
http://www.norges-bank.no/en/statistics/historical-monetary-statistics/
Exports and imports (nominal and real) Grytten (2003)
http://www.norges-bank.no/en/statistics/historical-monetary-statistics/
Finland: http://www.stat.fi/til/vtp/tau_en.html
Hjerppe (1989)

References

Bambrick, S. (1970). Australia's long-run terms of trade. *Economic Development and Cultural Change, 1*, 1–5.

Bértola, L. (1990). *The manufacturing industry of Uruguay, 1913–1961: A sectoral approach to growth, fluctuations and crisis*. Publications of the Department of Economic History.

Bértola, L. (2016). *El PBI per capita de Uruguay 1870–2015: Una reconstrucción* (No. 48). *Progama de Historia Económica y Social. Documentos de Trabajo* (Vol. 48). Montevideo.

Baptista, B., & Bértola, L. (1999). Uruguay 1870–1913: Indicadores de comercio exterior. *Segundas Jornadas de Historia Económica*. AUDHE.

Bértola, L., Higachi, H., & Porcile, G. (2002). Balance-of-payments-constrained growth in Brazil: A test of Thirlwall's Law, 1890–1973. *Journal of Post Keynesian Economics, 25*(1), 123–140.

Bértola, L., & Ocampo, J. A. (2012). *The economic development of Latin America since independence*. Oxford University Press.

Bértola, L., & Lanzilotta, B. (2021). Trends and cycles: The Uruguayan economy, 1870–2019, paper presented at the RIDGE Economic History Workshop, December 8–9, 2021, Montevideo.

Bértola, L., & Porcile, G. (2006). Convergence, trade and industrial policy: Argentina, Brazil and Uruguay in the international economy, 1900–1980. *Revista de Historia Económica-Journal of Iberian and Latin American Economic History, 24*(1), 37–67.

Bjerke, K., & Ussing, N. (1958). *Studier over Danmarks nationalprodukt 1870–1950*. København: Københavns økonomiske institut, G E C Gads forlag.

Blattman, C., Hwang, J., & Williamson, J. G. (2007). Winners and losers in the commodity lottery: The impact of terms of trade growth and volatility in the Periphery 1870–1939. *Journal of Development Economics, 82*(1), 156–179.

Bohlin, J. (2005). Tariff protection in Sweden, 1885–1914. *Scandinavian Economic History Review, 53*(2), 7–29.

Bolt, J., & van Zanden, J. L. (2020). *Maddison style estimates of the evolution of the world economy. A new 2020 update* (Maddison-Project Working Paper No. 15). Groningen.

Briggs, P. (2003). *Looking at the numbers: a view of New Zealand's economic history*. NZ Institute of Economic Research.

Butlin, M., Dixon, R., & Lloyd, P. J. (2014). *Statistical appendix: Selected data series, 1800–2010*. Cambridge University Press.

Butlin, M., Dixon, R., & Lloyd, P. J. (2015). Statistical appendix: Selected data series, 1800–2010. In S. Ville & G. Withers (Eds.), *The Cambridge economic history of Australia* (pp. 555–594). Cambridge University Press.

Diaz Alejandro, C. F. (1970). *Essays on the economic history of the Argentine republic*. Yale University Press.

Edvinsson, R. (2014). The gross domestic product for Sweden within its present borders, 1620–2012. In R. Edvinsson, T. Jacobsson, & D. Waldenström (Eds.), *House prices, stock returns, national accounts, and the Riksbank balance sheet, 1620–2012* (pp. 101–182). Ekerlids.

Fagerberg, J. (1987). A Technology gap approach to why growth rates differ. *Research Policy, 16*(2–4), 87–99.

Fagerberg, J. (1994). Technology and international differences in growth rates. *Journal of Economic Literature, 32*, 1147–1175.

Ferreres, O. J. (2010). *Dos siglos de economía Argentina 1810–2010: Historia Argentina en cifras*. El Ateneo, Fundación Norte y Sur.

Gerchunoff, P., & Llach, L. (2011). Dos siglo en las economías del Plata, 1810–2010. In L. Bértola, & P. Gerchunoff (Eds.), *Institucionalidad y desarrollo económico en América Latina* (pp. 287–321). CEPAL. AECID.

Grytten, O. H. (2003). The gross domestic product for Norway 1830–2003. In Ø. Eitrheim, J. T. Klovland, & J. F. Qvigstad (Eds.), *Historical monetary statistics for Norway 1819–2003* (pp. 241–288). Norges Bank.

Grytten, O. H. (2015). Gross domestic product by industry 1830–1930. *Norges Bank Working Paper, 19*.

Hansen, S. A. (1974). *Økonomisk vækst i Danmark. Bind II: 1914–1970*. Akademisk forlag.

Hausmann, R., Hwang, J., & Rodrik, D. (2007). What you export matters. *Journal of Economic Growth, 12*(1), 1–25.

Hjerppe, R. (1989). *The Finnish economy 1860–1985: Growth and structural change*. Bank of Finland.

Houthakker, H. S., & Magee, S. P. (1969). Income and price elasticities in world trade. *Review of Economics and Statistics, 51*(2), 111–125.

Hutchinson, D. (2015). Manufacturing. In S. Ville, & G. Withers (Eds.), *The Cambridge economic history of Australia*. Cambridge University Press.

Johansen, H.C. (1985). *Danmarks historie, bind 9, Dansk økonomisk statistik 1814–1980*. København: Gyldendal (Danmarks historie, 9).

Johansson, Ö. (1967). *The gross domestic product of Sweden and its composition 1861–1955*. Almqvist & Wicksell.

Jörberg, L., & Krantz, O. (1973). The industrial revolution in the Nordic countries. In *The Fontana economic history of Europe vol. 4. The emergence of Industrial societies* (pp. 375–485). Collins/Fontana.

Jörberg, L., & Krantz, O. (1976). Scandinavia 1914–1970. In *The Fontana economic history of Europe vol. 6. Contemporary economies*. Collins/Fontana.

Katz, J., & Kosacoff, B. (1989). *El proceso de industrialización en la Argentina: Evolución, retroceso y perspectivas*. Cepal.

Katz, J., & Kosacoff, B. (2000). Technological learning, institution building and the microeconomics of import substitution. In E. Cardenas, J. A. Ocampo, & R. Thorp (Eds.), *An economic history of twentieth-century Latin America vol. 3: Industrialization and the state in Latin America: The postwar years*. Palgrave.

Krugman, P. (1989). Differences in income elasticities and trends in real exchange rates. *European Economic Review, 33*(5), 1031–1046.

López, G. J., & Cruz, B. A. (2015). "Thirlwall's Law" and beyond: The Latin American experience. *Journal of Post Keynesian Economics*, 22(3), 477–495. https://doi.org/10.1080/01603477.2000.11490253

López, P., & Thirlwall, A. (2006). Trade liberalization, the income elasticity of demand for imports, and growth in Latin America. *Journal of Post Keynesian Economics., 29*(1), 41–61. https://doi.org/10.2753/PKE0160-3477290103

Maddison Project. (2020). *Maddison project database*. https://www.rug.nl/ggdc/historicaldevelopment/maddison/releases/maddison-project-database-2020?lang=en

McLean, I. W. (2013). *Why Australia prospered: The shifting sources of economic growth*. Princeton University Press.

Mitchell, B. R. (2003). *International historical statistics: Europe, 1750–2000 (5)*. Palgrave Macmillan.

Mitchell, B. R. (1983). *International historical statistics. The Americas and Australasia*. Macmillan.

Ocampo, J. A., & Parra-Lancourt, M. (2010). The terms of trade for commodities since the mid-19th century. *Revista De Historia Económica / Journal of Iberian and Latin American Economic History, 28*(01), 11.

Ølgaard, A. (1966). *Growth, productivity and relative prices* (p. 10). Københavns Universitets økonomiske institut (Studier fra Københavns universitets Økonomiske Institut.

O'Rourke, K. H., & Williamson, J. G. (1999). *Globalization and history: The evolution of a nineteenth-century Atlantic economy*. MIT.

Pesaran, M. H., Shin, Y., & Smith, R. J. (2001). Bounds testing approaches to the analysis of level relationships. *Journal of Applied Econometrics, 16*(3), 289–326. https://doi.org/10.1002/jae.616

Rankin, K. (1992). New Zealand's gross national product: 1859–1939. *Review of Income and Wealth, 38*(1), 49–69.

Schlueter, A. (2014). *Institutions and small settler economies. A comparative study of New Zealand and Uruguay, 1870–2008*. Palgrave Macmillan.

Schön, L. (2010). *Sweden's road to modernity: An economic history*. SNS.

Schön, L., & Krantz, O. (2015). *New Swedish historical national accounts since the 16th century in constant and current prices* (Lund Papers in Economic History no. 140 No. 140).

Schvarzer, J. (1996). *La industria que supimos conseguir. Una historia política y social de la industria argentina*. Planeta.

Senhadji, A. (1998). Time-series of structural import demand equations. *IMF Staff Papers, 45*(2), 236–268.

Senhajidi, A., & Montenegro, C. (1998). Time series analysis of export demand functions: A cross-country analysis. *IMF Working Papers*, (149), 1–29.

Setterfield, M. (2012). The remarkable durability of Thirlwall's Law. *PSL Quarterly Review, 64*(259), 393–427.

Thirlwall, A. (1997). Reflections on the concept of balance-of payments-constrained growth. *Journal of Post Keynesian., 19*(3), 377–385.

Thirlwall, A. P. (1979). The balance of payment constraint as an explanation of international growth rate differences. *Banca Nazionale Del Lavoro Quarterly Review, 32*(128), 45–53.

Thirlwall, A. P. (1983). Foreign trade elasticities in centre-periphery models of growth and development. *Banca Nazionale Del Lavoro Quarterly Review, 36*(146), 249–261.

Thirlwall, A. P. (1991). Professor Krugman's 45-degree rule. *Journal of Post Keynesian Economics, 14*(1), 23–28.

Thirlwall, A. P. (2011a). Balance of payments constrained growth models: History and overview. *PSL Quarterly Review, 64*(259), 307–351.

Thirlwall, A. P. (2011b). The balance of payments constraint as an explanation of international growth rate differences. *PSL Quarterly Review, 64*(259), 429–438.

Thirlwall, A. P. (2013). *Economic growth in an open developing economy. The rule of structure and demand*. Edward Elgar.

Thirlwall, A. P., & Hussain, M. N. (1982). The balance of payments constraint, capital flows and growth rate differences between developing countries. *Oxford Economic Papers, 34*(3), 515–519.

Thorp, R. (1986). Latin America and the international economy from the First World War to the World Depression. In L. Bethell (Ed.), *The Cambridge history of Latin America IV* (pp. 57–81). Cambridge University Press.

Verspagen, B. (1993). *Uneven growth between interdependent economies: An evolutionary view on technology gaps, trade and growth*. Avebury.

Wilson, R. (1931). *Capital imports and the terms of trade. Examined in the light of sixty years of Australian borrowing*. Melbourne University Press, Macmillan.

CHAPTER 5

Coming Full Circle: Brazilian/Swedish Labour Productivity Ratios in Manufacturing, 1912–2014

Cecilia Lara and Svante Prado

1 Introduction

Economic history research typically stresses the importance of manufacturing in driving economy-wide productivity. Hirschman (1958) stressed the backward and forward linkages emanating from manufacturing, and Kaldor (1967) expounded the idea that growth of productivity in manufacturing always spilled over into growth of productivity in the aggregate according to a growth law. These old and influential ideas have resurfaced in discussions about the drivers of income convergence across countries. Most countries that have experienced convergence over a longer time

C. Lara
Universidad de La República, Montevideo, Uruguay

S. Prado (✉)
University of Gothenburg, Göteborg, Sweden
e-mail: svante.prado@econhist.gu.se

J. Álvarez and S. Prado (eds.), *Scandinavia and South America—A Tale of Two Capitalisms*, Palgrave Studies in Economic History,
https://doi.org/10.1007/978-3-031-09198-8_5

frame have also undergone industrialization (Bénétrix et al., 2015). In the jargon of the literature on income convergence, industrialization is a requisite that makes catching up with the productivity leaders much more likely to occur (Amsden, 2001).

Yet the empirical evidence for this manufacturing convergence nexus relates mostly to developed countries for the long-term assessment, associated with the works of for instance Broadberry (1993), or to cross-country comparisons of large country samples for the relatively short-term assessment, associated with for instance Rodrik (2013). The long-term assessment á la Broadberry (1993) indicates that the productivity ratio in manufacturing, comparing productivity levels in one country with that of the other, remains quite stable over long stretches of time. This stability would indicate that structural transformations and productivity growth rates in sectors other than manufacturing play a bigger role than manufacturing itself for economy-wide income convergence. The short-term assessment for a large set of countries suggests in contrast convergence at the level of manufacturing. Rodrik (2013) suggests that deindustrialization or sluggish performance in sectors other than manufacturing explains the lack of economy-wide convergence for mostly less developed countries.

In this chapter, we compare the productivity levels in manufacturing of Brazil and Sweden. We follow in the footsteps of Broadberry's research design, aiming for the long-term assessment. We believe in the importance of long-term studies, advised as we are by previous work showing that the comparative record is subject to wide swings (Lara & Prado, 2022). If we only capture a brief spell of a volatile, comparative record, we run the risk of drawing misguided conclusions. Contrary to Broadberry, though, we compare the levels of productivity in manufacturing of a developed country with that of a less developed country, which means that the comparison comprises two countries that set out with radically different preconditions in terms of labour productivity levels and composition of output at the beginning of the investigated period (Fig. 1 and Table 1). Large productivity gaps across countries are commonplace as soon as we venture to expand the narrow sample of developed countries. The result of our binary comparison can hopefully also gain us some generic insights into the nexus between manufacturing and convergence in less developed countries.

In addition, both Sweden and Brazil depended largely on manufacturing. This dependence on manufacturing is important since so much

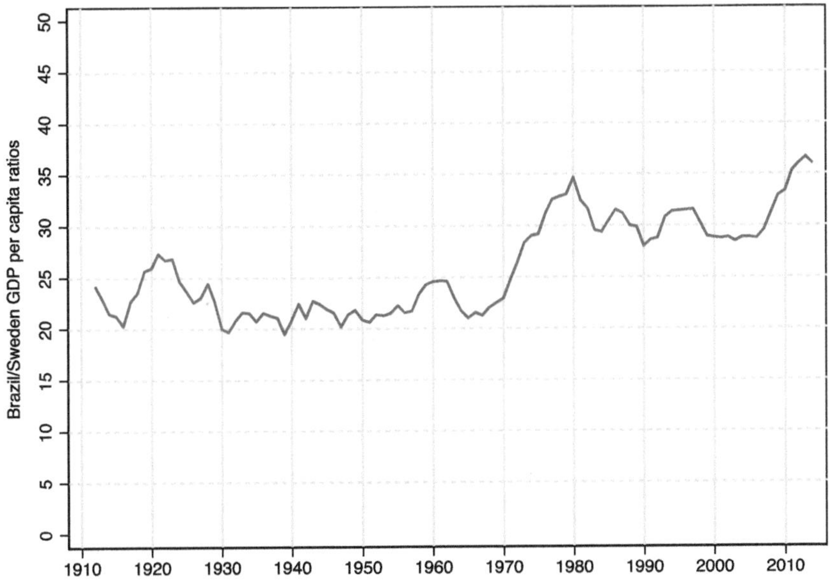

Fig. 1 Brazil/Sweden GDP per capita ratios, 1912–2014 (*Source* Sweden, Schön and Krantz [2015]. The Maddison Project Database, version 2020. https://www.rug.nl/ggdc/historicaldevelopment/maddison/releases/maddison-project-database-2020. *Note* The Maddison project has released three different versions of long-term series of GDP since 2014. The series displayed in this figure originates from the most recent release [2020], which depends on Maddison's original 1990 benchmark for backward extrapolation. For Brazil/Sweden, this version places itself in the middle of the two previous versions as to the rate of Brazilian convergence across the whole period)

economic history research has conditioned convergence in GDP per capita on industrialization. Brazil has developed the greater dependence on manufacturing in a Latin American context, rivalled only by Mexico (Bértola & Ocampo, 2012; Haber, 2006).[1] Besides being relatively large, the Brazilian manufacturing sector also came to host at least one firm—Embraer, in aerospace—operating at the cutting edge of new production technologies. Brazil was a latecomer to industrialization. The wave of

[1] In 1974, the share of manufacturing in GDP was 17% for Latin America. For Brazil, however, it was 30%, rivalled only by Mexico (Bértola & Ocampo, 2012: 184).

Table 1 Sectoral composition (%) of GDP for Brazil and Sweden, 1950–1995

	Brazil				*Sweden*			
	Sectoral shares (sum total = 100)				*Sectoral shares (sum total = 100)*			
	Agriculture	*Industry*	*Services*	*Manufacturing*	*Agriculture*	*Industry*	*Services*	*Manufacturing*
1950	24	24	52	19	11	42	46	38
1955	23	26	51	20	10	43	47	38
1960	18	32	50	26	8	43	49	37
1965	16	32	52	25	6	43	51	38
1970	12	36	53	27	4	41	55	36
1975	11	40	49	31	4	40	56	36
1980	10	41	49	31	3	34	63	29
1985	11	42	47	32	3	34	63	29
1990	10	37	53	26	2	32	65	27
1995	11	31	57	21	2	32	67	27

Sources Brazil, *Estatísticas do Século XX*; Sweden, Krantz and Schön (2007)
Note Industry includes manufacturing, mining, construction, and utilities

industrialization that swept across Western Europe and its offshoots missed much of Latin America, Africa, and most of Asia. Most of the development within manufacturing in Brazil occurred in the post-World War II era of state-led development until the debt crisis of the early 1980s. Table 1 shows that the manufacturing share of GDP peaked at about 30% between 1975 and 1985. Still, with this centre of gravity in manufacturing, one would venture to conjecture that the dynamic properties of Brazilian manufacturing provided an added impetus to accelerating economy-wide growth rates. Like other Latin American countries, however, Brazil has failed to close the gap to the leading countries in GDP per capita. Figure 1 shows how the Brazilian GDP per capita fared relative to the Swedish. Some catching up certainly took place yet the Brazilian level has barely exceeded 35% of the Swedish.

Sweden has developed the greater dependence on manufacturing in a Scandinavian context (Jörberg, 1973). Historically, two features distinguish the Swedish manufacturing industry from the Brazilian: first, Sweden joined the second wave of industrialization in the closing decades of the nineteenth century. The country thus enjoyed the benefits of an early start. This early start meant that the manufacturing sector swallowed up a relatively large share of employment in the 1960s, before declining (Feinstein, 1999); indeed, a much larger share than in Brazil. Table 1 shows that the share of manufacturing in GDP peaked at 38% in the mid-1960s. Second, industrialization was accompanied by rapid and sustained improvements in labour productivity, which implies that catching up with the leaders of the US and the UK was accomplished as the twentieth century was coming to an end (Prado & Sato, 2021). In a sense, Sweden conforms well with Gordon's (1999) identification of "One Big Wave" that started in the late nineteenth century and ebbed out in the early 1970s. Sweden began climbing the ranks of countries in terms of GDP per capita as the "Wave" gathered strength in the late nineteenth century, and Sweden reached the top in the 1960s as the wave began to lose its momentum.

In this chapter, we show dramatic swings in the comparable levels of labour productivity of Brazil and Sweden. The empirical strategy is a two-tier framework, drawing on methods that were established by Paige and Bombach (1959), van Ark (1993), and Broadberry (1993). First, we will document the labour productivity gap between Brazil and Sweden for groups of industries (roughly 2-digit level) and manufacturing at large for the benchmark year of 1975. This productivity benchmark will be based on the industry-of-origin method (unit value ratios) using each country's industrial census. The justification for establishing a benchmark in 1975 is the availability of an Industrial Census for Brazil in that particular year (*Censo Industrial, Produção Física*). This census is the first to provide a detailed list of output in physical units, e.g. tons of cement produced, alongside the corresponding gross value in cruzeiro. Maddison and van Ark (1989) used this census in their comparison of Brazil and the US in 1975. We have matched products in the Brazilian census with similar products in the Swedish Industrial Statistics (*SOS, Industri, Del 2, 1975*). The final procedure combines the products together as shares of value added to form an overall price ratio of the two countries' currencies. This price ratio, used as a common unit of accounts, enables us to establish a labour productivity ratio for 1975.

Second, we will extrapolate time series of labour productivity from the benchmark in 1975 to cover the period between 1912 and 2014. We have striven to create time series that accommodate the organized formal part of manufacturing, hence excluding the informal sector that otherwise influences the perceived growth rates of labour productivity. In addition, we stick to the manufacturing sector proper, so excluding mining and public utilities. The time series of the two countries were readily available thanks to two parallel projects (Hamark & Prado, 2021; Lara & Prado, 2022). With this long-term picture at hand, the chapter proceeds to examine how the ratio behaved over time against the background of the historical context and previous discussions about convergence in productivity at the whole economy level and convergence in productivity in manufacturing.

2 Data and Method

Following van Ark (1993), we have compared productivity levels in manufacturing in Sweden and Brazil to establish a benchmark in 1975. In order to avoid using the exchange rate, whose magnitude is determined by tradable goods and subject to the influence of capital movements, the literature on cross-country productivity comparisons has elaborated two methodological solutions, commonly referred to as "industry-of-origin approaches" (van Ark, 1993). The first of these solutions, due to Rostas (1948), compares output in physical terms for similar products and establishes labour productivity measures as physical output per worker in each country. This solution is ideal when the industrial censuses, as for pre-1952 Sweden, fail to offer output as value added. It has so far been used mostly for pre-World War II benchmarks. The second solution, due to Paige and Bombach (1959), establishes so-called unit value ratios by product, and aggregates these ratios up to industry level, branch level, and manufacturing as a whole, using value-added weights. The overall unit value ratio converts different currencies into a single unit of account, yielding a measure of real output at comparable levels. We have used the second option, unit value ratios, following the convention for most post-World War II benchmarks. The two sub-sections that follow review the qualities of the two country's information on output by product in physical and monetary terms, and value added and employment by industry, while the third expands on the methodology employed.

2.1 Swedish Industrial Statistics

The Swedish Industrial Statistics have been published annually since the mid-nineteenth century, based on a comprehensive sample of establishments.[2] We used the Swedish Industrial Statistics of 1975, which coincides with the publication of the Brazilian Industrial Census. The Swedish Industrial Statistics of 1975 were published in two volumes, both of which are indispensable for our productivity comparison (*SOS, Industri, 1975*).[3] Volume one offers information by industry: number of establishments, gross output and value added, cost data, including quantity and cost of individually important raw materials consumed during the period, employment data, capacity of power equipment, and capital formation. This information by industry in volume one meets two essential requisites for the industry-of-origin method: first it allows us to aggregate unit value ratios from product level to industry, from industry to branch, and finally from branch to manufacturing as a whole; second, it allows us to establish value added per worker in current prices for similar manufacturing industries as in Brazil. It classifies industries using the Swedish Standard of Industrial Classification (SNI), which is reminiscent of the International Standard Industrial Classification of All Economic

[2] The annual publications of industrial statistics do not count as industrial censuses. Statistics Sweden only carried out three actual Industrial Censuses during the twentieth century: in 1931, 1951, and 1972. These censuses, however, do not offer output in physical terms, and cannot therefore be used for the industry-of-origin method.

[3] https://www.scb.se/sv_/hitta-statistik/historisk-statistik/sok-publikationer-efter-amne/?Statistikserie=Industri+1911-1996.

Activities (ISIC). The industries are broken down into several subdivisions, sometimes down to 5-digit level. The classification of industries is just about as disaggregated as it is in many other countries' industrial censuses.

The second volume offers information on production by product: output in physical quantities, mostly in tons, and corresponding product value (gross output), as well as imports and exports. We have used the second volume to match Brazilian products and then establish unit value ratios for as many products as possible. The products are presented by two classification schemes: The Standard International Trade Classification (SITC) and the Brussels nomenclature with numerous subdivisions. We have used the classification scheme of the Brussels nomenclature because it offers more details on product attributes. The number of individual items totals almost 5000 units.

Despite this seemingly large supply of products, the coverage ratio of the Swedish sample is quite low (Table 2). Three factors explain the low coverage ratio: First, the Swedish Industrial Statistics do not come close to the number of items that are recorded in the census of, for example, the US, the UK, and Brazil. The Swedish statistics only cover about a third of the number of products in the Brazilian census. Second, the Swedish Industrial Statistics have circumscribed the number of products given in physical units in the mechanical engineering industry, which is a drawback for a project aimed at international productivity comparisons. Third, a benchmark year of 1975 is rather recent by the standard of international productivity comparisons. In general, the more recent the benchmark year, the more the variety of products expands; it lies in the nature of modern economic growth to diversify the supply of product qualities with the passage of time. Therefore, the best-covered benchmarks originate from the pre-World War II period. In sum, the combined effect of the limitations inherent in the Swedish Industrial Statistics and a recent benchmark year explains the rather low share of matched products in the benchmark.

2.2 Brazilian Industrial Census

The first industrial census of Brazil that offers output by product in physical units was published in 1975 (*Censo Industrial, Produção Física*). The second, and last, Industrial Census that offered this information was published in 1985. The previous censuses of 1919, 1939, and 1949

Table 2 Coverage ratio and unit value ra tios by industries, 1975

	(1) Geometric coverage ratio (%)	*(2) Initial UVR*		*(3) Final UVR*			*(4) Final UVR Fisher/exchange rate (%)*
		Brazil	*Sweden*	*Brazil*	*Sweden*	*Fisher*	
Total manufacturing industry	21	0.70	2.10	0.61	2.21	1.16	59.14
Food, beverage and tobacco	56	0.83	1.35	0.58	1.20	0.83	42.34
Textile, apparel, leather and rubber	17	0.17	1.03	0.22	1.15	0.51	25.92
Wood and furniture	39	1.88	2.42	1.88	2.42	2.13	108.69
Pulp, paper, and printing	39	1.44	1.51	1.44	1.51	1.48	75.37
Chemical, petro, and plastic	4	2.83	3.50	0.70	2.10	1.21	61.91
Non-metallic minerals	13	1.83	2.48	0.70	2.10	1.21	61.91
Metals	23	1.78	6.58	1.78	6.58	3.42	174.55
Mechanical engineering	2	0.77	2.97	0.70	2.10	1.21	61.91

Sources Estimates based on *Censo Industrial, Produção Física*, 1975 for Brazil and *SOS, Industri*, 1975 for Sweden

Notes (1) Geometric coverage ratio is an average Fisher ratio of coverage ratio of Brazil and Sweden; (2) initial unit value ratio (UVR) is the unweighted unit value ratio; (3) final UVR is calculated using the initial unit value ratios weighed by value added, and final UVR Fisher is a geometric average of the final UVR of Brazil and Sweden; (4) and the relative price levels are the ratio of final UVR Fisher divided by the official exchange rate. The official exchange rate is 1.96 cruzeiro per krona

failed to provide this information (*Censo Industrial*). All the Brazilian Censuses were produced by the national statistical agency of Brazil, *Instituto Brasileiro de Geografia e Estatística* (IBGE). The industrial census of 1975 has nationwide coverage, and it comprises 183,824 establishments and 3,816,545 employees. As in the Swedish Industrial Statistics, the subject of investigation is establishments (not companies), i.e. production units (factory, mill, etc.) at which one or a group of products are manufactured. Information on products includes output in physical terms and corresponding product value. The products are listed with a sequence of numbers from 1 to 13,678. Hence the number of Brazilian products exceeds the Swedish by a factor of about 2.7. Products are listed by manufacturing branches named *generos*. This nomenclature does not correspond with the usual international classifications, which implied additional efforts to match products. In addition, the information on product attributes is often scant.

Apart from information on output by products, the Census also offers information on output by industry, including number of establishments, employment, wages, hours worked, and value added. This part of it has a nomenclature that is reminiscent of volume one of the Swedish Industrial Statistics. As for Sweden, we have used this information on value added by industry to aggregate from product to industry level and from industry level to branch level.

2.3 *Methodology of Productivity Benchmark*

The industry-of-origin approach applied here aims to compare the volume produced in one country with the volume produced in the other country. This is achieved by using two sets of weights, own country weights, and foreign country weights, in order to render nominal output into volume output. The methodology is reminiscent of the idea of inter-temporal index formulas, such as Paasche and Laspeyres, used to translate a series of outputs in current prices into a series of volumes of output. This procedure produces two sets of volume measures and the geometric mean of the two yields a so-called Fisher index.

Matching similar products in each country's statistics is the starting point of this exercise. After identifying a set of products with similar characteristics, the somewhat convoluted weighting procedure begins, which serves to aggregate output from product level to manufacturing at large. The weighting scheme draws on van Ark (1993). The first step separates quantities (Q) from gross output (P^*Q), computing unit values (P) by product (i) for a specific country (c), as in (1). Then, using these unit values, we calculate the unit value ratios (UVR) for each matched product as in (2), dividing Brazilian prices by Swedish prices. Any product whose UVR differs widely from the average UVR of all matched products will be excluded because the product does not therefore seem to be equivalent in the two countries.

Unit value:

$$P_i^c = P_i^c Q_i^c / Q_i^c \tag{1}$$

Unit value ratio:

$$UVR_i = \frac{P_i^{Br}}{P_i^{Sw}} \tag{2}$$

The next step aggregates the matched products into industries (j). We compute the average unit value ratio by industry, weighting the product UVRs by the corresponding quantity for one of the two countries. The UVR by industry (j) weighted by quantities for Brazil is expressed as in (3) and the unit value ratio by industry weighted by quantities for Sweden as in (4):

$$\mathrm{UVR}_j^{\mathrm{Br}} = \frac{\sum_{\mathrm{i\epsilon j}} P_i^{\mathrm{Br}} Q_i^{\mathrm{Br}}}{\sum_{\mathrm{i\epsilon j}} P_i^{\mathrm{Sw}} Q_i^{\mathrm{Br}}} = \frac{\sum_{\mathrm{i\epsilon j}} \left(\mathrm{UVR}_i \cdot P_i^{\mathrm{Sw}} Q_i^{\mathrm{Br}}\right)}{\sum_{\mathrm{i\epsilon j}} P_i^{\mathrm{Sw}} Q_i^{\mathrm{Br}}} = \frac{\sum_{i\epsilon j} P_i^{\mathrm{Br}} Q_i^{\mathrm{Br}}}{\sum_{i\epsilon j} \left(P_i^{\mathrm{Br}} Q_i^{\mathrm{Br}} / \mathrm{UVR}_i\right)}, \tag{3}$$

$$\mathrm{UVR}_j^{\mathrm{Sw}} = \frac{\sum_{i\epsilon j} P_i^{\mathrm{Br}} Q_i^{\mathrm{Sw}}}{\sum_{i\epsilon j} P_i^{\mathrm{Sw}} Q_i^{\mathrm{Sw}}} = \frac{\sum_{i\epsilon j} \left(\mathrm{UVR}_i \cdot P_i^{\mathrm{Sw}} Q_i^{\mathrm{Sw}}\right)}{\sum_{i\epsilon j} P_i^{\mathrm{Sw}} Q_i^{\mathrm{Sw}}}, \tag{4}$$

The second identity of (3) illustrates that the UVR by industry can also be obtained by weighting the product UVR by gross output expressed in the Brazilian price, and the third identity of (3) that there is yet another way. The third step entails aggregation into groups of industries, called branches. The UVR for a branch (k) is obtained by weighting the industry UVR by the value added for each subgroup in one of the two countries, as in (5), using value added by industry for Brazil, and as in (6), using value added by industry for Sweden.

$$\mathrm{UVR}_k^{\mathrm{Br}} = \frac{\sum_{j\epsilon k} \mathrm{VA}_j^{\mathrm{Br}}}{\sum_{j\epsilon k} \left[\mathrm{VA}_j^{\mathrm{Br}} / \mathrm{UVR}_j^{\mathrm{Br}}\right]}, \tag{5}$$

$$\mathrm{UVR}_k^{\mathrm{Sw}} = \frac{\sum_{j\epsilon k} \left[\mathrm{UVR}_j^{\mathrm{Sw}} \cdot \mathrm{VA}_j^{\mathrm{Sw}}\right]}{\sum_{j\epsilon k} \mathrm{VA}_j^{\mathrm{Sw}}}, \tag{6}$$

The final step aggregates the branch UVRs as in (5) and (6), which yields UVR^{Br} and UVR^{Sw}. The geometric mean of these two country-specific UVRs provides the UVR for manufacturing at large, converting output given in Brazilian cruzeiros into Swedish kronor.

We end this methodological detour with a brief note on shortcomings. It is impossible to match perfectly every item produced in Brazil with an equivalent in Sweden regarding quality, shape durability, and size. There are product quality differences between the two countries, and we also find products in one country that are not produced in the other. As expected, Sweden manufactured a great variety of goods that were not manufactured in Brazil. Furthermore, there are difficulties in reconciling some product varieties. What complicates this matter further is the lack of a harmonized product coding system; some items require additional aggregation in order to obtain a correct match between the two countries, e.g. beef in Brazil comprises three products while in Sweden it comprises two.

3 Results of Productivity Benchmarks

Table 2 shows that the coverage ratio based on 164 product matches for manufacturing at large and for separate branches. The value of matched output to total output of manufacturing at large is 21%. This coverage ratio is similar to other cases in which a developing country is compared to a developed country (van Ark, 1993). The highest coverage ratio is found for the Food, Beverages, and Tobacco industry, which records an average of 56%, followed by the Wood and Furniture industry and the Pulp, Paper, and Printing industry, both of which have a coverage ratio of 39%. At the other end of the scale, we find the Chemical, Petro, and Plastic industry with 4% and the Mechanical Engineering industry with 2%.

Table 2 also presents the UVR for manufacturing at large as well as for separate branches. In the aggregate, the UVR arrives at 1.16 cruzeiro per krona. The final column compares this price relation with the official exchange rate at 1.96 cruzeiros per krona.[4] It shows that the UVR was 59.14% of the official exchange rate. This discrepancy between the

[4] This exchange rate is calculated using the cruzeiros per dollar rate (8.13) and the Swedish kronas per dollar rate (4.17) (van Ark & Timmer, 2001: 46).

two units of accounts highlights the potential pitfall of employing the exchange rate to convert Brazilian output in cruzeiro to Brazilian output in kronor. We would have overestimated the Brazilian labour productivity level by about 59.14%. It also suggests that the Brazilian exchange rate policy aimed to keep the value of the cruzeiro rather high relative to other currencies. The overvalued cruzeiro made it possible to import capital equipment and intermediate consumption at low prices, which was a deliberate aim of the policies known as import substitution industrialization (Baer, 1972). Brazilian manufacturing may, though, have been disadvantaged by the overvalued cruzeiro rendering their products unnecessarily expensive to purchase, thereby curtailing export rates.

The discrepancy between the UVRs and the exchange rate varies by branch, as the last column shows. The lower the ratio, the more Brazil has a comparative advantage in that industry. Brazil has a competitive edge in the production of food, beverages, and tobacco; and in the production of textiles, apparel, and leather products. This is consistent with the fact that the Brazilian economy was, despite industrialization, heavily skewed towards processed agricultural products and natural resources, sectors from which most of the export commodities originated.

The UVR for manufacturing at large is used to convert value added given in each country's currency into a common unit of account. Table 3 shows labour productivity ratios by branch and manufacturing, computed by using UVRs in Brazilian and Swedish prices as well as the geometric mean of the two, yielding a Fisher ideal index. For total manufacturing, Brazilian labour productivity was about 74% of the Swedish level in 1975. This result seems somewhat high if we compare it with van Ark and Maddison's (1994) previous Brazil/US benchmark for 1975. They found that the Brazilian level was 46.5% of the American. Prado and Sato (2021) found that Sweden's labour productivity was 75.7% of the American in 1975. By implication, as a rough cross-check, the Brazilian level would be about 61% of the Swedish (100*48.5/74.7 = 61%). There is thus no perfect symmetry between the different estimated productivity levels. A possible source of error in all comparisons involving Sweden is the lack of information on output in physical terms for mechanical engineering, which was the Swedish manufacturing industry par excellence. This failure to include mechanical engineering probably underestimates the Swedish overall productivity advantage relative to Brazil.

Looking across the productivity ratios disaggregated by industries in Table 3, the Swedish levels remain superior in absolute terms except

Table 3 Labour productivity ratios by industries and manufacturing at large, 1975

	Value added by manufactures (thousand kronor) using UVR		*All employees*		*Value added per employee using UVRs*		*Productivity ratio (Sw = 100) using UVR*
	Brazil	*Sweden*	*Brazil*	*Sweden*	*Brazil*	*Sweden*	
Total manufacturing	261,233,546	87,559,654	3,747,162	925,299	69.72	94.63	73.67
Food, beverage, and tobacco	52,275,948	8,654,854	575,406	72,076	90.85	120.08	75.66
Textile, apparel, leather, and rubber	73,143,293	4,636,634	718,242	70,954	101.84	65.35	155.84
Wood and furniture	7,065,597	6,386,089	342,400	76,758	20.64	83.20	24.80
Pulp, paper, and printing	12,884,313	13,069,780	213,150	104,145	60.45	125.50	48.17
Chemical, petro, and plastic	45,703,968	6,501,669	260,908	54,484	175.17	119.33	146.79
Non-metallic minerals	15,789,724	3,041,613	320,304	33,127	49.30	91.82	53.69
Metals	11,335,608	6,037,837	442,379	70,702	25.62	85.40	30.01
Mechanical engineering	56,733,366	38,784,083	789,849	436,587	71.83	88.83	80.86

Sources Brazil, *Censo Industrial, Produção Física*, 1975; Sweden, *SOS, Industri*, 1975

for two branches: Textiles, Apparel, Leather, and Rubber and Chemicals, Petroleum, and Plastic. For Textiles, Apparel, Leather, and Rubber this Brazilian productivity edge squares with the result of Table 2, which showed that this branch had lower costs for inputs in production. The result is expected because the textile industry has propelled Brazilian industrialization since the late nineteenth century (Stein, 1957). In Sweden, this sector has receded in importance as much production has been outsourced to countries with much lower labour costs. For Chemicals, Petroleum, and Plastic, a possible explanation is harder to pin down precisely. The possible spillover effects from the Brazilian extraction of oil can perhaps offer some clues, even though offshore oil drilling only commenced in the early 1970s (Ryggvik, 2021). In addition, Sweden may not have access to raw oil but began to establish a petrochemical industry in the 1960s that transformed imported raw oil into refined oil products, most of which were sold in the world markets (Berglund, 2010). We should at any rate avoid attaching much importance to this observation since the coverage ratio for this industry is very low (Table 2).

4 Establishing the Long-Term Record

Ideally, the series of output should indicate the movement of value added in volume terms, constructed by deflating both the current value of gross output and the current value of intermediate inputs, and subtracting the volume of intermediate inputs from the volume of gross output. In this ideal solution, the final series of volume of value-added incorporates changes in the volume of intermediate inputs to volume output, the so-called technical coefficients; for instance, how much paper pulp does it require to produce a certain amount of paper. In addition to the technical coefficients, the series also incorporates the changes in relative prices of intermediate inputs to final goods. In historical national accounts, however, a second-best solution is to let volume gross output for separate industries, combined into a series of manufacturing at large by using value-added shares for benchmark years, indicate the movement of value added in volume. Since value-added shares pertain to a single or to a few years, the final series does not incorporate changes in either technological coefficients or relative prices. If data constraints render the ideal and the second-best solution impracticable, we have recourse to series of gross output in constant prices weighted by gross output shares. For practical reasons, the second-best solution has been most commonly applied in historical national accounts before World War II (Thomas & Feinstein, 2003).

Obviously, the conditions for constructing time series vary by country and by the time period covered. We have taken pains to construct time series that are comparable and have small inter-temporal heterogeneities. To this end, we have attempted to include only the organized formal part of manufacturing, affecting above all our choice of data source for the Brazilian time series, but also affecting the Swedish time series pre-1950. We have also excluded the mining sector, which is more dependent on factor endowments than on capabilities, and public utilities, which are not generally considered manufacturing proper.

4.1 Time Series for Sweden

The annual publications of industrial statistics form the basis of the Swedish time series of output and labour pre-1950. The Board of Trade (Kommerskollegium) annually requested a large sample of establishments to report output and number of workers, along with some additional information, beginning in the mid-nineteenth century. The coverage of industries was expanded in 1913 to include the entire manufacturing sector, although all establishments with less than ten employees were excluded. Considering the scope and ambition of the annual industrial statistics, we may place them on equal footing with other countries' industrial censuses.

For productivity studies, the Swedish Industrial Statistics suffer from a major flaw, namely, they do not report the value of intermediate consumption required to compute value added. This information was only reported from 1952 onwards. This means that we have to resort to the second-best solution in order to establish a measure of constant volume output pre-1952: indicators of volume of gross output weighted by value-added shares for benchmark years. This was the solution preferred by Schön (1988) in his contribution to historical national accounts, who deflated gross output in current prices by a price index from Ljungberg (1988) (with some modifications) and multiplied the volume of gross output thus obtained by value-added shares for benchmark years.[5] The

[5] To be fair, Schön (1988) actually used a more refined method to estimate volume of value added. The account of the procedure employed is, however, not sufficiently transparent to make its replication worthwhile.

problem with this final series of volume of value added is that it grows too fast to be credible in the 1940s (Hamark & Prado, 2021). In addition, the series includes mining and public utilities, as well as an estimate of handicraft production, so it fails to satisfy our requirement that output figures should simply include manufacturing proper.

Instead of depending on Schön (1988), we have taken as our departure the Board of Trade's (*Kommerskollegium*) industry-specific series of volume of gross output that begins in 1913.[6] The Board of Trade tapped the rich supply of physical quantities reported in the Swedish Industrial Statistics in order to establish series of volume of gross output. We use these series for different industries, together with value-added shares for the same industries in 1913, 1918, and 1926, to construct a series of volume value added for manufacturing at large, beginning in 1913 and ending in 1930. Johansson (1985) improved the series of Borad of Trade by adding annual value-added shares based on archival sources from 1939 to 1950. The Board of Trade's series from 1913 to 1930, and Johansson's (1985) from 1930 to 1950, have thus furnished us with an annual time series of volume of value added constructed on the basis of the so-called second-best solution. As Hamark and Prado (2021) show, this optional and preferred series of output displays a slightly faster growth rate from 1913 to 1950 than Schön's (1988) previous series. Finally, we have gathered a series of labour input from the industrial statistics by compiling the annual number of workers for manufacturing proper.

From 1950, Statistics Sweden began reporting national accounts on an annual basis, reporting volume of value added for manufacturing proper. We have continued the series of labour inputs by collecting the number of workers from the industrial statistics until 1989. From then onwards output and labour inputs were taken from the EUKLEMS database.[7]

4.2 *Time Series for Brazil*

For Brazil, the long-term record is much more difficult to establish because annual information on output and labour only began to be published in 1952. Prior to this date we depend on the industrial censuses

[6] We have also included the year 1912 based on the industrial statistics (Hamark & Prado, 2021).

[7] http://www.euklems.net.

of 1919 and 1939 and on the so-called *imposto de consumo* for annual figures of output (*Estatísticas Históricas do Brasil: 366–7, 383–4*). The *imposto de consumo* was a tax levied on sold output. Thanks to this tax, we have information on the units of goods purchased by industries and the corresponding sales value back to at least 1912. The number of products subjected to this tax expanded gradually. The sample included the most important capital goods and nondurable consumables. Although one could raise several objections to this source of information as a measure of total manufacturing output (Haber, 1992), it provides the only comprehensive measure of annual output before 1949. It constitutes the basis for Haddad's (1978) historical national accounts.

This industry-specific evidence of current gross output needs to be aggregated so as to indicate the movement of volume of value added. Haddad (1978) multiplied these series by value-added shares from the Industrial Censuses of 1919 and 1939. So did Versiani (1984) but he revised the aggregate series in 1919–1923. We accept his revision. This approach to establish a measure of volume of value added is essentially the same as for Sweden, setting aside the inferior quality of the Brazilian data sources: series of volume of gross output for different industries are multiplied by value-added weights to yield a measure of volume of value added for manufacturing at large. So, in a methodological sense, we have compared like with like when it comes to the series of volume of value added.

The great challenge with the Brazilian time series of labour productivity concerns the evidence on labour inputs. No annual statistical information on employment accompanies the series of output before 1949; we merely have the three complete censuses of 1919, 1939, and 1949 at our disposal. In a previous study we offered an informed guesstimate to circumvent the lack of annual information (Lara & Prado, 2022). We begin by computing the change in labour productivity between the three census years. Then we draw on an assumed relationship between output and labour productivity, known as Verdoorn's Law. An elasticity of, let us say, 0.5 would indicate the extent to which labour productivity would change in response to a percentage change in output: as output increased by 1%, labour productivity would increase by 0.5%. By applying an elasticity of 0.76 to project the movement of employment, the time series of employment is rendered consistent with the change in labour productivity across the census years, and we can also extrapolate the series of employment, and hence labour productivity, backwards to

1912. For the gap between 1949 and 1952, we follow Colistete (2007) who interpolated linearly the time series of employment.

From 1952 onwards, we rely on IBGE's annual industrial surveys (*Pesquisa Industrial Annual*, PIA). They provide value added in current prices and employment. Colistete (2007) and Aldrighi and Colistete (2015) gathered this data along with price deflators (*Índices de Preços ao Atacado*, IPA) from 1945 to 1990. We draw on their previous efforts.[8] We also continue to use IBGE's annual industrial surveys for value added in current prices and price deflators after 1990. However, we refrain from using the raw series of labour provided by the Industrial Surveys between 1985 and 1990. Bonelli (2015) has levelled well-founded critique against this series of labour and constructed an optional series that stretches from 1950 to 2013. It deviates in important regard from the raw series of industrial surveys, particularly for the 1985 and 1990 period. This deviation can be seen in Fig. 2, showing Bonelli's revised series of labour and the raw series of the industrial surveys. Between 1984 and 1990, the raw series of the industrial surveys declines by 2.6% annually, whereas Bonelli's revised series increases by 4.1% annually. We have incorporated Bonelli's revision into our series of labour based on the industrial surveys between 1985 and 1990. The difference between Bonelli's series and the raw series of the industrial surveys is rather small from 1990 to 2013. If we set the two series to 100 in 1990, both series arrive at 132 in 2013, notwithstanding divergence in the second half of the 1990s. We have made an additional adjustment of the raw series of the industrial surveys. Between 1995 and 1996, the number of workers increased by more than 60%, obviously because the sample was enlarged to also include a fair proportion of small-scale establishments. We smoothed this discontinuity in the series backwards to 1990.

4.3 Comparative Levels of Labour Productivity

To yield the comparative levels of labour productivity, we have extrapolated the growth rates of the time series from the benchmark in 1975 backward to 1912 and forward to 2014. This is the same methodology as that used by Angus Maddison to obtain long-term comparisons of GDP per capita, according to the formula (7),

[8] We thank the author for sharing their spreadsheet with us.

Fig. 2 Comparing different series of employment in Brazilian manufacturing, 1949–2014 (1975 = 100) (*Sources* Bonelli [2015]; *Pesquisa Industrial Annual*, [PIA])

$$\text{Brazil/Sweden labour productivity ratio}_t = \frac{LP_{t+1}^{Br(Kr)}}{LP_{t+1}^{Sw(Kr)}} = \frac{LP_t^{Br(Kr)} * \left[LP_{t+1}^{Br(R)}/LP_t^{Br(R)}\right]}{LP_t^{Sw(Kr)} * \left[LP_{t+1}^{Sw(Kr)}/LP_t^{Sw(Kr)}\right]}, \tag{7}$$

which shows how the extrapolation is designed. The labour productivity (*LP*) benchmark of 1975, expressed in Swedish kronor (*Kr*), is extrapolated by annual changes in the time series of labour productivity expressed in each country's currency, i.e. Brazilian real (*R*) in the numerator and Swedish kronor (*Kr*) in the denominator. The two time series of labour productivity in 1912–2014 appear in Fig. 3, which has a logarithmic scale on the y-axis. In 1975, we have pegged the Brazilian level at 73.67 and the Swedish level at 100, mirroring the estimated productivity gap according to our industry-of-origin benchmark (Table 3). Table 4 subdivides the whole period and presents the estimated annual growth rates.

Brazilian productivity grew faster than Swedish until the early 1980s. Between 1912 and 1949, Brazil grew annually by 1.96%, whereas Sweden grew by 1.02%. The difference diminished in the next period, from 1950 to 1980, when Brazil grew by 2.28% and Sweden by 1.76%. A quite remarkable shift occurred after 1980, when Brazilian productivity decelerated into complete stagnation, whereas Swedish productivity accelerated to an impressive 2.25% annual growth rates. As conventionally described, in absolute terms Brazilian growth rates of productivity in manufacturing were impressive during the post-World War II decades until the debt crisis of the early 1980s; yet in relative terms, they look more impressive between 1912 and 1949. As previously discussed, a caveat applies to the quality of the Brazilian time series before 1952, and in particular before 1919.

To appreciate the vast shifts in comparative levels across time, we have divided the Brazilian series by the Swedish. The outcome of the varying growth rates of productivity in manufacturing across the two countries comes to the fore in Fig. 4, depicting the Brazil to Sweden ratios from 1912 to 2014. The triangle indicates the benchmark of 1975 from which the times series are extrapolated. From the beginning of our investigated period to the 1930s, the Brazilian level of labour productivity increased from about 20% to about 25% of the Swedish level. From the mid-1930s, the Brazilian level began to converge towards the Swedish level, incrementally at first, then gathering speed in the 1940s. As a result, the ratio increased from about 25 to 50. This is the first major spell of convergence. The ratio then continued on its upward drift in the 1950s but an interlude reversed its effect during the 1960s. The second major spell of convergence occurred in the 1970s, which elevated the Brazilian level to more than 70% of the Swedish. In the early 1980s, the Brazilian productivity level peaked at about 80% of the Swedish. The rest of the period, from the early 1980s to the late 2000s, witnessed a dramatic reversal of the comparative record. The ratio literally collapsed in just about three decades. This conspicuous bout of divergence contracted the ratio so much that the Brazilian standing in the early 2010s had almost come full circle: in 2014, Brazilian labour productivity had arrived at a level less than a fourth that of the Swedish, a relative level not witnessed since before the 1920s.

How much confidence can we have in this long-term picture? The critique levelled against Angus Maddison's extrapolation of GDP per capita levels also applies to our approach. Maddison's contenders argue

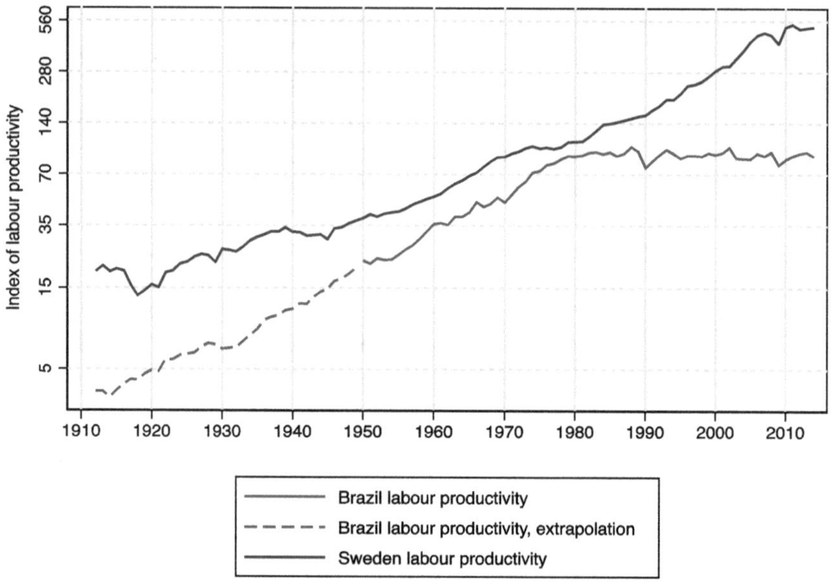

Fig. 3 Brazilian and Swedish series of labour productivity, 1912–2014 (*Sources* Brazil, Lara & Prado [2022]; Sweden, Hamark & Prado [2021]. *Notes* Logarithmic scale on the y-axis. In 1912–1949, the Brazilian series of labour productivity is taken from the projection described in Sect. 4.2. In 1975, the Brazilian series is pegged at 73.67, whereas the Swedish series is pegged at 100, which conforms with the gap established by our industry-of-origin benchmark for 1975 [Table 3])

Table 4 Growth rates of labour productivity, 1912–2014

	Mean annual growth rate rates (%)			
	Brazil	*Sweden*	*Diff (Brazil–Sweden)*	*Characteristics*
1919–1949	2.01	1.17	0.84	Convergence
1912–1949	1.96	1.02	0.94	Convergence
1950–1980	2.28	1.76	0.52	Convergence
1980–2014	–0.08	2.25	–2.33	Divergence

Source see Fig. 3

Fig. 4 Brazil to Sweden labour productivity ratios, 1912–2014 (*Source* The ratios are derived from the time series of labour productivity in Fig. 3. *Note* The triangle denotes the benchmark of 1975 established by the industry-of-origin method [Table 3])

that the further off the benchmark used for extrapolation, the higher the likelihood that the time series drift away from the "true" comparative level (Prados de la Escosura, 2000; Ward & Devereux, 2003). A solution to this problem is to establish several benchmarks over time besides the one used for extrapolation. The additional benchmarks are then used to indicate whether the time series tend to drift away suspiciously (Broadberry, 1997). In this study, however, we do not have the additional benchmarks that could serve as cross-checks. In the literature discussing extrapolations, the assumed mechanism behind the potential drifting away may be summed up as an "index number problem". The benchmark has a fixed basket of goods, whereas the composition of output changes considerably over time. Arguably, though, the structural change component to which this discussion refers is more problematic for long-term comparisons of GDP in which sectoral shares of output changes significantly, and most notably through a dwindling share of agriculture. The comparison of manufacturing comprises a narrower selection of components subject to such dramatic shifts over time. Since we do not have additional benchmarks besides that for 1975, used for extrapolation, we cannot offer a cross-check to the projected productivity levels. Instead, the coming section attempts to make sense of the estimated levels by adding some historical context.

5 The Comparative Record in Historical Context

The following sections aim to bring history to bear on the comparative record we have outlined so far, drawing above all on the industrialization chronologies of the two countries. Unlike comparisons of the developed countries, in other words the pioneers of industrialization that would form the group known as OECD countries, there is no obvious set of sub-periods that fits both Sweden and Brazil. As a result, one has to lean towards one more than the other in drawing lines of demarcation between the various sub-periods. We have chosen sub-periods that mostly reflect the development of Brazil, whose delayed industrialization in the mid-twentieth century deserves attention. The account is unbalanced in the sense that we emphasize the features that lay behind the Swedish acceleration in the late nineteenth and early twentieth century when industrialization had barely begun in Brazil, while offering a thorough treatment of the Brazilian industrialization experience of the post-World War II period.

5.1 Industrialization Pre-World War II

The early industrialization in Sweden grew swiftly thanks mostly to increased foreign demand for timber in the third quarter of the nineteenth century. In addition, the application of the steam engine made it possible to locate the saw mills closer to the coast as the generation of motive power no longer required running water. This early industrialization also gained from expansions of textile production and steel and iron production. Overall, however, this early industrialization was never sufficiently powerful to bring about productivity convergence in manufacturing with the UK and the US (Prado & Sato, 2021). There was a large backlog of productivity to catch up on relative to these two forerunners around the year 1870: the US/Sweden productivity ratio was about 240 and the UK/Sweden ratio was 170. In GDP per capita terms the gap was equally wide (Edvinsson, 2013). It would require an intensified industrialization process to enable manufacturing to propel the economy forward fast enough to close the gap with the leaders.

In the fourth quarter of the nineteenth century, an era in which economic historians often coin the Second Industrial Revolution (Landes, 1969), industrialization in Sweden gathered speed (Gustafsson, 1996). The composition of output and industries moved upwards along the value-added chain, exemplified by the output expansion and exports of pulp and paper, accompanying the exports of timber which continued apace. At the heart of this acceleration and reallocation of industrialization lay the ironware and foundry industry and mechanical engineering. The ironware and foundry industry delivered iron and steel products, either in the relatively crude form of manufacturing plates, rails, tubes, wires, and nails, or further processed into various machine-made products. The mechanical engineering industry developed in close association with iron and steel production, and this development is a stellar example of how processing and adding of value to the raw materials and semi-finished goods, such as tack pig iron and bar iron, vitalized industrialization. Mechanical engineering had roots back in the 1830s, grew steadily in the latter half of the nineteenth century, and blossomed in the 1890s into an industry that was highly competitive in the world market and still able to supply the domestic market until World War I with an almost infinite variety of manufacturing machines, some of which were based on Swedish inventions.

Electricity is at the heart of the swift Swedish transition. Schön (2010) argues that electricity was the new technology on which a new development block was created in the 1890s. Few countries could match the pace at which the Swedish manufacturing industry adopted electricity as a source of motive power in production processes. In 1912, about half of the installed horsepower came from electric motors, whereas the US and Germany had a corresponding share of about 20%. This spurt in the use of electricity stemmed from the country's abundant supply of suitable sites for harnessing energy from water. Prado (2014) has shown that the pattern of productivity growth rates became much uniform across industries after the turn of the century. Whereas only a handful of industries accounted for overall productivity growth from 1869 to 1901, productivity increases were spread across a broad spectrum of industries thereafter. Using the metaphors of Harberger (1998), he concludes that the productivity pattern was mushroom-like before 1901, i.e. sporadic improvements in some industries, but yeast-like in 1901–1909, i.e. regular improvements across the board. He surmises that the reason the productivity pattern became yeasty was the productivity lever of electricity, affecting a broad swath of manufacturing processes.

Parallel with the rise of electricity and development of the mechanical engineering industry, the electromechanical industry grew vigorously in importance, accompanied by successive improvements in productivity, and an unending flow of product innovations. It would become one of the most important export industries in the twentieth century. The movement of prices makes it easier to appreciate the attractiveness of this new prime mover. The prices of electric motors plummeted in the two decades preceding the First World War. In relation to a price index for manufactured goods, they fell by 60% from 1893 to 1913, and Edquist's (2010) hedonic price index for electric motors shows an even greater decline from 1900 to 1913. The decline of prices for this new technology mirrors that shown in Crafts' (2004) investigation of steam in the latter half of the nineteenth century: the capital cost and annual cost of steam horsepower declined after the mid-nineteenth century. Was the drop in the price of electric motors particularly steep in Sweden? It is most probable that dramatic price declines were commonplace because the Swedish company ASEA met stiff competition in the world market for electric motors, in particular from German firms.

For Brazil, as for Argentina, Uruguay, Chile, Mexico, there is plenty of evidence of an "early industrialization" before the 1930s, which is key to explaining the growth of manufacturing after the Great Depression in the early 1930s (Haber, 2006). It is wrong to assume that industrialization in Brazil only began as a result of the state-led development associated with the post-World War II decades. However, the general view that comes across in the economic history literature of Brazil is that its pre-WWII industrialization was delayed and relied largely on foreign technology and incomes generated by exports of coffee. The use of electricity also lagged behind. In 1907, only 4.2% of the power used by industry was based on electricity. The corresponding number in Sweden in 1906 was 24%.

Much discussion has concerned the role of coffee exports. Dean (1969) argued that the export of coffee was a lever of investments in domestic manufacturing plants. Without it, there would not have been sufficient savings for large-scale investments in new technology. A later interpretation fears instead that the export boom diverted incomes away from manufacturing and contributed to deindustrialization; in short, the Dutch disease argument applied to an historical context (Gómez-Galvarriato & Williamson, 2009). But the Brazilian economy did witness growing industrialization as the coffee boom occurred, so the argument, if it is to be sustained, must imply that industrialization would have been faster without the coffee boom. Aldrighi and Collistete (2015: 166–171) cast serious doubt on the Dutch disease argument for Brazilian coffee exports; it does not hold up to scrutiny, they argue. One may recall, moreover, that the Swedish economic history literature is completely devoid of argument for the Dutch disease, yet Sweden was heavily dependent from at least the mid-nineteenth century on exports of several raw materials. To our knowledge, no one in the Swedish historiography has ever put forward the idea that Swedish development would have been more favourable without the export booms in timber and oats (Chapters 3 and 4).

How do our established levels of labour productivity compare with previous studies? Most of them have used as a reference point the US, the leading country in GDP per capita since at least the last quarter of nineteenth century, and a country equipped with particularly good data sources for international comparisons. Because the US was way ahead of most other countries by the early twentieth century, the gap between it and most other countries appears very large (Broadberry et al., 2015), and relative to peripheral economies, such as Brazil and China, astronomical. The Chinese level was just 7% of the American in 1935 (Yuan et al., 2010). The US level of productivity was more than twice that of the Swedish in the early twentieth century (Prado & Sato, 2021). Lara and Prado (2022) suggest that the Brazilian level was about 10–15% that of the US in the 1910s. By reference, if these numbers concurred, the Brazilian level of productivity should have been about 20–30% of the Swedish level. This is what our Brazil/US ratio indicates, hence we may conclude that the different studies display internal consistency at least within a certain error range.

The small size of the Brazil/Sweden productivity ratios in the 1910s inform us that the Brazilian preconditions for early industrialization were poles apart from the Swedish. The economic history literature long suffered from a blind eye with regard to development in today's less developed countries. Overviews of industrialization often referred to the Scandinavian countries as late industrializers. But they were only late relative to the UK, which was first, and to the US, which was second. Sandberg famously called Sweden an "impoverished sophisticate", arguing that it was a paradox that Sweden was poor yet sophisticated in terms of human capital and state capacity. The quite high levels of labour productivity in manufacturing that Sweden had achieved by the outbreak of World War I bear witness to the dynamic properties of its manufacturing sector. Moreover, even if we look at comparative levels in the 1870s, which is as far back in time as our data permit us to project, the gap between Sweden and the US was never remotely as wide as it was for Brazil and the US before the 1930s. Sweden merits the epithet of sophisticate, but the impoverished label sits quite uneasily if one views productivity levels in manufacturing from an international perspective.

Provided the small size of the Brazil/Sweden productivity ratio, the composition of output in the two countries was very different. For Brazil, most authors emphasize the preponderance of consumer goods industries, above all textiles and food, and the deficiency in capital goods industries, like the iron and steel industry and the mechanical engineering industry.[9] Fishlow (1972: 322) argued that: "as a whole, industrial production was limited and unsophisticated". The textile industry dwarfed most other industries, with a quarter of total output in 1920. It was rivalled only by all food processing industries combined, which accounted for 33% of output (Fishlow, 1972: 323). This Brazilian consumer goods bias also comes across in Table 5, which compares output in the two countries in the Brazilian census years of 1919, 1949, and 1975. In 1919, food and textiles combined, the two epitomes of consumer goods industries, accounted for 78% of output, whereas in Sweden, those industries accounted for a modest 30%. Mechanical engineering, a typical example of capital goods industry, accounted for merely 3% of Brazilian output in 1919, whereas in Sweden, it accounted for an impressive 18%. Even in 1975, almost at the very peak of comparative levels of labour productivity in Brazilian manufacturing, the share of output in mechanical engineering in Sweden was still twice that of Brazil.

[9] See, for instance, Villela and Suzigan (1973: 50); Topik (1987: 155–157); and Fishlow (1972: 322–323). The patent record recently unearthed by Colistete (2010) shows that most patents were allotted to the mechanical engineering industry, and the majority of these patents concerned special-purpose machinery for coffee processing.

Table 5 Shares of value added across manufacturing industries (%), 1919–1975

	1926/1919		*1952/1949*		*1975*	
	Sweden	*Brazil*	*Sweden*	*Brazil*	*Sweden*	*Brazil*
Total manufacturing industry	100	100	100	100	100	100
Food, beverage, and tobacco	17	40	21	37	10	15
Textile, apparel, leather, and products	13	38	10	25	4	11
Wood and furniture	9	5	7	5	7	5
Pulp, paper, and printing	18	1	14	5	15	6
Chemical, petro, rubber, and plastic	5	7	7	10	9	20
Non-metallic minerals	6	3	3	5	3	6
Metals	13	2	12	8	7	13
Mechanical engineering	18	3	26	5	45	23

Sources Brazil, Censo Industrial do Brasil, 1919, 1949; Censo Industrial Produção Física, 1975. Sweden, Hamark and Prado (2021); *SOS, Industri*, 1952, 1975

5.2 *Brazilian Zeal and Swedish Maturity: ca 1950–1980*

The heyday of Swedish manufacturing industry occurred in the 1950s and 1960s. The peak in manufacturing's share of employment occurred in the mid-1960s. Labour productivity in Swedish manufacturing outpaced that of the US in the 1960s, and the US to Sweden labour productivity ratio dropped from 200 to 150 (Prado & Sato, 2021). The foundation for that boom was laid during the previous growth spurt in manufacturing output, which commenced in the fourth quarter of the nineteenth century and continued with unabated force during the first half of the twentieth century, and was moreover fuelled by the growing demand for consumer goods and capital goods from the war-ravaged countries of Western Europe in the 1950s. We need to keep in mind that Sweden in the 1950s had a level of labour productivity in manufacturing which was equal to that of the UK (Prado & Sato, 2021).

The Swedish growth regime of post-World War II decades conforms well with the expression "golden years", used to capture the experiences of Western Europe and North America. The demand for labour was so high that imports of labour from Finland, above all, but also from former Yugoslavia and Southern Europe, were deemed necessary (Lundh & Ohlsson, 1997). The mechanical engineering industry was again the foremost engine driving output and productivity levels forward.

In particular, the branch of mechanical engineering producing transport equipment put its mark on this development. Two car manufacturers, Volvo and Saab, grew swiftly as the frequent use of private cars spread across Sweden. They were also early users of the assembly line, which spread across much of the mechanical engineering industry in the post-World War II period. The assembly line would transform work places, much as the use of small electric motors reshaped the design of factories in the first quarter of the twentieth century. Relative to electrification, though, the assembly line only made inroads into a limited numbers of manufacturing industries.

International competition grew as technological improvements in shipping lowered transportation costs. At the same time, successive efforts to lower tariff levels exposed many industries to international competition. Some of these tariffs dated back to the last quarter of the nineteenth century, whereas others had been introduced, or reinforced, in the 1930s (Bohlin, 2005). For consumer goods, such as textiles, shoes, and clothing, this competitive environment was completely new. In Sweden, the clothing and shoe industries sprang up only after the introduction of tariffs in the 1890s. It is fair to say that these industries did not fare well without protection when consumer goods industries developed quickly in Southern Europe based on wage levels much lower than in Sweden. These consumer goods industries became the first victims of the dawning globalization. Shipyards were the next Swedish victim. They had grown vigorously in the 1950s and 1960s, and by the 1970s had made deep imprints in the city ports of Gothenburg, Malmö, and Uddevalla. The Swedish ship building industry was specialized in the building of large oil tankers. Stiff competition from Japanese shipyards lowered profitability, and the oil crisis of the early 1970s inflicted heavy losses on Swedish shipyards. Attempts were made to save them through a public holding company, Svenska Varv, but the fate of the shipyards was sealed, and they disappeared in the 1980s (Bohlin, 1999).

Gordon (2016) argued that the technologies of the Second Industrial Revolution continued to push economic development in the post-World War II era. No major new innovations can explain the rapid growth of productivity that most developed countries enjoyed in the 1950s and 1960s. Instead, it was the spread and refinement of the macro-innovations of the early twentieth centuries, in particular electricity and the combustion engine, that explain the golden years. When the potential of these innovations to serve as a lever of productivity became exhausted, many countries' productivity growth rates decelerated significantly. This appears to be an apt characterization of the Swedish economy. From the vantage point of the present, the forces propelling the economy forward appear to have petered out in the 1970s. As in most of the countries pioneering industrialization in the nineteenth century, economy-wide productivity growth rates decelerated in the 1970s and 1980s, as did growth rates in the manufacturing industry. Nevertheless, the Swedish rate continued to outpace that of the US and the UK, two other countries that suffered structural crises during the 1970s. Convergence of productivity levels in manufacturing with the US was a fait accompli in the 1980s (Prado & Sato, 2021).

Until the 1970s, the industrial policies that underpinned the progress of manufacturing are best described as generic. In general, the state refrained from supporting specific industries through subsidies and ownership. Instead, it aimed to establish a level playing field for all industries through investments in infrastructure, education, and research and development (Bohlin, 1999). This generic policy stance stands in sharp contrast to the emergence of the model of state-led development in much of Latin America. In Sweden, the exception to this rule occurred in the 1970s, when the state gathered all the resources that it could muster to rescue industries from sliding into decay. The 1980s witnessed a return to generic policies. We may also count the so-called solidaristic wage policy as an industrial policy, even though it was originally laid down and handled by the large blue-collar workers union (LO) and the employers' organization (SAF) (Davies & Henrekson, 2005). The wage policy was designed to level out wage differentials across worker categories, affecting above all low-wage workers and low-wage industries, granting them relatively higher wages. The policy followed on from the centralization of power in the hands of LO and SAF by the Saltsöbad agreement in 1938. The egalitarian symbolism of this reform notwithstanding, the foremost motive behind its implementation in the 1950s was in fact to speed up structural transformation and promote productivity and real wage improvements (Hibbs & Locking, 2000). Although globalization would finally have spelled the end of the Swedish consumer goods industries, the solidaristic wage policy entailed a rapid shift away from low-wage and labour-intensive production towards high-wage and highly mechanized production.

As in other Latin American economies, industrialization was the major force propelling economy-wide progress in Brazil from the 1930s to the

1980s. However, the industrial basis in Brazilian development stands out. The share of industry in GDP peaked at about 40% in the latter half of the 1970s and the first half of the 1980s (Table 1). The share of manufacturing proper peaked at about 30% in the same period. No other Latin American country could rival the size of the manufacturing basis in Brazilian development. The rise of industry also spurred urbanization. As more people migrated to cities, the supply of workers for industry and service increased, and so did the demand for consumer goods, which provided a growing internal market for industrial production. The nexus between industry and the growing size of the urban population was particularly strong in the case of São Paulo, whose industrial work force and population at large grew rampantly in the post-World War II decades, fuelled by an influx of internal migrants from more backward areas of Brazil (Cano, 2015).

In Brazil, under the government of Getúlio Vargas, and especially after 1937, economic policies became gradually more interventionist in order to speed up industrialization and structural transformations. New industries were founded and supported by public subsidies and other interventionist mechanisms such as tariff discrimination, direct trade controls, and prohibition of competing imports. The state also became involved in the generation of electricity, construction, and transport in order to provide infrastructure to the industrial sector (Thorp, 1998). The share of value added of capital-intensive industries (metallurgical, mechanical engineering) in relation to the total increased steadily in the second and third quarters of the twentieth century. As Table 5 depicts, the share rose from 5 to 36% between 1920 and 1975. On the other side, traditional industries based on natural resources (food for example) or labour (textiles) decreased their shares in total value added. This manifest effort by the state led to a relatively successful process of learning and technological advances across manufacturing firms, and catching up with the developed countries (Colistete, 2010).

This model of state-led industrial development ran into problems by the outbreak of the debt crisis of the early 1980s. The Economic Commission of Latin American, ECLAC, was among the first to level harsh criticisms of the way that industrialization had developed (Macario, 1964). It filed complaints against alleged excessive protectionism, distortions caused by indiscriminate and complex policies, and poor results in terms of productivity performance. Many critical voices concurred with the view that state-led policies had stalled innovations, fed vested interests through unending flows of subsidies, and made entrepreneurs unwilling to invest in new technologies. In combination, this had a significantly negative effect on Latin American economic performance, and on Brazil as well (Bértola & Ocampo, 2012; Bulmer-Thomas, 1994; Colistete, 2010). In addition, many authors with a leaning towards market liberal views dismissed the entire possibility that state-led development could have any positive spillover effects in terms of companies' learning capacities (Balassa, 1980).

The view that the state-led development model only spelled doom and gloom sits uneasily with the evidence presented in this book chapter, as well as in Lara and Prado (2022), who compare Brazil with the US. The Brazilian/Sweden productivity ratio increased from about 50 to 80 in the 1950–1980 period that coincides with the pinnacle of the state-led development model. Neither before, nor since, has Brazilian labour productivity in manufacturing grown so fast. We need to remember that Sweden in the same post-World War II period was a moving target, enjoying the country's most long-lasting acceleration in labour productivity. Thus, the catching up of Brazil with Swedish levels of productivity in manufacturing was no mean feat. Moreover, the Brazilian level in 1975 was half that of the US, which implies that there had been a narrowing of the gap with several of today's developed countries. As a comparison, the Brazilian/US ratio actually increased from about 25 to 50 in the 1950–1980 period (Lara & Prado, 2022).

Furthermore, capital-intensive industries, such as metallurgical and metalworking, increased their export volumes (Teitel & Thoumi, 1986). This achievement runs counter to the litany of complaints against import substitution industrialization. Instead, it illustrates how the state-led policy fostered development of heavy industries, which played an important role in promoting exports. Unlike other small Latin American countries, the large domestic market in Brazil allowed firms to reap the benefits from economies of scale and made it profitable to produce capital goods, durable consumption goods, and transport equipment. However, besides the achieved improvements in manufacturing productivity at large, heterogeneity across firms and industries continued to plague Brazil, giving food for thought that through its generous subsidies state-led development delayed sustainable economic growth and structural change (Colistete, 2010).

5.3 *Swedish Boom and Brazilian Bust: 1980–*

The foremost manifestation of the Swedish predicament occurred in the early 1990s, when the country was struck by a severe economic downturn. When further devaluations were no longer feasible, the competitive edge Swedish firms had in export markets disappeared, and the manufacturing industry could no longer carry the cost burden implied by raising nominal wages. Although the real estate and banking sector was hardest hit by the financial turmoil that also accompanied the crisis, the total loss of employment in manufacturing was manifest: from 1989 to 1993 it declined by 20% (Krantz & Schön, 2007).

As a result of the crisis, Sweden suffered a precipitous decline in the income rank of countries. Growth rates had sunk to levels well below the OECD average, and previous laggards had outstripped the Swedish GDP per capita level. Against this backdrop, there followed heated debate about the causes and consequences of this fall down the ladder, including political overtones to the messages that the contenders attempted to convey. One camp argued that the move down the rank in the 1980s and 1990s was an inevitable outcome of the Swedish head start in the early post-World War II era. Unlike the laggards, such as the countries of Southern Europe and Finland, Sweden enjoyed minor convergence gains. As a result, Sweden underperformed only relative to those countries whose initial GDP per capita levels were relatively lower, but did just as well as the already rich countries (Korpi, 1996). The other camp instead maintained that much of the falling behind stemmed from policy failures, distorted incentives, regulated markets, and weak competition (Henrekson, 1996). Much of what formed the recommendations of the Economics Commission (SOU, 1993: 16) took it for granted that policy-failure views were correct in identifying the causes of Swedish retardation. The prescriptions of the Lindbeck report would prove to have an enduring impact on economic policy throughout the 1990s and 2000s (Lindert, 2004: ch. 11).

The effects of the crisis, however, proved conducive to productivity growth rates. In fact, the growth rate of labour productivity in manufacturing picked up as the economic crisis of the early 1990s unfolded. Before the political repercussions of the crisis had evaporated, the Swedish economy had already started following an upward trajectory. To some extent, the crisis itself was the catalyst for acceleration in productivity. Hordes of unprofitable companies went out of business and those that remained raised the average level of productivity. This is reminiscent of Field's (2003) contention that the surging growth rates of American productivity during the 1930s were a corollary of the Great Depression. However, the most important factor behind the surge in productivity was information and communication technologies (ICT), as a similar productivity spurt is also identifiable in countries that, unlike Sweden, did not plunge into a severe crisis in the early 1990s. Japan also had a deep economic crisis in the early 1990s but did not share in the productivity upswing centred on ICT (Fukao, 2013).

Sweden belonged to the forerunners in the development and application of ICT technologies. Swedish Industrial Statistics allow us to trace the beginning of the ICT revolution through the information by commodity they provide. From the late 1960s, one can trace the emergence and growing importance of computers under the heading "office machines". It took a while for firms to figure out how to reap the benefits of this new technology, and the use of networks required complementary investments in infrastructure. But the famous quote due to Solow (1987) that "we see computers everywhere but in the productivity statistics" seems hasty with hindsight; the appearance of computers in the productivity statistics was just around the corner. Evidence of widespread ICT usage placed Sweden at the very top of the league across developed countries in the 1990s (Ilshammar, 2002: 325). Van Ark and Smits (2007) furthermore document large effects on labour productivity due to market services and investments in ICT in Europe and the US in 1987–2003. They note that the penetration of ICT investments was as high in Sweden as in the US in 2004, putting Sweden among the topmost users of ICT in industry and services. Anecdotal evidence, such as famous ICT-related innovations originating in Sweden (Spotify, Skype, etc.) also points in this direction.

What role did industrial policy play in this productivity spurt that is attributable to the technologies of the Third Industrial Revolution? As we discussed previously, setting aside the brief interlude of the 1970s, Swedish industrial policy has been designed to establish general conditions that are conducive to industrialization. The state has not engaged itself with either ownership or subsidization of industries. Arguably, the productivity surge related to ICT was to some extent the corollary of some of those generic policies, such as widespread access to broadband, subsidization of home computers, investments in research and development, and investments in higher education.

For most of Latin America, the debt crisis of the early 1980s was a cataclysm that spelled the end of the previous modus operandi; it paved the way for neoliberal policies and prompted a change in the institutional environment. The neoclassical perspective that many Latin American governments embraced advocated outward-oriented policies with the aim of improving competitiveness and productivity in a context of hyperinflation (Palma, 2011). The debt crisis that ushered in the new policy era coincided with the end of convergence and beginning of divergence. As we have shown, the Brazilian/Swedish ratio began to decline precipitously, and almost uninterruptedly, by the early 1980s. The reason for this relative decline is that Brazilian labour productivity stopped growing, whereas Swedish labour productivity continued growing apace, even accelerating in the 1990s.

The Brazilian stagnation and the repercussions of the debt crisis stirred controversy about the legacy of the state-led development model. We may differentiate between three camps that offered conflicting explanations as to the causes of the economic crisis of the early 1980s and the stagnation that followed in its wake. The first camp attributes Brazil's post-1980 problem to the state-led model's failure to promote exports of manufactured products. Unlike East-Asian economies, such as South Korea, Taiwan, and later China, Brazil never adopted sustainable policies aiming at increasing the share of exports of manufactured products in GDP. As the argument goes, countries should specialize in the production of those goods in which they have a comparative advantage (Balassa, 1980). The second camp focuses on the growing external debt during the 1960s and 1970s. Fishlow (1981) argues that Brazil implemented a debt-led growth model between 1968 and 1978: the external debt increased from 10% of total GDP in 1967 to 17% in 1973 and 25% in 1978. After 1973, external debt grew at more rapid rates in order to support the II Development National Plan carried out by the military government. The third camp has argued that the state-led industrialization model did not make sufficient efforts to increase the capacity to generate new technology, through investments in, for instance, national innovation systems and a stronger educational system (Thorp, 1998; see Chapter 6).

It is difficult to associate a particular set of policies, be it import substitution industrialization or neoliberal trade policies, with a development trend that has persisted over a considerable time period. The shift towards a new development strategy focusing on openness occurred gradually. Trade liberalization, for instance, began in the late 1980s but gathered momentum only in the mid-1990s (Kume et al., 2003).[10] At that time, the stagnation in productivity had already been ongoing for at least a decade. This time difference between the policy shift and beginning of stagnation begs the question of whether the two phenomena have an intrinsic connection. On the other hand, it becomes far-fetched to associate the Brazilian productivity failure since the early 1980s with the policies of import substitution industrialization. After all, the stagnation in productivity continued until at least the early 2010s, which means that 3–4 decades have elapsed since the heydays of import substitution industrialization.

The sluggish performance of Brazilian productivity after the mid-1990s has something to do with a failure to reap the benefits of ICT technologies. Research on the nexus between growth and technology has identified a brief spell of productivity acceleration beginning in the mid-1990s and propelled by the innovations of the Third Industrial Revolution, in particular those associated with ICT (Gordon, 2016; Oliner et al., 2007). This momentary spurt occurred in several developed countries, such as the US, Germany, and Canada (Colecchia & Schreyer, 2002). Rather than discussing the legacies of the import substitution industrialization of the post-World War II decades, research should perhaps direct attention to the quality and the distribution of primary and secondary education, or the intersections between market service sectors and manufacturing industries, which are the breeding ground for new technologies.

The 1980s witnessed the transition to democracy. The first free presidential election since 1960 was held in 1989, and saw Fernando Collor gaining power. He was impeached by the National Congress in 1992, accused of serious corruption. With hindsight, corruption was a weakness symptomatic of democracy in Brazil, as similar events were about to unfold. Although the Brazilian democracy has struggled to cope with recurrent problems of corruption and lack of professional conduct, it has so far proved resistant to all attempts made to undermine its foundation. Recently, some researchers have argued that several key institutions conducive to economic growth and egalitarianism were created as a result of the transition to and consolidation of democracy in the latter half of the 1990s and early 2000s, coinciding with the era of Fernando Henrique

[10] The first two tariff reforms between 1987 and 1989 reduced the average effective tariff from 68 to 39%. In 1993, the tariff was down to 15% (Kume et al., 2003).

Cardoso (Alston, 2017; Alston et al., 2016). They argue that the strong belief in fiscally sound social inclusion and the establishment of institutions framed to achieve those objectives have prepared the ground for growth and prosperity for decades to come. This upbeat message contrasts, however, with the economic downturn and political turmoil of the 2010s. In addition, productivity in manufacturing has not yet responded to these stimuli.

Finally, our evidence that the Brazil/Sweden productivity ratio in manufacturing continues to decline throughout the 2000s is perhaps surprising against the backdrop of the economy-wide prosperity that Brazil enjoyed after 2004, notwithstanding a mild recession in 2009. The growth rate of GDP per capita between 2004 and 2013 was 2.8%. Since the contribution from manufacturing to this economy-wide spurt was almost nil, other sectors must have grown considerably. The impetus from the commodity price boom in the world market is probably the most important contribution to the economy-wide acceleration, fuelling large-scale investments in agriculture, mining, and other raw-material-based activities. The growth rates of productivity in these sectors increased in the 2000s as a result of the increasing demand (Aldrighi & Colistete, 2015). Nevertheless, growth in Brazil was largely driven by external factors that were short-lived by default rather than domestic factors that were conducive to sustainable growth rates in productivity; in other words, Brazil was growing without progressing.

6 Conclusion

From the Brazilian vantage point, the long-term record of comparative productivity that we have established is quite disconcerting. The productivity frontier, here exemplified by Sweden, has behaved like a moving target throughout the twentieth century. This target is by the 2010s as remote as it was in the 1910s, which marks the beginning of our study period. However, those similar levels at the start and end points of our investigation mask the conspicuous narrowing of the productivity gap that occurred in the post-World War II decades. This episode of convergence proved short-lived and elusive, as since the early 1980s the gulf between Sweden and Brazil has reverted to the same size as in the 1910s. This productivity collapse is an important explanation for Brazilian difficulties in sustaining high growth rates in the aggregate since the early 1980s.

The brief acceleration in growth rates of GDP per capita in 2004–2012 owed to temporary gains from the worldwide boom in commodity prices.

The wide swings in productivity levels have implications for the scholarly debate on the role of manufacturing in income convergence among countries. Our study shows that the productivity ratio between a developed and less developed country is susceptible to quite dramatic changes. The notion that the ratio somehow should remain stable over time is refuted. Moreover, Rodrik's (2013) notion of unconditional catching up in manufacturing does not square with the Brazilian experience. Catching up in productivity in manufacturing is conditioned on country-specific capabilities. Rodrik worries that deindustrialization in less developed countries will halt economy-wide convergence. But the scale of manufacturing will not help if productivity growth rates stagnate. The experience of Brazil shows instead that the combined effect of deindustrialization and an extended period of productivity stagnation in manufacturing is a recipe for macro-economic hardships. Industrialization does not automatically translate into sustainable growth rates in GDP per capita unless it has the dynamic properties of research and development and technological change. Otherwise, the spillover effects from manufacturing to other sectors that we associate with the epochal studies of Hirschman (1958) and Kaldor (1967) will cease to appear. The performance of manufacturing weighs heavier than its size.

References

Official Publications

Brasil

Censo Industrial do Brasil, 1919, 1939, 1949. IBGE.

Censo Industrial Produção Física 1975. IBGE.

Estatísticas Históricas do Brasil: Series Economicas, Demograficas, e Sociais, 1550 a 1988, 1990. IBGE.

Índices de Preços ao Atacado (IPA). Conjuntura Econômica. FGV.

Pesquisa Industrial Annual (PIA). IBG.

Sweden

SOS, Industri. Sveriges offentliga statistik. Statistiska Centralbyrån. Stockholm.

SOU 1993:16. *Nya villkor för ekonomi och politik: Ekonomikommissionens förslag och betänkande*. Stockholm: Allmänna förl.

Books and Articles

Aldrighi, D., & Colistete, R. (2015). Industrial growth and structural change: Brazil in a long-run perspective. In W. Naudé, A. Szirmai, & N. Haraguchi (Eds.), *Structural change and industrial development in the BRICS* (pp. 162–198). Oxford University Press.

Alston, L. J. (2017). Beyond institutions: Beliefs and leadership. *Journal of Economic History, 77*(2), 353–372. https://doi.org/10.1017/S0022050717000523

Alston, L. J., Melo, M. A., Mueller, B., & Pereira, C. (2016). Brazil in transition: Beliefs, leadership, and institutional change. *Princeton University Press*. https://doi.org/10.1515/9781400880942

Amsden, A. H. (2001). The rise of "the Rest": Challenges to the West from late-industrializing economies. *Oxford University Press*. https://doi.org/10.1093/0195139690.001.0001

Baer, W. (1972). Import substitution and industrialization in Latin Amercia: Experiences and interpretations. *Latin American Research Review, 7*(1), 95–122.

Balassa, B. (1980). The process of industrial development and alternative development strategies. *Essays in International Finance, 141*, 1–34.

Bénétrix, A., & S., O'Rourke, K. H., & Williamson, J. G. (2015). The spread of manufacturing to the poor periphery 1870–2007. *Open Economics Review, 26*(1), 1–37. https://doi.org/10.1007/s11079-014-9324-x

Berglund, B. (2010). *Den petrokemiska revolutionen: svensk petrokemisk industri 1960–2010*. Rydin.

Bértola, L., & Ocampo, J. A. (2012). The economic development of Latin America since independence. *Oxford University Press*. https://doi.org/10.1093/acprof:oso/9780199662135.001.0001

Bohlin, J. (1999). Sweden: The rise and fall of the Swedish Model. In J. Foreman-Peck & G. Federico (Eds.), *A century of European industrial policy* (pp. 152–176). Oxford University Press.

Bohlin, J. (2005). Tariff protection in Sweden 1885–1913. *Scandinavian Economic History Review, 53*(2), 7–29.

Bonelli, R. (2015). Comparações internacionais de produtividade na indústria e tendências setoriais: Brasil e EUA. In N. Barbosa, N. Marconi, M. Canêdo-Pinheiro, & L. Carvalho (Eds.), *Indústria e desenvolvimento produtivo no Brasil* (pp. 487–517). Editora Elsevier.

Broadberry, S. N. (1993). Manufacturing and the convergence hypothesis: What the long run data show. *Journal of Economic History, 53*(4), 772–795. https://doi.org/10.1017/S0022050700051317

Broadberry, S. N. (1997). *The productivity race: British manufacturing in international perspective, 1850–1990*. Cambridge University Press.

Broadberry, S. N., Fukao, K., & Zammit, N. (2015). How did Japan catch-up on the West? A sectoral analysis of Anglo-Japanese productivity differences, 1885–2000. *CEPR Discussion Paper No. DP10570*.

Bulmer-Thomas, V. (1994). *The economic history of Latin America since independence*. Camridge University Press.

Cano, W. (2015). Crise e industrialização no Brasil entre 1929 e 1954: A reconstrução do estado Nacional e a política nacional de desenvolvimento. *Revista De Economia Política, 35*(3), 444–460. https://doi.org/10.1590/0101-31572015v35n03a04

Colecchia, A., & Schreyer, P. (2002). ICT investment and economic growth in the 1990s: Is the United Stantes a unique case? A comparative study of nine OECD countries. *Review of Economic Dynamics, 5*(2), 408–442. https://doi.org/10.1006/redy.2002.0170

Colistete, R. (2007). Productivity, wages, and labor politics in Brazil, 1945–1962. *Journal of Economic History, 67*(1), 93–127. https://doi.org/10.1017/S0022050707000046

Colistete, R. (2010). Revisiting import-substituting industrialisation in Post-War Brazil. *MPRA Paper No. 24665,*.

Crafts, N. (2004). Steam as a general purpose technology: A growth accounting perspective. *Economic Journal, 114*(April), 338–351.

Davies, S. J., & Henrekson, M. (2005). Wage-setting institutions as industrial policy. *Labour Economics, 12*, 345–377. https://doi.org/10.1016/j.labeco.2004.01.002

Dean, W. (1969). The Industrialization of São Paulo, 1880–1945. *University of Texas Press*. https://doi.org/10.2307/980623

Edvinsson, R. (2013). New annual estimates of Swedish GDP 1800–2010. *Economic History Review, 66*(4), 1101–1126. https://doi.org/10.1111/1468-0289.12004

Edquist, H. (2010). Does hedonic price indexing change our interpretation of economic history? Evidence from Swedish electrification. *The Economic History Review, 63*(2), 500–523. https://doi.org/10.1111/j.1468-0289.2009.00504.x

Feinstein, C. H. (1999). Structural change in the developed countries during the twentieth century. *Oxford Review of Economic Policy, 15*(4), 35–55.

Field, A. J. (2003). The most technologically progressive decade of the century. *American Economic Review, 93*(4), 1399–1413. https://doi.org/10.1257/000282803769206377

Fishlow, A. (1972). Origins and consequences of import substitution in Brazil. In L. E. Di Marco (Ed.), *International economics and development: Essays in honor of Raúl Prebisch* (pp. 311–365). Academic Press.

Fishlow, A. (1981). A dívida externa latinoamericana: Um caso de desenvolvimento com incerteza. *Pesquisa e Planejamento Econômico, 11*(2), 283–322.

Fukao, K. (2013). Explaining Japan's unproductive two decades. *Asian Economic Policy Review, 8*, 193–213. https://doi.org/10.1111/aepr.12020

Gómez-Galvarriato, A., & Williamson, J. G. (2009). Was it prices, productivity or policy? Latin American industrialisation after 1870. *Journal of Latin American Studies, 41*(4), 663–694. https://doi.org/10.1017/S0022216X09990551

Gordon, R. J. (2016). *The rise and fall of American growth: the U.S. standard of living since the Civil War*. Priinceton University Press.

Gustafsson, B. (1996). The industrial revolution in Sweden. In M. Teich & R. Porter (Eds.), *The Industrial Revolution in national context: Europe and the USA* (pp. 201–225). Cambridge University Press.

Haber, S. H. (1992). Business enterprise and the Great Depression in Brazil: A study of profits and losses in textile manufacturing. *Business History Review, 66*(2), 335–363. https://doi.org/10.2307/3116941

Haber, S. H. (2006). The political economy of industrialization. In V. Bulmer-Thomas, J. Coatsworth, & R. Cortes-Conde (Eds.), *The Cambridge Economic Hisotry of Latin America* (Vol. Part IV Sectoral development and equity, pp. 537–584). Cambridge University Press.

Haddad, C. L. S. (1978). *Crescimento do produto real no Brasil, 1900–1947*. FGV.

Hamark, J., & Prado, S. (2021). Output and productivity in Swedish manufacturing, 1870–1950. *Unpublished manuskript*.

Harberger, A. C. (1998). A vision of the growth process. *American Economic Review, 88*(1), 1–32.

Henrekson, M. (1996). Sweden's relative performance: Lagging behind or staying on top? *Economic Journal, 106*(439), 1747–1759. https://doi.org/10.2307/2235215

Hibbs, D. A., & Locking, H. (2000). Wage dispersion and productivity efficiency: Evidence for Sweden. *Journal of Labor Economics, 18*(4), 755–782. https://doi.org/10.1086/209976

Hirschman, A. (1958). *The Strategy of economic development*. Yale UP.

Ilshammar, L. (2002). *Offentlighetens ny arum: teknik och politik i Sverige 1969–1999*. Örebro universitet.

Johansson, M. (1985). *Svensk industri 1930–1950: produktion, produktivitet, sysselsättning*. Ekonomisk-historiska föreningen.

Jörberg, L. (1973). The industrial revolution in the Nordic Countires. In C. M. Cipolla (Ed.), *The Fontana Economic History of Europe, vol 4 1700–1914* (pp. 375–479). Collins.

Kaldor, N. (1967). *Strategic factors in economic development*. Ithaca.

Korpi, W. (1996). Eurosclerosis and the sclerosis of objectivity: On the role of values among economic policy experts. *Economic Journal, 106*(439), 1727–1746. https://doi.org/10.2307/2235214

Krantz, O., & Schön, L. (2007). *Swedish historical national accounts 1800–2000*. Almqvist & Wicksell International.

Kume, H. R., Piani, G., & de Souza, C. F. B. Z. (2003). A política Brasileira de importação no período 1987–1998: Descrição e avaliação. In C. H. Corseuil & H. R. Kume (Eds.), *A abertura comercial Brasileira nos anos 1990: Impacto sobre emprego e salário*. IPEA.

Landes, D. S. (1969). *The Unbound Prometheus: Technical change and industrial development in Western Europe from 1750 to the Present*. Cambridge University Press.

Lara, C., & Prado, S. (2022). From boom to gloom: Brazilian labor productivity in manufacturing relative to the US, 1912–2019. Forthcoming in *Economic History Review*

Lindert, P. (2004). *Growing public: Social spending and economic growth since the eighteenth century* (Vol. 1). Cambridge University Press.

Ljungberg, J. (1988). *Historiska nationalräkenskaper för Sverige: Deflatorer för industriproduktionen*. Ekonomisk-historiska föreningen.

Lundh, C., & Ohlsson, R. (1997). *Från arbetskraftsimport till flyktinginvandring. Andra reviderade upplagan*. SNS.

Macario, S. (1964). Protectionism and industrialization in Latin America. *Economic Bulletin for Latin America, 9*, 61–101.

Maddison, A., & van Ark, B. (1989). International comparison of purchasing power, real output and labour productiivity: a case study of Brazilian, Mexican and U.S. Manufacturing, 1975. *Review of Income and Wealth, 35*(1), 31–55. https://doi.org/10.1111/j.1475-4991.1989.tb00581.x

Oliner, S. D., Sichel, D. E., & Stiroh, K. J. (2007). Explaining a productive decade. *Finance and economics discussion series divisions of research & statistics and monetary affairs. Federal Reserve Board, Washington, D.C.*

Paige, D., & Bombach, G. (1959). *A comparison of national output and productivity of the United Kingdom and the United States*. OECD.

Palma, J. G. (2011). Why has productivity growth stagnated in most Latin America countries since the neo-liberal reforms? In J. A. Ocampo & J. Ros (Eds.), *Oxford Handbook of Latin American Economics* (pp. 568–607). Oxford University Press.

Prado, S. (2014). Yeast or mushrooms? Productivity patterns across Swedish manufacturing industries, 1869–1912. *Economic History Review, 67*(2), 382–408. https://doi.org/10.1111/1468-0289.12018

Prado, S., & Sato, Y. (2021). Sweden chasing the US and UK productivity frontiers in manufacturing, 1870–2010 *Unpublished manuskript*.

Prados de la Escosura, L. (2000). International comparisons of real product, 1820–1990: An alternative data set. *Explorations in Economic History, 37*(1), 1–47. https://doi.org/10.1006/exeh.1999.0731

Rodrik, D. (2013). Unconditional convergence in manufacturing. *Quarterly Journal of Economics, 128*(1), 165–204. https://doi.org/10.1093/qje/qjs047

Rostas, L. (1948). *Comparative productivity in British and American Industry*. Cambridge University Press. https://doi.org/10.1038/164295a0

Ryggvik, H. (2021). Oil and industry in Norway and Brazil. In C. Ducoing & J. Peres-Cajías (Eds.), *Natural resources and divergence: A comparison of Andean and Nordic trajectories* (pp. 219–256). Palgrave Macmillan. https://doi.org/10.1038/164295a0

Schön, L. (1988). *Historiska nationalräkenskaper för Sverige: Industri och hantverk 1800–1980*. Lunds universitet.

Schön, L. (2010). *Sweden's road to modernity: An economic history*. SNS.

Solow, R. (1987). We'd better watch out. *New York Times Book Review, July 12*, 36.

Stein, S. J. (1957). *The Brazilian cotton manufacture: Textile enterprise in an underdeveloped area, 1850–1950*. Harvard University Press.

Teitel, S., & Thoumi, F. E. (1986). From import substitution to exports: The manufacturing exports experience of Argentina and Brazil. *Economic Development and Cultural Change, 34*(3), 455–490. http://www.jstor.org/stable/1154049

Thomas, M., & Feinstein, C. (2003). The value added approach to the measurement of economic growth. In T. W. Guinnane, W. A. Sundstrom, & C. W. Whatley (Eds.), *History matters. Essays on economic growth, technology, and demographic change* (pp. 425–458). Stanford University Press.

Thorp, R. (1998). *Progress, poverty and exclusion: An economic history of Latin America in the 20th Century*. Inter-American Development Bank.

Topik, S. (1987). *The political economy of the Brazilian state, 1889–1930*. University of Texas Presshttps://doi.org/10.7560/765009

van Ark, B. (1993). *International comparisons of output and productivity: Manufacturing productivity performance of ten countries from 1950–1990*. Groningen Growth and Development Centre Monograh Series 1.

van Ark, B., & Maddison, A. (1994). "An international comparisons of real output, purchasing power and labour productivity in manufacturing industries: Brazil, Mexico and the USA in 1975. *Research memorandum 569. Groningen Growth and Development Centre, Groningen.*

van Ark, B., & Smits, J.-P. (2007). Technology regimes and productivity growth in Europe and the United States. In B. Eichengreen, B. Stiefel, & M. Landesmann (Eds.), *The European economy in an American mirror* (pp. 41–61). Roultedge.

van Ark, B., & Timmer, M. (2001). The ICOP manufacturing database: International comparisons of productivity levels. *Groningen Growth and Development Centre, Groningen.*

Versiani, F. R. (1984). Índices de produção industrial para a década de 1920: Um reexame. *Estutdos Economicos, 14*(1), 43–55.

Villela, A. V., & Suzigan, W. (1973). *Política do governo e crescimento da economia Brasileira, 1899–1945*. IPEA/INPES.

Ward, M., & Devereux, J. (2003). Measuring British decline: Direct versus long-span income measures. *Journal of Economic History, 63*(3), 826–851. https://doi.org/10.1017/S0022050703542000

Yuan, T., Fukao, K., & Wu, H. X. (2010). Comparative output and labor productivity in manufacturing between China, Japan, Korea and the United States for ca. 1935 - a production-side PPP approach. *Explorations in Economic History, 47*, 325–346. https://doi.org/10.1016/j.eeh.2009.08.003

CHAPTER 6

The Role of Education in Modernization Drives in Brazil and in Sweden

Thomas Kang and Anders Nilsson

1 Introduction

In the early nineteenth century, neither Brazil nor Sweden could be characterized as a modern country. They were sparsely populated, had small and undeveloped urban sectors and a fairly low GDP per capita. Both countries were affected by globalization in the course of the nineteenth century mainly as exporters of primary products, for Brazil chiefly coffee, for Sweden above all iron and timber. However, the institutional settings were very different. Brazil had a long colonial past during which slavery was widespread until the end of the nineteenth century, whereas Sweden had an even longer existence as an independent country where, despite

T. Kang (✉)
Department of Economics and International Relations, Universidade Federal do Rio Grande do Sul (UFRGS), Porto Alegre, Brazil
e-mail: kang.thomas@gmail.com

A. Nilsson
Lund University, Lund, Sweden

J. Álvarez and S. Prado (eds.), *Scandinavia and South America—A Tale of Two Capitalisms*, Palgrave Studies in Economic History,
https://doi.org/10.1007/978-3-031-09198-8_6

feudal strains, the peasantry was basically free. Land ownership was much more unequal in Brazil and the local community had more autonomy in Sweden, to mention just a few differences. We develop the institutional settings in the two countries further in the text. These differences had vast implications for the structure and reach of schooling in the two countries, in the decades around the turn of the century 1900, and in the post-World War Two period.

In this chapter, we aim to undertake a comparative analysis of education performance in Sweden and Brazil focusing on two periods: 1870–1910 (extended until 1930 in the case of Brazil) and 1945–1973. Our reason for concentrating on two separate periods, instead of covering the whole period, is that we want to examine how the education system in the two countries responded to the great international challenges that occurred in those years. During the first period, while industrialization was in its early stage in Brazil, Sweden embarked on the Second Industrial Revolution. The second period was the heyday of import-substitution industrialization (ISI) in Brazil, while Sweden witnessed large transformations as the European economy recovered after 1945. The two countries clearly experienced diverse paths of modernization and development. According to Robert Allen (2011), mass education is one of the crucial aspects in successful experiences of catch-up industrialization. One of the major differences between the experiences of Brazil and Sweden is that the latter already had a relatively well-educated population when industrialization arrived. By the mid-nineteenth century, Sweden had a low GDP per capita, compared to other West European countries, but comparatively high levels of human capital, thanks to religious demands for a literate population—an 'impoverished sophisticate' in the words of Sandberg (1979). By the early twentieth century, Sweden's GDP per capita had caught up with most countries in Western Europe.

A comparative analysis of the evolution of education in these two countries imposes some challenges. Differences in regulations on school-age definitions, length of the school year and organization of the education system create hurdles to comparative studies. Despite this, several studies have attempted to create comparable datasets on education attainment (Barro & Lee, 1993, 2013; Cohen & Soto, 2007; Lee & Lee, 2016; Morrison & Murtin, 2009; Van Leuween & Van Leuween-Li, 2014). For

Table 1 Average years of schooling of the population aged between 15 and 64 years, Brazil and Sweden, 1870–2000

Year	*Brazil*			*Sweden*			*Ratio (a)/(b)*
	Male	*Female*	*Total (a)*	*Male*	*Female*	*Total (b)*	
1870	0.24	0.01	0.14	3.74	3.47	3.60	0.04
1900	0.71	0.41	0.56	4.04	4.56	4.32	0.13
1920	1.09	1.07	1.07	4.64	5.03	4.84	0.22
1940	1.77	1.55	1.66	6.34	6.00	6.16	0.27
1950	2.31	1.91	2.11	7.18	6.72	6.95	0.30
1960	2.71	2.34	2.53	7.83	7.55	7.69	0.33
1970	3.45	3.11	3.28	8.84	8.47	8.65	0.38
2000	6.58	6.93	6.76	11.53	11.93	11.72	0.58

Source Lee and Lee (2016)

the sake of comparison, we have decided to use the well-known Barro and Lee (2013) and Lee and Lee (2016) datasets.[1]

Information on education performance exposes the stark difference between the Brazilian and Swedish education systems since the mid-nineteenth century. In Table 1 we show average years of schooling among the adult population from 1870 to 2000. The table demonstrates very clearly that an educational gap existed between the two countries, but also that the Brazilian education system underwent a slow catch-up process with Sweden (as the last column of Table 1 shows) from as early as around 1900. However, that process only gained momentum in the 1990s. For a long time, education was clearly not a top priority among Brazilian policy-makers. By 1970 Brazil still had not achieved the level of average years of schooling that Sweden reached a century earlier.

In Table 2 we compare the performance of Brazil and Sweden with a couple of relevant countries, namely Argentina and the USA. In this table we focus on enrolment in primary education between 1850 and 1930. The table shows that in 1870 Sweden's gross enrolment rate had already reached 100%, while the Brazilian rate had not even reached 10%.[2]

[1] Country-specific indicators exist; Maduro (2007) and Kang et al. (2021) for Brazil and Ljungberg and Nilsson (2009) for Sweden, but they are not directly comparable with each other.

[2] Lee and Lee (2016) defined a ceiling at 100%, even though gross enrolment ratios can be larger than 100%.

Table 2 Gross enrolment rate (%) in primary education, selected countries, 1870–1930

Country	*1850*	*1870*	*1890*	*1910*	*1930*
Brazil	3.4	8.2	9.6	17.1	29.5
Argentina	9.0	21.0	31.5	50.5	66.9
Sweden	89.4	100.0	100.0	100.0	100.0
USA	80.1	100.0	100.0	100.0	100.0

Source Lee and Lee (2016)

Swedish indicators were close to those reported by the USA, one of the leaders of the Second Industrial Revolution, while Brazil was a laggard even compared to its neighbour Argentina (21.0% in 1870). Even in 1930, the gross enrolment ratio in Brazil was lower than 30%, while the same indicator was close to 67% in Argentina.

These initial differences in schooling apparently had long-lasting effects that also reflect on recent educational performance. In 2010, Brazilians aged between 15 and 64 years attained 8.2 years of schooling on average, while the average years of schooling reached 12.0 in Sweden (Barro & Lee, 2013). PISA results show that Brazilian 15-year-old students only achieved a score of 382 in the math test, whereas Swedes broke the 500 points mark in 2018 (OECD, 2019). Despite the geographical, institutional and cultural differences between a large Latin American country and a Scandinavian one, a comparative analysis of the evolution of education in Brazil and Sweden during critical historical periods may be an illuminating exercise for a better understanding of diverse experiences of modernization.

2 Brazil, 1870–1930

2.1 *Background*

Since colonial times, the Brazilian economy has been based on the export of agricultural products to the world market. In the early nineteenth century there was a gradual decline in the previously dominant sugar and cotton exports from the north-east region, while coffee production was on the rise in the south-east. During the Empire period, the gap between the Brazilian economy and the world's economic leaders widened as more countries joined the industrialized world (Villela, 2013).

In contrast to some European countries, which already had some modern features before the arrival of industrialization, Brazil was far from modern. As mentioned earlier, coffee had been the main export product since the 1830s. Lack of capital and cheap energy sources, low education levels and the absence of an integrated market contributed to the late arrival of industrialization (Bethell & Carvalho, 1995).

Modernization and industrialization received a boost in the final decades of the nineteenth century. Brazil was the last country in the region to formally abolish slavery (1888) and the Empire's fall made way for the Republic in 1889. Some decentralization took place under the republican regime, but Brazil continued to be a centralized country in several respects.[3] Provinces were transformed into states, but continued to have the major responsibility on education matters. Despite the lay character of the Republic, Roman Catholic orders maintained an important role in providing schooling.

The arrival of immigrants (in large numbers since 1870) and infrastructure investments contributed to the expansion of coffee production.[4] Linkages and externalities related to agricultural export growth fostered structural change in the Brazilian economy (Aldrighi & Colistete, 2015). Between 1872 and 1920, the population share living in larger cities (more than 20,000 inhabitants) increased from 7.9 to 13.0% (Merrick & Graham, 1979). In the 1920s, coffee exports boomed and investments in the manufacturing sector rose sharply. These investments not only reached traditional sectors (textile and food processing, for example), but also boosted the burgeoning intermediate and capital goods' sectors (Suzigan, 2000; Villela, 2013). Even under an elite democracy, the country was apparently taking its path to modernity.[5]

Despite these social and economic changes, the achievements of the central government on education matters were meagre: the Empire

[3] While the power of states (formerly provinces) increased, the central government had more financial resources and armed forces than all states combined (Topik, 1987).

[4] On the role of immigrants in the industrialization of São Paulo, see Dean (1969). Summerhill (2003) argues that railroads built from the late nineteenth century led to efficiency gains of between 6 and 8% of GDP in 1913. On the expansion of the coffee economy and modernization, see Cano (1977) and Hanley (2005).

[5] In cultural terms, this was epitomized by the 1922 Modern Art Week in São Paulo, which attracted attention to modern Brazilian artists and scandalized more conservative members of the elite.

created an elite secondary school (*Colégio Pedro II*) and a few higher education institutions. A large share of the existing primary and secondary schools belonged to the church. Roman Catholicism was the official religion and was practised by the large majority of the population. Unlike Sweden, there were few Protestant groups in the country, mostly located in the south, where most German immigrants settled in small properties during the nineteenth century. In several provinces, slaves were not allowed to attend classes.

2.2 *Education Reforms*

Since the country was barely urbanized, there was not a significant demand for education in the early nineteenth century. Illiteracy was widespread even among the free population and nearly the entire slave population was illiterate. In 1810, almost two-thirds of the population were mixed or black and more than half of them were slaves (Alden, 1987).

After independence from Portugal in 1822, the 1824 Constitution of the Empire declared that 'primary instruction was free for all citizens'. A decade later, the 1834 Additional Act (*Ato Adicional*) made provinces responsible for providing primary and secondary education. However, financial centralization left provinces with few resources to fund the expansion of mass schooling throughout the Empire period. On the other hand, the delegation of power to provincial assemblies left local governments with little (if any) role in education matters (Colistete, 2017).

Basic literacy remained an elite privilege during the period. In the early 1870s, illiterates comprised 81.4% of the Brazilian population. Moreover, illiteracy was more prevalent among women according to the 1872 Census: 76.6% of men and 86.6% of women were illiterate. A somewhat faster growth of school enrolment and falling illiteracy rates began by the turn of the century (Colistete, 2016; Musacchio et al., 2014). From 1890 to 1930, Brazil (together with Colombia and Peru) reported the largest growth of per capita enrolment rates in the region (Colistete, 2016). The federalist structure of the First Republic (1889–1930) contributed to the expansion of schooling (Musacchio et al., 2014). The 1920s were marked by the surge of a national movement in favour of mass schooling (Schwartzman et al., 1984). The less centralized structure of the First Republic allowed more experimentalism in state-level education policies.

Reformers, some of whom would later be known as members of the progressive *Escola Nova* movement, brought pedagogical innovations in several states (Nagle, 1974). The relationship of these reforms to an increase in enrolments has not been established yet, since quantitative information is scarce for the period.

Of course, this expansion did not benefit all groups evenly. Havighurst and Moreira (1969) stressed that the expansion was concentrated to cities of richer states, leaving behind rural and poorer areas. Musacchio et al. (2014) pointed out that the black population benefited less from this expansion. Moreover, enrolment rate growth did not necessarily mean that the children completed the primary level. According to Komatsu et al. (2019), the proportion of the population that completed primary schooling remained relatively constant (around 5%) from 1890 to 1930. By 1920, the illiteracy rate had fallen to 75.5%, with a persistent gender gap. According to the 1920 Census, illiteracy rates for men and women were 71.1 and 80.1%, respectively. All these statistics include both children and adults, since the 1872 Census did not present illiteracy rates for the adult population alone.[6]

2.3 Education, Globalization and Modernization

Several scholars have attributed Brazilian educational backwardness to colonial origins and institutions. Engerman and Sokoloff (1997) considered initial factor endowments as the main determinant of long-term growth in the Americas. According to the authors, initial conditions led to the adoption of large-scale plantations and other activities with pervasive effects on institutions in Latin America. Land ownership inequality and low levels of education would have arisen from these colonial origins. Following this line of research, later studies investigated the evolution of schooling institutions in the Americas (Engerman et al., 2009). The same idea was applied to within-country contexts: several studies found an association between higher land ownership inequality and lower levels of schooling within Brazil (de Carvalho Filho & Colistete, 2010; de Carvalho Filho & Monasterio, 2012; Wegenast, 2010).

[6] Considering only the population over 15 years of age in 1920, 57.1% of men over were illiterate, while the illiteracy rate for women in the same age group reached 62.8%.

However, this literature leaves little room for the effects of the first wave of modern globalization on education in Brazil. Besides the intellectual movement in favour of mass schooling mentioned in the previous section, the opportunities provided by the expansion of trade and factor movements were another reason for the expansion of education during the period. In the case of Brazil, two specific channels must be considered: (i) the export boom combined with a more decentralized structure after the fall of Imperial Brazil and (ii) migration flows to Brazil, which had a significant impact on both the demand and supply of schooling.

The first channel linking globalization to education was the combined effect of the expansion of trade with the less centralized structure of the First Republic on education spending and outcomes. In the 1880s, Brazil's supply share in the world coffee market was around 60% (Abreu & Lago, 2014). Export taxes, though inefficient, provided the most important source of revenue for states such as São Paulo, where most coffee was grown. As a result, the state was a major beneficiary of the coffee boom in the world market. Other states that exported coffee, rubber and cattle also benefited from positive trade shocks, while states that relied on sugar and cotton did not perform well in fiscal terms. These positive trade shocks allowed a considerable increase in state-level tax revenues and education expenditures (Musacchio et al., 2014). The state of São Paulo, for instance, expanded its primary education system following an increase in tax revenues (Colistete, 2016). Despite the existence of groups in favour of further decentralization of education matters to local governments, initiatives in that direction were short-lived. According to Colistete (2016), the lack of decentralization likely limited the expansion of mass education in the state of São Paulo.

Immigration was the second channel. In the mid-nineteenth century, coffee plantations relied predominantly on slave labour, but the situation changed with the gradual demise of the slave trade and the arrival of immigrants (Graham, 1983). Most newcomers were Italian and Iberian, but a significant contingent of German, Lebanese, Japanese and other immigrant groups arrived in Brazil during that period (Levy, 1974; Stolz et al., 2013). Musacchio et al. (2014) pointed out that Brazil attracted the poorest Europeans, with lower levels of education, but even these poor migrant groups had on average better access to schooling in their countries of origin than in Brazil. In fact, Stolz et al. (2013) found that nineteenth-century immigrants in general possessed higher skills than native Brazilians according to numeracy measures.

Several studies showed a positive long-term impact of immigration on Brazilian education (De Carvalho Filho & Colistete, 2010; De Carvalho Filho & Monasterio, 2012; Rocha et al., 2017; Witzel de Souza, 2018). Rocha et al. (2017), for instance, found that municipalities in the state of São Paulo that received immigrants presented higher levels of schooling and income. In addition, communities that received skilled migrants (and therefore had a higher initial level of human capital stock), took more advantage of the industrialization process years later (Rocha et al., 2017).

The story told so far naturally needs qualifying in some respects: foreign groups were heterogeneous and some migrants 'had little concern about the education of their offspring' (Witzel de Souza, 2019: 242). On the other hand, Colistete (2016) revealed that several illiterate people, including locals and migrants, signed petitions to the government asking for schools. In spite of these qualifications, on the whole, immigrant groups apparently demanded more schooling than the locals. On the other hand, immigrants apparently had a larger impact through supply rather than demand, as part of the literature has emphasized (De Carvalho Filho & Colistete, 2010; Rocha et al., 2017; Witzel de Souza, 2018). Among immigrant groups, Japanese and German communities were especially active on the supply side through the foundation of schools, which is probably related to the higher literacy rates among immigrants from these communities (Kreutz, 2000; Witzel de Souza, 2019).

3 Sweden, 1870–1910

3.1 Background

As pointed out in the introduction, Sweden could hardly be characterized as a modern country in the early nineteenth century. Nevertheless, by that time, an impressive agricultural transformation had begun with the large-scale redistribution of land, as the old open-field system was replaced by private ownership of land, agricultural as well as forested. In addition, extensive land reclamation took place, and new crops were introduced, in particular potatoes. As a result, agricultural production increased rapidly, which stimulated the domestic proto-industry. Another result was growing social differences, as landowners tended to become fairly well-to-do, whereas the landless, day-workers and other agricultural workers increased substantially in numbers. Another feature in nineteenth-century Sweden was rapid population growth, which resulted in substantial emigration from the 1860s onwards. The country benefitted from fortunate factor endowments, as timber and iron were in particular demand from the industrializing regions of Western Europe. This induced industrialization on a modest scale from the mid-nineteenth century, including steam-powered sawmills and large-scale converters for iron production. From the 1870s, industrialization became more widespread as the successful agricultural sector demanded industrial products. The construction of railways from the 1850s onwards also contributed to such demand. Much of the demand was directed towards the mechanical industry, which soon became a leading sector in the Swedish economy.

One important factor for future development was that by 1800 almost all Swedes, women as well as men, already possessed limited literacy. This was the result of a massive literacy campaign launched in the eighteenth century. The campaign, motivated by religious reasons, was carried out almost completely without schools. Instead, the main responsibility lay with the parents through the so-called home instruction. To ensure that the necessary skills were taught, the vicar in each parish held catechetical examinations on a regular basis. These included reading specified religious texts and knowledge of prayers and hymns (Johansson, 1987).

3.2 Education Reforms in the Nineteenth Century

From the early nineteenth century, however, the system of home instruction was considered inadequate. In 1842, the Swedish *Riksdag* decided to introduce primary schools throughout the country. The decision meant that every parish should have at least one school and, in addition, defined a minimum standard of knowledge and skills that all pupils should attain (Westberg, 2014). But the decision did not define to what extent children had to participate in primary schools. As a result, there existed large variations in access to schooling and the quality of schools. Most of the costs of schooling fell on the local parishes, and their ability and willingness to defray such costs varied. Instead of an ordinary primary school (*folkskola*), a parish could opt for less-expensive alternatives. The 'minor school' (*småskola*), where pupils seldom spent more than two or three years in school, was one option. In sparsely populated parishes, there could even be ambulatory schools with a teacher travelling between villages (Ljungberg & Nilsson, 2009). As Johannes Westberg (2019) has pointed out, this meant that most children received only a basic education, consisting of reading, writing, arithmetic and religious knowledge.

Still, the level of education they received increased gradually, from 3.3 school years on average in 1870 to 4.0 school years in 1910 (Lee & Lee, 2016). The increasing number of years that children spent in school meant that other subjects were also taught, mainly history and geography at an elementary level. From 1877 practical subjects were also taught: woodwork for boys and needlework for girls.

Engineers played a crucial role during industrialization, not least in the Second Industrial Revolution (Fox & Guagnini, 1999; Mokyr, 2017). In Sweden, the best engineers were educated at the two technical colleges in Stockholm and Gothenburg founded in 1826 and 1876,[7] respectively (Ahlström, 1982; Torstendahl, 1975). These students were recruited from grammar schools or from the four technical schools that were founded in the 1850s and 1860s (Lundh Nilsson & Grönberg, 2019). Primary schools were more important for people who applied for other types of school. That included the technical schools, mentioned above, but also training facilities in new activities, including postal services, the telegraph and the railway. From the 1860s, schools were also founded to provide specially trained personnel for the agricultural sector, including dairy schools and 'yeomen schools' (*lantmannaskolor*) (Nilsson, 2008). These schools were part and parcel of a bigger movement, namely the founding of a large number of Folk high schools from the 1860s onwards. These schools provided secondary education to a large number of young men and women in rural areas. In addition to theoretical courses, the schools often also had agrarian practical courses. In the towns, and at a lower level of skill provision, the so-called Sunday and evening schools in basic vocational education expanded from the 1870s onwards. In the beginning, these schools mainly provided further training in writing and arithmetic, but as the standard in primary schools improved, more time could be devoted to actual vocational training in these schools (Nilsson, 2008). In addition, several mechanical enterprises functioned in reality as a sort of 'training centre' for mechanics, smiths and other skilled workers, and access to them in turn contributed to the expansion of several other branches of industry. As a result of all these training opportunities, the skills of many young workers increased (Lundh Nilsson, 2007).

[7] The technical college in Gothenburg was founded as early as 1829 but the school was initially more a vocational school. In 1850, an 'upper part' was added, with high-quality technical education lasting three to four years.

From a gender perspective, boys and girls received almost the same education in primary school.[8] But at all other levels, there were big differences. The prestigious State grammar schools were closed to girls for a long time. Instead, they could attend the Girls' schools that had existed since the beginning of the nineteenth century. Their primary target of these schools was to raise girls to become wives and mothers, but in most cases the education was more comprehensive than this. Many girls who were educated in these schools could enter 'respectable' jobs in the service sector, for example in the postal service or telegraph companies, or work as a governess or teacher (Richardson, 2004). The vast majority of the Girls' schools were private and it was quite costly for a family to put a girl through such schools. From 1874 state grants were given, which increased the popularity of the Girls' schools. Starting in 1905, new educational opportunities opened up for girls. That year, the grammar schools were divided into upper and lower secondary schools. The lower secondary school was called *realskola* and many (but far from all) of these became open to girls. After 1905, an increasing number of municipalities also introduced lower secondary schools, where girls as well as boys were admitted. In 1909 municipal intermediary schools were started. They corresponded to lower secondary schools and were open to both boys and girls. Thus by 1910 girls had access to most of the schools at the lower secondary level. But the state-run upper secondary grammar schools remained closed to girls until 1927.

3.3 Education, Globalization and Modernization

The preceding paragraphs clearly demonstrate that an increasing amount of human capital was formed during the second half of the nineteenth century. One crucial question is to what extent this was useful in the transformation of Swedish society. By and large, both the early industrialization and the transformation of agriculture could be achieved without large amounts of human capital. Most of the tasks involved were well-known and mainly involved manual labour. On the other hand, the increasing 'sophistication' (Sandberg, 1979) meant that the recruitment base for

[8] As we have seen, boys and girls had separate courses in the practical subjects, and there is some anecdotal evidence that girls received less education in history and geography (Aquilonius, 1942).

further studies became larger. And well-educated specialists were needed in many areas.

The background to the demand for skills of various types was the accelerating industrialization that took place in Sweden from the 1870s. As mentioned above, the country had benefitted from exporting primary products to Western Europe. This had generated income and demand for industrial goods. The ongoing agricultural transformation had also resulted in increasing income and a demand for industrial goods from the agricultural sector (Schön, 2000).

With the advent of the Second Industrial Revolution towards the end of the nineteenth century, the advantages of having a literate population, skilled industrial workers and a large number of engineers became obvious. The country possessed the technological capability to make use of the strong stream of international inventions and improvements in the industrial sector. A large number of new enterprises were founded in various branches: pulp and paper, textiles, shoemaking and the graphics industry. But the most important element of all was the mechanical industry, and several companies that were founded in the late nineteenth century were soon among the leading companies in their field, for example ASEA (now part of ABB) in the electrical industry, LM Ericsson (now Ericsson) in telecommunications, and SKF, which made ball bearings. Most of the new companies, however, concentrated on the domestic market. Growing towns stimulated the demand for processed food, ready-made clothing, shoes, in addition to new consumer goods such as bicycles. As a result of all these changes, economic growth increased very fast. It is estimated that Sweden's GDP grew by 2.4% annually between 1890 and 1910. That figure was higher than other European countries' and even exceeded that of the USA (Schön, 2000).

4 Comparative Analysis 1870–1930

Brazil and Sweden were both deeply affected by the first wave of globalization, not least by the expanding possibilities for migration, but the patterns for the countries were completely different. When discussing the factors behind Sweden's high growth rate (which was to continue from 1910 until 1930), Lennart Schön's analysis is quite plausible. From the 1880s onwards Sweden had a high emigration rate, which meant that the labour supply in Sweden grew slowly. At the same time, capital imports were very high. Relative factor prices changed in favour of labour, i.e.

real wages increased substantially, with two important consequences. One was that the demand for consumption goods increased, which further stimulated industrial production for the domestic market. The other, more important consequence, was that companies tried as far as possible to replace labour with capital. The resulting productivity growth was a central part of the high GDP growth rate (Schön, 2000). The previous discussion on education and human capital formation in the second half of the nineteenth century supplements the analysis. Companies were more likely to increase the wages of skilled labourers, who as we have seen were available in larger numbers. Even unskilled labour possessed some human capital and was, for example, able to read and understand written work instructions. This good access to human capital was thus, from an international perspective, an important factor in the economic modernization of Sweden in the period 1870–1910.

In Brazil, by contrast, access to human capital was very limited. This helps to explain why that country's response to increasing foreign demand was different from Sweden's. Both countries possessed natural resources that could be exploited without large amounts of human capital: timber and iron in Sweden; coffee and rubber in Brazil. The large inequalities in Brazil meant, however, that domestic demand for everyday industrial products remained low. Thus there was little stimulus for domestic industrial production, and more sophisticated industrial products were almost impossible to manufacture without substantial amounts of human capital, precisely what Brazil lacked. Sweden, on the other hand, had a less unequal distribution of income and better access to human capital. Domestic demand factors as well as domestic supply thus favoured industrial production early on, and gave Sweden good prerequisites for active participation in the Second Industrial Revolution. During this period, Brazil remained chiefly an exporter of primary products.

Another crucial difference between Brazil and Sweden was migration flows. Whereas Sweden was a country of emigration, i.e. an 'exporter' of labour and skills, Brazil exhibited the opposite characteristics. In Brazil, even though immigrants on average possessed only limited amounts of human capital, they represented an important contribution, since the human capital level among Brazilians was abysmally low. On the other hand, the huge contingent of migrants contributed to the persistence of low salaries.

The literate population was also an important factor for the political development and in the emergence of a strong civil society in Sweden.

On the political level, widespread literacy was important above all in local politics. In the course of the nineteenth century, parishes became more autonomous in relation to the State. Poor relief and, after 1842, primary schools were the responsibility of the parishes, and in 1862 further important changes took place. The parish was divided into two separate organizations; the parish 'proper' handled all Church affairs and education matters including primary schools. The other organization, the 'civil' parish (*kommun*) was given responsibility for all matters that were important to the inhabitants of the *kommun*. The *kommun* also gained the right to raise necessary taxes, and voting rights were given to all men who paid taxes. However, the right to vote was graded by the level of taxes the voter paid, which meant that in some parishes a single person could possess the majority of votes. The local autonomy increased the value of being literate in several ways. Voters could get information from written material. Each *kommun* set up several committees to prepare and decide in internal matters and it was of necessary to be literate to sit on these committees. The *kommun* also set up an administration, albeit quite rudimentary in the beginning, which provided work for literate people.

In the long run, the relationship between local autonomy and education was very important, but more immediate effects can be observed in the popular movements that grew strong during the second half of the nineteenth century. These movements, which included the temperance movement, the Free Churches, and (a little later) the trade unions, recruited hundreds of thousands of members and performed extremely important tasks in civil society. They depended on the knowledge and skills of their members and this is where literacy and education come in. The members were all literate and thus able to read pamphlets, newspapers and books published by the popular movements. They were also able to write minutes in meetings and formulate speeches and petitions. Such specialized skills were not taught in primary schools, so the popular movements had to provide active members with training in these matters. They organized courses and even set up their own Folk high schools. In fact, the popular movements could be regarded as centres for further education that enabled many people to take up important positions in the political arena.

By contrast there were few incentives for the formation of a strong civil society in Brazil. Attempts to increase local autonomy were ill-fated according to Colistete's (2016) study on education in São Paulo. Provinces (and later states under the Republic) were responsible for most decisions that affected people's daily lives. Since literacy was required, voting rights were highly restricted—suffrage never surpassed 5.7% of the population until 1930 (Love, 1970). Moreover, local elites often resorted to vote corralling schemes to manipulate elections (Nunes Leal, 1975). On the other hand, the urban labour sector was becoming a more significant social force in response to increasing industrialization, as demonstrated by the organization of the first general strike in 1917.

5 Brazil 1945–1973

5.1 *Structural and Political Change*

Facing the closure of world markets in the 1930s, Brazil engaged more fully with an import-substituting industrialization (ISI) strategy: a set of policies to restrict imports of manufactured goods and promote domestic industries—often through protection and state-led investment. The policies initiated in the 1930s were extended after World War Two. Between 1945 and 1980, the country reported high rates of economic growth (7.3% per annum on average) and even higher rates of industrial growth (8.8%). Industrial activities outstripped agriculture as a proportion of national output in the 1950s (Aldrighi & Colistete, 2015; see Chapter 5). This period also witnessed a significant growth of labour productivity in Brazil (Ark & Timmer, 2001). Primary exports, nonetheless, still retained an important role given the high anti-export bias of the Brazilian manufacturing sector (Doellinger, 1973). Economic growth was associated with the allocation of labour towards more productive activities and urbanization: a clear example is the rise of migration from the historically poorer north-east to the industrial south-east. The rapid industrialization created a large industrial labour force in cities. Unlike Sweden, however, labour relations were confrontational and far removed from the 'social compact for growth' in Western Europe (Colistete, 2007).

The world economic crisis contributed to political turmoil in the early 1930s. A coup led to the fall of the First Republic, and Getúlio Vargas, who had been defeated in the presidential election, took over the government. This period under Vargas' rule (1930–1945) is characterized by several institutional changes with increasing centralization and state intervention in the economy.[9] The country returned to democracy in 1945, but ISI policies remained a key aspect, as state intervention and industrialization were hailed as a crucial instrument to overcome underdevelopment at the time. In the second half of the 1950s, the Kubitschek administration deepened the ISI strategy through the *Programa de Metas*, a big push industrialization programme. Despite success in achieving economic growth, the costs of the programme were mostly felt some years later, when political conditions were highly sensitive; the early 1960s witnessed intense political unrest as the Cold War escalated in Latin America, particularly after the Cuban Revolution in 1959. The left-wing government of João Goulart inherited rising inflation and external debt, a consequence of the expensive investment programme in the 1950s. After increasing political polarization, the military ousted Goulart and took over the government in April 1964.

The regime change did not mean the rejection of ISI. Despite carrying out several institutional reforms and anti-inflation policies from 1964 to 1967, the military administrations forcefully stimulated industrialization during the most repressive period under dictatorship between 1968 and 1973. Expansionary policies led the average rate of economic growth to reach 11.1% per annum during this period. The 'economic miracle', however, was halted by the oil crisis in 1973.[10]

5.2 *Increasing Demand for Education*

The country continued its modernization process in the post-war era, but mass education kept lagging behind (Birdsall et al., 1996; Frankema, 2009; Kang, 2017; Plank, 1996; Wjuniski, 2013). In 1945, more than half the population was still illiterate and the average schooling of the working age population was approximately 1.8 years (Barro & Lee, 2013). The gross enrolment ratio in primary schooling was 54.6% while the middle school enrolment rate was only 3.3% (Lee & Lee, 2016).

[9] The Vargas period (1930–1945) is formally divided into three stages: provisional (1930–1934), constitutional (1934–1937) and the openly autocratic *Estado Novo* (1937–1945).

[10] The country managed to keep the ISI strategy alive until the second oil shock, but the second oil shock and the subsequent debt crisis hit the Brazilian economy in the late 1970s/early 1980s.

The return to democracy was followed by an increase in enrolment rates after 1945. In the case of primary education (*ensino primário*), there was at least a fivefold increase in absolute enrolments during the period. The gross enrolment ratio in primary education increased from 54.6% in 1945 to 87.1% in 1965 according to Lee and Lee (2016). The latter figure does not mean that almost 90% of children aged between 7 and 11 years were enrolled at primary schools. Far from it, the *gross* measure included many older children who were stuck at the primary level, since some students entered late in school and repetition rates were astoundingly high in Brazil (Ribeiro, 1991; Schiefelbein, 1975). In fact, nearly 40% of the population aged between 5 and 14 years did not attend school in 1960.

The former middle school (*ensino médio*) level witnessed an even larger expansion during the period: enrolment increased from 377,976 to 2,154,430 students between 1945 and 1965. The gross enrolment rate, which had reached 3.3% in 1945, increased to 11.1% in 1965 (Lee & Lee, 2016).[11] In spite of the impressive enrolment growth in two decades, the country still failed to educate a large fraction of the school-age population.

The increase in secondary-level graduates, however, heightened the pressure on the higher education system. In 1945, the gross enrolment rate in higher education was only 0.3% (Lee & Lee, 2016). After pressure from middle- and upper-class families, the system was expanded in 1968 (Ames, 1973; De Mattos, 1988; Kang, 2019). However, this came at a cost since it siphoned off resources from other education programmes, as described in the next section.

Despite the general delay in the expansion of mass education, the distribution of enrolments was at least egalitarian in pre-tertiary education. Girls comprised 48.9% of the enrolments in primary education in 1945 and 49.7% in 1970. The situation was similar in higher schooling levels: girls made up the majority in high schools and represented 52.5% of enrolments in 1970. In fact, the patterns were similar in several Latin American countries. Frankema (2009) argued that the high proportions of female enrolments were related to income inequality in Latin America: richer families had enough resources to send all their children to school, irrespective of gender, while poorer ones could not afford to send any of

[11] From 1970 onwards, Lee and Lee's (2016) figures consider the new eight-grade primary level (after the 1971 reform). These figures cannot be compared to earlier periods.

them. However, similar patterns of enrolments could be found in most Western countries around the mid-twentieth century. More research is needed to understand the high proportions of female enrolments in Brazil and Latin America in the period.

5.3 Conflicts and Changes in the Education System

The 1946 Constitution called for a Law of Directives and Bases (*Lei de Diretrizes e Bases—LDB*) to organize the national education system. The Minister of Education sent a draft to the National Congress in 1948, but disputes over financial support to private/religious schools paralysed the decision-making process for 13 years. After some concessions that allowed private schools to receive government subsidies, the LDB was approved in late 1961.

Little was done to promote the expansion of mass education until the early 1960s. Perhaps this was to be expected, since states were mostly responsible for the provision of schooling (except for higher education). However, states were not able to finance the expansion of the system by themselves, as tax resources were concentrated in the hands of central government. Instead of increasing support for basic education, the central government focused on capital deepening industrialization policies at the expense of mass education, particularly during the 1950s (Kang, 2017). An illustrative example is the *Programa de Metas*: one of the architects of the programme admitted that education was included in the plan at the very last minute under pressure from the Minister of Education, Clóvis Salgado (Brasil—MEC, 1967). Nonetheless, the same minister asserted that central government *chose* to spend on tertiary education to meet industrialization needs, *at the expense* of other levels (Kang, 2017; Pires, 2010). Around that period, education expenditure per pupil in tertiary education was nearly 50 times higher than at the primary level (Lindert, 2010).

In the early 1960s, left-wing President Goulart advocated for extensive social reforms. In this context, enrolment growth in primary education accelerated during the period, which is probably related to the implementation of the LDB and the Goulart administration's support for mass education (Kang, 2017). In terms of adult education policy, Goulart called on the well-known educator Paulo Freire to coordinate the 1964 National Literacy Campaign, but his method was considered subversive, for attempting to produce 'a change in the consciousness' of students

(Kirkendall, 2010). The campaign never took off as the military coup took place later that year.

Despite the regime change, basic education received attention in the early years under military rule. Several technocrats who took positions in the new regime favoured the human capital approach and considered basic education as an important tool for increasing long-term economic growth (De Mattos, 1988). The military government initially deployed more resources for education in general and, after a wide-ranging tax reform that benefited all government levels, education funding increased permanently. As a result, spending and enrolments in primary and lower secondary education kept increasing from 1964 to 1973 (Kang, 2019).[12]

Two issues were among the priorities of the technocrats in charge of education matters: (i) decreasing illiteracy rates among adults and (ii) decreasing school dropout rates after the completion of primary education. These issues required changes at the primary and secondary levels. At that time, the school system was divided into elementary (four to six grades), middle (seven to eight grades) and higher education. The middle school (*ensino médio*) had several segments that included the more academic secondary school, as well as technical education (commercial, industrial, agricultural, etc.) and 'normal schools' (i.e. teacher training). Admission to secondary school required students to take an examination, which excluded many of them from advancing up the educational ladder. Secondary schools, in turn, trained students for the *vestibulares*, entrance examinations promoted by higher education institutions. The system was, therefore, highly elitist as only a few were able to progress to the higher education system.

As a consequence of this structure, there was a growing unmet demand for higher education among middle and upper classes, which later became a movement that demanded expansion of the higher education system. Despite the reservations of technocrats, this political pressure led to the Higher Education Reform in 1968. This reform created the conditions for a large increase in the number of available places in both the public and private higher education systems in the ensuing years (Ames, 1973; De Mattos, 1988).

The priority given to the expansion of the university system affected other education initiatives. The launch of a large-scale programme to

[12] Tax revenues increased from 16.0% of GDP in 1963 to 26.0% in 1969.

fight adult illiteracy (MOBRAL), which was supposed to start in 1967, was postponed to 1970. Furthermore, the Primary and Secondary Education Reform, which merged the former primary education to the lower secondary level, was only enacted in 1971. This reform created a new primary level comprised of eight grades (7–14 years old) and eliminated the former track system at the middle level. In its stead, vocational education started to be offered as part of a unified general secondary level. The reform also led to the gradual elimination of the entrance examination for the former lower secondary level. These changes did not however, lead to the universalization of the eight-grade primary level nor solved the issue of high repetition rates. These two problems were only addressed in the 1990s—after the extension of suffrage to illiterates and the consolidation of democracy.

5.4 Education and Modernization

Industrial activities, particularly the production of durable consumer goods, markedly increased between 1945 and 1973. The development of the automobile sector, a symbol of the period, was boosted by closing the market to imported vehicles, which attracted foreign direct investments from car companies such as Volkswagen, Ford and General Motors. The state of São Paulo was the epicentre of this structural transformation, and nearly half the industrial workforce was located here in 1960 (Colistete, 2001). Other sectors such as food products, metalworking, machinery, chemicals and pharmaceuticals also made important contributions to productivity growth throughout the period (Aldrighi & Colistete, 2015, see Chapter 5).

Since access to formal schooling was limited, the growing manufacturing sector had to count on specific industry training. Still under the *Estado Novo*, the manufacturing sector lobbied for the creation of the National Service of Industrial Apprenticeship (*Serviço Nacional de Aprendizagem Industrial*—SENAI) in 1942. SENAI was inspired by the German corporatist training experience, but run only by industrialists; labour representatives were voiceless. Nonetheless, SENAI received funds from the national government and became a major source of technical training for workers in sectors such as metalworking and textiles (Colistete, 2001). This solution to the scarcity of skilled workers may have met immediate needs, but was insufficient for the formation of a world-class competitive labour force.[13]

Structural transformations also led to a demographic boom. During the 1950s, the total population increased by 3.0% per annum on average, while in the 1960s annual population growth reached 2.9% on average (Hasenbalg, 2003). Urbanization also grew considerably: while 31% of the population lived in urban areas in 1940, the urbanization rate reached 56% in 1970. These changes led to an increase in the demand for schooling, but the supply side did not respond accordingly. As a result, the combination of rapid growth in the population and urbanization with low levels of schooling generated a large group of unskilled workers in urban areas, who were mostly employed in low-productivity informal sectors. The priority given to vocational and higher education proved to be short-sighted: the modest increase in average schooling levels between 1950 and 1980 only placed Brazil (3.1 years) in front of Haiti (2.1 years in 1980) among all the Latin American and Caribbean countries (Ferreira & Veloso, 2013).[14]

In labour markets, demand for skilled labour in the modern sectors increased, but education was consistently losing its race with technology (to use Tinbergen's apt expression). The consequences of income inequality are not hard to envisage. Rates of return estimates on schooling reveal the extent of the skills scarcity in the Brazilian economy. According to Langoni (1974), four years of schooling yielded a return of 48.1%, while completing eight years of schooling yielded a return of 23.8% in 1960. These and other results led Langoni to assert that the expansion of education was the most efficient means to increase long-term growth.[15]

[13] This does not deny the importance of SENAI. Former President Lula, a trade union leader, was trained at SENAI, like several of his colleagues, in the metallurgical sector (Weinstein, 1996).

[14] Barro and Lee (2013) may have underestimated average years of schooling figures in Brazil, particularly from 1970 to 1980. An ongoing research by Julia Walter and Thomas Kang has found 4.2 years in 1980. While the methodology of this study was specifically devised for Brazilian data and is not comparable to Barro and Lee's, the difference is large enough to call our attention. Nevertheless, 4.2 years is still a low level even bearing in mind Latin American standards at the time.

[15] The most important factor behind the rise in income inequality during the 1960s. Langoni may have overlooked the effect of the wage-setting policies of the military regime on inequality, as Fishlow (1972) pointed out, but his general point remains important.

Similarly, other markers of modernization and human development, such as health conditions, did not improve markedly during the period. Alongside a slow decrease in infant mortality rates, life expectancy in Brazil was lower than the figures presented by poorer countries such as Paraguay and Belize in 1960 (Ferreira & Veloso, 2013). Moreover, the number of unskilled workers occupying the outskirts of cities increased dramatically, living under poor conditions in terms of security, sanitation and social services. In a nutshell, economic growth and industrialization came with restricted schooling and limited modernization in Brazil.

6 Sweden 1945–1973

6.1 *Structural Changes in Society and Economy*

After the Second World War, the world economy recovered within a few years and during the following quarter-century the economic growth rate was higher than ever before in the industrialized countries. Sweden took part in that development. The country had managed to remain neutral during World War Two, with intact production capacity and without loss in manpower. It could also, like other West European countries, take advantage of the technological lead the USA had created, by borrowing, buying or renting new technology. In addition, the emerging international institutions increasingly favoured movements of trade and capital, which were essential to a small, export-oriented country such as Sweden.

As a result of these favourable circumstances Sweden's GDP per capita grew by 3.2% annually between 1950 and 1973 (Schön, 2000). The basic reason was rising productivity made possible by the technological catch-up with the USA. In addition, structural changes took place that favoured the growth rate. Branches with lower productivity, such as the textile industry, could not remain competitive and more or less disappeared. These and other changes in the economic structure facilitated the conversion of some of the economic growth into continuous wage increases throughout the period. The strong trade unions were able to reach favourable collective agreements with the employers; in return there was peace and stability for a very long time in the Swedish labour market (Lundh, 2002). The agricultural sector went through a rationalization process and shrank considerably. Small farms were abandoned or combined into larger units, and the net effects were higher productivity but far fewer employed in agriculture.

High economic growth also generated resources for the service sector. The Social Democratic Party, which had been in power since the mid-1930s, launched numerous social reforms that became known as the Welfare State. These included a general, i.e. non-means tested, family allowance in 1948, general sick assurance in 1955 and a reformed pension system in 1959, to name some of the most important ingredients. The end result was a massive transfer system that was further expanded in the 1960s and 1970s, leading to substantial growth of the public sector. But the public sector grew for other reasons, too. Large investments were made in infrastructure, in particular roads, telecommunications and electricity networks. Healthcare was a public undertaking and expanded rapidly, especially from the 1960s, with zero or low costs to the individual. From the perspective of this paper, the high spending on education is of particular interest. All levels of the education system expanded at a quick pace, with no cost to the individual. It should be added that private services also expanded, for example in banking and retail. The expansion of the service sector led to rising demand for labour with a diverse range of skills and this had repercussions for the demand for education.

6.2 *Increasing Demand for Education*

In parallel with investigations and political discussions during the 1940s, 1950s and 1960s, popular demand for education increased markedly. The number of graduates from lower secondary school increased from about 7000 in 1940 to about 28,000 in 1960 (Richardson, 2004). Most of them continued to upper secondary, technical or commercial schools (Ohlsson, 1986).[16] But many of those who completed all eight years in elementary school also continued their education, albeit in more practical forms. Folk high schools (*folkhögskolor*)[17] became increasingly popular,

[16] In 1960, about 45% of the graduates from lower secondary school continued to upper secondary school and about 15% to technical or commercial schools (Ohlsson, 1986, figures X:4 and X:5).

[17] The first Folk high schools (*folkhögskolor)* were founded in Denmark, based on Grundtvig's ideas on citizenship for the rural masses. In Sweden, the first schools were established in 1868. Citizenship as well as practical knowledge in agriculture were core subjects in the Swedish schools. The concept was later used also by other organizations; in 1901, for example, the labour movement (Social democratic party and the trade unions) founded a Folk high school (Lundh Nilsson & Nilsson, 2010).

but above all the number of full-time students in vocational education increased substantially, in particular after 1950.

One could rightfully pose the question why the demand for education of all kinds increased after the Second World War. In the interwar years, the situation had been almost the opposite. One fundamental reason for the demand for education was structural changes in the labour market. The Swedish economy experienced a number of boom years, with a higher demand for labour as a result. That demand was concentrated in particular on skilled and semi-skilled workers and included both the manufacturing industry and the service sector. A second factor was that Sweden had become significantly richer since the interwar years. This meant that a teenager's income was becoming of little or no importance to a family's income, which allowed them to continue their education. Thus, there were minimal obstacles for young people who wanted to qualify for better-paid jobs in the future. A third factor was related to the first, the structural changes in the labour market. Those changes were not only noted but actively promoted by politicians at the national and local levels. For that reason alone politicians were willing to spend a lot of money on education. In addition, the ruling Social Democrats in particular saw education as an important tool for the promotion of a more equal society.

6.3 *Transformation of the Education System*

After World War Two, Sweden, like the rest of Europe, lagged behind the USA in several respects, including technological knowledge and human capital in general (Goldin & Katz, 2008). That had been apparent even before the war, and action was taken in two separate ways. The first action concerned vocational education and training. The Swedish system for vocational training was in poor shape and the labour market organizations (the Employers' Federation and the blue-collar trade union movement) agreed to set up a joint council to develop and promote vocational education. In some ways, they tried to copy the German corporatist and apprentice-based system. But apprenticeships never became very popular among young people and in the 1950s the labour market organizations became less involved in vocational training. Instead, the State took the initiative by giving generous financing to municipal vocational schools. The result was a very diverse 'system'. Apprentice-based training still existed in many companies, and the municipal courses and programmes vary in length, from less than six months up to four years.

A large number of courses, mainly attended by young adults, were part-time (Nilsson, 2014). That diversity ended with the reform of secondary education discussed below.

The second action concerned reforms in primary and lower secondary education. During the war period, a very extensive investigation of the school system was carried out. This was followed by a School Commission, which presented proposals for a new school system that started a political struggle that lasted most of the 1950s. The proposals meant that the existing *parallel school system* was to be replaced by a *comprehensive* one. In the parallel system, pupils could leave elementary school[18] after four or six grades and continue their studies in lower secondary grammar schools (*realskola*). Successful studies at this level gave pupils access to upper secondary schools and technical schools and commercial schools. Most pupils, however, remained in the elementary school. In addition, the gender-based parallel system with Girls' schools (discussed above) still existed, although girls had access to upper secondary grammar schools since 1927. These schools were mainly frequented by girls from the middle classes, whose parents wanted to give them a 'proper upbringing'. Girls' schools were quite popular, but to an increasing extent also considered to be outdated. They were gradually dismantled after the decision to implement the comprehensive school system in 1962 (Richardson, 2004).

After a long political debate, the decision to replace elementary schools, lower secondary schools and girls' schools with comprehensive schools was taken in 1957 and after a transition period, it was fully implemented by 1962. Comprehensive schools have nine grades with a (virtually) common curriculum for everyone, and schooling begins at the age of seven. The basic structure has remained almost intact since its introduction in 1962 (Richardson, 2004).

The next step was to reform the upper secondary school level, which consisted of general upper secondary school, technical school, commercial school and vocational school. The first three types of school had a similar structure with three or four years of full-time studies that prepared pupils for white-collar jobs or higher studies. Vocational schools were, as we have seen, very diverse. Most of the vocational education prepared for blue-collar jobs, and with a few exceptions these programmes did not

[18] The elementary school built on the previous primary school, which was extended to seven grades in the 1930s and 1940s and to eight grades in the early 1950s.

qualify pupils for higher studies. The political struggle concerned whether to integrate vocational education with the other, more theoretical, forms of education. Since the labour market organizations had a very strong influence on vocational education, their position was crucial for the decision to actually include vocational education. The end result, called the integrated upper secondary school, was launched in 1971. It consisted of a blend of two-year programmes, which were either theoretical or practical (Richardson, 2004). The latter programmes more or less replaced vocational schools.[19] In addition, there were three-year programmes that replaced the previous upper secondary schools, commercial schools and technical schools.[20]

During the period 1945–1973, the gender compositison in the education system began to change. In the early twentieth century, male dominance was strong. In 1910, female graduates constituted 22% at the lower secondary level and 12% at the upper secondary level. In 1945, the male predominance had almost disappeared in lower secondary education and females made up 47% of graduates that year. In 1951, the gender composition was absolutely even, and after that, the female proportion increased to 53% in 1960.[21] At the upper secondary level,[22] a similar process started a little later. In 1945, 32% of graduates were female. Their share started to increase from 1952, when females constituted 36% of graduates. By the mid-1960s, the mix was almost even, when 48% of graduates from upper secondary schools were female (Promemorier från SCB, 1977).

The result of the reforms in education was, above all, an increase in attainment. The average number of years in school among adults rose from 6.5 in 1945 to 9.6 in 1975. The bulk of the increase was in secondary education, which increased from 1.5 to 3.7 years of schooling (Lee & Lee, 2016). The increasing share of young women in secondary

[19] Part-time vocational courses were not included. Instead, they became the bulk of a new form of schools, called municipal education for adults, which started in 1968 (Nilsson, 2014).

[20] For students in the technical programme, there also existed a fourth, optional, year, mainly for those who wanted to enter the labour market rather than continue studies in technical colleges or universities.

[21] With the transformation of the education system discussed above, the lower secondary level became part of the mandatory comprehensive school.

[22] The figures refer to general, commercial and technical upper secondary school.

education is reflected in average years of schooling at that level; for women it increased by 269% whereas it went up by 224% for men. All in all it meant that human capital was available in much higher quantities than before.

6.4 Education and Modernization

It is not an easy task to disentangle education and modernization in the post-war period, since education constituted an integrated part of the modernization process. We can, however, discuss a number of areas where education strengthened various processes of modernization, but also how such processes influenced the demand for education.

Manufacturing industry had already become the dominant sector of the Swedish economy before the war and that position became even more pronounced in the 1950s and 1960s. Opportunities to borrow and modify foreign technology were realized by the large and increasing number of engineers that graduated from technical universities, colleges and schools. This development was particularly noticeable in the mechanical industry, where several old and new companies took prominent positions in the world market: ASEA in electrical equipment, SKF in ball bearings, Götaverken and Kockums in shipbuilding and Volvo in cars and trucks, to name but a few. The success of these and a multitude of other companies in the mechanical industry was further favoured by the increasing availability of skilled and semi-skilled workers from the vocational schools. In a similar vein, the success of the pharmaceutical industry was closely connected to the increase in the number of graduates from medical schools and science departments at the universities (Norgren, 1989). At the same time, the existence of successful companies that could offer secure and well-paid jobs, encouraged people to undertake several years of education and training. A very different example is seen in the important forestry industry. Here, productivity increased markedly with the introduction of chainsaws in the late 1940s. In this case, the necessary training to master the new tool only took a couple of weeks, but it is still an example of how education contributed to modernization (Lundh Nilsson, 2013).

The interaction between education and modernization is perhaps even more obvious in the public sector, where the construction of the welfare state required a large number of well-educated workers: teachers, doctors, nurses, social workers and administrators. The continuous expansion of the public sector meant that the jobs offered were attractive and encouraged young people to apply for the education needed. A similar development took place in urban planning. Sweden was undergoing rapid urbanization, which created demand for planners, architects and construction workers. Outside the public sector, companies in private services also demanded educated workers and could offer good positions. In short, education played an important role in the modernization of Sweden after the Second World War, and modernization stimulated people to educate themselves at a high rate. The positive effects are clear in the wage premium for jobs in education, which was quite high (about 8%) in Sweden during the 1960s (Björklund et al., 2010). Other studies based on less comprehensive wage material indicate the wage premium was also high in the 1940s and 1950s (Ohlsson, 1986). But in the 1970s the wage premium plummeted to only about 4% in 1980, partly as a result of the economic crisis in the 1970s, and partly because of the very high supply of graduates in the 1960s.

7 Comparative Analysis 1945–1973

Brazil and Sweden exhibited large differences during this period. One extremely important difference concerned the overall economic policy. Brazil continued its import-substitution strategy, shielded itself partly from the world market and tried to build a strong industrial base. To some extent, this inward-looking strategy modernized the country in several respects but, partly because of insufficient human capital, the industrial products were not competitive in the world market. Even in the domestic market, a significant proportion of Brazilian manufacturers was only competitive behind high tariff walls. Sweden, by contrast, seized the opportunities that the increasing world trade provided and much of the prosperity that the population experienced during the period was a result of the very successful export industries.

There were also major differences in the education area. The most striking difference is of course the large and persistent illiteracy rate in Brazil, which was non-existent in Sweden. Widespread illiteracy implies low levels of human capital formation, since it excludes a large part of the population from basic as well as further education. In addition, it made participation in political life more difficult, since literacy was a prerequisite to vote in Brazil up to 1988.

There are, nevertheless, some interesting parallel developments in the educational field. The drawn-out debates in the 1950s concerning the structure of the education system exhibit some common traits. In both countries, progressive forces (*Escola Nova* and left-wing political parties, respectively) stood against more established interests (proponents for religious and private schools and right-wing political interests). Although the debated topics were somewhat different in the two countries, the outcome was quite similar: an extended elementary education, corresponding to primary and lower secondary schooling, followed by non-compulsory upper secondary training consisting of both theoretical and vocational options. The new systems were clearly inspired by the American high-school model, but did not solve all problems in the education system. Although the 1971 reform formally inserted vocational education into the school system in both countries, results were disappointing. In Sweden, the new system was criticized only a few years after the reform (Lundahl, 1997) and in many ways, the inclusion of vocational education in upper secondary school has remained problematic (Olofsson, 2005). In Brazil, the outcome was even worse. Vocational education was left aside during the last few decades, and the problem remains: debates on the curricula of the secondary education remain alive in Brazil.

8 Concluding Remarks

We noted in the introduction that Sweden was an 'impoverished sophisticate' at the time when industrialization started on a larger scale, and this was probably one of the factors behind the rapid growth in the decades surrounding 1900. In Brazil, the opportunities created by globalization in the same period benefitted the spread of education, but for various reasons only at a limited rate. For a long time, education was clearly not a top priority among Brazilian policy-makers. As shown in the introduction, by 1970 Brazil still had not achieved the level of average years of schooling that Sweden had reached a century earlier.

We consider it very likely that the large resources spent on the education system in Sweden at certain points in time contributed to the fast and thorough modernization of Sweden. The introduction of a nationwide system of primary schools in the mid-nineteenth century meant that the country had a sufficient supply of human capital to take advantage of the First Globalization and successfully take part in the Second Industrial Revolution. In a similar fashion, the massive investments in education during the 1950s and 1960s facilitated the country's participation in the rapidly growing world trade and the export industries were dependent on skilled labour. Unlike Sweden, few resources were devoted to primary and secondary education in Brazil. The country relied for a long time on the production and export of primary materials, where skilled labour was less important. The import-substitution strategy that was prevalent for a long time also meant that only a small part of the workforce had to be skilled. Most Brazilian companies were sheltered from world markets through exceptionally high tariffs, which may have dampened the demand for skills.

This is reflected in the attempts to solve skill shortages in manufacturing industry during and after the Second World War. At that time, industrialists in Brazil and the labour market organizations in Sweden were both promoting apprentice-based blue-collar labour training. Thus, in both countries it was interest groups rather than the State that tried to reform parts of the education system. In the long run, company-based training proved to be insufficient in both countries, but the reactions were different. In Sweden, policy-makers took new initiatives and created an extensive school-based system for vocational education. Such training was not as thorough as the apprentice-based training but was sufficient for many tasks in the Swedish economy at the time. A similar development did not take place in Brazil, which reflects the relatively smaller interest in education matters in that country.

In conclusion, education seems to have played somewhat different roles in response to globalization forces and modernization in the two countries. In Brazil, education expanded as a weak and delayed *response* to the challenges posed by globalization. In our first period, the response did not come until the very end, in the 1920s when the international challenges were weaker than before the Great War. Also during our second period, the educational response in Brazil was late. Thus, education did not play an important role in the limited modernization that took place in the hundred-year period from the 1870s to the 1970s. In Sweden by contrast, education was an *integral part* of modernization processes that were strengthened by globalization forces. The country's head start, with a relative abundance of human capital even before the onset of industrialization, was an asset, and it was even more so between 1945 and 1970, when education played a vital role in the building of the welfare state.

References

Abreu, M. P., & Lago, L. A. C. (2014). A economia brasileira no Império, 1822–1889. In M. P. Abreu (Ed.), *A Ordem do Progresso*. Campus.

Ahlström, G. (1982). *Engineers and industrial growth*. Croon Helm.

Alden, D. (1987). Late colonial Brazil (1750–1808). In L. Bethell (Ed.), *Colonial Brazil*. Cambridge University Press. https://doi.org/10.1017/CHOL9780521395250.033

Aldrighi, D., & Colistete, R. P. (2015). Industrial growth and structural change: Brazil in a long-run perspective. In W. A. Naudé, A. Szirmai, & N. Haraguchi (Eds.), *Structural change and industrial development in the BRICS*. Oxford University Press. https://doi.org/10.1093/acprof:oso/9780198725077.003.0007

Allen, R. C. (2011). *Global economic history: A very short introduction*. Oxford University Press.

Ames, B. (1973). *Rhetoric and reality in a militarized regime: Brazil since 1964*. Sage Publications (CA).

Aquilonius, K. (1942), *Svenska folkskolans historia, andra delen. Det svenska folkundervisningsväsendet 1809–1860*. Albert Bonniers förlag.

Ark, B., & Timmer, M. (2001). The ICOP manufacturing database: International comparisons of productivity levels. *International Productivity Monitor, 3*, 44–51.

Barro, R. J., & Lee, J.-W. (1993). International comparisons of educational attainment. *Journal of Monetary Economics, 32*(3), 363–394. https://doi.org/10.1016/0304-3932(93)90023-9

Barro, R. & Lee, J.-W. (2013). A New Data Set of Educational Attainment in the World, 1950–2010. *Journal of Development Economics*, 104, 184–198. https://doi.org/10.1016/j.jdeveco.2012.10.001

Bethell, L., & Carvalho, J. M. (1995). Brazil, 1822–1850. In L. Bethell (Ed.), *The Cambridge History of Latin America*. Cambridge University Press (pp. 305–311). https://doi.org/10.1017/CHOL9780521395250.052

Birdsall, N., Sabot, R. H., & Sabot, R. (1996). *Opportunity foregone: Education in Brazil*. IDB.

Björklund, A., Fredriksson, P., Gustafsson, J.-E., & Öckert, B. (2010). *Den svenska utbildningspolitikens arbetsmarknadseffekter: vad säger forskningen?* Rapport 2010:13, Institutet för arbetsmarknads- och utbildningspolitisk utvärdering.

Cano, W. (1977). *Raízes da concentração industrial em São Paulo*. Difel São Paulo.

Cohen, D., & Soto, M. (2007). Growth and human capital: Good data, good results. *Journal of Economic Growth, 12*(1), 51–76. https://doi.org/10.1007/s10887-007-9011-5

Colistete, R. P. (2001). *Labour relations and industrial performance in Brazil: Greater São Paulo, 1945–1960*. Palgrave.

Colistete, R. P. (2007). Productivity, wages, and labor politics in Brazil, 1945–1962. *The Journal of Economic History, 67*(1), 93–127. https://doi.org/10.1017/S0022050707000046

Colistete, R. P. (2016). *O atraso em meio à riqueza: Uma história econômica da educação primária em São Paulo, 1835 a 1920* [Tese de livre docência]. Universidade de São Paulo.

Colistete, R. P. (2017). Iniciativas locais e mobilização por escolas primárias em São Paulo, 1830–1889. *Revista de História (São Paulo), 176*, 1–33. https://doi.org/10.11606/issn.2316-9141.rh.2017.120263

Dean, W. (1969). *The Industrialization of São Paulo 1880–1945*. The University of Texas Press.

de Carvalho Filho, I., & Colistete, R. P. (2010). Education performance: Was it all determined 100 years ago? Evidence from São Paulo, Brazil. *MPRA Paper*, 24494. https://mpra.ub.uni-muenchen.de/24494/

de Carvalho Filho, I., & Monasterio, L. (2012). Immigration and the origins of regional inequality: Government-sponsored European migration to southern Brazil before World War I. *Regional Science and Urban Economics, 42*(5), 794–807. https://doi.org/10.1016/j.regsciurbeco.2011.08.002

De Mattos, P. L. C. (1988). *The politics of education funding in Brazil, 1964–1984.* [PhD Thesis]. London School of Economics and Political Science (United Kingdom).

Doellinger, C. (1973). *Transformação da estrutura das exportações brasileiras: 1964–70*. IPEA/INPES.

Engerman, S. L., & Sokoloff, K. L. (1997). Factor endowments, institutions, and differential paths of growth among new world economies: A view from economic historians of the United States. In S. Haber (Ed.), *How Latin America fell behind* (pp. 260–304). Stanford University Press.

Engerman, S. L., Mariscal, E. V., & Sokoloff, K. L. (2009). The evolution of schooling institutions in the Americas, 1800–1925. In D. Eltis, F. Lewis, & K. Sokoloff (Eds.), *Human capital and institutions: A long-run view* (pp. 93–142). Cambridge University Press. https://doi.org/10.1017/CBO9780511605390.006

Ferreira, P. C., & Veloso, F., et al. (2013). O desenvolvimento econômico brasileiro no pós-guerra. In P. C. Ferreira (Ed.), *Desenvolvimento econômico: Uma perspectiva brasileira* (pp. 129–165). Elsevier.

Fishlow, A. (1972). Brazilian size distribution of income. *The American Economic Review, 62*(1/2), 391–402. https://www.jstor.org/stable/1821573

Fox, R., & Guagnini, A. (1999). *Laboratories, workshops, and sites: Concepts and practices of research in Industrial Europe, 1800–1914*. Office of the History of Science and Technology, University of California.

Frankema, E. (2009). The expansion of mass education in twentieth century Latin America: A global comparative perspective. *Revista De História Economica / Journal of Iberian and Latin American Economic History, 27*(3), 359–395. https://doi.org/10.1017/S0212610900000811

Goldin, C. & Katz, L. (2008), *The race between education and technology*, Cambridge (Mass.), Belknap Press of Harvard University Press.

Graham, R. (1983). Escravidão e desenvolvimento econômico. *Estudos Econômicos (São Paulo), 13*(1), 223–257. https://www.revistas.usp.br/ee/article/view/156728

Hanley, A. G. (2005). *Native capital: Financial institutions and economic development in Sao Paulo, Brazil, 1850–1920.* Stanford University Press.

Hasenbalg, C. (2003). Estatísticas do século XX: Educação. *Estatísticas Do Século XX. CDDI/IBGE.*

Havighurst, R. J., & Moreira, J. R. (1969). *Society and education in Brazil.* University of Pittsburgh Press.

Johansson, E. (1987). Literacy campaigns in Sweden. In R. Arnove, & H. Graff, (Eds.), *National Literacy Campaigns.* Plenum Press.

Kang, T. H. (2017). Educação para as elites, financiamento e ensino primário no Brasil, 1930–1964. *Latin American Research Review, 52*(1), 35–49. http://doi.org/10.25222/larr.42

Kang, T. H. (2019). *The political economy of education under military rule in Brazil, 1964–1985*, PhD Thesis (Economics), Universidade Federal do Rio Grande do Sul.

Kang, T., Paese, L., & Felix, N. (2021). Late and unequal: Measuring enrolments and retention in Brazilian education, 1933–2010. *Revista De Historia Económica/Journal of Iberian and Latin American Economic History, 39*(2), 191–218. https://doi.org/10.1017/S0212610921000112

Kirkendall, A. J. (2010). *Paulo Freire and the cold war politics of literacy.* University of North Carolina Press.

Komatsu, B., Menezes-Filho, N., Oliveira, P., & Viotti, L. (2019). Novas medidas de educação e de desigualdade educacional para a primeira metade do século XX no Brasil. *Estudos Econômicos, 49*(4), 687–722. https://doi.org/10.1590/0101-41614943bnpl

Kreutz, L. (2000). Escolas comunitárias de imigrantes no Brasil: Instâncias de coordenação e estruturas de apoio. *Revista Brasileira de Educação, 15*, 159–176. https://www.scielo.br/j/rbedu/a/JYYxCr33QdTvPLpDTBYWXFg/?format=pdf&lang=pt

Langoni, C. G. (1974). *As causas do crescimento econômico do Brasil.* Apec.

Lee, J., & Lee, H. (2016). Human capital in the long run. *Journal of Development Economics, 122*, 147–169. https://doi.org/10.1016/j.jdeveco.2016.05.006

Levy, M. S. F. (1974). O papel da migração internacional na evolução da população brasileira (1872 a 1972). *Revista De Saúde Pública, 8*, 49–90. https://doi.org/10.1590/S0034-89101974000500003

Lindert, P. H. (2010). The unequal lag in Latin American schooling since 1900: Follow the money. *Revista De História Economica/Journal of Iberian and Latin American Economic History, 28*(2), 375–405. https://doi.org/10.1017/S0212610910000066

Ljungberg, J., & Nilsson, A. (2009). Human capital and economic growth: Sweden 1870–2000. *Cliometrica, 3*(1), 71–95. https://doi.org/10.1007/s11698-008-0027-7

Love, J. L. (1970). Political participation in Brazil, 1881–1969. *Luso-Brazilian Review, 7*(2), 3–24. https://www.jstor.org/stable/3512756

Lundahl, L. (1997). *Efter svensk modell. LO, SAF och utbildningspolitiken 1944–1990*, Umeå, Boréa.

Lundh, C. (2002). *Spelets regler. Institutioner och lönebildning på den svenska arbetsmarknaden 1850–2000*. SNS förlag.

Lundh Nilsson, F. (2007). Lönande lärande: Teknologisk förändring, yrkesskicklighet och lön i svensk verkstadsindustri omkring 1900 (diss.), Almqvist & Wiksell International.

Lundh Nilsson, F. (2013). De specialiserade yrkesutbildningarna. Exemplet skoglig utbildning. In P. Håkansson, & A. Nilsson (Eds.), *Yrkesutbildningens formering i Sverige 1940–1975*. Nordic Academic Press.

Lundh Nilsson, F., & Grönberg, P.-O. (2019). For the promotion of industrialization: Technical upper secondary schools in Sweden 1855–1920. *Ferrum – Nachrichten aus der Eisenbibliothek* (Vol. 91, pp. 50–57).

Lundh Nilsson, F., & Nilsson, A. (Eds.). (2010). *Två sidor av samma mynt?* Nordic Academic Press.

Maduro, P. R. R. (2007). *Taxas de matrícula e gastos em educação no Brasil*, Master's Thesis, Fundação Getúlio Vargas, Rio de Janeiro.

Merrick, T. W., & Graham, D. H. (1979). *Population and economic development in Brazil: 1800 to the present*.

Mokyr, J. (2017). *A culture of growth: The origins of the modern economy: The Graz Schumpeter lectures*. Princeton University Press.

Morrisson, C., & Murtin, F. (2009). The century of education. *Journal of Human Capital, 3*(1), 1–42. https://doi.org/10.1086/600102

Musacchio, A., Fritscher, A. M., & Viarengo, M. (2014). Colonial institutions, trade shocks, and the diffusion of elementary education in Brazil, 1889–1930. *The Journal of Economic History, 74*(3), 730–766. https://doi.org/10.1017/S0022050714000588

Nagle, J. (1974). *Educação e sociedade na Primeira República*. Editora Pedagógica e Universitária São Paulo.

Nilsson, A. (2008). *Yrkesutbildningen i Sverige 1850–1910*. Årsböcker i svensk undervisningshistoria.

Nilsson, A. (2014). The unknown story: Vocational education for adults in Sweden 1918–1968. *History of Education: Journal of the History of Education Society, 43*(5), 615–634. https://doi.org/10.1080/0046760X.2014.930187

Norgren, L. (1989). Kunskapsöverföring från universitet till företag: En studie av universitetsforskningens betydelse för de svenska läkemedelsföretagens produktlanseringar 1945–1984. Reprocentralen HSC.

Nunes Leal, V. (1975). *Coronelismo, enxada e voto: O município e o regime representativo no Brasil*. Alfa-Omega.

OECD. (2019). PISA 2018 Database, OECD, https://www.oecd.org/pisa/data/2018database

Ohlsson, R. (1986). *Högre utbildning och demografisk förändring*, Lund, Skrifter utgivna av Ekonomisk-historiska föreningen, Vol. XLVII.

Olofsson, J. (2005). Svensk yrkesutbildning. Vägval i internationell belysning. Stockholm: SNS Förlag.

Pires, J. M. (2010). Desenvolvimentismo versus liberalismo econômico no período populista e o gasto público social. *Economia e Sociedade, 19*(3), 529–556. https://doi.org/10.1590/S0104-06182010000300005

Plank, D. N. (1996). *The means of our salvation: Public education in Brazil, 1930–1995*. Westview Press.

Promemorier från SCB. (1977). *Elever i icke-obligatoriska skolor 1864–1970* (Vol. 11). Statistiska Centralbyrån.

Ribeiro, S. C. (1991). A pedagogia da repetência. *Estudos Avançados, 5*(12), 7–21. https://doi.org/10.1590/S0103-40141991000200002

Richardson, G. (2004). *Svensk utbildningshistoria, sjunde reviderade upplagan*. Studentlitteratur.

Rocha, R., Ferraz, C., & Soares, R. R. (2017). Human capital persistence and development. *American Economic Journal: Applied Economics, 9*(4), 105–136. https://doi.org/10.1257/app.20150532

Sandberg, L. (1979). The case of the impoverished sophisticate: Human capital and Swedish economic growth before World War I. *Journal of Economic History, 39*(1), 225–241. https://doi.org/10.1017/S0022050700096418

Schiefelbein, E. (1975). Repeating: An overlooked problem of Latin American education. *Comparative Education Review, 19*(3), 468–487. https://doi.org/10.1086/445853

Schön, L. (2000). *En modern svensk ekonomisk historia*. SNS förlag.

Schwartzman, S., Bomeny, H. M. B., & Costa, V. M. R. (1984). *Tempos de capanema*. Paz e Terra Rio de Janeiro.

Stolz, Y., Baten, J., & Botelho, T. (2013). Growth effects of nineteenth-century mass migrations: "Fome Zero" for Brazil? *European Review of Economic History, 17*(1), 95–121. https://doi.org/10.1093/ereh/hes019

Summerhill, W. (2003). Big social savings in a small laggard economy: Railroad-led growth in Brazil. *The Journal of Economic History, 65*(1), 72–102. https://doi.org/10.1017/S0022050705050035

Suzigan, W. (2000). Industrialização brasileira em perspectiva histórica. *História Econômica & História de Empresas, 3*(2), 7–25. https://doi.org/10.29182/hehe.v3i2.143

Topik, S. (1987). *The political economy of the Brazilian state, 1889–1930.* University of Texas Press.

Torstendahl, R. (1975). *Dispersion of engineers in a transitional society. Swedish technicians 1860–1940.* Almqvist & Wicksell International.

Van Leeuwen, B., & Li, J. (2014). Education since 1820. In J. L. van Zanden, et al. (Eds.), *How was life? Global well-being since 1820* (pp. 87–100). https://doi.org/10.1787/9789264214262-9-en

Villela, A. (2013). O desenvolvimento econômico no Brasil pré-1945. In P. C. Ferreira, et al. (Eds.), *Desenvolvimento econômico: Uma perspectiva brasileira* (pp. 91–128). Elsevier.

Wegenast, T. C. (2010). Cana, café, cacau: Agrarian structure and educational inequalities in Brazil. *Revista De Historia Económica/journal of Iberian and Latin American Economic History, 28*(1), 103–137. https://doi.org/10.1017/S0212610909990024

Weinstein, B. (1996). *For social peace in Brazil: Industrialists and the remaking of the working class in São Paulo, 1920–1964.* Univ of North Carolina Press.

Westberg, J. (2014). *Att bygga ett skolväsende: Folkskolans förutsättningar och framväxt 1840–1900.* Nordic Academic Press.

Westberg, J. (2019). The production of impoverished but sophisticated emigrants: Emigration, human capital, and economic growth in Sweden. In D. Mitch & G. Capelli (Eds.), *Globalization and the rise of mass education*, Palgrave Studies in Economic History, Springer International Publishing. https://doi.org/10.1007/978-3-030-25417-9_7

Witzel de Souza, B. G. (2018). Immigration and the path dependence of education: The case of German-speakers in São Paulo, Brazil (1840–1920). *The Economic History Review, 71*(2), 506–539. https://doi.org/10.1111/ehr.12575

Witzel de Souza, B. G. (2019). Organizations matter: German schools and educational performance amid Brazilian coffee plantations (1840–1940). In *Globalization and the rise of mass education* (pp. 219–250). Springer. https://doi.org/10.1007/978-3-030-25417-9_8

Wjuniski, B. S. (2013). Education and development projects in Brazil (1932–2004): Political economy perspective. *Brazilian Journal of Political Economy, 33*(1), 146–165.

CHAPTER 7

Land-Ownership Systems and Agrarian Income Distribution in Denmark, New Zealand and Uruguay During the First Globalization Era and Beyond

Jorge Álvarez and María de las Mercedes Menéndez

1 Introduction

Understanding the factors involved in the divergent development paths of Scandinavia and South America was a central concern of the literature that summarizes Chapter 2 and the principal issue of this book. This chapter seeks to analyse in depth the link between domestic institutions, income

J. Álvarez (✉) · M. de las Mercedes Menéndez
Universidad de La República, Montevideo, Uruguay
e-mail: jorge.alvarez@cienciassociales.edu.uy

M. de las Mercedes Menéndez
e-mail: mercedes.menendez@cienciassociales.edu.uy

J. Álvarez and S. Prado (eds.), *Scandinavia and South America—A Tale of Two Capitalisms*, Palgrave Studies in Economic History,
https://doi.org/10.1007/978-3-031-09198-8_7

distribution and economic performance as factors involved in the divergent development paths followed by the Scandinavian countries and the Southern Settler Economies, as shown in Chapters 3 and 4. To do that, we focus on the cases of Denmark, New Zealand and Uruguay as small representative countries of each region.

Denmark, New Zealand and Uruguay enjoyed a peripheral integration into the world economy during the First Globalization era (1870–1913), as small, export-oriented countries with abundant natural resources for producing goods derived from livestock rearing, such as wool, leather, meat and dairy products. The agrarian sector was the engine of growth of the three countries: more than half of their exports between 1870 and 1930 were products derived from livestock (meat, dairy products, wool) which mainly supplied European markets. This pattern of insertion in the global economy enabled Denmark, New Zealand and Uruguay to achieve some of the highest levels of income per capita in the world at the beginning of the twentieth century. Despite their initial shared success, the three countries experienced different economic growth trajectories during the period of analysis. Denmark rapidly moved away from the income levels per capita experienced by Uruguay and converged with the New Zealand levels. New Zealand outperformed Denmark and Uruguay throughout the period. Finally, Uruguay lagged behind the other two countries (see Table 1).

The fact that the three countries share common features and yet have performed so differently in terms of economic growth makes them interesting cases for comparative analysis. Since the beginning of the twentieth century, the similarities in agrarian specialization and the differences in economic performance achieved among the three countries have attracted the attention of economists, academics and politicians of settler economies that conceived the Scandinavian country as an example to follow in areas such as agrarian scientific knowledge, land distribution and social laws. In this regard, a considerable contribution was made by the pioneering comparative work of Senghaas (1985) which examined the long-term development dynamics of the three countries. The author highlights the relevance of the agrarian structure of each country in their potential to generate links with other productive sectors. Furthermore, Senghaas questions why, despite having similar natural conditions for agrarian production and facing the same world economic context, the export-orientated growth dynamics of Denmark resulted in the emergence of a typical metropolitan society and economy, while the export-orientated

Table 1 Population, GDP per capita as share of core and exports (% of agricultural exports and composition)

	Years	*Denmark*	*New Zealand*	*Uruguay*
Population (thousands)	**1870**	1887	291	420
	1914	3017	1146	1169
	1930	3542	1507	1727
GDP per capita as a share of core = 100	**1870**	77	119	89
	1913	84	111	65
	1930	103	96	72
Agricultural exports as a share of total exports (%)	**1870–1879**	89	54	87
	1900–1909	90	65	88
	1920–1929	77	81	86
Top three products exports	**1870–1880**	(1) Grains (2) Butter, Bacon (3) Meat	(1) Wool (2) Forestry (3) Gold	(1) Hides and skin (2) Meat (3) Wool
	1901–1910	(1) Butter (2) Bacon (3) Other agricultural products	(1) Wool (2) Meat (3) Dairy products	(1) Wool (2) Hides and skin (3) Meat
	1921–1930	(1) Butter (2) Bacon (3) Industrial products	(1) Dairy products (2) Wool (3) Meat	(1) Meat (2) Wool (3) Hides and skin

Sources Population in Denmark from Hansen (1984), New Zealand from Briggs (2003), Uruguay from Bértola (2016). GDP per capita as a share of core (France, Germany, United Kingdom, United States), based on sources of Chapter 3, Table 1. Agricultural exports in total and main export products in Denmark from Johansen (1985), New Zealand from Briggs (2003), Uruguay from Millot and Bertino (1996) and Finch (2005)

growth dynamics of Uruguay resulted in a peripheralization process in the capitalist world economy. New Zealand is considered as an "intermediate case" between Denmark and Uruguay since it carried out a series of transformations in the distribution and tenure of land at the end of the nineteenth century that allowed this country to achieve an equitable distribution of land and the intensification of agriculture. Senghaas' analysis applied a general approach using mainly secondary sources, emphasizing the key role of the agricultural sector and the institutional, productive and technological transformations that took place in each country during the First Globalization. These differences showed up in the distribution of land, which was initially the most important factor of production in the three countries.

Recently, Senghaas' results have been proved by empirical studies (Álvarez, 2013; Álvarez & Willebald, 2013, Willebald & Juambeltz, 2018) comparing settler economies using new evidence and new measures of inequality. Among this literature, several authors have explained the uneven economic performance among New Zealand and Uruguay, by analysing how different land distribution patterns conditioned wealth and income distribution in the agrarian sector of the two countries and thus affected the potential of domestic market growth to enhance structural change and industrialization (Álvarez et al., 2011; Bértola & Willebald, 2013). In this sense, Chapter 3 explains the link between income distribution, structural change and economic growth in the Scandinavian countries and the Southern Settler Economies of Australasia and the River Plate countries. Through Senghaas' approach and the empirical studies mentioned above, this chapter seeks to address, from a comparative perspective, to what extent the processes of configuration of the property structure and land tenure explain the differences in income distribution in the agrarian sector and hence the economic performance of Denmark, New Zealand and Uruguay during the period 1870 to 1930.

Our central hypothesis predicts that the differences in economic performance among the three countries, from 1870 up to 1930, are in part explained by the emergence of different systems of property rights and land tenure that generate different patterns of wealth and income distribution. We assume that the configuration of these systems should be interpreted as the interaction of three main features: (a) the domestic institutions that are reflected in the government land distribution policies and by the state's power to impose efficient ownership rights; (b) the expansion of trade, increasing integration of factor markets and convergence of commodity prices in the world market during the First Globalization (Lindert & Williamson, 2003; O'Rourke & Williamson, 1999); and (c) the natural characteristics of the land, relative endowments of labour, agricultural specialization and technology available. Based on primary sources for Denmark and secondary sources for the other two countries published in previous research (Álvarez, 2014; Álvarez & Willebald, 2013), we test the hypothesis by presenting empirical evidence on the number of properties and their distribution according to size and type of tenure. Furthermore, we study the different patterns of income distribution by analysing the income of landowners and wage-earners through land prices and wages (rental/wage ratio) and estimating the functional income distribution of the agricultural sector in the three countries.

In regards to the methodology, this chapter will approach the study of institutional transformations through a qualitative, systematic, contextualized and macro-causal comparison. We will proceed according to Stuart Mill's logic of difference method. Denmark, New Zealand and Uruguay shared several features (e.g. size, population, productive specialization and trade partners), but there are differences among them in the causal variables—institutions associated with the definition of property rights and the historical land distribution processes—and in the phenomena to be explained, that is the agrarian income distribution and hence, economic performance. The aim, therefore, is not to give a detailed description of the three countries' history but to find the causes that led to their development and distributive patterns (Skocpol & Somers, 1980).

This chapter arrives at two main results. First, it is verified that institutional differences existed between the countries in the processes associated with the configuration of the structure of ownership and land tenure in terms of timing, agents involved and productive factors endowments. These factors were key in consolidating the family farm, medium-sized farms and large estates—latifundio—as the main economic unit in Denmark, New Zealand and Uruguay respectively. Second, the land ownership and tenure structures formed in each of the countries were crucial to setting up different distributive patterns in the agricultural sector and, as is emphasized in Chapter 3, to the potential of each country to transform its productive structure and initiate a process of industrialization and sustainable growth. Denmark had a relatively egalitarian ownership structure, which translated into widespread income growth on account of growing export receipts to a greater portion of society. In New Zealand, the distribution and tenure structure of land allowed that the agrarian income was distributed among small and medium-sized producers. Finally, in Uruguay, the domestic institutions associated with land ownership structure consolidated large estates as the main productive unit and the agrarian income was concentrated mainly among the landowners.

2 Landholding Systems and the Distribution of Ownership Rights

Landholding systems are considered a collection of norms (legal or derived from custom) that regulate the rights of individuals, groups and institutions regarding the use, transfer and inheritance of land and natural resources (Norton, 2002). The stability of landholding systems depends on agents' perceptions of how securely they hold these rights (Dale & McLaughlin, 2000). The state plays a key role in establishing and guaranteeing possession and ownership rights by legislating, enforcing justice and having the power to impose compliance (North, 1984).

In the following subsections, we outline the historical process associated with the configuration of land ownership rights and landholding systems in the three countries. In Denmark, the land distribution processes intensified in the last decades of the eighteenth century, during the transition between absolute monarchy and the nation state, when land reform was implemented. In the case of New Zealand and Uruguay, both new settlement economies, the processes took place during the nineteenth century, in the context of the formation of capitalist liberal regimes. As land distribution and the emergence of landholding systems are long-term processes that involve changes and breaks with the past, our analysis in this section covers a wider time frame.[1]

2.1 Denmark

Danish land tenure presented the same pattern of development as the rest of north-western Europe (Jensen, 1937). The spread of Enlightenment ideas, such as the enclosure movement, altered the traditional form of peasants' life and labour in the Danish countryside and were determinant in the subsequent economic ascent of Denmark (Lampe & Sharp, 2019). The major agrarian reforms, proposed by the Great Rural Commission, chaired by the landlord Christian Ditlev Reventlow and its secretary Christian Colbjørnsen, took place between 1788 and 1807.

[1] For further information on the case of Denmark see Menéndez (2021: Ch. 5), Álvarez (2008), Álvarez (2014: Ch. 4 and Ch. 8), and Álvarez (2017) for the cases of New Zealand and Uruguay.

These reforms included the abolition of adscription,[2] the regulation of tenancy relations, the confirmation of peasants' right to tenancy for life, measures to make the sale of freeholds to tenants easier, the enclosure of open fields and transformations in rent relations between landlords and tenants (Herlitz, 1983).

The significant changes in Danish land tenure were influenced by the decision of landlords to sell their agricultural land to their tenants, thus transforming the tenure from leasehold to predominantly freehold (Henriksen, 2003). As a result, between 1780 and 1850 the landowners sold 90% of their land to their tenants, who became free owners. This process was mainly concentrated between 1790 and 1807 (Smout, 1987). The decision of the owners to sell the land was influenced by three aspects: first, the difference in productivity between peasants who worked on manor farms (demesne) and those who worked on their own farms (Fæstegaarde); second, the costs of collecting taxes for landowners; and third, the greater efficiency of land use by farmers due to their knowledge of the potential of farms (Henriksen, 2003). Østergaard (2006) points out that it was more profitable for the landowners to sell the land and hire labour for the demesne.

The consolidation of the small farm structure was a subject of extensive debate throughout the nineteenth century and well into the twentieth century. The agrarian reforms at the end of the eighteenth century notably improved the situation of the peasantry. However, towards the end of the nineteenth century more than 70% of the properties of the small owners were Husmænd.[3] Generally, the legislation approved in this period sought to fulfil the objective of preserving small farmers' farms, as well as encouraging the establishment of new farms of sustainable dimensions for family productive development (Kristensen, 1930).

In 1870 Det Forende Venstre (United Left) was established, mainly comprising small farmers, and managed to achieve a parliamentary majority around 1872. Despite this, the Danish king appointed landowner

[2] This system—also known as the "compulsory residence system" (Skrubbeltrang, 1961)—emerged in 1733 and limited the movement of men in the countryside, guaranteeing military recruitment. However, the main aim was to maintain the required labour force in the manor's farms (Skrubbeltrang, 1961, Sharp & Lampe, 2019).

[3] *Husmænd* makes reference to small-holders whose production is less than 1 Tdr. Hartkorn, and hence its productivity was below what was considered the sustainable size for a family farm (Henriksen, 2008).

Jacob Estrup (1825–1913) as prime minister, who ruled from 1875 to 1894 (Paldam, 1990). During this period the Venstre party adopted a strategy known as Visnepolitikken, which consisted of rejecting government proposals—including the budget law—in parliament, which meant that only emergency projects were approved to finance projects existing (Paldam, 1990). Christiansen and Togeby (2006: 2) point out that the "battle for parliamentarianism" contributed to the mobilization of the peasantry in the political arena, in the same way as the formation of agrarian cooperatives during the last three decades of the nineteenth century and its active role in peasants education.

In 1899, a series of land laws enacted by Parliament changed the regulation of property size. The "Small Holding Act" introduced state loans to small properties to retain some workers in agriculture and alleviate the movement of workers from the countryside to the city, which was leading to rising wages. However, the law limited the size of the farm to four hectares, which meant that the small owner and his family also had to seek employment on large and medium-sized farms (Henriksen, 2008).[4] During the 1901 election, the Hojre party (Conservative Party), which had the support of the king, was defeated by Venstre. Hence, the class of peasant owners of medium-sized properties became the dominant political force, one hundred years after the agrarian reform. In the year 1903, a modern tax law was introduced, eliminating the hartkorn[5] as a measure of land productivity and replacing it with a progressive income and property taxes (Silagi & Faulkner, 1994) in an attempt to adjust to the land yield transformations introduced in the nineteenth century (Madsen et al., 1992). However, the tax reform was unfavourable for small landowners, whose farms had a higher proportion of buildings and structures intended for agricultural activity (Silagi & Faulkner, 1994).

The Venstre party remained united until 1905, when it divided into two factions: the Venstre (also translates as the Left) made up of the

[4] The conditions of the 1899 law would be partially modified in 1909 under the *Venstre* government: the size of properties would be expanded and loans would be increased (Henriksen, 2008).

[5] Between 1662 and 1903, "Tønde hartkorn" represented a measure of the taxable value of land and its quality that fit the area of each parcel. Very fertile land could therefore reach 1 Tønde hartkorn in a very small area, while land that was less fertile would require a larger area (Lampe & Sharp, 2019). Tønder of Hartkorn (1 Tdr. Hrtk) is on average for the whole of Denmark 18.0 tønde of land (Td. Ld) which is approximately 10 hectares (Danmarks Statistik, 1908: 40, Table 38).

wealthiest owners and Det Radikale Venstre (also translates as the Social-Liberal party) made up of small owners and intellectuals. The Det Radikale Venstre party did not see its interests being fulfilled under the liberal economic ideas of the Venstre. On the contrary, they were more influenced by the ideas of Stuart Mill and Henry George, proposing in their programme a new system of small farms based on the parcelling of large properties, and a tax policy that would reduce inequalities (Jespersen, 2019; Kærgård, 2001). Smallholders supported obtaining tax revenue from unimproved lands and abolishing all direct and indirect duties and taxes on property and personal wages (Silagi & Faulkner, 1994).

During World War I many small farms were sold because they depended on imported inputs, especially those that were dedicated to animal production, and these were later annexed by larger farms (Kristensen, 1930). At the same time, during the conflict, an increase in the price of land was observed, limiting the ability of new buyers to acquire properties (Henriksen, 2008). The government tried to preserve small farms through declaring that the properties between 2.5 and 18 acres should be protected. The land could be sold, but a parcel of between 18 and 25 acres, depending on their quality, should remain with the buildings (Jensen, 1937: 131). These rules were permanently stated in an act dated 1925. After the end of the war, Denmark incorporated the north of Schleswig into its territory, which expanded the territory by 4000 square kilometres, reaching the current geographical limits (Johansen, 1987).

The government sought to sub-divide the largest estates of land, to expand the supply of land. To meet this objective, the Land Rent Holding Act (1919) introduced land leases to support a new generation of family farms (Henriksen, 2008) through proclaiming available for sub-division the ecclesiastical (glebe land) and public lands (Kristensen, 1930). Furthermore, the law abolished the right to own land through the entailed estates, which was a form of tenure originating from Danish absolutism (Jespersen, 2019). According to the author, the law provided that the owners of the estates could keep their land, but pay 10% of the value of the estate to the government and give 25% of the land in return for their compensation, to be divided into small farms. Furthermore, Jespersen (2019) highlights that around 10% of the country's agricultural land was under this type of feudal form of tenancy, so their redistribution represented a change in land ownership comparable to the agrarian reforms of the eighteenth century, as the smallholder farmers benefited the most. Until 1930, many farms were established under the 1919 act. However, the Danish agricultural sector was highly mechanized, so it became increasingly difficult to live in small farms and it was therefore no longer efficient to create them.

2.2 *New Zealand*

In New Zealand, the distribution of land was based on English common law. This was formalized by the Treaty of Waitangi, which was signed with the chiefs of the main Māori tribes in 1840.[6] Article II of the English version of the treaty established that the Māori communities ceded sovereignty over their lands to the British Crown, and in exchange, the Crown guaranteed the indigenous communities' possession of land rights, which included ownership rights. If Māori wanted to cede or sell land they could only do so to the Crown. This treaty is considered a milestone in the foundation process and history of New Zealand, but its legal ramifications have caused considerable controversy.

The acquisition of Māori lands by the state since the Treaty of Waitangi can be studied in two phases (Boast, 2008). The first phase (1840–1860) was dominated by the Crown's right to pre-emption in land purchases. This preferential right was grounded in the doctrines of British imperial law and established under the Treaty of Waitangi (Boast, 2008). This enabled the colonial government to purchase land at low prices, sell at high prices and use the profits from this arrangement to finance the settlement of new immigrants. It also amounted to a legal restriction on the activities of colonists who sought to acquire land purely for speculation. By 1860, based on this legal disposition, more than 60% of the occupied land had been sold. Most of this land was in South Island, but there were also some regions in North Island similarly affected (Boast, 2008, 2016). By the 1850s, a large part of the highlands in South Island had been leased to big livestock producers (Fairweather, 1985).

The second phase (1862–1873) took place under the provisions of the Native Land Act of 1862, which introduced two radical changes to the

[6] The treaty was signed on 6 February 1840 by 43 Māori chiefs from Northland, and in the subsequent eight months nearly 500 Māori chiefs from all over the country signed it. According to recent estimates, the Māori population amounted to some 70,000 and the European population amounted to some 2000 in 1840 when the Treaty of Waitangi was signed (Belich, 1996: 178, 193).

landholding system. The first was that the legal statute governing Māori community ownership rights was superseded by the British system of individual private ownership or freehold. The second was that the preferential Crown purchase system was abolished, which eliminated the state's monopoly on the right to buy certain categories of land. The effects of these new laws were extremely negative as they seriously prejudiced the indigenous communities' rights, changed how the land market functioned and opened the door to speculation. They also contributed to the concentration of land ownership in a few hands in South Island as well as in the more accessible areas in North Island (Condliffe, 1959). At around this time, the Māori communities fought a series of bitter wars (1845–1872) against the government, which was supported by British Empire troops. These armed conflicts were rooted in the points of dispute between the Māori communities and the government concerning the sale of land (Belich, 1996).

In 1876 the province system was abolished and the central government intensified its policy of distributing land to colonists by simplifying the legislation and incorporating some important changes. The Torrens system for registering land ownership was established, which made land purchase and sale transactions easier and more economical. In 1877 the Land Act was passed, overturning all previous statutes by introducing a system of land auctions with deferred payment. An important innovation in this legislation was that it provided an incentive to lease public land. The main aim of this policy was to keep public land under state control in anticipation that its value would rise in the future. This meant that the state was disposed to renounce the income it gained from land sales in exchange for potentially greater income in the future. Various amendments to the Land Act of 1877 were introduced in 1882 and 1884, which included provisions for leasing in perpetuity.

Between the signing of the Treaty of Waitangi in 1840 and the start of the 1890s, successive governments bought and sold land and favoured the leasing of public land. Through these land sales the government pursued three main objectives: to obtain income, to bring about the settlement of rural areas by Europeans, and to develop the agrarian sector. However, between 1870 and 1890 land ownership became highly concentrated. Large rural estates emerged and formed the basis of extensive livestock production geared to the export market. There were also large numbers of smallholdings engaged in subsistence production oriented towards the domestic market (McAloon, 2009).

It was not until the 1890s that "suitable conditions" were established to carry out the final transformations in the land ownership system, especially in the large estates. Those conditions were population growth and rising unemployment rates, coupled with the arrival of refrigeration, which made farming production more relevant and led to the victory of the Liberal Party in the elections of 1891, which brought with it a radical programme of land reforms (Álvarez & Willebald, 2013).

The Liberal Party was in power for twenty years, from 1891 to 1912 and, in that period it succeeded in carrying out a good part of its programme of reforms, which included dismantling the large rural estates. The main measures it adopted for this purpose included expropriating large estates by purchase and subdividing the land, imposing a specific tax on large estates to pressure landholders to divide them into smaller units, the settlement of new agrarian producers on land in North Island (which favoured the leasing of public land over private purchase) and the development of a public financing scheme to help rural producers improve land productivity (McIntyre, 2007).

The main debate that dominated the land question in the 1890s revolved around whether the best landholding regime was the leasing system (mainly of public land) or the private property (freehold) system. The government defended the leasing system, arguing that people's capital should be used to improve production (increasing the numbers of livestock, erecting wire fences and so on) and not to make mortgage payments for land. If the best-quality land was already in private hands by 1892, as Condliffe (1959) emphatically stresses, a question arises about which lands could be given over to leasing. The system was implemented on deforested lands in North Island, which were incorporated into production between 1891 and 1911, and highlands in South Island, which were turned over to grazing. However, it was in South Island that the leasing system predominated, under a modality known as Crown Pastoral Lease, which had been in force since the 1850s. Between 1874 and 1911 a very large proportion of the land devoted to agrarian production (between 60% and 30% of the total occupied area in New Zealand) was crown lands located in South Island (McIntyre, 2007).

The most important land laws passed by Liberal Party governments were the Land and Income Tax Act (1891), the Land for Settlements Act (1892, 1894) and the National Endowment Act (1907). The evidence shows that the area controlled by large estates was effectively reduced from 3.2 million hectares in 1891 to 1.4 million in 1910 (Greasley & Oxley, 2005; Hawke, 1985), but it is also clear that market forces played a key role in this change in the structure of land ownership. International demand was expanding and refrigeration had a big impact in rural areas because it made production systems that were more intensive, like dairy farming, more profitable in capital and labour (Bertram, 2009; Easton, 1997; Hawke, 1985). This caused a steady rise in land prices and tended to make large estates less important as an agrarian system based on small and medium family holdings became consolidated. On this point, Gould (1965) reports that only 26% of the reduction in the area of the big estates between 1892 and 1910 was due to the state expropriating land.

In 1912, the Reform Party led by William Massey came to power, and many small producers in North Island, who had been favoured by the Liberal government's land distribution policies and able to accede to land through the leasing regime, claimed the right to own their land outright. One of Massey's main policies was to help many leasers become owners at the original price valuation of their land. Land prices were rising strongly at that time, and the new owners succeeded in appropriating the profits from changing land values. This policy of privatizing small and medium holdings in North Island ushered in a phase during which "the farmers take over [as] the backbone of the country" (Fairburn, 1991: 185). A landholding system and ownership structure with very particular characteristics became established. There was a wide base of small and medium family production units (freehold) located in North Island and on the lowlands of South Island, combined with large production units on low-productivity public lands leased for livestock grazing (Crown pastoral lease) in the highlands of South Island.

2.3 Uruguay

In the case of Uruguay, the distribution of land began during the colonial period: the owner of the land was the king of Spain and the mechanisms for acquisition and transfer of land were established in the Laws of the Indies. In the second half of the eighteenth century, a new phase of land occupation and border expansion was observed due to the Royal Instruction of 1754, which repealed the real confirmation of titled lands and the Pragmática de Libre Comercio (Decree of Free Trade) (1778) that not only promoted agricultural exports but also increased land property rights. Regarding the indigenous population, which was smaller than in New Zealand, the Spanish Crown did not recognize any rights to land ownership (Álvarez, 2014) and their presence in the territory was a problem for the settlement of the population in the rural environment.

The most common form of land acquisition during the colonial period was through direct appropriation or mere occupation, which enhanced the consolidation of latifundio. According to Álvarez (2014), several factors explain its strengthening: the inability of local governments to ensure property rights, high land/population ratio, the pattern of productive specialization based on livestock production and the border status of the Banda Oriental.

The definition of property rights during the decades of independent life was progressive, on one hand due to the lack of legitimacy of governments and their frequent changes, and on the other hand to the limited ability of the state to maintain registers and control systems in the entire territory (Bértola & Ocampo, 2013). These factors combined meant that during the first decades of the nineteenth century (after Uruguay became an independent nation) there were massive transfers of public lands to private hands. Between 1830 and 1836, private property increased from 20% to 42% of the total land area (Álvarez & Willebald, 2013: 39).

In the 1870s the political power of the state became stronger and this secured the ownership rights in rural areas. The consolidation of the state's power was associated with the formation of a regular army, which muscled into political life and established a series of military dictatorships in the ten years from 1876 to 1886, and with the introduction of a series of technological changes such as modern weapons, the railway and the telegraph that were at the service of the state. These changes and the introduction of wire fencing—a technological innovation that made it possible to physically divide rural plots—contributed to the consolidation of private ownership rights in the rural sector and the emergence of capitalist markets for land and labour (Jacob, 1969). The enclosure of rural land had important economic and social repercussions. It reduced the demand for rural workers, caused the displacement of around 10% of the rural population, contributed to the concentration of land ownership in few hands and allowed the private appropriation of residual public land, estimated at 25% of the total in 1878, by the de facto occupation (Álvarez, 2014; Barrán & Nahum, 1972). These processes contributed to the emergence of an agrarian system based on large livestock production units oriented towards exports and a very concentrated land ownership structure (Barrán & Nahum, 1967, 1972; Finch, 2005).

In 1903 a faction of the Colorado Party led by José Batlle y Ordóñez formed a government and remained in power for more than a decade

(1903–1915).[7] Its main political and social support was based on the middle classes and urban workers, and in this period they implemented a policy programme geared to widening the state's orbit of action, competing with British capital in strategic areas of the economy. As regards land ownership, there were intense debates in parliament about whether it was economically and politically feasible to preserve an agrarian ownership structure dominated by large livestock estates (Barrán & Nahum, 1978, 1979). In 1912, the Batlle government enacted legislation to establish a system whereby land was purchased and divided into small family farm units and to promote the use of private funds to expropriate land on the outskirts of provincial cities and distribute it among small producers. There was also an effort to identify lands that were still state property (legislation of 1904 and 1912). In most cases, these areas had been incorporated into private holdings through the fact of occupation, and represented around 15% of the country's total territory (Álvarez, 2014). The government's most consistent initiative was to impose a modest increase in the land ownership tax—a mere 0.6% to 1% of the assessed value (Frega et al., 1985).

However, none of these Batlle faction initiatives came to fruition. This was due to a collection of factors, including opposition from the big livestock-producing landowners who had great economic and political power, the unresolved contradiction in the government's agenda between implementing land-expropriation policies and respecting property rights, and Battle's conviction that at the end of the day the sub-division of the large rural estates would come about as a natural result of the development of the agrarian sector and growth of agriculture, in other words, of market forces (Álvarez, 2014). The Batlle governments were unable to essentially change either the landholding system or the structure of land ownership in the country because their land policy initiatives were limited and they lacked political conviction as to the advisability of undertaking reforms that would call established ownership rights into question. As a result, in the first decades of the twentieth century, an agrarian system, dominated by large estates engaged in extensive livestock production, became entrenched.

Based on Sects. 2.1–2.3, Table 2. synthesizes and compares the main characteristics of the land tenure and distribution process described above:

[7] Batlle y Ordoñez was president in two constitutional periods (1903–1907 and 1911–1915). In the gap between 1907 and 1911, the president was Claudio Williman, an ex-minister in the Batlle administration, who continued with the same policies.

Table 2 Comparison of ownership and land tenure in Denmark, New Zealand and Uruguay

	Denmark	*New Zealand*	*Uruguay*
Timing	De-feudalization started at the end of the eighteenth century Changes in land distribution and land tenure continued during the nineteenth century and the first decades of the twentieth century	Relevant changes in land distribution and land tenure occurred during the nineteenth century. Uruguay liberal policy towards land ownership from 1830, New Zealand from 1860s	
Main goal	Consolidation of the family farm as an economic unit	Reduction of the extension of large estates and expansion in medium-sized farms	Consolidation of land market, private property and livestock rearing big estates
Main agents	**Eighteenth century and nineteenth century**: members of the elites, landlords **Last decades of nineteenth century and twentieth century**: farmers and their action through the *Venstre* party	**1840–1860**: crown right to pre-emption in land purchases **1862–1890**: liberal reforms, individual property rights **1890–1912**: the government, mainly represented by the Liberal Party **1912 onwards**: Union Party in government and shift of leasing system of public land to land free-holding, mainly in the small holding of North Island	**Until the end of the nineteenth century**: caudillos and landlords, the state was weak **1870 onwards**: state promotes the consolidation of rural property. Rural Association of Uruguay (landlords association)
Tenancy system	Private property	Maintained political and economic control of the land, keeping an average of 40% of public lands under lease between 1881 and 1940	Private property

(continued)

Table 2 (continued)

	Denmark	*New Zealand*	*Uruguay*
Productive frontier	No expansion of the productive frontier. Restoration of northern Schleswig (400,000 ha)	Expansion of the productive frontier	Consolidation of the current territory in the nineteenth century

Source Own elaboration

3 Distribution of Land Ownership and Tenancy Systems

The historical processes of land occupation and land distribution in the three countries discussed in Sect. 2 were key in shaping the structure of land ownership and the tenure system. In this section, we examine the structure of ownership by comparing a set of indicators such as the number of properties and their distribution according to size, occupied area and land tenure systems. We then explore the relationship between agrarian specialization and the property structure in each of the three countries. When comparing land ownership distribution some problems have to be resolved in the statistical information. It is not easy to make comparisons between the three land ownership structures using official agrarian statistics because the three countries have used different criteria for collecting and presenting the information. These differences have to do in particular with the categories of land holdings by size, the unit of measurement used in each country (acres/hectares/hartkorn) and the frequency with which this kind of information was published.

Regarding the distribution of land ownership by property according to its size, Table 3 shows the number of farms in Denmark, New Zealand and Uruguay between 1891 and 1937. In Denmark, the number of farms was higher than in New Zealand and Uruguay during this period. At the beginning of the twentieth century a medium-sized Danish farm was less than 10% of the size of a medium-sized farm in New Zealand or Uruguay. In New Zealand, between 1891 and 1931, the number of properties increased by almost 90%. This increase could be explained by the effect of the expansion of the productive frontier from 12 to 16 million hectares in almost the same period and the sub-division of larger properties. The average area of all holdings in New Zealand decreased from 283

Table 3 Number of farms (*in thousands), occupied land (*in thousands ha) and the average size of rural holdings (ha) in Denmark, New Zealand and Uruguay

Years			*Denmark*			*New Zealand*			*Uruguay*		
DK	*NZ*	*UY*	*Farms 000*	*Land 000*	*Avg ha*	*Farms 000*	*Land 000*	*Avg ha*	*Farms 000*	*Land 000*	*Avg ha*
1895	1891		270.9[1]	3,800	14	45.3	12,833	283			
1905	1906	1908	289.1	3,800	13	69.9	15,053	215	43.6	17,177	394
1919	1913	1916	206.0	3,200	16	77.2	16,698	216	58.5	17,177	293
1933	1931	1937	204.2	3,200	16	83.8	17,498	209	73.4	16,745	228

Sources Denmark Johansen (1985). The land occupied is the total agricultural area. One estimate includes the island of Bornholm. New Zealand: Gould (1965: 139), Fairweather (1985: 18, Table 3). Uruguay: Agriculture censuses and Barrán and Nahum (1977: 270, 277)

hectares in 1891 to 209 hectares in 1931. In Uruguay, between 1908 and 1937, the number of properties increased by 70% and the average size of holdings decreased from 394 hectares in 1908 to 228 hectares in 1931. Both transformations occurred in an agrarian area that remained relatively constant in terms of size, so the process mainly involved the partition of existing holdings. This trend is explained by three factors: division on inheritance, properties being divided to avoid taxes, and the fact that agriculture was expanding into regions originally devoted to livestock (Bértola, 2005). However, the increase in the number of holdings mainly took place in the lower reaches of the agrarian structure and involved holdings of less than 100 hectares, and it did not substantially alter the fact that land ownership was highly concentrated (Menéndez, 2021).

The different forms of land tenure in the three countries during the period are shown in Table 4. For Denmark, since the end of the nineteenth century, we not only identify a progressive growth in farms working under the system of a freehold, but also a reduction in the farms under the traditional system of faeste.[8] This last fact was a response to the abolition of forms of tenure characteristic of the feudal period during the first decades of the twentieth century. In the settler economies, half of

[8] This is a type of traditional land tenure in which the land is occupied by tenant farms but the property is owned by the manor.

the properties were under the freehold system. New Zealand maintained political and economic control of the land, keeping an average of 40% of public lands under lease during the analysis period. This allowed the state to obtain income and achieve a social appropriation of income. In Uruguay, the percentage of public lands was lower and, in fact, they had private possession. The tenants represented 40% on average between 1916 and 1937, which meant an appropriation of the rent by private agents.

The land ownership structure and the tenancy system set up in each country resulted from land distribution processes, described in Sect. 2, along with natural resources endowment and agricultural specialization patterns. These factors fostered the configuration of three different agricultural systems dominated by livestock production. In particular: an intensive-type livestock system that combines animal production and cereal and forage production (Denmark); an intensive-type livestock system based on soil improvement and the use of artificial pastures (New Zealand); and an extensive livestock system based on the intensive use of natural pastures (Uruguay) (Menéndez, 2021).

In Denmark, the less concentrated ownership structure and smallholders encouraged a type of capital and labour intensive farming. By 1933, small farms (between 0.5 and 30 hectares) were those with the highest proportion of cattle per 100 hectares, with dairy cattle being the predominant herd (Danmarks Statistik, 1969: 50–51, Table 28–29). Also, by 1933, cereal production was predominant in the Islands and Jutland region, with approximately 40% of the land allocated to farms of all sizes (Danmarks Statistik, 1968: 34, Table 14). Additionally, the percentage of hectares allocated for the production of green forage and pasture was higher in Jutland than in the Islands (Danmarks Statistik, 1968: 183, Table 107). In New Zealand, changes in distribution and tenure allowed a reduction in the extent of large estates and the expansion of medium-sized properties, encouraging a type of intensive livestock farming based on the improvement of land productivity devoted to livestock rearing. The small farms also specialized in dairy farming, while the medium-sized properties specialized in the production of cattle and sheep (Álvarez, 2008). The productive specialization of the farms in Uruguay was chosen for the extensive production of cattle and sheep based on the natural conditions of grasslands.

The different patterns of landholding distribution and the fact that the ownership structure was less concentrated in Denmark than in the settler

Table 4 Farm tenancy in Denmark, New Zealand and Uruguay

Years			*Denmark*			*New Zealand*			*Uruguay*		
DK	*NZ*	*UY*	*Free-hold*	*Fæste*	*Other*	*Free-hold*	*Lease Private*	*Public*	*Free-hold*	*Lease Private*	*Other*
1873	–	–	81	19	0	–	–	–	–	–	–
1901	–	–	85	4	11	–	–	–	–	–	–
1919	1916	1916	92	1	7	52	8	40	47	43	11
–	1937	1937	–	–	–	58	8	40	58	43	8

Sources Denmark 1873– Statistiske Årbog, several years; 1901– Danmarks Statistik (1903) containing general information about land use for the date 15 March 1901; 1919– Danmarks Statistik (1921) containing information about the use of land for the date 15 July 1919. New Zealand and Uruguay: extracted from Álvarez (2008)

economies—and less concentrated in New Zealand than in Uruguay—explain the emergence of different income distribution patterns in the three countries' agrarian sectors. These patterns are analysed in the next section by comparing the evolution of the rental-wage ratio and the functional distribution of income in the agrarian sector.

4 The Evolution of Factor Prices and the Functional Distribution of Income in the Agrarian Sector

The First Globalization era was characterized by the expansion of trade on a global scale, the increasing integration of factor markets and the convergence of commodity prices, and hence had a big impact on income distribution all over the world. A string of influential research has argued that in the Old World, where there was a relative abundance of labour and scarcity of natural resources such as land, inequality decreased (Lindert & Williamson, 2003; O'Rourke & Williamson, 1999), whereas in the New World where there was a relative abundance of natural resources and scarcity of labour, inequality tended to increase. The power of this research programme is the contrast between the two types of economies. In this regard and following Greasley (2006), the analysis of the impact of globalizing forces on distribution, through the study of the evolution of wage-earners' and landowners' income, is particularly interesting for Denmark and New Zealand, as well as for Uruguay, because they are small and open economies with a similar productive structure.

Figure 1 shows the evolution of the wage-rental ratio for Denmark, New Zealand and Uruguay. For the case of Denmark, the evolution of the wage-rental showed an increasing trend that reflects a distributional bias towards wages during the period. Greasley (2006) suggests that, until 1914, urban wages showed strong development but the capital value of land did not collapse. It is rightly mentioned that this evolution took place at the same time the Danish economy experienced a profound structural change in its productive structure from an exporter of grain to an exporter of livestock goods. After World War I there was a steep reduction in land prices as well as a sharp increase in wages that reflected the success of wage negotiations by the unions in this country and the reduction in the working day from nine and a half hours to eight hours between 1919 and 1920, which was also accompanied by an increase in unemployment benefits.

The evolution of the wage/rental ratio in New Zealand and Uruguay shows a declining trend that reflects a distributional bias towards landowners. In the settler economies, land prices went up during this period as a result of the export boom in raw materials and food-stuffs. It might be thought that the ratio between wages and the price of land should have decreased more rapidly in Uruguay than in New Zealand because Uruguay did not expand its productive frontier during

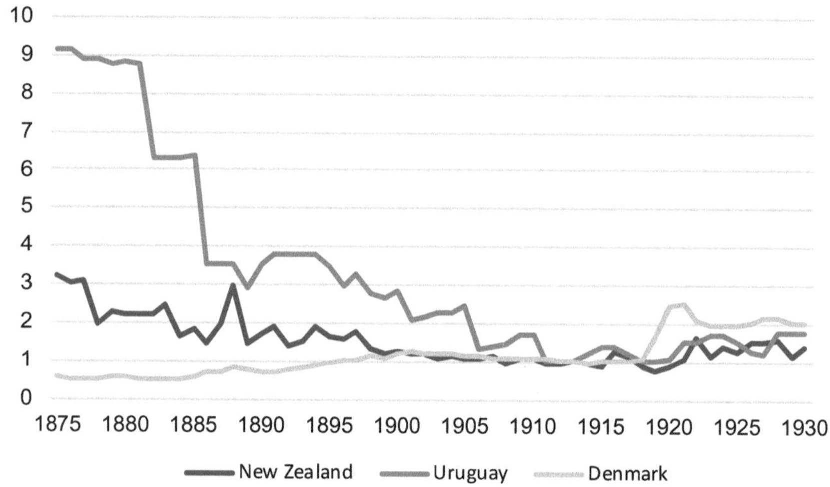

Fig. 1 Evolution of the wage/rental ratio 1875–1930 (1913 = 1) (*Sources* Denmark: data extracted from Greasley [2006: 135–136]. The nominal wages correspond to urban unskilled labour and are extracted from Johansen [1985]. The land prices are extracted from Christensen [1985] and Statistisk Årbog for several years. The consumer prices are extracted from Pedersen [1930] and Johansen [1985]. New Zealand: data extracted from Greasley & Oxley [2005: 43–44]. The nominal wages correspond to non-agricultural labourers. The estimates up to 1913 are extracted from Greasley & Oxley [2004] and for the period up to 1939 the estimates of wages are extended taking into consideration the average of labourers' wages in five activities: building, baking, brewing, meat freezing and saw mills. Uruguay: real land is estimated based on the nominal land price index from the PHES Dataset and the price index is extracted from Bértola et al. [1999]. Real wage estimate was based on Bértola et al. [1999])

the period, whereas New Zealand did (see Table 1). However, in New Zealand this trend was counterbalanced by the intensity of migratory flows over the period, receiving twice as many immigrants as Uruguay (Chapter 3). From 1915 onwards it is possible to detect a distributional bias towards wages in the settler economies, but more modest than in the Scandinavian country. As we will see below, the extent of the rise in inequality depended on the domestic institutions that determined the distribution of land ownership rights in each country (Álvarez & Bértola, 2013; Álvarez & Willebald, 2013; Álvarez et al., 2011). The evolution of the wage/rental ratio, which indicates a similar trend towards inequality in New Zealand and Uruguay, conceals the fact that land ownership distribution patterns were different in the two countries. As we could see in the previous section (see Table 3), there were more rural producers in New Zealand during the First Globalization, and more producers owned land, which meant that the income derived from exports was captured by a greater number of rural producers in New Zealand than in Uruguay. In Uruguay, the increased income derived from the rise in land prices was more beneficial to the big livestock landowners.

An alternative approach for studying income distribution is given by estimating the agrarian functional income distribution in terms of the share of wages, rents and profits in agricultural GDP. This perspective reflects an interest in analysing the link between institutions and growth and its implications for income distribution as proposed by the neo-Ricardian and post-Keynesian schools. Table 5 shows the functional income distribution in the agrarian sector of the three countries for the period 1870–1930. The estimates for New Zealand and Uruguay are extracted from previous research (Álvarez, 2014; Álvarez & Willebald, 2013) and the figures for Denmark were estimated by Menéndez (2021).[9]

As shown in Table 5, during the golden age of the First Globalization and its crisis, the income derived from land ownership was proportionally greater in Uruguay (an average of 50% over the period) than in New Zealand (which averaged 41% in the period) and Denmark (which averaged 19% in the period). The table also shows that profits and wages represented a greater share of agrarian GDP in Denmark (an average of 80%) and New Zealand (59%) than in Uruguay (50%).

[9] More information on the estimates is available in the Appendix in the end of this chapter.

Table 5 Functional distribution of income in the agrarian sector (as % of agrarian GDP)

DK|NZ-UY	*Denmark*			*New Zealand*			*Uruguay*		
Years	*Wages*	*Rents*	*Profits*	*Wages*	*Rents*	*Profits*	*Wages*	*Rents*	*Profits*
1876|1874	45	23	32	23	33	44	37	46	17
1881	47	24	29	35	42	22	26	49	24
1896|1891	51	19	30	30	41	29	21	49	29
1908|1901	43	17	40	26	48	26	25	48	27
1925|1911	32	16	52	30	51	20	21	68	11
1930	30	16	53	41	33	26	32	41	27
Average	**41**	**19**	**39**	**31**	**41**	**28**	**27**	**50**	**23**

Sources Denmark: Menéndez (2021). New Zealand and Uruguay: 1874–1911, Álvarez and Willebald (2013); 1911 onwards, Álvarez (2014: Table IX.3)

In the case of Denmark, profits experienced an increase during the period of analysis, from 32% to 53% of the agrarian GDP. This could be explained by the early adoption of capital-intensive labour-saving technology (Khaustova & Sharp, 2015). According to the authors, who based their analysis on Allen (2009), the transformations at the level of technological change and capital accumulation could be explained by the high wages achieved in Denmark during the First Globalization era, which encouraged the adoption of intensive forms of capital production. The contribution of capital to the Danish economy is reflected in the early growth account of Danish Agriculture proposed by Hyldtoft (1999). In this regard, when comparing the periods 1875–1895 and 1895–1910 the contribution of capital in agriculture rose from 21% to 32%. Henriksen (2008) points out that this growth is explained by the construction of new buildings for herds and by the increased use of machinery such as threshing machines. This growth led to a doubling of labour productivity between the two periods, during which there is also an increase in the labour force in the agricultural sector, which Henriksen (2008) attributes to changes in land policy.

In the case of the settler economies, from the beginning of the period analysed, New Zealand offered a higher reward for labour and reproducible capital than Uruguay. In the South American country, land renters captured 50%, capitalists 23% and workers 27% of the total agricultural output. For New Zealand, the figures were 31, 41 and 28% respectively. In this country, capital investments were a condition for expanding livestock production into deforested areas. Meanwhile, in Uruguay, the simple possession of land suitable for animal feed allowed the owner to seize a significant part of the total agricultural output. By assuming that capitalists' profits are determined in the short term by consumption and investment decisions, it could be inferred that the greater share of the benefits in the distribution of Denmark and New Zealand reveals higher levels of investment in the agricultural sector than in Uruguay. Additionally, profit and land rent were distributed among a broad base of small and medium producers in the former countries. Meanwhile, in Uruguay, the simple possession of the highly concentrated land allowed landowners to obtain a good portion of the agricultural GDP.

This result has a direct impact on the potential of the three countries for inclusion in a virtuous process of structural change and industrialization as is discussed in Chapter 3. Based on Álvarez et al. (2011), the homogeneous distribution of property rights and agrarian income in Denmark and New Zealand is more likely to generate a higher demand for basic manufactures. By contrast, in Uruguay, the concentrated distribution of property rights and agrarian income in the hands of landowners stimulates the consumption of imported luxury goods by high-income sectors and inhibits the demand for locally produced manufactures and their profitability (Bilancini & D'Alessandro, 2005).

5 Concluding Remarks

Denmark, New Zealand and Uruguay were the wealthiest economies in the world in terms of income per capita at the end of the nineteenth century. This economic growth was sustained by the opportunities derived from integration in the global economy through the export of products obtained from livestock rearing. Despite the initial shared success, the three countries experienced different economic growth trajectories during the period 1870–1930.

The focus of the comparative analysis of this chapter was to study to what extent the different institutions associated with the definition of property rights and the historical land distribution processes impact on agrarian income distribution and hence the economic performance of the three countries during the First Globalization and the interwar period. Thus, we hypothesized that the emergence of different property rights systems and land tenure generated different wealth and income distribution patterns in the three countries, and hence different conditions for the economic performance from 1870 up to 1930.

Denmark intensified the land distribution process in the late eighteenth century, replacing the traditional open field system with reallocation of land to individual farms. At the end of the nineteenth century, agricultural modernization grew out of a viable and well-established family unit. Its relatively more egalitarian ownership structure translated into widespread income growth based on productivity increases. The evolution of the wage-rental relationship and the functional distribution of income, in which profits and wages accounted for a more significant proportion of agricultural GDP, seem to confirm this.

New Zealand and Uruguay showed different results in terms of land ownership distribution, despite sharing several similarities. Uruguay had a concentrated land ownership pattern dating back to the colonial period and was characterized by extensive pastoral farming. At the end of the nineteenth century, the country consolidated this highly unequal ownership structure, which translated on one hand into an increase in income for landowners relative to wage-earners, and on the other hand, into an agrarian sector income distribution pattern in which land ownership, capturing agrarian rents, was the most significant source of income. In New Zealand, the ways in which land ownership rights were distributed created an agrarian structure that was less concentrated and relatively more egalitarian than in Uruguay. The New Zealand agrarian sector contained a broader base of small and medium-sized producers. This land ownership structure caused income derived from exports to be captured by a broader section of rural producers than in Uruguay. Finally, and aligned with the arguments put forward by Senghaas (1985) and Álvarez et al. (2011), we assert that the agrarian ownership structure and the resulting income distribution pattern may create better conditions for structural change and industrialization in Denmark and New Zealand than in Uruguay, as is discussed in Chapter 3.

Appendix: Sources for Data

We present the general data sources, assumptions and methodological options for the functional income distribution estimates.

Agrarian GDP

Denmark

To estimate Danish agrarian GDP, we consider the Gross Domestic Product in million kroner at factor cost (in current prices) according to Mitchell (1998). We use the agricultural share of the GDP at factor cost estimated from Hansen (1984: 229–234 and 238–243) extracted from Henriksen (2008: 140–141) to calculate the agrarian product in current prices.

New Zealand and Uruguay

Data extracted from (Álvarez, 2008) and updates (Álvarez & Willebald, 2013; Álvarez, 2014).

Wages

Denmark

We have to estimate the wage mass in the agrarian sector, which is understood as the number of wage-earners multiplied by the annual salary in current prices in the agrarian sector. We obtain the wage per kroner per day from rural labourer (male and female) from Khaustova and Sharp (2015) for the period 1870–1913. For the agricultural wage series construction, the authors use Pedersen's (1930) estimates for the period between 1859 and 1913 for the municipality of Fladså. We assume that the number of *days* of *employment was 25 days per month.* For the 1870–1913 period, we use Hansen's (1984) estimates of the number of labourers in the agricultural sector *"defined as working men and woman aged from fifteen to sixty-four according to the censuses and with interpolation between the census years"* (footnote Henriksen, 2008: 136). Therefore, to calculate annual wages we assume that the rural wage in the economy is the simple average of the male and female wages. To cover the period 1914–1930, we first calculate the agricultural salary for the year 1914 assuming that the growth rate between 1913 and 1914 was the same as the industrial nominal wages provided by Greasley (2006). We then use the nominal index from Kærgård (1991) extracted from Henriksen (2008: 136) estimated for wage-earners in agriculture and for self-employed with wives in agriculture to calculate the salary mass for the remaining years.

New Zealand and Uruguay

Data extracted from (Álvarez, 2008) and updates (Álvarez & Willebald, 2013; Álvarez, 2014).

Rents

Denmark

We obtain the land values per Tønder Hartkorn, in kroner from Christensen (1985: Table VII.2, 106–107) for the period (1870–1900). We assume that one Tønder Hartkorn is equivalent to 18 Tønder land, and this is approximately equal to 10 hectares. For the 1900–1930 period we extracted land values from Statistik Årbog. In this sense, from 1900 to 1912, we consider the sale price of rural properties (propriétés rurales vendues [sans monture et à l'exclusion des ventes par adjudication, entre parents, etc.]) per Tønder Hartkorn. For the period 1913–1930 we consider the ordinary sale price of rural properties (including land and constructions) per Tønder Hartkorn. Finally, we obtain the total agricultural area (total crop area plus fallow areas) in Johansen (1985: Table 2.2, 129–130).

New Zealand and Uruguay

Data extracted from (Álvarez, 2008) and updates (Álvarez & Willebald, 2013; Álvarez, 2014).

Profits

Profits are obtained by difference for the three countries.

References

Allen, R. C. (2009). *The British industrial revolution in global perspective*. Cambridge University Press. https://doi.org/10.1017/CBO9780511816680

Álvarez, J. (2008). *Instituciones, cambio tecnológico y distribución del ingreso. Una comparación del desempeño económico de Nueva Zelanda y Uruguay (1870–1940)*. MSc Thesis. in Economic History. *Programa de Historia Económica y Social*. Universidad de la República-Uruguay. https://hdl.handle.net/20.500.12008/7714

Álvarez, J. (2013). The evolution of inequality in Australasia and the River Plate, 1870–1914. (Documentos de Trabajo On Line / FCS-PHES; 31). Udelar. FCS-UM. https://doi.org/10.2139/ssrn.3962473

Álvarez, J. (2014). *Instituciones, cambio tecnológico y productividad en los sistemas agrarios de Nueva Zelanda y Uruguay. Patrones y trayectorias de largo plazo (1870–2010)*. PhD Thesis *Programa de Historia Económica y Social*. Universidad de la República, Montevideo. https://hdl.handle.net/20.500.12008/8022

Álvarez, J., & Bértola, L. (2013). So similar, so different: New Zealand and Uruguay in the world economy. In C. Lloyd, J. Metzer, & R. Sutch (Eds.), *Settler economies in world history* (pp. 493–520). Brill. https://doi.org/10.1163/9789004232655_019

Álvarez, J., Bilancini, E., D'Alessandro, S., & Porcile, G. (2011). Agricultural institutions, industrialization and growth: The case of New Zealand and Uruguay in 1870–1940. *Explorations in Economic History, 48*(2), 151–168. https://doi.org/10.1016/j.eeh.2010.05.004

Álvarez, J. y Willebald, H. (2013). Agrarian income distribution, land ownership systems, and economic performance: settler economies during the First globalization. (Documentos de Trabajo On Line / FCS-PHES; 30). Udelar. FCS-UM. https://doi.org/10.2139/ssrn.3993969

Barrán, J. P., & Nahum, B. (1967). *Historia rural del Uruguay moderno* (Vol. I–VII). Ediciones de la Banda Oriental.

Barrán, J. P., & Nahum, B. (1972). *Historia rural del Uruguay moderno. Historia social de las revoluciones de 1897 y 1904* (Vol. IV). Ediciones de la Banda Oriental.

Barrán, J. P., & Nahum, B. (1977). *Historia rural del Uruguay moderno: La civilización ganadera bajo Batlle (1905–1914) (Vol.VI)*. Ediciones de la Banda Oriental.

Barrán, J. P., & Nahum, B. B. (1978). *Historia rural del Uruguay Moderno. Agricultura, crédito y transporte bajo Batlle (1905–1914)* (Vol. VII). Ediciones de la Banda Oriental.

Barrán, J. P., & Nahum, B. (1979). *Batlle, los estancieros y el Imperio Británico: Un diálogo difícil, 1903–1910* (Vol. 2). Ediciones de la Banda Oriental.

Belich, J. (1996). *Making peoples: A history of the New Zealanders, from Polynesian settlement to the end of the nineteenth century*. Penguin Book.

Bértola, L. (2005). A 50 años de la curva de Kuznets: Crecimiento económico y distribución del ingreso en Uruguay y otras economías de nuevo asentamiento desde 1870. *Investigaciones de Historia Económica, 1(3), 135–176.* https://doi.org/10.1016/S1698-6989(05)70022-9

Bértola, L. (2016). El PBI per capita de Uruguay 1870–2015: una reconstrucción. *(Documentos de Trabajo On Line / FCS-PHES; 48). Udelar. FCS-UM.*

Bértola, L., & Ocampo, J. A. (2013). *El desarrollo económico de América Latina desde la independencia*. Fondo de Cultura Económica.

Bértola, L., Calicchio, L., Camou, M. & Porcile, G. (1999). Southern Cone real wages compared: a purchasing power parity approach to convergence and divergence trends, 1870 – 1996. (DOL (Documentos On-line) Reedición / FCS-UM; 19). Udelar. FCS-UM. https://hdl.handle.net/20.500.12008/4664

Bertram, G. (2009). The New Zealand economy, 1900–2000. In G. Byrnes (Ed.), *The New Oxford History of New Zealand*. (pp. 537–572). Oxford University Press.

Bilancini, E., & D'Alessandro, S. (2005). Functional distribution, land ownership and industrial takeoff. The B.E. *Journal of Economic Analysis y Policy*, 8(1). https://doi.org/10.2202/1935-1682.1912

Boast, R. (2008). *Buying the land, selling the land: Governments and Māori land in the north island 1865–1921.* Victoria University Press.

Boast, R. P. (2016). *Māori land and land tenure in New Zealand: 150 years of the Māori Land Court*. NZACL, No. 22. Wellington.

Briggs, P. (2003). *Looking at the numbers. A view of New Zealand economic history*. NZIER, Wellington.

Condliffe, J. B. (1959). *New Zealand in the making: A study of economic and social development*. George Allen & Unwin Ltd.

Christensen, J.(1985). *Landbostatistik: Håndbog i dansk landbohistorisk statistik 1830–1900*, LandbohistoriskSelskab.

Christiansen, P. M., & Togeby, L. (2006). Power and democracy in Denmark: Still a viable democracy. *Scandinavian Political Studies, 29*(1), 1–24. https://doi.org/10.1111/j.1467-9477.2006.00139.x

Dale, P., & McLaughlin, J. (2000). *Land administration. OUP Catalogue*. Oxford University Press.

Danmarks Statistik (1903). *Statistiske Meddelelser* 4.12.7

Danmarks Statistik. (1908). *Statistisk Årbog 1907*. Denmark.

Danmarks Statistik. (1921). *Statistiske Meddelelser* 4.61.2

Danmarks Statistik. (1968). *Landbrugsstatistik 1900–1965*. Statistiske undersøgelser. Nro.22.

Danmarks Statistik. (1969). *Landbrugsstatistik 1900–1965*. Statistiske undersøgelser. Nro.25

Easton, B. (1997). *In stormy seas: The post-war New Zealand economy*. University of Otago Press.

Fairburn, M. (1991). The farmers take over (1912–1930). In K. Sinclair (Ed.), *The Oxford illustrated history of New Zealand* (pp.185–210). Oxford University Press.

Fairweather, J. R. (1985). Land Policy and land settlement in New Zealand. An Analysis of Land Policy Goals and an Evaluation of their Effect. Agricultural Economics Research Unit, Research Report No. 165, Lincoln College, Canterbury, New Zealand.

Finch, H. (2005). *La economía política del Uruguay contemporáneo, 1870–2000*. Ediciones de la Banda Oriental.

Frega, A., Maronna, M., & Trochón, Y. (1985). La reforma del agro. Una encrucijada para el batllismo. 1911–1933. *Serie Investigaciones CLAEH*, *2*(44–45).

Gould, J. (1965). The occupation of farm land in New Zealand, 1874–1911: A preliminary survey. *Business History and Archives*, *VI*, 123–141.

Greasley, D. (2006). A tale of two peripheries: Real wages in Denmark and New Zealand 1875–1939. *Scandinavian Economic History Review*, *54*(2), 116–136. https://doi.org/10.1080/03585520600759470

Greasley, D., & Oxley, L. (2004). Globalization and real wages in New Zealand 1873–1913. *Explorations in Economic History*, *41*(1), 26–47. https://doi.org/10.1016/S0014-4983(03)00044-5

Greasley, D., & Oxley, L. (2005). Refrigeration and distribution: New Zealand land prices and real wages 1873–1939. *Australian Economic History Review*, *45*(1), 23–44. https://doi.org/10.1111/j.1467-8446.2005.00126.x

Hawke, G. R. (1985). *The making of New Zealand. An economic history*. Cambridge University Press.

Hansen, S. A. (1984). *Økonomisk vækst i Danmark* (Vol. II). Akademisk Forlag.

Henriksen, I. (2003). Freehold tenure in late eighteenth century Denmark. In Advances in Agricultural Economic History (Vol. 2, pp. 21–39). Emerald Group Publishing Limited. https://doi.org/10.1016/S1569-4933(03)02013-X

Henriksen, I. (2008). The contribution of agriculture to economic growth in Denmark, 1870–1939." In P. Lains & V. Pinilla (Eds.), *Agriculture and economic development in Europe since 1870* (pp. 117–147). Routledge.

Herlitz, L. (1983). Landlords' agrarian reforms? *Scandinavian Economic History Review*, *31*(1), 68–73. https://doi.org/10.1080/03585522.1983.10408001

Hyldtoft, O. (1999). *Danmarks økonomiske historie 1840–1910*. (Vol. 2). Systime.

Jacob, R. (1969). *Consecuencias sociales del alambramiento (1872–1880)*. Ediciones de la Banda Oriental.

Jensen, E. (1937). *Danish agriculture, its economic development: a description and economic analysis centering on the free trade epoch, 1870–1930*. JH Schultz.

Jespersen, K. (2019). *A history of Denmark* (3rd ed.) Macmillan Essential Histories. Red Globe Press.

Johansen, H. C. (1985). *Danish historical statistics, 1814–1980*. Gyldendal.

Johansen, H. C. (1987). *The Danish economy in the twentieth century*. Croom Helm.

Kærgård, N. (1991). *Økonomisk vækst: en økonometrisk analyse af Danmark 1870–1981.* Jurist-og Økonomforbundets Forlag.

Kærgård, N. (2001). Economic theory and economic development in Denmark 1848–1914. In M. Psalidopoulos, & M. Mata (Eds.), *Economic thought and policy in less developed Europe – The nineteenth century.* (pp. 21–36). Routledge.

Khaustova, E., & Sharp, P. (2015). A note on Danish living standards through historical wage series, 1731–1913. *Journal of European Economic History, 44*(3), 143–172.

Kristensen, K. (1930). Public guidance in rural land utilization in Denmark. *The Annals of the American Academy of Political and Social Science, 150*(1), 230–237. https://doi.org/10.1177/000271623015000130

Lampe, M., & Sharp, P. (2019). *A land of milk and butter: how elites created the modern Danish dairy industry.* The University of Chicago Press.

Lindert, P., & Williamson, J. G. (2003). Does globalization make the world more unequal? In M. D. Bordo, A. M. Taylor, & J. G. Williamson (Eds.), *Globalization in historical perspective* (pp. 227–276). University of Chicago Press. https://doi.org/10.7208/chicago/9780226065991.003.0006

Madsen, H. B., Nørr, A. H., & Holst, A. (1992). The Danish Soil Classification. Atlas of Denmark I, 3. *The Royal Danish Geographical Society*, C.A. Reitzel.

McAloon, J. (2009). The New Zealand economy 1792–1914. In G. Byrnes (Ed.), *The New Oxford History of New Zealand* (pp. 197–217). Oxford University Press.

McIntyre, R. (2007). *Historic heritage of high-country pastoralism: South Island up to 1948.* Department of Conservation. Science & Technical Publishing.

Menéndez, M. (2021). Transformaciones productivas, institucionales y tecnológicas en el sector agrario de Dinamarca, Nueva Zelanda y Uruguay (1870–1930). MSc Thesis in Economic History. Programa de Historia Económica y Social. Facultad de Ciencias Sociales, UdelaR. https://hdl.handle.net/20.500.12008/27488

Millot, J., & Bertino, M. (1996). *Historia económica del Uruguay (1860–1910).* Fundación de Cultura Universitaria.

Mitchell, B. (1998). *International historical statistics: Europe 1750–1993.* Springer.

North, D. (1984). *Estructura y cambio en la historia* (económica). Alianza.

Norton, R. D. (2002). *Agricultural development policy: concepts and experiences.* John Wiley & Sons.

O'Rourke, K. H., & Williamson, J. G. (1999). *Globalization and history: The evolution of a nineteenth-century Atlantic economy.* MIT. https://doi.org/10.7551/mitpress/3310.001.0001

Østergaard, U. (2006). Denmark: a big small state–the peasant roots of Danish modernity. In Campbell, J.; Hall, J; Kaj, O: *National Identity and the Varieties of Capitalism–The Danish Experience*. (p. 53–98). McGill-Queen's University Press.

Paldam, M. (1990). El desarrollo de un próspero Estado benefactor en Dinamarca. In M. Blomström, & P. Meller (Eds.), *Trayectorias Divergentes: Comparación de un Siglo de Desarrollo Económico Latinoamerico y Escandinavo* (pp. 83–114). CIEPLAN-Hachette.

Pedersen, P. J.(1930). *Arbejdslønnen i Danmark Under Skiftende Konjunkturer i Perioden ca. 1850–1913*. Akademisk Forlag.

Skocpol, T., & Somers, M. (1980). The Uses of Comparative History in Macrosocial Inquiry. *Comparative Studies in Society and History*, 22(2), 174-197. https://doi.org/10.1017/S0010417500009282

Senghaas, D. (1985). *The European experience: A historical critique of development theory*. K. H. Kimmig.

Silagi, M., & Faulkner, S. N. (1994). Henry George and Europe: In *Denmark* the Big Landowners Scuttled the Age-Old Land Tax, but the Smallholders, Moved by George, Restored It. *The American Journal of Economics and Sociology*, 53(4), 491–501. https://www.jstor.org/stable/3487193

Skrubbeltrang, L. F. (1961). Developments in tenancy in eighteenth-century Denmark as a move towards peasant proprietorship. *Scandinavian Economic History Review*, *9*(2), 165–175. https://doi.org/10.1080/03585522.1961.10411438

Smout, T. C. (1987). Landowners in Scotland, Ireland and Denmark in the age of improvement. *Scandinavian Journal of History*, *12*(1–2), 79–97. https://doi.org/10.1080/03468758708579109

Willebald, H., & Bértola, L. (2013). Uneven Development Paths among Settler Societies, 1870–2000. In C. Lloyd, J. Metzer, & R. Sutch (Eds.), *Settler economies in world history* (pp. 105–140). Brill. https://doi.org/10.1163/9789004232655_006

Willebald, H., & Juambeltz, J. (2018). Land Frontier Expansion in Settler Economies, 1830–1950: Was It a Ricardian Process?. In V. Pinilla, & H. Willebald (Eds.), *Agricultural Development in the World Periphery*. (pp. 439–466). Palgrave Studies in Economic History. Palgrave Macmillan, Cham. https://doi.org/10.1007/978-3-319-66020-2_17

CHAPTER 8

Poles Apart? Living Standards and Inequality by Labour Market Outcomes in Brazil and Sweden, ca. 1830–1920

Jakob Molinder, Thales Pereira, and Svante Prado

1 Introduction

Today, South America and Scandinavia appear to be poles apart in the range of economic inequality across the world: inequality is very high in South America and very low in Scandinavia. For South America, two positions emerge from the previous research on the origin of today's high inequality: the first camp underscores the role of persistence and

J. Molinder
Uppsala University and Lund Universitiy, Uppsala and Lund, Sweden

T. Pereira
São Paulo School of Economics, São Paulo, Brazil

S. Prado (✉)
University of Gothenburg, Göteborg, Sweden
e-mail: svante.prado@econhist.gu.se

J. Álvarez and S. Prado (eds.), *Scandinavia and South America—A Tale of Two Capitalisms*, Palgrave Studies in Economic History,
https://doi.org/10.1007/978-3-031-09198-8_8

argues that high levels of inequality reach all the way back to the colonial past (Acemoglu et al., 2001; Engerman & Sokoloff, 1997). The other camp argues that today's high inequality is attributable to developments during the second and third quarters of the twentieth century, when the developed countries, such as those in Scandinavia, witnessed a compression of the income distribution. Williamson (2015) asked whether Latin America missed the "twentieth-century levelling" and responded in the affirmative. In fact, similar standpoints have recently emerged in the discussion about the roots of Swedish equality (Bengtsson, 2019). Some scholars claim that Scandinavian egalitarianism was shaped in the pre-industrial period (Rothstein & Uslaner, 2005), while more recent research provides evidence that the low-income concentration of today is the result of developments in the twentieth century (Bengtsson et al., 2018; Gärtner & Prado, 2016; Piketty, 2020).

This chapter is motivated by a quest to trace the historical roots of this present-day pattern of inequality, contrasting Brazil with Sweden. Both these countries are at the frontier of the inequality debate: Brazil, despite decreasing inequality in the 2000s, remains one of the most unequal countries in the world, and Sweden, despite increasing inequality since the early 1980s, remains one of the most equal. To succeed in our quest, we began by examining the years between 1830 and 1920, which mark a period that begins with the first evidence of inequality in Brazil and ends before the Great Levelling of the twentieth century. We then turned our focus on the labour market and on the rewards to different kinds of worker attributes. Three motives warrant our labour market focus. First, wages are an important component of earnings for people from most social strata. Second, wages allow us to examine different dimensions of inequality, such as differentials across sexes, skills, and regions. Third, the availability of evidence on wages for specific groups of workers is also quite good for periods prior to industrialization, when other evidence of income distribution is in short supply, which makes it possible to push the comparisons further back in time.

Our empirical study is separated into two parts. In the first, we examine the evolution of comparative standards of living over time. By looking at both GDP per capita and real wage records, we can determine whether inequality was driven by the forces associated with Lewis' (1954) and Kuznets' (1955) notions of a duality between the modern and the traditional sector. Since the trajectory of real wages followed GDP per capita quite closely for both countries, we conclude that neither Lewis' nor

Kuznets' models offer much guidance in our search for the roots of inequality. A close examination of the relative levels, on the other hand, shows that standards of living were comparable in the two countries until about the late 1880s. We also show evidence of slaves' welfare ratios, although evaluation of the true welfare ratio of slaves is a thorny issue because of the unknown level of slaves' earnings that was due to their masters. After the 1880s, the welfare ratios of Swedish workers surged ahead, whereas those of Brazilian workers of all kinds faced a long-term absolute stagnation and relative decline. The similar levels of welfare ratios before the fourth quarter of the nineteenth-century contrast with the GDP per capita record, which indicates a two-to-one Swedish advantage. This discrepancy between the two measures warrants us to bring additional inequality considerations into the picture.

In the second empirical section, we therefore examine the spread of earnings across space, skills, and sex. Among these different inequality dimensions, the regional element separates Brazil from Sweden. Regional inequality in Brazil was higher than in Sweden. The gap in standards of living between the dry and often poverty-stricken Northeast and prosperous and industrialized Southeast is a perennial theme of Brazilian historiography (Leff, 1982; Prado Júnior, 1945). Also, whereas regional inequality in Brazil has remained until the present-day, much of the regional earnings differentials in Sweden were initially wiped out in the early twentieth century, and subsequently after the 1940s. However, earnings differentials across skills and sex were seemingly no higher in Brazil than in Sweden in the early twentieth century.

We conclude that the major divergence in workers' welfare took place in the fourth quarter of the nineteenth century, whereas most aspects of inequality began to diverge on different trajectories during the twentieth century. Barring the regional dimension, the colonial legacies of Brazil and the possibly ancient roots of Swedish equality seem to offer few insights into today's patterns of inequality. Although the colonial legacy of present-day inequality is still a matter of dispute, we argue that Brazil missed an opportunity of growth and equality during the twentieth century. The colonial past cannot entirely explain this missed opportunity.

2 Overview of Labour Markets

As in other countries outside of the heartlands of industrialization and modernization, the vast majority of workers in Brazil toiled in the agricultural sector throughout the nineteenth century. Figures based on the census show that as late as the 1940s, a staggering 70% of the male workforce was employed in agriculture (Fig. 1). Aside from the agricultural bias, the presence of large number of slaves distinguished the function and evolution of the Brazilian labour markets. Between the early sixteenth and mid-nineteenth century, Brazil was the country that received most slaves from the transatlantic trade. After the end of the slave trade in 1850, slavery persisted in Brazil until 1888, leaving a mark on racial inequality that persists to this day. Slavery also had inevitable implications for the development of the labour markets in Brazil. The highly elastic supply of enslaved labour most likely influenced the wages of the free population, although we do not have quantitative studies that demonstrate this impact convincingly. The standard hypothesis is that, with the presence of slaves in multiple sectors of the economy, wages in Brazil did not increase during most of the nineteenth century. The presence of slaves also made Brazil a less attractive destination in the eyes of European immigrants. Counterfactually, a larger inflow of European immigrants, equipped with higher levels of human capital, could have elevated the average level of wages. The next section will show that the evidence we have for Bahia and Rio de Janeiro indicates that wages in Brazil remained stagnant during the lifetime of slavery. One may surmise that the large supply of slaves has something to do with that stagnation.

With the end of slavery, immigration increased rapidly, which transformed the labour market in south-eastern Brazil. Between 1850 and 1887, the average number of immigrants arriving in Brazil was 17,500 per year, while in the two decades after abolition in 1888 it increased to an average of 89,400 people. During the period after abolition, 26.5% of the migrants came from Portugal and 42.7% from Italy (Willcox, 1929). The rapid increase in immigration after the end of the slave trade was mostly concentrated in São Paulo and 80% of immigrations were subsidized by the government (Holloway, 1980: 40). Data from the census show that 18% of São Paulo's population was foreign-born in 1920. The pattern of those decades was transitory, and the country returned to receiving few immigrants in the following decades, especially after Vargas' restrictions in

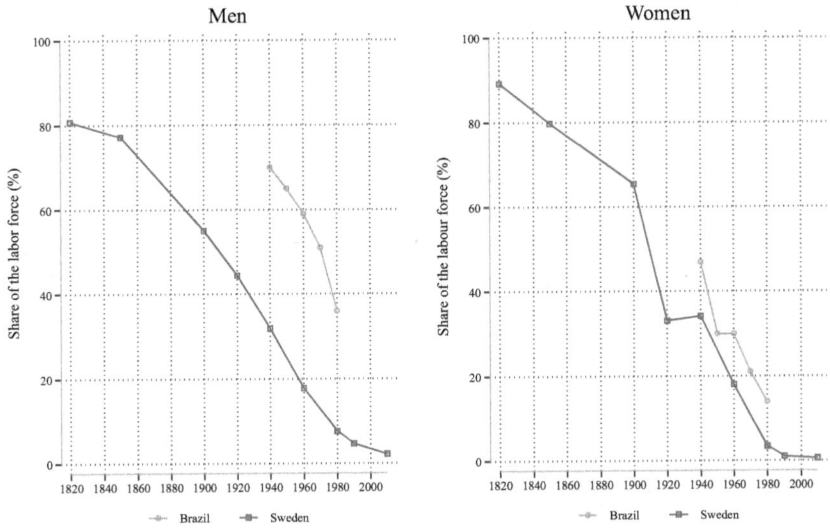

Fig. 1 Share of the labour force in agriculture by sex, 1820–2010 (*Sources* Brazil: Merrick and Graham [1979]; Sweden: Unpublished manuscript by Pernilla Jonsson, Inger Jonsson and Fredrik Sandgren)

1934. The existence of state subsidies to maintain a greater flow of immigrants, however, kept wages low in São Paulo between 1890 and 1930. Ball (2013) shows that real wages for skilled and unskilled workers in the city of São Paulo were stagnant during the 1889–1930 period.

In Sweden, the formation of a modern labour market occurred gradually during the second half of the nineteenth century. The Swedish economy was overwhelmingly agrarian before the mid-nineteenth century since manufacturing then was still in its infancy. Most estimates suggest that the share of workers in agriculture was about 80%. From the 1860s, the share of agriculture declined rapidly owing to the rapid progression of manufacturing and urbanization (Fig. 1). In addition to structural transformation, changes in labour market institutions also paved the way for a modern labour market. In agriculture, individual employment contracts between two equal parties replaced older forms of coercive labour relations in the manors, and cash wages and short-term notice replaced payments in kind and yearly employment agreements (Lundh, 2010).

The impact of manufacturing on the wages of farm workers was negligible at least until the 1850s, when the sawmills along the northern Baltic coast expanded. The rapid growth of manufacturing in the fourth quarter of the nineteenth-century mark increased integration between rural and urban labour markets (Collin, 2016). In addition, much industrialization occurred in the countryside close to rivers, to harness the energy, and close to the natural resources used in production, as illustrated by the sawmills scattered throughout Sweden before the arrival of the steam engine. Many people earned a living through a combination of farm work and industrial work, and short-distance and circular migration was the norm (Dribe & Lundh, 2005; Gadd, 2011).

With the advent of new transportation and communication technologies, labour mobility increased. In 1860, 7% of the population were born outside their county of residence (Institute for Social Sciences, 1941: 42; Lundh, 2006). In 1900 and 1930, the corresponding percentage figures were 16 and 22, respectively, indicating a substantial increase in long-distance internal migration. Emigration to the United States took off in the late 1860s and accelerated in the 1880s and 1900s (Bohlin & Eurenius, 2010; Hatton & Williamson, 1998, pp. 197–198). Emigration reduced the supply of labour relative to other factors of production in the late nineteenth and early twentieth centuries, and it has often been assumed that, above all, this affected the rewards for unskilled workers (O'Rourke and Williamson, 1995; Williamson, 1995). The evidence for a major effect is however uncertain (Ericsson & Molinder 2020; Prado, 2010a). Enflo et al. (2014) provide econometric evidence that emigration and internal migration before World War I diminished regional wage differentials. Emigrants left low-wage counties in particular. The diminished supply of workers in low-wage counties spurred faster growth in wages in these counties than in high-wage counties, which resulted in declining wage differentials across all counties. In the post-World War II decades, Sweden turned from being a country of emigration to one of immigration.

Labour market institutions, through unions, employers' organizations, and collective agreements, have played a major role in the evolution of the labour market and the development of wages in Sweden. In the beginning of the twentieth century, wage formation was local and laid down in collective agreements between trade unions and firms or local employers' associations. Only a few nationwide collective agreements were formed to impose standardized employment conditions, working hours, and wage rates. Prior to World War I, union membership was still quite low (ca. 15%), but since the collective agreements also included non-union members employed by firms that practiced collective bargaining, they actually covered about half the workforce in manufacturing. Unionization increased rapidly during the interwar period; in the early 1930s, half of all blue-collar workers in the manufacturing industry were union members. The coverage of collective agreements reached between 60 and 80%, depending on the industrial branch (Lundh, 2010: 105). Unlike Britain, where unions were organized by occupation, trade unions and employers in Sweden were largely organized by industry (Lundh, 2010). A likely effect of the collective agreements is that within-industry differences in wages across regions diminished. Collective bargaining was not restricted to norms governing within-industry wage harmonization; trade unionist norms that favoured increasing wage equality between occupational groups and across industries were also part of the collective bargaining system.

3 Comparing Standards of Living, ca. 1830–1920

In this empirical section, we establish comparative standards of living in Sweden and Brazil for the period from 1830 to 1920, beginning with a review of the historical national accounts for Brazil and then examining at length nominal earnings and prices, combined into welfare ratios. The GDP per capita records for the so-called periphery, in particular the peripheral countries of Europe, such as Finland, Greece, Norway, Portugal, Spain, and Sweden, indicate that differences among them were quite small by the mid-nineteenth century. By 1900, GDP per capita for some of those countries, including Sweden, had increased by approximately 50%, but not so in Brazil, however; the record shows that GDP per capita barely increased during the latter half of the nineteenth century, even though, as we shall examine below, the quality of Brazilian historical accounts leaves a great deal to be desired.

3.1 GDP Per Capita

Brazil's economic stagnation during the nineteenth century has been the subject of numerous studies. The first one that sought to measure economic growth in the period was Furtado (1959), who presented an optimistic view. He concluded that while stagnation marked the first half of the century, GDP per capita grew by 1.5% annually in the second half, which is respectable compared to the world economy at the time. According to Furtado, growth in the aggregate after 1850 was largely the result of surging coffee exports in the southeast and rubber production in the north of the country. Northeast Brazil, in contrast, stagnated, which spurred regional disparities that would persist throughout the twentieth century.

Following Furtado, Contador and Haddad (1975) gathered data on exports, imports, and government spending to generate a series of real incomes by principal component analysis beginning in 1861. For the nineteenth century, however, their estimate of nominal output depends entirely on data on imports and exports. A critical aspect of their national accounts is their dependence on the price deflator of Ónody (1960), employed in order to establish a series of volume outputs. This deflator is based on official prices for imported products used to calculate customs revenues, which are not representative of market prices for the nineteenth century. Contador and Haddad (1975) painted a much more pessimistic picture of income growth than Furtado (1959); they concluded that between 1861 and 1900, the growth rate in GDP per capita was only 0.4%. By comparison, the United States grew by 1.3% annually during the same period.

Subsequently, Goldsmith (1986) reached a result similar to that of Contador and Haddad (1975), also resorting to data on exports, imports, government spending, as well as the wage series from Lobo (1978). He reckoned that Brazil's per capita growth was 0.3% per year for the second half of the nineteenth century. Another contribution of his was to estimate production disaggregated by regions based on the work of Buescu (1970). The regional distribution of GDP, however, allocated 71% of the national economy to the southeast, putting excessive weight on the coffee economy and possibly underestimating other regions.

The attempts to estimate Brazilian growth rates, fraught as they are with problematic assumptions, are usually overlooked because most scholars draw on the historical income statistics provided by the so-called Maddison project. It is, therefore, important to subject the Brazilian series in the Maddison project to scrutiny. The roots of the Brazilian series go all the way back to Maddison's unpublished working paper, titled "Brazilian Development Experience from 1500 and 1929". In this working paper, Maddison cites all the work we have discussed above and presents annual growth rates between 1889 and 1986, using Goldsmith's (1986) GDP deflator. In a follow-up paper, he presents some estimates for 1820 and 1890 (Maddison, 2000). Since this paper was based on a lecture, it does not include references, so the source of the figures prior to 1850 is unclear.

The different versions of the Maddison project have, on the one hand, reproduced Maddison's data, and on the other, replaced Maddison with more recent updates. In the first version of the Maddison project database (2010), there are two more estimates, for 1850 and 1870, and a linear interpolation between 1870 and 1890. The next version of the Maddison project (2013) provides almost the same figures, reaching back to 1850, but also includes an estimated value of GDP for 1800. According to the description of the sources, the estimates between 1800 and 1870 are from Prados de la Escosura (2009), who employs Maddison's approach to calculate long-term estimates of GPD per capita, extrapolating from a recent benchmark (Bolt & van Zanden, 2014: 645). Prados de la Escosura extrapolates backwards from the benchmark of International Comparisons Project (ICP), drawing on the GDP data from Goldsmith (1986), whose series, however, begins in 1850. So, building on the work of Leff (1982: 33), Prados de la Escosura assumes that there was zero per capita income growth for the first half of the nineteenth century. Later versions of the Maddison project (2018, 2020) have maintained this assumption (Bolt & van Zanden, 2020; Bolt et al., 2018). In the most recent update of the Maddison project (2020), there is a new historical time series for the period between 1850 and 1899 originating from Barro and Ursúa (2008). They claim to have improved the linear trend between 1870 and 1890, but the paper does not include any information on the procedure and sources. We are told that a continuous series starting in 1850 was constructed by "combining various sources" (Barro & Ursúa, 2008: 77). The authors have not provided justification for their claimed improvement to the Brazilian series.

It is thus clear that there are no real GDP estimates for Brazil prior to 1850, which is often ignored because most scholars depend on the historical time series of GDP offered by the Maddison project. Moreover, even the data on nominal GDP used to estimate income during the second half of the nineteenth century has many limitations, as our minor digression has highlighted. Bold claims made with reference to Brazilian GDP per capita figures should be regarded with a certain amount of scepticism.

Given these limitations, we seek to contribute to this debate using data on real wages to measure both differences in the level of Brazilian income with the European periphery—in this case, Sweden—and to compare trends over time. The reason is that other measures of well-being show results that conflict with what we know from GDP. Anthropometric evidence suggests that there was some improvement in living conditions in southeast Brazil after the 1870s (Franken, 2019). Moreover, previous comparative evidence for wages also shows a different pattern than GDP estimates. Williamson (1995) compares trends in real wages for 17 countries between 1830 and 1988. One of the surprising results is that Brazil had higher wages than Sweden until the early twentieth century. Looking closer at Williamson's series, several problems with the underlying data become apparent, however. For Sweden, Williamson uses agricultural wages for the period 1830–1860, but uses a flawed series of unskilled industrial wages between 1860 and 1913 (Prado, 2010a). For Brazil, wages are an unweighted average for labourers, carpenters, bricklayers, and porters in Rio de Janeiro, which had wages higher than the average in the country at the time (Pereira, 2019). We provide several improvements from these earlier attempts to estimate real wages in the following sections.

3.2 Comparing Workers' Standards of Living

We draw on Allen's (2001) approach to measure comparative standards of living in a two-step procedure. We first establish nominal wages for similar worker categories, and then the cost of buying a fixed basket of consumer items yielding a certain amount of calories. By combining the nominal wage income and the cost of the consumption basket, living standards can be expressed in terms of welfare ratios which measure the number of such consumption baskets that a family could afford. The assumption following Allen (2001) is that a male worker had to support his wife and two children. Expressed in consumption units, the four family members needed to consume the equivalent of three adults. To arrive at the welfare ratio, nominal income is divided by the cost of the consumption basket times three in the following way:

$$\text{Welfare ratio} = \frac{\text{Nominal wage income}}{\text{Cost of consumption basket} * 3}$$

As with our previous review of GDP per capita, our treatment of the sources for nominal wages and prices of consumables is heavily skewed towards Brazil. The reason for this Brazilian bias is the scarcity of previous research on Brazilian nominal wages and prices.

For Brazil, we depend on nominal wages for Rio de Janeiro in 1827–1930 and for Bahia in 1801–1889 (Lobo et al., 1971; Mattoso, 1986). We begin by using information on carpenters and masons, which have counterparts in Swedish statistics. We have collapsed these two worker categories into one labelled skilled labour. For Bahia, the wages of carpenters and masons move in tandem. They were stagnant until the late 1820s; they doubled during the early 1830s; they were stagnant from then until the mid-1850s; and then they almost doubled again by the late 1880s. This stair-like pattern is not present in the wage series for Rio de Janeiro. They instead show a trend of continuous growth. Since all the series originate from evidence from health institutions, the geographical difference might stem from measurement errors. Interpolation on the part of researchers is one such possible error; another is the procedure used by the institutions to record their expenses for labour. Because we do not know anything about the error margins, we take the arithmetic mean of the wages in Rio de Janeiro and Bahia.

For Sweden, we depend on Ericsson and Molinder's (2020) series of day wages for construction workers for the 1831–1900 period. This evidence was originally sourced from the price currents for building materials and labour services that local authorities submitted to the state. We have included the series of nominal wages for carpenters and masons in Stockholm and Gothenburg in order to establish wage measures similar to those for Brazil. We multiply the day wage by 250 to arrive at yearly wages. Complementing Ericsson and Molinder (2020), Bagge et al. (1935) offer evidence of wages for urban construction workers for nine Swedish towns between 1890 and 1930 based on payrolls from municipalities. They present one series, labelled unskilled, that begins in 1890 and another, labelled skilled, that begins in 1894. A comparison between the overlapping decade of the 1890s suggests that the wages for carpenters in Ericsson and Molinder (2020) are similar to the series of wages labelled unskilled in Bagge et al. (1935), while the wages of masons in Ericsson and Molinder (2020) are similar to the series of wages labelled skilled in Bagge et al. (1935). Starting in 1913, evidence of wages for construction workers is also available in the official wage statistics. Until 1925, they present figures for the average yearly wages of adult male workers in construction; thereafter, they present wage figures for workers hired by municipal and state construction projects. While the series of

Bagge et al. and the series of the official wage statistics are in close correspondence up to 1920, they diverge thereafter. We have drawn on the series of the official wage statistics because of its broader coverage.

To build the cost of the subsistence basket for Brazil, we use the prices collected by Mattoso (1986) for Bahia and the price index by Lobo et al. (1971) for Rio de Janeiro.[1] To cover the period before 1864 in Rio de Janeiro, we collected monthly prices for the period 1834–1865 from *Jornal do Commercio*. To create the consumption basket, several historical sources indicate that manioc flour, black beans, and meat were the staple diet of Brazilians. For example, James Henderson, who visited Brazil during the late 1810s, wrote that many families "subsisted" on manioc flour, and sometimes ate black beans and dried beef (Henderson, 1821: 74). Reports from workers, many of them slaves, in the whale-hunting business during the early nineteenth century relate that they consumed dried meat, manioc flour, black beans, salt, and tobacco (Ellis, 1969: 86). Although meat consumption was relatively common, poor workers could afford to eat beef only in small quantities for much of the nineteenth century. J. B. Debret reported (around the 1820s) that small traders ate only a "miserable piece of meat" (dried meat, not beef) for dinner. The main food was manioc flour with "some" beans (Campos, 2010: 202). The merchant John Luccock, around the same time, reported that:

> The beef, thus brought to market, used to be employed almost entirely as a basis for soup. At a later period, it appeared at table in pieces, and in the form of steaks; in this state it was chiefly confined to the higher ranks. Others seldom tasted of it, except household slaves, who, in many families, had, with their regular allowance of *feijam* [corrected in the document as *farinha*], a small quantity of boiled beef or bacon. The *carne-seca*, which is beef killed at a distance from the city, cut into flitches, and dried in the sun, was in much more common use. (Luccock, 1820: 43)

Luccock's mention of the increase in meat consumption at a "later period" owes to the abolishment of several restrictions to the meat trade in 1822 that made meat less expensive after independence (Graham, 2010: 119). Manioc meal, nonetheless, was by far the main source of calories. The merchant reported that a "plate of *farinha*, with orange-juice squeezed over it, forms a frequent dinner for the inferior traders and

[1] We use the 1919 weights, since the 1856 weights overestimate price trends.

artisans; others eat it with gravy, and the negroes give it a slight boiling" (Luccock, 1820: 46). Information from Salvador's grains market from the mid-nineteenth century shows that manioc meal accounted for 87% of sales, which included beans, rice, and corn (Graham, 2010: 95). Therefore, despite the supply of various foods in Brazil most food consisted of manioc meal, beans, and meat.

Given the meagre diet of Brazilian workers, how can we establish a consumption basket similar to those used in studies of other regions? Many sources from the nineteenth century mention that "the standard daily ration of manioc meal for slaves, soldiers, sailors, prisoners, employees, and pensioners" was 0.907 L (1.25 pounds or 0.56 kilos). This meal, which supplied between 2000 and 2500 cal, was equivalent to military rations of other grains from European nations (Graham, 2010: 84–85). Troops also received some meat alongside beans, bacon, and rice. Records from workers in the Brazilian navy show similar information. Slaves who worked for the navy in 1832 received 140 réis to buy manioc, beef jerky, black beans, rice, and bacon. They also received uniforms—two shirts, two trousers, and a jacket—every six months (Rocha, 2012: 50). Another record from 1829 shows that a daily ration in the navy had 344.2 g of beef jerky or 459 g (1 lb) of fresh beef, 28.68 g (one *onça*) of bacon, 244 g (1/120 *alqueire*) of black beans, and 734 g (1/40 *alqueire*) of manioc flour. There was also some rice and tobacco (Rocha, 2012: 126). These amounts are similar to what workers received in private companies. Slaves who worked in industrial establishments in Minas Gerais during the late 1840s had daily rations with an average of 185.7 g of beef, 28 g of bacon, 428 g of corn flour (*fubá*), 242 g of black beans, and small quantities of manioc flour, coffee, rum, and rice (Rocha, 2012: 119).

The way to build a basket of comparable consumption, therefore, is from the caloric consumption of these foods instead of the quantities consumed. Modern estimates show that there are approximately 340 kcal in each 100 g of manioc flour. The annual consumption for manioc flour presented above ranges from 204 to 267 kg, which gives an average of 2200 kcal a day, which is already higher than Allen's (2001) widely used so-called subsistence basket of 1960 kcal. The quantities consumed in Brazil actually suggest that the "subsistence basket" was probably too low for a worker during the nineteenth century. Allen et al. (2012: 873) use 165 kg of maize in their estimates for real wages in colonial America, which corresponds to 1655 kcal a day. For 1655 kcal a day, the consumption of manioc meal would be 487 g, amounting to 178 kg per year.

Table 1 shows our Brazilian basket alongside those of Allen (2001) for Europe and Allen et al. (2012) for colonial America. The European basket in the first column includes only the foods that are comparable to the other baskets, which gives 1665 kcal from the total 1941 kcal of the complete basket. If we use the latter figure, it would by inference be 75.8 kg of beans or peas for 187 kcal, which is closer to our estimates for black beans in Brazil. For meat, however, consumption was much higher. The consumption basket used for Europe is similar to those used to calculate welfare ratios in other parts of the world, except when it comes to legumes, the second most important component of the diet. The calorie figure for beans/peas for colonial America's bare-bones subsistence basket is much higher than the corresponding figure for Europe, implying that the colonial America basket is cheaper. In his basket for Europe, Allen (2001) assumes that 100 g of peas/beans has 90 kcal, but for the American basket beans/peas produce 340 kcal. This higher number is the same for the basket used to calculate Asian welfare ratios (Allen et al., 2011: 38). As the number of calories for each food has a significant impact on the price of the basket, we adopted a conservative estimate for the Brazilian basket with the aim of bringing it closer to the European basket.

For Sweden, our estimate of the cost of a subsistence basket is based on the work of Gary (2018) and Ericsson and Molinder (2020). Gary (2018) presents the development of welfare ratios for casual workers on construction sites in Stockholm, Malmö, and Kalmar over the 1500–1914 period. She calculates the cost of a subsistence basket as well as a respectability basket. She follows the composition of goods in Allen (2013) but substitutes half of the consumption of meat for fish in order to reflect a Scandinavian diet. Ericsson and Molinder (2020) calculate welfare ratios using respectability baskets for Swedish construction workers over the 1831–1900 period. They draw on Gary (2018) and use the same source for prices but create regionally disaggregated series. As a baseline, they assume that workers consumed 2.5 kilos of meat and 2.5 kilos of fish but show that the cost of the basket is not greatly affected by substituting fish for meat.

Both Gary (2018) and Ericsson and Molinder (2020) depend on the price series of Jörberg (1972), which are based on market price scales for each county in 1732–1914. To extend the series of the cost of a subsistence basket up to 1920, we depend on the official price statistics from

Table 1 Subsistence baskets for Europe, colonial America, Brazil, and Sweden

Europe *Allen (2001)*	*Colonial America* *Allen et al. (2012)*	*Brazil* *This study*	*Sweden* *This study*
Bread 182 kg 100 g = 245 kcal amount: 1223 kcal	Maize 165 kg 100 g = 366 kcal amount: 1655 kcal	Manioc 178 kg 100 g = 340 kcal amount: 1655 kcal	Rye 170 kg 100 g = 390 kcal amount: 1816 kcal
Beans/Peas 52 L 100 g = 90 kcal amount: 160 kcal	Beans/Peas 20 kg 100 g = 338.3 kcal amount: 187 kcal	Black Beans 38 kg 100 g = 180 kcal amount: 187 kcal	Peas 20 kg 100 g = 341 kcal amount: 187 kcal
Meat 26 kg 100 g = 250 kcal amount = 178 kcal	Meat 5 kg 100 g = 250 kcal amount = 34 kcal	Beef Jerky 3 kg 100 g = 410 kcal amount = 34 kcal	Meat 5 kg 100 g = 248 kcal Amount = 34 kcal
Butter 5.2 kg 100 g = 728 kcal amount = 104 kcal	Butter 3 kg 100 g = 727 kcal amount: 60 kcal	Bacon 4.6 kg 100 g = 476 kcal amount: 60 kcal	Butter/cheese 3 kg 100 g = 730 kcal Amount: 60 kcal
Sum: 1665 kcal	Sum: 1936 kcal	Sum: 1936 kcal	Sum: 2097 kcal

Sources Allen (2001: 421) and Allen (2015). Calorie information from Food and Nutrient database for dietary studies (https://fdc.nal.usda.gov/). *Note* The basket for Sweden depicted in Table 1 follows the application by Gary (2018) and Gary and Olsson (2020) of the Allen subsistence basket to the Swedish context, and as applied by Ericsson and Molinder (2020). We make one change compared to that work, however. Because of the easier access to sources for the price of meat than for fish for our period, we assume consumption of 5 kg of meat, rather than a 50/50 split between meat and fish. Also note that the Swedish basket is based on Allen's most recent update (Allen, 2015), which includes a higher calorie total in the subsistence basket

Statistics Sweden starting in 1913 (*Detaljpriser och indexberäkningar åren 1913–1930*). The overlap in 1913–1914 allows us to assess the impact of the shift in sources. Gary (2018) and Ericsson and Molinder (2020) depend on Jörberg's price notation for barrels of rye to capture the cost of grain. In the official statistics, the cost is instead provided for rye flour. Our comparison for 1913 reveals that a kilo of unprocessed rye amounted to about half the price of a kilo of rye flour. If we apply this price ratio and double the price of a barrel of rye as reported by Jörberg (1972), the cost of a subsistence basket in 1913 is almost the same using the two different sources. In order to match our subsistence basket for Brazil, which includes manioc flour, we opt to use the price of rye flour instead of rye in our subsistence basket for Sweden.

We begin our assessment of comparative standards of living by looking at GDP per capita (Fig. 2) as provided by the Maddison project (2020). By the third quarter of the nineteenth century, the Swedish level of GDP per capita was about twice that of Brazil: That is, a substantive lead well before industrialization and modern economic growth even began in Sweden. The gap then began to widen after the mid-1870s and continued to do so until the outbreak of World War I. At that time the Swedish level was about 5 times that of Brazil. The Swedish level then continued to range between 4 and 5 times the Brazilian until the 1970s. As the previous review of historical national accounts bore out, great uncertainty about the Brazilian levels as well as growth rates in GDP per capita remains for the entire nineteenth century, however.

The welfare ratios of different unskilled and skilled workers paint a picture that is somewhat different from GDP per capita (Fig. 3–4). First, welfare ratios indicate that the gap in living standards between the two countries was quite narrow until the third quarter of the nineteenth century. The welfare ratio comparisons show that for both skilled and unskilled workers, welfare ratios in Rio were higher than in Stockholm

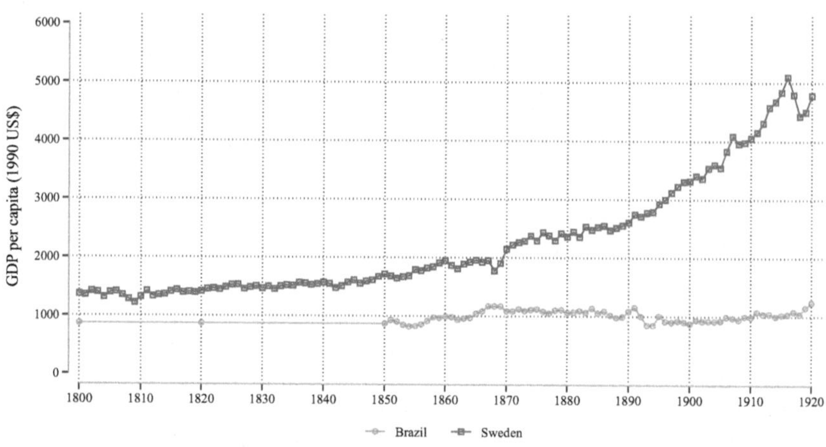

Fig. 2 GDP per capita in Brazil and Sweden, 1800–1920 (*Sources* Brazil, Barro and Ursúa [2008]; Prados de la Escosura [2009]; Sweden, Schön & Krantz [2015]; Maddison Project Database, version 2020); https://www.rug.nl/ggdc/historicaldevelopment/maddison/releases/maddison-project-database-2020?lang=en

and Gothenburg until the 1860s. Moreover, aside from some year-to-year swings, the average of the Rio welfare ratio is a full four times the subsistence level. This quite high level suggests that a carpenter in Rio could provide the required amount of food for himself and his family without major difficulties. For slaves, following some historical evidence, we have assumed that half of their nominal earnings were due to their masters (Andrade, 1988; Reis, 2019: 66). As a result, the slaves in Bahia and Rio had welfare ratios close to unity for the whole period. The helpers in Gothenburg had welfare ratios at a similarly scanty level until 1860 but they began to increase steadily thereafter. Since previous research has shown that Swedish workers' welfare ratios were respectable in an international perspective (Ericsson & Molinder, 2020), urban workers in Brazil earned quite high wages. Italy, for example, which served as a main source of migrants to Brazil in the late nineteenth century, had higher GDP per capita than Sweden but lower real wages (Federico et al., 2019). This pecuniary advantage explains the attractiveness of Brazil as a destination country for European workers in the latter half of the nineteenth century.

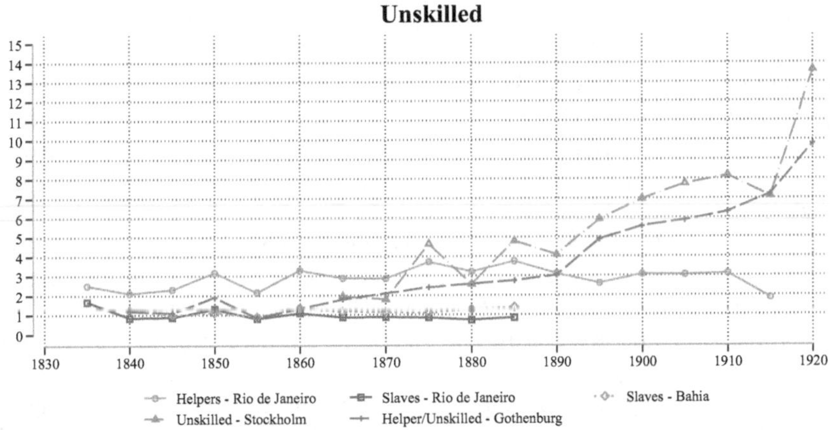

Fig. 3 Welfare ratios for Brazilian and Swedish unskilled workers, 1835–1920 (*Sources* Brazil, Lobo [1978]; Mattoso [1986]; Sweden, nominal wages, Bagge et al. [1935] and Ericsson and Molinder [2020]; prices, Jörberg [1972] and Detaljpriser och indexberäkningar åren 1913–1930. *Note* All series are five-year moving average)

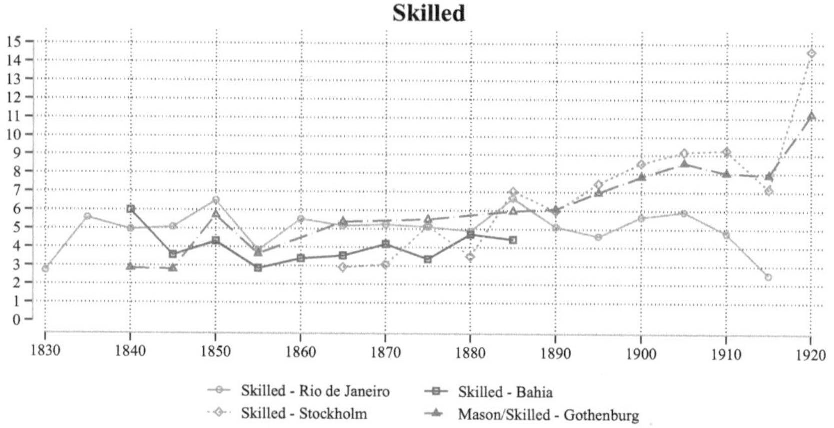

Fig. 4 Welfare ratios for Brazilian and Swedish skilled workers, 1830–1920 (*Sources* See Fig. 3)

Second, the divergence in levels of welfare ratios occurred later than in levels of GDP per capita. Swedish wages began to progress by the 1860s and growth rates gathered pace from the 1890s. In Brazil, however, the welfare ratio began to decline somewhat in the mid-1880s after displaying some progress in the 1870s and early 1880s. As a result, a gap between the two countries began to appear in the 1890s. This result deviates from that of Williamson (1995) whose comparative real wage levels indicate that Brazil was on a par with Sweden as late as in the early 1910s. As Pereira (2019) has illustrated, Williamson's pioneering comparison lacked a careful consideration of worker characteristics and due attention to the large wage differentials across Brazilian regions.

Third, over the long haul, the Brazilian welfare ratios—just as the GDP per capita figures—testify to a remarkable standstill in standards of living. Consequently, it appears that real wages followed the trajectory of economy-wide developments in Brazil. There is thus no evidence of a disconnect between rates of GDP per capita growth and of living standards following the predictions of Lewis' (1954) model of unlimited supply of labour. Moreover, this stagnation regarding the purchasing power of workers coincides with the first era of Globalization and the beginning of Brazilian industrialization, two forces that potentially could have acted as a lever for growth rates and workers' welfare. Despite initially favourable conditions for workers as measured by welfare ratios in an international perspective, a long-term relative decline distinguished the Brazilian experience through much of the nineteenth and twentieth centuries. The Swedish welfare ratios also tracked rather well the growth of GDP per capita. If anything, real wages may have outstripped the growth of GDP per capita. In contrast to Brazil, economy-wide forces, in particular industrialization and possibly also emigration, acted as a lever for real wages (Ericsson & Molinder, 2020; Prado, 2010a).

Admittedly, there are some caveats which concern the validity of our conclusion that the welfare ratios of Brazilian workers were on an equal footing with those of Swedish workers until about 1890. First, the approach employed to establish these standards of living probably favours the Brazilian standing relative to the Swedish. Food weighs heavily in the subsistence basket, which tends to minimize differences in living standards between developed and less developed countries. This aspect becomes increasingly important by the time of the transition to modern economic growth and hence increased consumption of non-agricultural goods in the developed countries (Deaton & Heston, 2010; Vollrath, 2011: 364). As we noted earlier, the quantities of grain and meat in the Allen (2001) type of basket seems too low for Brazilian urban areas during the nineteenth century, so a measure of subsistence will not capture broader consumption patterns. If the basket had also included a fair share of manufactured goods, perhaps the Swedish workers would have appeared more well off relative to the Brazilian workers. This argument is reminiscent of the point made by Broadberry and Gupta (2006) in the Great Divergence debate, namely, that the British lead relative to India and China in silver wages, which included manufactured goods, was more pronounced than that in grain wages. There are also several items missing from the Allen basket that figured prominently in working class consumption in Sweden at the time, in particular potatoes and milk.

Second, the welfare ratios of skilled labour, such as masons and carpenters in Rio de Janeiro, were not indicative of the general living conditions of urban workers in Brazil. Most workers were low-skilled, including slaves, who worked for daily wages. Self-employed slaves, known as "*escravos de ganho*", were fairly common in large urban areas during the nineteenth century (Soares, 1988). We can assume that reported daily wages for self-employed slaves were an upper bound, as they had to hand over part of their income to their owners. Evidence is scarce, but information for Salvador in 1849 suggests that slaves passed on more than half of their daily earnings to their masters (Andrade, 1988; Reis, 2019: 66). Moreover, many free workers who worked as "*ganhadores*" could be former slaves as rates of manumission were notoriously high in Brazil (Nishida, 1993). Given this characteristic of the Brazilian labour market, we use nominal wage series for construction helpers (*servente de obras*) from Rio de Janeiro and slaves who worked as craftsmen in Salvador. We also use hire rates for slaves in Rio de Janeiro, assuming they worked 250 days a year (Lobo, 1978: 803; Mattoso, 1986: 443–460; Mello, 1977: 66). As expected, the hire rate for slaves was lower than for construction workers yet the overall trend for the whole period is similar.

Finally, inequality considerations for both countries should be brought into the picture to better assess comparative standards of living. The GDP per capita figures used reflect production in the aggregate, whereas the welfare ratios reflect the wage conditions in the urban labour markets. The composition of output in both countries leaned heavily towards agriculture, and farm workers made up the vast majority of the labour force (Fig. 1). If the rift between the rural and urban sectors was greater in Brazil than in Sweden, this would somewhat undermine the welfare ratios as a generic yardstick for standards of living. Moreover, in Brazil, the high demand for skilled workers in construction might also play a part in the high welfare ratios of Brazilian workers. These and other inequality considerations related to the labour market form the topic of the coming section.

4 Inequality by Labour Market Outcomes

The aim of this section is to provide new inequality measures for labour market outcomes for both countries. For most of these measures, we depend on benchmark years that provide us with cross-sectional data on wages and prices. The first of these years is 1912/1913 and the second is 1920. The motivation for the selected years has to do with the availability of wage evidence for Brazil through public investigations or population censuses. We have matched this with similar data for Sweden. In addition to new measures of inequality for those years, we also offer a brief review of some other inequality measures in particular for Sweden. We begin our treatment of inequality with the regional dimension followed by differences in pay by occupation, skills, and sex.

4.1 Regional Wage Differentials

For Brazil, we use the estimates from Pereira (2019) to examine regional wage differentials. For 1912, he uses nominal wages and food prices from municipal surveys carried out by the Ministry of Agriculture between 1910 and 1913. The government supposedly carried out these surveys in all Brazilian states, although documents are only available for twelve states, totalling 753 municipalities. For 1920, he uses the 1920 census, which offers information on industrial wages divided into 13 branches, comprising 341 industries.[2] Since different states had different industrial sectors, all averages presented in this chapter are weighted by the number of workers recorded in each sector. For non-industrial wages, information is recorded for 748 municipalities in 20 different states, and this is divided into 10 categories, including skilled workers, such as carpenters and blacksmiths. To achieve comparability between the two benchmark years of 1912 and 1920, we have lumped together states into two macro-regions: South/Southeast and Northeast.

For Sweden, we have grouped the county-specific information on nominal wages and prices of consumables into seven regions: East, Småland and the Islands, South, West, Bergslagen, Lower North, and Upper North. These regions correspond to the NUTS2 level in the Nomenclature of Territorial Units for Statistics. Besides being commonly used in regional studies, this regional classification has been used by the Social Board and Statistics Sweden to adjust nominal wages of public employees for variations in cost of living. In addition, it has formed the basis for collective agreements in the private sector. For nominal wages, we draw on the official wage statistics for farm workers available since 1865, which includes wages for male and female servants, married workers on yearly contracts (*statare*), and day labourers. Besides an economy-wide average for these different labour categories, wages were also reported by the 24 Swedish counties until 1945, constituting the basis for our new estimates of regional welfare ratios.

We have chosen male farm servants as the basis for our comparison. They were unskilled workers and ubiquitous throughout Sweden (Utterström, 1957). The other option would have been day workers,

[2] The sectors include textiles; leathers and furs; wood; metalworking; ceramics; chemical; food; clothing; furniture; construction; transport; power transmission; and science, arts, and luxury goods.

which formed the evidential basis for previous studies on regional wage convergence; however, the use of day workers would have required a bold assumption as to the number of workdays. By choosing farm servants, we have a direct measure of annual earnings. The annual earnings include the estimated monetary value of payments in kind, food, and shelter, which were obtained from the official wage statistics. The final figure for each region is the arithmetic mean of the county-specific annual earnings. Nominal wages were highest in lower Norrland followed by Bergslagen and the South. The lowest monetary wages were found in Småland and the islands, followed by the West. In general, wages were lowest in those areas that were dependent on agriculture and specialized in small-scale farming. One may surmise that manufacturing did not exert a sufficiently large pull on farmworkers' wages in those regions.[3]

We have multiplied the quantities of the food basket used in the previous section by the corresponding regional prices. We have regional prices for all food items thanks to a public investigation (*Detaljpriser och indexberäkningar åren 1913–1930*). For a few non-food items, however, prices are national (Ljungberg, 1990). Because we have applied the same consumed quantities to all regions, we have not controlled for regional differentials attributable to relative prices and consumer preferences. In all likelihood, workers would obtain a larger fraction of their calories from grains on the plains in the south and the east, while meat and dairy were more prevalent and cheaper in the regions specialized in livestock production. Moreover, the prices that we have collected reflect the cost to obtain a basket in urban areas. Lundh (2012, 2013) has documented that the price of unprocessed foodstuff was significantly lower in the countryside than in urban areas. Farm workers could often buy goods at farm-gate prices (Collin, 2016). The same is true also for rent, which, following Allen, in the absence of any actual data has been estimated at 5% of the total budget.

The cost of buying a subsistence basket did not vary a great deal across the seven regions in 1913 and 1920. In general, the prices of grains were

[3] Space constraints prevent us from displaying the within-region differences in earnings levels, yet the very high wage level of lower Norrland warrants a brief note. The reason for its outstanding level is the very high earnings level of farm servants in Jämtland. Jämtland was by far the least populous county of Sweden; in the 1910s, about 120,000 people lived there, which equates to about 2% of the population. Thus, we should not allow this particular observation to have a great impact on our overall assessment.

lowest in the East because it specialized in grain production, and highest in the North, which lacks a climate suitable for grain production. The specialization in grain production resulted in high prices of meat and dairy products in the East. Fuel was particularly cheap in the region of Bergslagen as well as in lower and upper Norrland, which had an abundance of forests (Bagge et al., 1933). The relative difference in the price of the basket is somewhat understated owing to the lack of regional data on prices for soap, linen, and candles. These goods made up a relatively small part of the budget, however. Table 3 shows one cost measure that includes only food and another that includes the additional items, such as textiles, soap, and rent. The costs did not very a great deal, which should come as no surprise; Prado et al. (2021) have shown that the price convergence of goods was almost completed in the 1910s, with a coefficient of variation at about 4%. The upper North has the highest cost level although this cost penalty might be somewhat exaggerated because our national basket is fixed, which means it does not consider the potential to substitute expensive products for similar but cheaper alternatives. Looking at the change between 1913 and 1920, prices rose rapidly during World War I and its immediate aftermath. As a result of this inflation, the cost of the subsistence basket rose by roughly 200% in most regions. The cost of the basket containing only food rose less because prices for fuel and manufactured goods, such as soap and linen, increased more than prices for foodstuffs.

Table 2 (Brazil) and Table 3 (Sweden) present the welfare ratios by region for the two benchmark years. For Brazil, the real wage advantage for southeast workers ranged from 30 to 70% depending on the workers' skills and occupations. The highest regional premium was granted to rural workers followed by industrial workers, while the smallest regional premium went to skilled workers. The regional difference between farm workers and industrial workers declined quite significantly from 1912 to 1920. These results indicate much smaller regional real wage differences than the previous study by Williamson (1999), who showed that workers in the Southeast earned six times higher real wages than workers in the Northeast. As Pereira (2019) has shown, Williamson's regional comparison was made without due consideration to homogeneity in worker categories. The four categories that make up Williamson's unweighted average for Rio de Janeiro contain professions, such as carpenters, that were among the highest paid in Rio de Janeiro at the time, as recorded in the census of 1920. In contrast, the wages used for Pernambuco are minimum wages for farm workers that originate from Levine (1978: 25). These minimum wages are about 25% lower than those found in the census of 1920. This discrepancy in the selection of workers and dependence on Pernambuco minimum wages lead to a massive over-estimation of the Southeast's real wage advantage. As Table 2 shows, the regional real wage difference was quite modest, albeit significantly larger than in Sweden.

For Sweden, the regional differences in welfare ratios were quite small. The welfare ratio was on average about 3.4 by 1913. For food alone, the average ratio was about 4.3. Nowhere was the ratio smaller than 3 (4 for food alone), which indicates that the welfare ratio was quite similar across regions. The welfare ratio increased to 3.8 by 1920 (5.8 for food alone). On the whole, the regional ranking that was determined by nominal wages has persisted, which means that the lower welfare ratios in Småland (and the islands) and in the west were driven by lower nominal wages. In 1920, the gap between the lower and upper north on the one hand and the regions further south has contracted because the increase in wages did not fully match the increase in prices during World War I and its aftermath. In sum, if we disregard the special case of Lower Norrland, there is essentially no regional difference in 1913. The regional differences increased until 1920; by then, the difference between the high value for Bergslagen and the low value for Småland was about 11%, which is still

Table 2 Welfare ratios and female/male wage ratios in Brazil

		South-Southeast	*Northeast*	*South-Southeast/Northeast*
Welfare ratios (no rent)				
Rural workers	1912	5.3	3.1	1.7
	1920	5.3	3.4	1.5
Skilled workers	1912	14.1	9.0	1.5
	1920	11.1	8.4	1.3
Industrial workers	1920	8.5	5.2	1.6
Female/Male wage ratios				
Industrial	1920	0.6	0.6	

Source Pereira (2019)

Table 3 Cost of basket, nominal wages, and welfare ratios for farm servants across 7 Swedish regions

	Cost of basket kr	*Cost basket (just food) kr*	*Nominal annual wage kr*	*Welfare ratio*	*Welfare ratio (just food)*
1913					
East	73	58	713	3.2	4.1
Småland and the islands	73	58	694	3.2	4.0
South	74	59	726	3.3	4.1
West	74	59	706	3.2	4.0
Bergslagen	73	58	752	3.4	4.3
Lower Norrland	74	59	910	4.1	5.2
Upper Norrland	74	59	729	3.3	4.1
1920					
East	207	133	2439	3.9	6.1
Småland and the islands	205	132	2168	3.5	5.5
South	209	134	2471	3.9	6.2
West	208	134	2164	3.5	5.4
Bergslagen	209	136	2416	3.9	5.9
Lower Norrland	209	137	2536	4.0	6.2
Upper Norrland	210	138	2347	3.7	5.7

Sources Nominal wages, Historiska lönedatabasen (HILD); Prices of consumer goods, Detaljpriser och indexberäkningar åren 1913–1930; Ljungberg (1990). *Note* Welfare ratios are calculated by dividing nominal income by the cost of the basket times three, following the methodology in Allen (2001) and described in Sect. 3.2

much smaller than the regional difference for farm workers in Brazil in 1920 (about 60%).

4.2 *Differences by Occupation, Skills, and Sex*

For Brazil, we only have very scarce evidence to bring to bear on the issue of wage differentials by occupation. Table 2, which comprises welfare ratios for both farm workers and industrial workers for 1920 based on the census, indicates that the welfare ratios of industrial workers exceeded those of farm workers. In the South/Southeast, the ratio between industrial workers and farm workers was about 1.6 (8.5/5.3), while in the Northeast, the corresponding ratio was about 1.5 (5.2/3.4). Although welfare ratios were a great deal higher in the South/Southeast for both farm workers and industrial workers, the real earnings gaps between the two sectors were about the same. The size of these real earnings gaps conforms quite well to what has been documented for other countries (Hatton & Williamson, 1993).

For Sweden, Table 4 lists several other occupations for which we have information on annual earnings thanks to wage quotations from Bengtsson and Prado (2020). The earnings of farm servants are set to 100. The upper panel shows the earnings ratio of salaried employees and the lower panel shows the earnings ratios of workers. All other occupations earned more than farm servants, even contract workers, despite their claimed inferior position in the labour market (Lundh, 2008). Some of the salaried employees have extraordinarily high earnings, about ten times as high as farm servants. But semi-skilled white-collar professions, such as law clerk and railway clerk, also earned about four times as much as farm servants. Taken at face value, these ratios underscore that by the first quarter of the twentieth century, huge inequalities in earnings permeated some segments of the Swedish labour markets. Inequalities aside, construction workers and manufacturing workers earned about twice as much. If we translate this superior nominal pay of urban workers using the welfare ratio of farm workers, by inference the welfare ratio of a typical worker in an urban or manufacturing setting was about 7 in the early 1910s and about 8 in the early 1920s. These high welfare ratios testify to the accelerated productivity gains of the Swedish industrialization and modernization of the agricultural sector that spilled over to improved standards of living in the late nineteenth and early twentieth century.

The welfare ratios of farm servants increased modestly between 1913 and 1920. This comes across in the comparison of other workers in Table 4. As Lundh and Prado (2015) have shown, this was a particularly unfavourable time for farm workers of all kinds. The urban to rural hourly nominal wage ratio increased from about 150 in the early 1910s to 230 in the early 1920s. Dissimilarities in labour market institutions explain the relative decline in farm workers' standing. First, farm workers were sidestepped by the reduction of working hours that took place in 1919. The return on labour input per hour increased for manufacturing workers but remained unchanged for farm workers. Second, without collective

Table 4 Annual earnings ratios by profession in Sweden, 1906–1926. Farm servants = 100

	Location	*1906–1910*	*1911–1915*	*1921–1922*	*1925–1926*
Salaried employees					
Lecturer, higher education	Stockholm	838	726	824	851
Professor	Sweden		1176	636	939
Clerk	Stockholm	632	704		735
Clerk	Sweden		668	678	668
Higher civil servant	Stockholm	1180	1219		1301
Law clerk	Sweden		1176	1089	1075
Warrant officer	Sweden	411	365	427	397
Captain (military)	Sweden	806	698	715	704
Railway clerk	Sweden	423	360	493	474
Workers					
Unskilled construction worker	Stockholm	197	184	265	257
Manufacturing worker	Sweden	189	187	194	222
Day worker in agriculture	Stockholm	112	115	108	118

Source Bengtsson and Prado (2020: 96–97)

agreements, the nominal wages of farm workers were cut by a significant fraction in the deflation of the early 1920s. The nominal wages of manufacturing workers also declined, but the drop was cushioned by collective agreements; by then, unionization had already gone quite far in manufacturing, whereas it had barely begun in agriculture (Back, 1961; Lundh, 2010).

The skilled to unskilled wage ratio is a numeraire for inequality that economists and economic historians have long cherished. It indicates the magnitude of the skill premium, and the return on investments in formal education or on-the-job training. In economic history research, studies of the skill premium often refer to the construction sector. Large construction sites hired many helpers whose only skill requirement was the capacity to carry out repetitive and laborious manual work. Their earnings are often compared with the earnings of those with professional skills, such as masons, carters, and carpenters. We make use of our series of welfare ratios in the previous section to compare the skilled to unskilled pay ratio, as illustrated in Fig. 5. The skill premium in Rio was higher than in Stockholm, particularly between 1890 and 1905, when the premium increases in Rio and declines in Stockholm. For the period at large, though, the premium declines in Rio, ranging from 2 to 2.5 pre-1850 to 1.5 to 2 post-1850. The premium in Stockholm also declines across the whole period. A possible explanation for the temporary increasing gap in Rio after 1890 is immigration to Brazil, which created a huge construction boom, and a possible explanation for the gradually decreasing gap in Stockholm is emigration from Sweden, which favoured the rewards of unskilled labour that did not emigrate.

The high skill premium in Rio de Janeiro tallies with other New World experiences. The scarce supply of skills applicable to construction also forced other New World countries to pay skilled construction workers very generously, as Shergold (1982) has demonstrated was the case for the United States relative to Britain in the early twentieth century. Whereas the supply of skilled construction workers was quite sufficient in Britain, the supply of those skills was scarce in the United States. Skilled construction workers were probably relatively more abundant in Sweden than in Brazil, partly as a result of the Swedish expansion of a great many so-called Sunday schools and evening schools in basic vocational education in the fourth quarter of the nineteenth century (Chapter 6). In contrast, for Brazil, Lobo (1978: 128) notes that in the lists of professions in

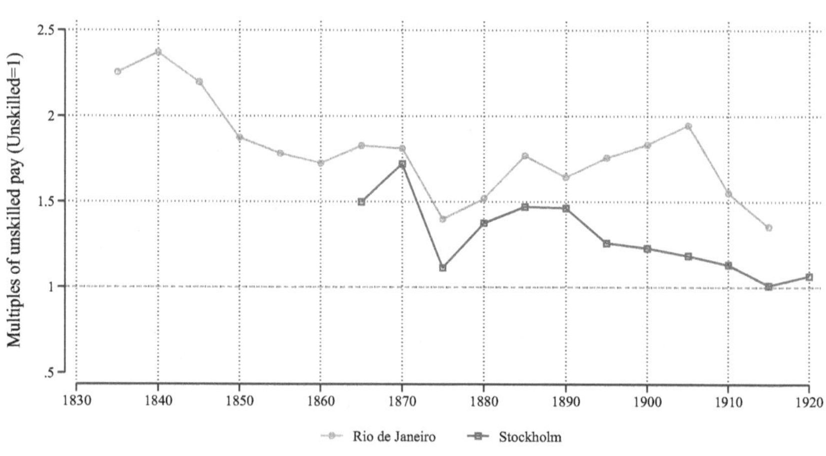

Fig. 5 Skilled to unskilled pay ratios in Rio de Janeiro and Stockholm, 1835–1920 (*Source* See Fig. 3. *Note* All figures are averages across five-year periods)

almanacs from the first half of the nineteenth century, "it can be seen that the number of masons and carpenters was very low to meet the need for an expanding [Rio de Janeiro] urban centre". This supply differential between the two countries probably spilled over to the pecuniary rewards for skilled construction workers, which might explain why Brazilian wages were higher than expected.

Besides this time series evidence, Table 2 offers some clues about the pay gap between skilled workers in the construction sector on one hand, and farm workers and industrial workers on the other in Brazil. In 1912, the ratio of skilled workers to rural workers was 2.7 in the South/Southeast and 3.0 in the Northeast. In 1920, the corresponding figures were 2.1 and 2.7. First, the skill premium was higher in the Northeast; and second, the skill premium, like the regional differentials, declined between 1912 and 1920. This early twentieth-century decline in the Brazilian premium is confirmed by the time series in Fig. 5, which shows a drop between 1905 and 1915. Figure 5 also shows that the skill premium among Swedish construction workers almost disappeared after 1900.

Studies of skill premiums in manufacturing are scarce. They are moreover fraught with problems of interpretation. Modern wage statistics rarely differentiate labour by skills, and the composition of the workforce with regard to skills varies greatly by industry depending on the technology in use. Based on the sample of manufacturing establishments with wages for both skilled and unskilled workers in Bagge et al. (1933), Prado (2010a) concluded that the skilled to unskilled ratio remained rather trendless between 1860 and 1912, fluctuating around an average of about 1.2. The size of the ratio varied greatly by industry, though. This average earnings advantage in favour of skilled workers does not seem large, in particular if we compare it with the average earnings gap between workers and salaried employees implicit in Table 4.

We conclude our review of inequality based on labour market outcomes with a brief note of pay differences by sex. In Brazil, the widespread use of slaves had an important bearing on the conditions for female labour both before and after the abolition in 1888. Slavery was an important reason why the share of women in the labour force was high throughout the nineteenth century. In addition to performing most of the household duties, enslaved women participated in the regular labour market, especially in urban areas. During the early twentieth century, the share of female workers was high for some industrial categories. Construction and mining aside, the manufacturing industry proper employed just as many women as men in 1920. Most of them were employed in the textile industry, which swallowed about 70% of all female workers in the industrial sector combined. As the twentieth-century progressed, however, the share of female workers in manufacturing decreased. Between 1920 and 1970, a crucial period for Brazil's industrial growth, the male labour force in manufacturing increased by 455%, while the female workforce increased by only 41% (Merrick & Graham, 1979: 158).

Examining wages, we find as expected that female workers earned less than male workers. Table 2 indicates that in Brazil, female workers earned 60% of the average male worker's wage in the overall industrial sector. Examining pay differences additionally in the census of 1920, it appears for instance that for textile workers in São Paulo, women had on average earnings that were 82% of men's earnings, controlling for the effect of different workers' skills. In aggregate, income inequality between men and women increased further in the following decades as the proportion of women in highly paid sectors decreased. Occupational information from the national census indicates that female labour moved away from the agricultural and industrial sectors towards the service sector, with lower-than-average wages. These changes in the proportions of female and male workers across sectors and industries point to a possible resolution of the increasing pay gap between men and women as Brazilian industrialization continued apace during the second and third quarters of the twentieth century.

Today, Sweden is known for far-reaching equality between the sexes. This achievement, however, is the outcome of several episodes of convergence during the twentieth century (Prado, 2010b; Svensson, 1996, 2003). Nothing in the wage records of the past indicates that equality between female and male workers was an inherent feature of Swedish society before the mid-twentieth century. Women in the labour force, as conventionally defined, toiled mostly in the textile industry and the food industry. Some also worked in the tobacco industry and the match-making industry. On average, female workers earned about 57% of male earnings in those industries between 1860 and the end of World War I. This crude metric, the average hourly female wage divided by the male wage, increased in the late 1910s, during World War II, and above all between 1960 and 1980. By 1920, the year for which we have a Brazilian reference point, female workers earned about 62% of the average male earnings in both the textile industries and in manufacturing at large. The female–male pay gap among industrial workers, thus measured, was actually wider in Sweden than in Brazil.

The ratio of female to male wages, however, is a raw figure that does not take into account several determinants of wage heterogeneity, such as formal education, on-the-job training and work tasks. The male wage advantage declines substantially if we account for some of those additional determinants, as shown by research from the tobacco industry and printing industry (Burnette & Stanfors, 2020; Stanfors et al., 2014). On the shopfloor, where men and women performed the same labour services, the hourly wage rates barely differed by sex. However, women were excluded from higher positions, which explains the average female-male wage gap at the industry level. In all likelihood, this kind of discrimination against female workers occurred in both countries' labour markets.

Manufacturing aside, the vast majority of women, in particular married women, worked in agriculture alongside their husbands without receiving any pecuniary gains. However, many women worked as farm servants before marriage. Table 5 shows that the female to male earnings ratio ranged widely across Swedish regions, from about 60 to 80% for farm servants and from 60 to 70% for day workers. The Brazilian female to male earnings ratio falls within these rather wide ranges, which inclines us to conclude that the gender gaps in agriculture were of similar magnitudes in the two countries.

Table 5 Female/male earnings ratios in Swedish agriculture

	1913		*1920*	
	Servants	*Dayworkers*	*Servants*	*Dayworkers*
East	0.79	0.62	0.77	0.60
Småland and the islands	0.73	0.61	0.71	0.59
South	0.72	0.65	0.70	0.63
West	0.72	0.69	0.70	0.67
Bergslagen	0.69	0.62	0.70	0.58
Lower Norrland	0.62	0.57	0.62	0.50
Upper Norrland	0.61	0.60	0.62	0.50

Source Historiska lönedatabasen (HILD) https://www.gu.se/handelshogskolan/ekonomi-samhalle/historiska-lonedatabasen-hild

5 Concluding Discussion

This chapter was motivated by a desire to cast new light on the historical roots of divergence in inequality and living standards in Brazil and Sweden. For Brazil, as well as for other South American countries with a similar legacy, it has been argued that today's inegalitarian traits have deep roots. The subjugation of indigenous populations and influx of slaves resulted in a dualist social structure, with the design of economic and political institutions in the hand of elites. According to this narrative, insufficient investments in human capital perpetuated the initially skewed income distribution and hampered the transition towards equality that the developed countries made in the twentieth century. In addition, labour markets remained segmented because the investments in public infrastructure necessary to spur labour mobility had been neglected. For Sweden, the conventional story is the opposite. Modern egalitarianism, it is argued, was rooted in a pre-modern and egalitarian social structure, signified by the strong political and economic position of peasant farmers and a lack of feudalism. Low levels of initial inequality then propelled the creation of inclusive institutions, spurring further equality. Following this line of thought, the two countries set out on divergent paths of societal disparities, which should be reflected by the level of inequality in the early twentieth century. These arguments of persistence have received pushback in recent years, however. Williamson (2015) has argued that Latin American inequality is the result of missing the levelling that took place in developed countries during the second and third quarters of the twentieth century. Gärtner and Prado (2016) and Bengtsson (2019) have contended that Swedish equality is the result of developments after World War I.

The first part of our empirical investigation into standards of living and inequality in Sweden and Brazil was concerned with rates of change and comparative levels of GDP and real wages. Beginning with a discussion of rates of change, the two frameworks of Lewis (1954) and of Kuznets (1955) have taken centre stage in the debate on the impact of economic growth on worker welfare. These two frameworks allow us to examine the economy as a split between a traditional sector, dominated by agriculture, and a modern sector, associated with urbanization and manufacturing. In both these frameworks, economic development is associated with expanding employment and growing productivity in modern industries, while labour shifts away from the farm sector. In Lewis' model, the traditional sector constitutes a source of unlimited supply of unskilled labour, keeping wages down in the modern sector. Inequality increases as capitalists and skilled workers reap the benefits of growing productivity. In Kuznets' model, workers in the traditional sector earn a subsistence wage, while incomes for workers in the modern sector grow with increasing productivity. Inequality, argues Kuznets, is higher in the capitalist sector, and together with growing income differentials between the traditional and modern sectors, the shift of employment towards urban manufacturing leads to rising disparities. Critically, both models suggest that workers' wages do not automatically rise with economic progress, something that has also been a recurrent theme in the debate over the impact of the first industrial revolution on the British working class (Allen, 2009; Williamson, 1985), and in discussions of early industrialization in the United States (Lindert & Williamson, 1980; Margo, 2000).

We find that real wages remained essentially stable in Brazil for the whole period of investigation. This stability contrasts with the pattern for Sweden, where wage growth rates accelerated by the 1880s. The GDP per capita record displays a similar trajectory: stagnation in Brazil and a gradual acceleration by the third quarter of the nineteenth century in Sweden. Consequently, real wages in both cases followed quite closely the trajectory of economic growth. There is no evidence of a disconnect between GDP per capita growth and living standards as theorized by either Lewis or Kuznets. Trailing worker income does not seem to be the main factor in the divergence of real wages between the two counties. The forces steering economy-wide development also steered the development of real wages. However, the Lewis model may wield some explanatory power for the Brazilian experience. The confluence of a large supply of slaves and stagnation of wages squares with the prediction of Lewis' notion of surplus labour. Perhaps slaves in such great numbers acted as a check on the growth of real wages for unskilled workers. A counter-argument is that the real wages of skilled workers also stagnated, which would suggest that other forces, such as weak institutions or lacklustre industrialization, hindered Brazilian real wages from taking off as they did in Sweden in the 1890s.

Besides rates of change, we have also investigated comparative levels. Our study revealed that the last quarter of the nineteenth century is crucial to an understanding of the rising gap in living standards that has persisted until today. Although it is true that Swedish GDP per capita was already twice that of Brazil before this period, this is still far from a spectacular difference in the context of cross-country differentials. What matters for income convergence is the long-term trajectory of economy-wide growth rates, and they began to diverge sharply in the last quarter of the nineteenth century. Brazil slid into relative decline as GDP per capita almost ceased to grow at all until the 1930s. To further examine comparative standards of living, we also employed the framework of welfare ratios for different worker categories. They revealed surprisingly small gaps between the two countries, and urban workers in Rio had welfare ratios ranging from 5 to 6 well into the 1880s. An apparent Swedish lead did not manifest itself until the 1890s. Thereafter, Swedish wages surged ahead, and the gap kept widening. The discrepancy between the records of GDP per capita and welfare ratios led us at any rate to suspect that inequality considerations are an important part of the story.

In the second empirical part of the chapter, we looked, therefore, at different dimensions of wage inequality, concentrating on differentials across regions, occupations, skills, and sex. The most remarkable difference in inequality between the two countries concerns the regional dimension. Differences in wages across regions in Sweden were already quite small by the early twentieth century, owing to a regional convergence in wages starting with industrialization in the 1860s and accelerating by the time of the mass emigration of the late nineteenth and early twentieth century. In Brazil, on the other hand, the regional divide has persisted. Instead of contracting, the gap between the prosperous South and Southeast on the one hand and the backward Northeast on the other widened further during the twentieth century.

For the other inequality dimensions, we do not come across very large differences between the two countries before the 1920s. True, the skill premium was higher in Brazil in 1890 to 1905, but declined thereafter. Wage differentials across workers' occupation and sex were vast in both places in the early twentieth century. For Sweden, the transition to equality in pay occurs after 1920, and in particular during two spells of convergence in the 1940s and between the late 1960s and the mid-1970s (Molinder, 2019; Prado & Waara, 2018). After the 1920s, the return on investment in skills fell continuously as a result of the democratization of education, which brought down the human capital advantage of skilled workers and white-collar professions. Occupational differences diminished as a result of widespread unionization and collective agreements (Lundh & Prado, 2015; Prado & Waara, 2018). In contrast to this egalitarian edge, Brazilian wage differentials remained high, and an expansion of adequate education for the masses never materialized (Chapter 6). The pattern is similar for sex. The wage disadvantage for women was large in both countries at the onset. The evolution of the sex differential is similar to that of skill, even though the levelling in Sweden came later in this case (Svensson, 1996), while the differentials in Brazil remained.

With such a late divergence in living standards and inequality patterns, it seems farfetched to blame the colonial legacy for every negative aspect of Brazilian economic development in the twentieth century. Admittedly, our knowledge about inequality levels is patchy, in particular for Brazil. Barring the regional dimension, our evidence of Brazilian inequality levels measured by labour market outcomes do not seem very different from the Swedish case by the early twentieth century. This result makes us gravitate towards the conclusion that future research should direct the searchlight on the twentieth century rather than on the colonial past in order to gain further insights into the roots of today's different inequality levels in Brazil and Sweden.

References

Acemoglu, D., Johnson, S., & Robinson, J. A. (2001). The colonial origins of comparative development: An empirical investigation. *The American Economic Review, 91*(5), 1369–1401. https://doi.org/10.1257/aer.91.5.1369

Allen, R. C. (2001). The Great Divergence in European Wages and Prices from the Middle Ages to the First World War. *Explorations in Economic History, 38*, 411–447. https://doi.org/10.1006/exeh.2001.0775

Allen, R. C. (2009). Engels' pause: Technical change, capital accumulation, and inequality in the British industrial revolution. *Explorations in Economic History, 46*(4), 418–435. https://doi.org/10.1016/j.eeh.2009.04.004

Allen, R. C. (2013). Poverty lines in history, theory, and current international practice. *University of Oxford, Department of Economics.*

Allen, R. C. (2015). The high wage economy and the industrial revolution: A restatement. *Economic History Review, 68*(1), 1–22. https://doi.org/10.1111/ehr.12079

Allen, R. C., Bassino, J.-P., Ma, D., & Moll-Murata, C. (2011). Wages, prices, and living standards in China, 1738–1925: In comparison with Europe, Japan and India. *Economic History Review, 64*(1), 8–38. https://doi.org/10.1111/j.1468-0289.2010.00515.x

Allen, R. C., Murphy, T. E., & Schneider, E. B. (2012). The colonial origins of the divergence in the Americas: A labor market approach. *Journal of Economic History, 72*(4), 836–894. https://doi.org/10.1017/S0022050712000629

Andrade, M. J. d. S. (1988). *A mão de obra escrava em Salvador, 1811–1860.* Corrupio.

Back, P.-E. (1961). *En klass i uppbrott: den fackliga lantarbetarrörelsens uppkomst och utveckling*. Framtiden.

Bagge, G., Lundberg, E., & Svennilson, I. (1933). *Wages in Sweden 1860–1930. Part One*. P. S. King & Son.

Bagge, G., Lundberg, E., & Svennilson, I. (1935). *Wages in Sweden 1860–1930. Part Two*. P.S. King & Son.

Ball, M. C. (2013). *Inequality in São Paulo's Old Republic: A wage perspective, 1891–1930*. University of California, Los Angeles.

Barro, R. J., & Ursúa, J. F. (2008). Macroeconomic crises since 1870. *The Brookins Institution, 39*(1), 255–350.

Bengtsson, E. (2019). The Swedish Sonderweg in question: Democratization and inequality in comparative perspective, c. 1750–1920. *Past & Present, 244*(1), 123–161. https://doi.org/10.1093/pastj/gtz033.

Bengtsson, E., Missiaia, A., Olsson, M., & Svensson, P. (2018). Wealth inequality in Sweden, 1750–1900. *The Economic History Review, 71*(3), 772–794. https://doi.org/10.1093/pastj/gtz033

Bengtsson, E., & Prado, S. (2020). The rise of the middle class: the income gap between salaried employees and workers in Sweden, ca. 1830–1940. *Scandinavian Economic History Review, 68*(2), 91–111. https://doi.org/10.1080/03585522.2019.1650293.

Bohlin, J., & Eurenius, A.-M. (2010). Why they moved - emigration from the Swedish countryside to the United States, 1881–1910. *Explorations in Economic History, 47*(4), 533–551. https://doi.org/10.1016/j.eeh.2010.07.001

Bolt, J., Inklaar, R., de Jong, H., & van Zanden, J. L. (2018). Rebasing "Maddison": new income comparisons of the shape of the long-run economic development. *GGDC Research Memorandum, 174*.

Bolt, J., & van Zanden, J. L. (2014). The Maddison Project: A collaborative data base. *Economic History Review, 67*(3), 627–651. https://doi.org/10.1111/1468-0289.12032

Bolt, J., & van Zanden, J. L. (2020). Maddison style estimates of the evolution of the world economy. A new 2020 update. *Maddison-Project Working Paper WP-15*.

Broadberry, S. N., & Gupta, B. (2006). The early modern great divergence: Wages, prices and economic development in Europe and Asia, 1500–1800. *Economic History Review, 59*(1), 2–31. https://doi.org/10.1111/j.1468-0289.2005.00331.x

Buescu, M. (1970). *História econômica do Brasil: Pesquisas e análises*. APEC.
Burnette, J., & Stanfors, M. (2020). Understanding the gender gap further: The case of Turn-of-the-Century Swedish compositors. *Journal of Economic History, 80*(1), 175–206. https://doi.org/10.1017/S002205071900086X
Campos, P. H. P. (2010). *Nos caminhos da acumulação. Negócio e poder no abastecimento de carnes verdes para a cidade do Rio de Janeiro (1808–1835)*. Alameda.
Collin, K. (2016). Regional wage gaps between agricultural and manufacturing workers in Sweden, 1860–1945. In *Regional wages and labour market integration in Sweden, 1732–2009* (pp. 117–158). Gothenburg Studies in Economic History No 17.
Contador, C. R., & Haddad, C. L. (1975). Produto real, moeda e preços: A experiência Brasileira no período 1861–1970. *Revista Brasileira De Estatística, 36*(146), 407–440.
Deaton, A., & Heston, A. (2010). Understanding PPPs and PPP-based national accounts. *American Economic Journal: Macroeconomics, 2*(4), 1–35. https://doi.org/10.1257/mac.2.4.1
Dribe, M., & Lundh, C. (2005). People on the move: Determinants of servant migration in Nineteenth Cenutry Sweden. *Continuity and Change, 17*(1), 53–91. https://doi.org/10.1017/S026841600400534X
Ellis, M. (1969). *A Baleia no Brasil colonial*. Melhoramentos.
Enflo, K., Lundh, C., & Prado, S. (2014). The role of migration in regional wage convergence: Evidence from Sweden 1860–1940. *Explorations in Economic History, 52*(2), 93–110. https://doi.org/10.1016/j.eeh.2013.12.001
Engerman, S. L., & Sokoloff, K. L. (1997). Factor endowments, institutions, and differential paths of growth among New World Economies: A view from economic historians of the United States. In S. Haber (Ed.), *How Latin America fell behind* (pp. 260–304). Stanford University Press.
Ericsson, J., & Molinder, J. (2020). Economic growth and the development of real wages: Swedish construction workers' wages in comparative perspective, 1831–1900. *Journal of Economic History, 80*(3), 813–852. https://doi.org/10.1017/S0022050720000285
Federico, G., Nuvolari, A., & Vasta, M. (2019). The origins of the Italian regional divide: Evidence from real wages, 1861–1913. *Journal of Economic History, 79*(1), 63–98. https://doi.org/10.1017/S0022050718000712
Franken, D. (2019). Anthropometric history of Brazil, 1850–1950: Insights from military and passport records. *Revista De Historia Economica - Journal of Iberian and Latin American Economic History, 37*(2), 377–408. https://doi.org/10.1017/S0212610919000077
Furtado, C. (1959). *Formacao econômica do Brasil* (1st ed.). Editôra Fundo de Cultura.

Gadd, C.-J. (2011). The agricultural revolution in Sweden: 1700–1870. In J. Myrdal & M. Morell (Eds.), *The agrarian history of Sweden: From 4000 BC to AD 2000* (pp. 118–165). Nordic Academic Press.

Gärtner, S., & Prado, S. (2016). Unlocking the social trap: Inequality, trust and the Scandinavian Welfare State. *Social Science History, 40*(1), 33–62. https://doi.org/10.1017/ssh.2015.80

Gary, K. (2018). *Work, wages and income: Remuneration and labor patterrns in Sweden 1500–1850*. Lund University.

Gary, K., & Olsson, M. (2020). Men at work: Wages and industriousness in southern Sweden 1500–1850. *Scandinavian Economic History Review, 68*(2), 112–128. https://doi.org/10.1080/03585522.2019.1704859

Goldsmith, R. W. (1986). *Brasil 1850–1948: Desenvolvimento financeiro sob um século de inflacão*. Harper & Row.

Graham, R. (2010). *Feeding the city: From street market to liberal reform in Salvador, Brazil, 1780–1860*. University of Texas Press.

Hatton, T. J., & Williamson, J. G. (1993). Labour market integration and the rural-urban wage gap in history. In G. D. Snooks (Ed.), *Historical analysis in economics*. Routledge.

Hatton, T. J., & Williamson, J. G. (1998). *The age of mass migration*. Oxford University Press.

Henderson, J. (1821). *A History of the Brazil*. Longman.

Holloway, T. H. (1980). *Immigrants on the Land: Coffee and society in São Paulo, 1886–1934*. The University Of North Carolina Press.

Institute for Social Sciences, U. o. S. (1941). *Population movements and industrialization: Swedish counties, 1895–1930*. P.S. King.

Jörberg, L. (1972). *A history of prices in Sweden 1732–1914. Volume 1. Sources, Methods, Tables*. Gleerup.

Kuznets, S. (1955). Economic growth and income inequality. *American Economic Review, 45*(1), 1–28.

Leff, N. H. (1982). *Underdevelopment and development in Brazil. Vol 1. Economic structure and change, 1822–1947*. George Allen & Unwin.

Levine, R. M. (1978). *Pernambuco in the Brazilian Federation, 1889–1937*. Stanford University Press.

Lewis, W. A. (1954). Economic development with unlimited supplies of labour. *Manchester School, 22*(2), 139–191.

Lindert, P. H., & Williamson, J. G. (1980). *American inequality: A macroeconomic history*. Academic Press.

Ljungberg, J. (1990). *Priser och marknadskrafter i Sverige 1885–1969: En prishistorisk studie*. Lunds universitet.

Lobo, E. M. L. (1978). *Historia do Rio de Janeiro, Vol. 1–2*. Instituto Brasileiro de Mercado de Capitais.

Lobo, E. M. L., Barbosa Madureira, L., Canavarros, O., Feres, Z., & Gonçalves, S. (1971). Evolução dos preços e do padrão de vida no Rio de Janeiro, 1820–1930 – resultados preliminares. *Revista Brasileira de Economia*, *25*(4), 235–266.

Luccock, J. (1820). *Notes on Rio de Janeiro, and the southern parts of Brazil; Taken during a residence of ten years in that country, from 1808–1818*. Samuel Leigh, In The Strand.

Lundh, C. (2006). Arbetskraftens rörlighet och arbetsmarknadens institutioner i Sverige 1850–2005. In D. Rauhut & B. Falkenhall (Eds.), *Arbetsrätt, rörlighet och tillväxt* (pp. 17–62). ITPS.

Lundh, C. (2008). Statarnas löner och levnadsstandard. In C. Lundh & M. Olsson (Eds.), *Statarliv - i myt och verklighet* (pp. 113–165). Gidlunds förlag.

Lundh, C. (2010). *Spelets regler: institutioner och lönebildning på den svenska arbetsmarknaden 1850–2000. Andra uppl.* SNS.

Lundh, C. (2012). Wage forms, costs of living and the urban-rural wage gap: Southern Sweden, 1881–1930. *Scandinavian Economic History Review*, *60*(2), 123–145. https://doi.org/10.1080/17546559.2012.693265

Lundh, C. (2013). Was there an urban-rural consumption gap? The standard of living of workers in southern Sweden, 1914–1920. *Scandinavian Ecoomic History Review*, *61*(3), 233–258. https://doi.org/10.1080/03585522.2013.794162

Lundh, C., & Prado, S. (2015). Markets and politics: the Swedish urban-rural wage gap, 1865–1985. *European Review of Economic History*, *19*(1), 67–87. https://doi.org/10.1093/ereh/heu022

Maddison, A. (2000). Brazilian economic performance since 1500: A comparative view. *Paper presented at XIII Fórum da Liberdade, April 4, 2000*.

Margo, R. (2000). *Wages and labour markets in the United States, 1820–1860*. University of Chicago Press.

Mattoso, K. M. Q. (1986). *Au nouveau monde, une province, d'un Nouvel Empire: Bahia au dix-neuviéme siécle*. Paris 4.

Mello, P. C. d. (1977). *The economics of labor in Brazilian coffee plantations , 1850–1888*. University of Chicago.

Merrick, T. W., & Graham, D. H. (1979). *Population and economic development in Brazil, 1800 to the present* Johns Hopkins U.P.

Molinder, J. (2019). Wage differentials, economic restructuring and the solidaristic wage policy in Sweden. *European Review of Economic History*, *23*, 97–121. https://doi.org/10.1093/ereh/hey005

Nishida, M. (1993). Manumission and ethnicity in urban slavery: Salvador, Brazil, 1808–1888. *Hispanic American Historical Review*, *73*(3), 361–391. https://doi.org/10.1215/00182168-73.3.361

Ónody, O. (1960). *A inflação Brasileira, 1820–1958*.

O'Rourke, K. H., & Williamson, J. G. (1995). Open economy forces and late nineteenth century Swedish catch-up. A quantitative accounting. *Scandinavian Economic History Review, 43*(2), 171–203. https://doi.org/10.1080/03585522.1995.10415900.

Pereira, T. A. Z. (2019). The north-south divide: real wages and welfare in Brazil during the early 20th century. *Journal of Iberian and Latin American Economic History*, 1–30 https://doi.org/10.1017/S0212610919000132

Piketty, T. (2020). *Capital and ideology*. Harvard University Press.

Prado Júnior, C. (1945). *História econômica do Brasil.*

Prado, S. (2010a). Fallacious convergence? Williamson's real wage comparisons under scrutiny. *Cliometrica, 4*(2), 171–205. https://doi.org/10.1007/s11698-009-0040-5

Prado, S. (2010b). Nominal and real wages of manufacturing workers, 1860–2007. In R. Edvinsson, T. Jacobsson, & D. Waldenström (Eds.), *Exchange rates, prices, and wages, 1277–2008* (Vol. 1, pp. 479–527). Ekerlids förlag.

Prado, S., Lundh, C., Collin, K., & Enflo, K. (2021). Labour and the 'law of one price': Regional wage convergence of farm workers in Sweden, 1757–1980. *Scandinavian Economic History Review, 69*(1), 41–62. https://doi.org/10.1080/03585522.2020.1740776

Prado, S., & Waara, J. (2018). Missed the starting gun! Wage compression and the rise of the Swedish model in the labour market. *Scandinavian Economic History Review, 66*(1), 34–53. https://doi.org/10.1080/03585522.2017.1405275

Prados De La Escosura, L. (2009). Lost decades? Economic performance in Post-Independence Latin America. *Journal of Latin American Studies, 41*(2), 279–307. https://doi.org/10.1017/S0022216X09005574

Reis, J. J. (2019). *Ganhadores: A greve negra de 1857 na Bahia.* Companhia das Letras.

Rocha, I. P. (2012). *Escravos da nação': O público e o privado na Escravidão Brasileira, 1760–1876.* Universidade de São Paulo.

Rothstein, B., & Uslaner, E. M. (2005). All for all: Equality, corruption, and social trust. *World Politics, 58*(1), 41–72. https://doi.org/10.1353/wp.2006.0022

Schön, L., & Krantz, O. (2015). "New Swedish historical national accounts since the 16th Century in Constant and Current Prices". Lund Papers in Economic History no. 140

Shergold, P. R. (1982). *Working class life: The "American Standard" in comparative perspective, 1899–1913.* University of Pittsburgh Press.

Soares, L. C. (1988). Os escravos de ganho no Rio de Janeiro do século XIX. *Revista Brasileira De História, 8*(16), 107–142.

Stanfors, M., Leunig, T., Eriksson, B., & Karlsson, T. (2014). Gender, productivity, and the nature of work and pay: Evidence from the late nineteenth-century tobacco industry. *Economic History Review, 67*(1), 48–65. https://doi.org/10.1111/1468-0289.12017

Svensson, L. (1996). Politics or market forces? The determinants of the relative wage movements of female industrial workers in Sweden, 1960–1990. *Scandinavian Economic History Review, 44*(2), 161–182. https://doi.org/10.1080/03585522.1996.10414629

Svensson, L. (2003). Explaining equalization: Political institutions, market forces, and reduction of the gender wage gap in Sweden, 1920–95. *Social Science History, 27*(3), 371–395. https://doi.org/10.1215/01455532-27-3-371

Utterström, G. (1957). *Jordbrukets arbetare: levnadsvillkor och arbetsliv på landsbygden från frihetstiden till mitten av 1800-talet*. Tiden.

Vollrath, D. (2011). The agricultural basis of comparative development. *Journal of Economic Growth, 16*(4), 343–370. https://doi.org/10.1007/s10887-011-9074-1

Willcox, W. F. (1929). Statistics of migrations, national tables, Argentina, Brazil, Paraguay, Uruguay, Chile. International Migrations, Vol.1: Statistics. In *International Migrations, Vol.1: Statistics*. NBER.

Williamson, J. G. (1985). The historical content of the classical labour surplus model. *Population and Development Review, 11*(2), 171–191.

Williamson, J. G. (1995). The evolution of global labour markets since 1830: Background evidence and hypotheses. *Explorations in Economic History, 32*(2), 141–196. https://doi.org/10.1006/exeh.1995.1006

Williamson, J. G. (1999). Real wages, inequality and globalization in Latin America before 1940. *Revista De Historia Económica, XVII*. https://doi.org/10.1017/S0212610900002287

Williamson, J. G. (2015). Latin American inequality: Colonial origins, commodity booms or a missed twentieth-century leveling? *Journal of Human Development and Capabilities, 16*(3), 324–341. https://doi.org/10.1080/19452829.2015.1044821

CHAPTER 9

Does Democratization Cause Redistribution? Evidence from Sweden and Brazil

Erik Bengtsson and Marc Morgan

1 Introduction

What is the relationship between democratization and economic redistribution? This is the question addressed in this chapter, by way of a comparative analysis of the case studies of Sweden and Brazil. In recent years a "redistributive" approach to democratization has become very influential.[1] Daron Acemoglu and James A. Robinson made a seminal

[1] This discussion has deeper roots, at least back to John Stuart Mill's fear that universal suffrage would mean that the poor would establish a "class government" with which they would oppress the rich, redistribute assets, and hamper the market economy (Weyland, 1996: 1–2).

E. Bengtsson (✉)
Lund University in Sweden, Lund, Sweden
e-mail: erik.bengtsson@ekh.lu.se

M. Morgan
Department of History, Economics and Society,
University of Geneva, Geneva, Switzerland

J. Álvarez and S. Prado (eds.), *Scandinavia and South America—A Tale of Two Capitalisms*, Palgrave Studies in Economic History,
https://doi.org/10.1007/978-3-031-09198-8_9

contribution in this regard with their article "Why did the West extend the franchise?", in which they argue that franchise extensions should be seen as "strategic decisions by the political elite to prevent widespread social unrest and revolution" (Acemoglu & Robinson, 2000). The disenfranchised masses under European oligarchies in the early twentieth century had an interest in redistribution, and political elites realized that they had to make concessions so that discontent would not boil over and cause a revolution. Toke S. Aidt and co-authors have also contributed a string of important studies on nineteenth- and twentieth-century franchise extensions, which highlight that popular unrest and the threat of revolution was essential driver of democratization (e.g. Aidt & Franck, 2019; Aidt et al., 2006).

Contrary to these studies, we examine democratization as the independent variable, not as the dependent outcome variable. The hypothesis is that recently enfranchised poorer groups are assumed to strive for social and economic reforms that benefit their material positions through the redistribution of economic resources. Dani Rodrik has argued that democratization can lead to higher wages, as the process of political participation and competition may raise workers' reservation wage by creating laws and institutions more "partial to workers' interests" (Rodrik, 1999: 727). An important institution in this regard is the tax office, emphasized strongly by Piketty (2014). The early twentieth century experienced the rise of direct taxes, such as progressive income taxes, inheritance taxes, and wealth taxes/capital levies, as populations gained more political rights.

The democratization–redistribution literature is profoundly connected to an older literature on democratization and the welfare state. Peter Lindert provided an important contribution to this literature with his paper on "the rise of social spending" from 1880 to 1930 (Lindert, 1994). He contrasted a functionalist argument, where social spending increases with economic development (proxied by GDP growth), with a "rise of democracy" argument where social spending on welfare and unemployment compensation, pension subsidies, health subsidies, and housing subsidies grows with popular power over policymaking, fundamentally proxied by democratization. The historical evidence marshalled by Lindert indicated that suffrage extension, to lower-income earners in general and also to women, increased social spending. Following Piketty and Lindert, in our two case studies, we will look for reforms in progressive taxation and social spending.

If the economic literature to some degree simplifies and just assumes that more labour mobilization equals more reforms, the institutionalist literature in political science points to some preconditions for efficient reforms, namely (a) intellectuals and reformist ideologues, and (b) a competent and willing bureaucracy (cf. Amenta, 2003; Orloff, 1988). Unless there is a competent state in place, with bureaucrats willing to implement reforms, reforms are impossible, as Rothstein (1986) showed in his study of the "Social Democratic state" in Sweden. Piketty (2020) examined these ideological preconditions more widely across time and space, highlighting how reformist ideas interact with sudden "ruptures" (mobilizations, wars, crises) to create multiple political-ideological bifurcations that follow power dynamics. Related to these mechanisms is the neorealist theory of political economy and institutional change, where social constraints—derived from contradictory interests and social demands among unequal citizens—inform states' strategies (Amable & Palombarini, 2008; Waltz, 1979).

The dominant approach of the literature on democracy, inequality, and redistribution employs quantitative large-N designs (Acemoglu & Robinson, 2000; Aidt et al., 2006; Albertus, 2017; Bronner and Skorge 2015). We instead employ an exploratory small-N design, using the logical sequencing and inference of "process tracing" to connect each piece of contextual evidence to the hypothesis under consideration. The strength of this approach is to tease out causal chains and the confluence of several factors, in comparison to the large-N design which is superior in estimating average effects (Ragin, 1997; also, Mahoney, 2000 and Fairfield, 2013). It also avoids problems of variable measurement and sample selection that limit the robustness of results in large-N design studies (cf. Eberhardt, 2019 in the literature on democracy and growth).

Sweden and Brazil can be considered examples of "most different" and "crucial" case designs, and this is precisely what makes them so interesting to compare (Chapter 1). A "most different" case design posits that if the independent variable of interest (in our case democratization) has a similar effect on the dependent variable of interest (in our case redistribution) in cases that are different in practically all other respects, then the causal importance of these variables is highlighted (Blyth, 2002). Sweden and Brazil can be seen as representing opposite ends of the socio-economic spectrum within parliamentary capitalist democracies in terms of social differentiation, industrial development, labour market integration, and nature of political institutions. Thus, taken together they can be considered as "crucial" cases in which the effect of interest is most likely to be found (in Sweden) and least likely to be found (in Brazil) (ibid).

In this work, we look at the effects of *democratization*, not democracy per se. The distinction is important. Democratization is a *change* of political regime in an extensive margin (from limited suffrage to full universal suffrage of the adult population). This change may have short-run and medium-run effects which are not necessarily reproduced by the continued existence of democracy (i.e. universal suffrage). Thus, we look for changes that gave all men and all women the right to vote over the legally defined adult age. In each of our case studies democratization took very different times to be completed. It took Brazil almost one hundred years (1891–1988) to pass the suffrage reforms Sweden passed in ten years (1909–1918), essentially because of the persistence of the literacy requirement in an underdeveloped country with a historical legacy of slavery and low educational standards. For this reason, we assess the impact of democratization in Sweden until 1950, while in Brazil we reach the twenty-first century. The years until 1950 mark a sufficiently long period to adequately detect the effects of democratization in Sweden, given that it was four decades after universal manhood suffrage and three decades after universal suffrage. By the second half of the 1930s and the 1940s, Sweden was a stable democracy, with no serious threats to the democratic system (cf. Lindström, 1983). In what follows, we analyse each case study separately, before synthesizing the lessons we draw from them in the conclusion.

2 The Swedish Case Study

2.1 Historical Background on Democratization

The national political system in Sweden was democratized in two steps. In 1909 all adult men got equal suffrage to the second chamber of parliament. In 1918 men and women got equal suffrage to the second chamber, and the extremely unequal suffrage system to the first chamber was abolished, replaced by an indirect but democratic election system. The 1866 reform, when the Swedish four estates diet—comprised of nobility, clergy, city burghers (merchants and artisans), and farmers—voted to abolish itself and instead instate a two-chamber parliament (in line with the European trend at the time; see Nilsson, 1994), is sometimes seen as a step to democracy but given the new system's plutocratic nature, this is a misleading description. The 1866 system before the 1909 reform is better described as a "competitive oligarchy" (Miller, 2015): there was a stable political system with elections, but voting was extremely unequal. A very exclusive first chamber (2% of the adult men could vote, and only 6000 men were electable; see [Rustow, 1969]) was combined with a broader representation in the second chamber. Low-income citizens lacked the right to vote, as did women, recipients of poor reliefs and other groups (cf. Lindgren, 2020). The fixed income threshold to vote meant that with rising real incomes and inflation, successively more people got the right to vote (Jusko, 2017). However, this process was slow. Figure 1 shows the evolution of suffrage for the two-chamber system, measured as the share of eligible adults over 18 years of age, and actual voting participation in elections to parliament, measured as votes cast as a share of adults over 18 years. We can clearly see the break between the 1908 and 1911 elections, and an even more important one between 1917

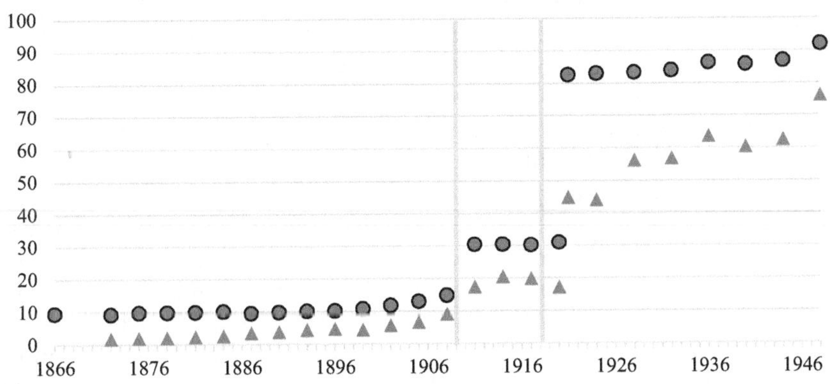

Fig. 1 Voting statistics, Sweden 1866–1948 (*Source* Lindgren [2020]. *Note* The numbers pertain to elections to the second chamber of parliament [*Riksdagen*]. Grey bars indicate the two years of democratization in 1909 [all adult men] and 1918 [all adult women])

and 1921. We also see that the share of those enfranchised who actually voted was very low in the beginning and grew over time, indicating increasing popular mobilization.

From the 1890s the democratization movement grew stronger and stronger. In this decade, the so-called "people's parliaments" gathered hundreds of thousands of votes for a pro-democratic mock parliament consisting of liberals and social democrats (Vallinder, 1962). The liberals formed a government for the first time in 1906, with suffrage reform the key issue on their agenda. However, as a minority government, they failed to carry their reform through parliament. As a consequence, they resigned and were replaced by a conservative government which inherited the suffrage issue and put through a reform.[2] Starting in 1909, all men could vote for the second chamber. However, the democrats were not satisfied. The first chamber was still an unequally appointed institution (since 1909, men were allocated votes on a 40-vote scale, with higher income and wealth carrying more votes), and women still did not have the right to vote. There was also severe political conflict in the 1910s over the issue of whether the government should be responsible to the King (its historical origins was as the King's council) or to the majority in the parliament, *Riksdagen*. As late as 1914, the King and the conservatives organized a non-violent uprising which overturned the Liberal government and ushered in a Conservative one (cf. Brusewitz, 1951: 59–78). This was however the last instance of royal power over the government.

Universal and equal suffrage for men and women, and for the first chamber too, was only put through during the age of revolutionary threats, in 1918, and was used for the first time in the election of 1921. The background to these changes was the very strong political polarization during World War I. The Conservative government, which with the King's support had replaced a Liberal government in 1914, became supremely unpopular as cold winters combined with blocked international trade caused a lack of food in 1916 and 1917. This lack of food led to protests, riots, and more or less spontaneous popular confiscations of food from merchants, traders, farmers, and others in the spring of 1917. At the same time, the revolutionary events in Russia influenced the Left

[2] The coming and inner life of the 1906–1909 Lindman government is discussed in Brusewitz (1951: 15–27). The government contained quite large differences of opinion on the design of the suffrage reform. Lindman did not wish to extend the suffrage but pragmatically saw it as unavoidable given public opinion: see Lewin (2010: 40-46).

in Sweden. The historian Carl Göran Andrae has in a thorough analysis of the events of these years shown that there was no serious threat of a Bolshevik-style revolution in Sweden, but that Social Democratic leaders did use the implied threat of unrest or revolution to push for reforms. For example, the Social Democratic leader Hjalmar Branting warned in a parliamentary debate on 9 June 1917 of what would happen if the government were to take a hard stance on demonstrations and food confiscations: "then we have the revolution here" (quoted in Andrae, 1998: 119). The social unrest was clearly a motivating factor for the 1918 democratic reform. Acemoglu and Robinson (2000: 1186) cite the political scientist Tim Tilton (1974) on the events of 1918: "Swedish democracy had triumphed without a revolution—but not without the *threat* of a revolution".

There are also good reasons to believe that the pro-suffrage movements from the 1890s onwards did expect that democratization would bring about redistribution. The historian Madeleine Hurd has shown that the suffrage movement spoke of how political inequality led to economic inequality and that "much of the propaganda implied that equal suffrage would lead to a redistribution of wealth" (Hurd, 2000: 132, cited in Lundberg, 2007: 94). The suffrage movement according to Lundberg (2007: 389, 405–406) had a "radical democratic, populist and anti-elitist" worldview and platform. This populism did not really theorize issues of political economy but emphasized that constitutional reform per se could create a more just society (cf. Bengtsson, 2021). Outside of the suffrage movement, which was to a large degree led by Liberals and characterized by Liberal/radical/democratic views, the major force for democratization was the Social Democrats.[3]

The Social Democratic Party (SAP) was founded in 1889 and the degree to which it was a Marxist party has been amply discussed in the literature; we may say that they took a reformist view to some degree and celebrated universal suffrage as the most important reform (Berman, 2006; Tingsten, 1941). Berman (2006: 154–155) makes the insightful observation that the very pronounced oligarchical system in

[3] On the working-class movements and the liberal middle class as the main drivers of democratization in Sweden, see the comprehensive, comparative analysis of Berins Collier (1999: 83–85).

Sweden meant that the Swedish Social Democrats became very appreciative of democracy, valued a possible suffrage reform, and didn't devalue it as "bourgeois", as labour movements in southern European countries did. For example, one of the leading Social Democrats of the 1880s, Axel Danielsson, stressed in 1889 that "Socialism cannot be realized in a country without free institutions. *Democracy* is necessary for *Social democracy*" (quoted in Zennström, 1983: 123). The concrete welfare policy proposals were less developed in the 1880s, but even at this early stage of the movement, the organizer August Palm listed reforms to strive for, which he deemed possible to achieve "under the current capitalist command". These were: progressive taxation of inheritances, the abolition of indirect taxes, the abolition of repression of the unemployed and vagrants, and public care of the sick, old, and victims of work injuries (Tingsten, 1967: 127).

Following this description, we need to study the development of inequality and public tax and spending policy before and after (a) the suffrage extension of 1909, which for the first time gave male workers significant influence over policy and (b) democratization in 1918, which for the first time was implemented in the 1921 election. To introduce the political distribution of power, Table 1 shows election results for the second chamber after the suffrage extension of 1909.[4] We see that the pro-redistribution Social Democrats are established as a major party immediately after the 1909 reform. The Liberals, who were a broad party that included some rather radical "free-spirited" liberals as well as more bourgeois politicians, were the leading force in Swedish politics in the 1910s but faded in the 1920s. There was a wave of politicization, with growing electoral participation, in 1914 and 1917, and then another wave after 1928 when participation increases from 53 to 55% in 1920–1924 to 67% in 1928 and 75% in 1936.

[4] Before 1909, parties were, with the exception of the Social Democrats, rather loosely organized. The national party of the Liberals (i.e. their organization which also encompassed non-MPs) was only founded in 1902, and the equivalent for the Conservatives in 1904. For example, for 1897 Wåhlstrand (1936: 177) classifies the second chamber's 230 MPs as 128 Country Party (a conservative agrarian party), 18 unaffiliated Conservatives, 53 unaffiliated Liberals, 30 Liberals, and 1 Social Democrat.

Table 1 Swedish election results, elections to the second chamber 1911–1950

Year	*Communists/Left Socialists*	*Social Democrats*	*Liberals*	*Farmers*	*Conservatives*	*Electoral participation*
1911	–	28.5	40.2	–	31.3	57.0
1914 (March)	–	30.1	32.2	–	37.7	69.9
1914 (September)	–	36.4	26.9	0.2	36.5	66.2
1917	8.1	31.1	27.6	5.3 + 3.1*	24.7	65.8
1920	6.4	29.7	21.8	7.9 + 6.2*	27.8	55.3
1921	4.6 + 3.2**	36.2	18.7	11.1	25.8	54.2
1924	3.6 + 1.5	41.1	13.0	10.8	26.1	53.0
1928	6.4	37.0	12.9	11.2	29.4	67.4
1932	3.0 + 5.3	41.7	9.8	14.1	23.1	68.6
1936	3.3 + 4.4	45.9	12.9	14.3	17.6	74.5
1940	4.2	53.8	12.0	12.0	18.0	80.3
1944	10.3	46.7	12.9	13.6	15.9	71.9
1948	6.3	46.1	22.8	12.4	12.3	82.7

Source Statistics Sweden (2018)
Note *In the 1917 and 1920 elections two separate farmers' parties participated in the elections. They merged in 1921
**In 1921, 1924, 1932, and 1936 elections two separate left socialist/communist parties participated

2.2 *Trends in Taxation, Social Spending, and Inequality*

For a historical setting like Sweden in the 1910s and 1920s, we have no thorough and detailed data on the distribution of post-tax, post-transfer incomes. Rather, we have to discuss the implications of democratization for redistribution using a combination of outcome variables. Figures 2, 3, and 4 present the evolution of a set of important outcome variables for the 1900–1950 period: the tax-to-GDP ratio with the top personal income tax rate, social spending, and the capital share of national income alongside top income shares. The first two are indicators of the welfare state, while the latter are indicators of how market inequality evolved.

The tax-to-GDP ratio, which between 1860 and 1900 was stable around 6–7%, started growing during the 1910s, especially during WW1 (Fig. 2). We should also add that the taxation system became more progressive in this period, as indirect taxation (consumption taxes and

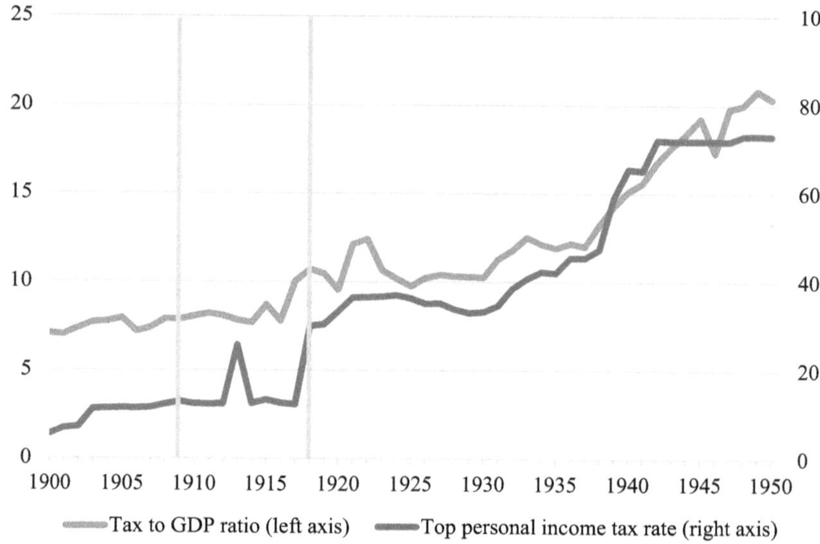

Fig. 2 Taxes and social spending, Sweden 1900–1950 (*Sources* Total taxation from Henrekson and Stenkula [2015: Fig. 1.2]; top personal income tax rate from Piketty [2020]. *Note* Grey bars indicate the two years of democratization in 1909 [all adult men] and 1918 [all adult women])

tariffs) was becoming less important, and direct taxation of incomes more important (cf. Lantz, 2019: 12). We know that at the height of the Swedish welfare state in the post-war period, taxation in itself was not more redistributive than in other countries (Steinmo, 1989: 516–520; Lindert, 2004: Chaps. 10–11). However, it is quite possible that before democratization, taxation was even more regressive. In the early twentieth century, income taxes made up about 30% of total tax revenues while consumption taxes made up about 50%. In the 1920s, 1930s, and 1940s, income taxes instead formed 50–60% of the total and consumption taxes 30–40% (Henrekson & Stenkula, 2015: 14). We will come back to specific taxes and tax reforms in the following section. Figure 2 also shows the top tax rate applied to personal incomes over the same period. Two important changes occur in the late 1910s when the top marginal rate jumps from about 10 to 30%, and the sharper upward trend in the 1930s and 1940s, which increases the rate to over 70%.

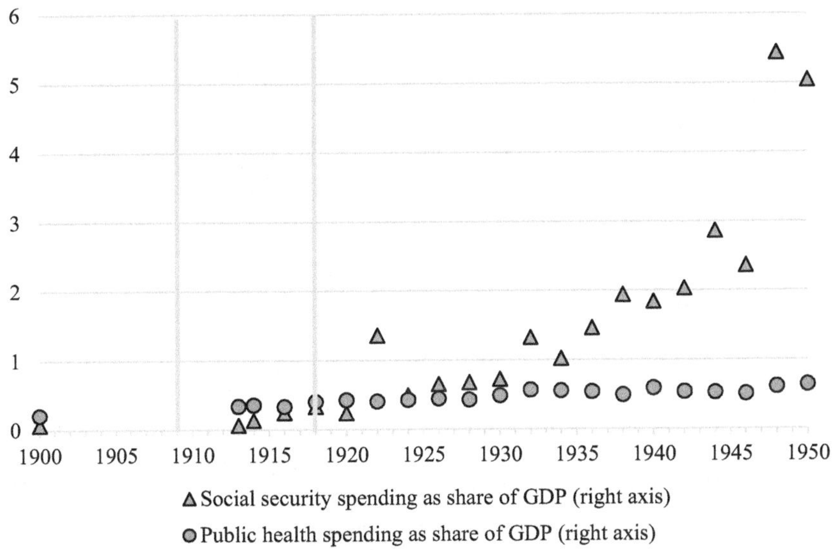

Fig. 3 Social spending, Sweden 1900–1950 (*Source* Information on social security spending and public health spending from Peter Flora's "Europe expenditure series", available as an Excel file from the UC Davis Global Price and Income History Group, http://gpih.ucdavis.edu/Government.htm. *Note* Grey bars indicate the two years of democratization in 1909 [all adult men] and 1918 [all adult women])

Figure 3 plots government spending on social security and public health as a share of GDP. Social spending grew rapidly in the 1930s and 1940s, owing in particular to the persistent rise in social security expenditures. These begin to increase prior to 1920, but pick up speed in the 1930s to outgrow public health spending, which only gradually increases from the 1910s, doubling between 1913 and 1950.

Pre-tax income inequality (Fig. 4) was high and stable in 1903–1913, with the top decile receiving 45–50% of total incomes. By 1916, 53% of total income accrued to the top decile. There was a steep decline to around 40% in the early 1920s, 35–40% in the 1930s, and a further decline to 30% in 1950. Roine and Waldenström (2008) do not discuss democratization as a potential driver of income inequality, even though in pure timing terms it is clear that inequality peaked during the tumultuous WWI years just before the democratizing reform of 1918, in the years of

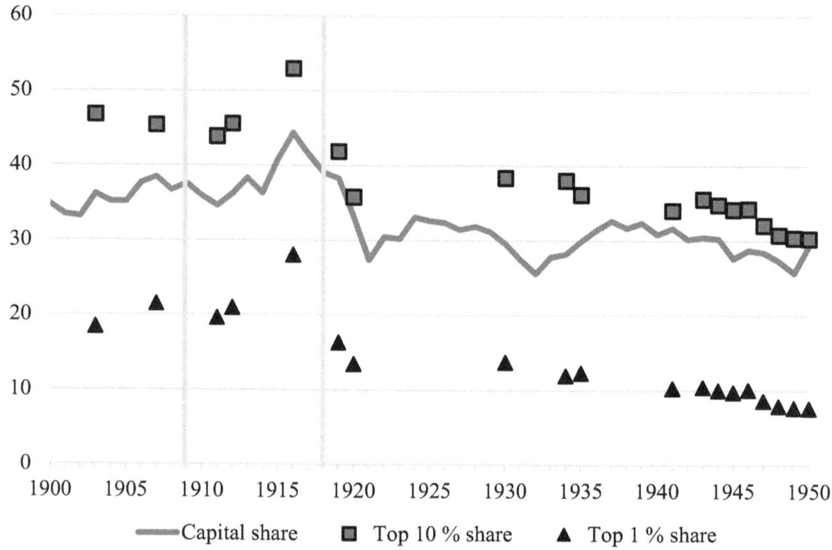

Fig. 4 Income distribution in Sweden, 1900–1950 (*Sources* Top 1% and top 10% shares from the World Inequality Database [wid.world]; Swedish shares from Roine and Waldenström [2008]; capital shares in gross terms from Bengtsson and Waldenström [2018]. *Note* Grey bars indicate the two years of democratization in 1909 [all adult men] and 1918 [all adult women])

food riots and unrest (cf. Andrae, 1998). In their analysis of the fall in inequality, Roine and Waldenström emphasize the role of falling capital incomes.

The income distribution between capital and labour (Fig. 3) is the measure here which shows the most immediate effect of democratization (cf. Bengtsson et al., 2020). The capital share fell from a peak of around 50% in 1916–17, the years of war-time profiteering, to around 35% in the 1920s and eventually to 25–30% in the 1950s and 1960s.

2.3 *Democratization and Redistributive Reforms*

Interestingly, major studies of the build-up of the welfare state in Sweden such as Edebalk (1996), Åmark (2005) and Sejersted (2005) do not present democratization as an important shift in the history of Swedish welfare policy. Edebalk (1996: 13, 51) does present the imposition of universal male suffrage in 1911 as one factor of relevance for the growth of social insurance in the 1910s, but this factor plays a subordinate role, alongside population aging and economic growth. Moreover, in the analyses of Sejersted (2005) and Åmark (2005: 43) the major period of build-up of the Swedish welfare state was the 1930s to the 1970s (cf. the timing of social security spending in Fig. 2). In Åmark's analysis, prior to this crucial reform period was a pioneer period from the 1880s to the 1930s, which did not see many successful reforms but many important debates. This pioneer period straddles the democratic breakthrough of the 1910s, which is not singled out as a break point. We will now discuss redistributive reforms and welfare state reforms from the 1880s to the 1940s and see whether the evolution of policy relates to democratization.

The first step towards a welfare state in Sweden was a motion in parliament for industrial injury insurance in 1884 from a radical liberal, S.A. Hedin. This led to a public commission and in the debate the threat of a socialist labour movement like that in Germany was highlighted (Åmark, 2005: 45–46; Baldwin, 1990: 85–88). This did not lead to a reform, but the fact that interest in social reforms began precisely then is an instance of ***anticipation***: political elites realized that there were threats to the social order, which could be co-opted by imposing innovative and popular reforms. However, given the reform failures, Åmark in his overview of the Swedish welfare system argues that by 1910 there was still no welfare system at all, only a highly heterogeneous combination of some residual insurances (Åmark, 2005: 58). Edebalk (1996: 10, 15) is more optimistic, arguing that a new social insurance system with universalist aspirations was already in place in the 1910s. In his criticism of this interpretation, Åmark stresses that benefit levels were very low and that coverage was patchy.

Regarding the degree of reforms before the advent of universal manhood suffrage in 1911, we may note that Edebalk (1996: 12) and Åmark (2005) agree: there were very few, if any redistributive, pro-egalitarian policies in place before 1911. Edebalk summarizes the situation before the 1910s as voluntary, independently organized sickness insurance associations and, since 1901, some obligation for employers to contribute to benefits after workplace accidents. In terms of social services, there had been mandatory provision of six years of schooling since 1842, but attendance was low (there was no compulsory attendance until 1882, and children often skipped school to work or for other reasons). Educational ambitions were initially weak, and the schooling system was heavily class-segregated. It was not until around 1900 that the first steps were taken to build a more integrated schooling system with higher ambitions, including for children in the lower class of schools. (Edgren, 2011: 104–111.) Both in the schooling literature and in the social insurance literature, growing reform ambitions in the 1910s and 1920s are related to the coming of democratic society (Edebalk, 1996; Edgren, 2011: 110–113). With this in mind, we can look at the timing of the reforms. We may point out that in relation to welfare state literature, which is often very much oriented either towards social insurance (e.g., Edebalk, 1996) or public service provision, while taxation literature is studied separately (Henrekson & Stenkula, 2015; Steinmo, 1989), here we consider a broader set of policies that have implications for income distribution.

- 1911: wealth tax introduced; level is 1/60 of wealth. From 1939 to 1947: 1% (Henrekson & Stenkula, 2015: 31).
- 1913: universal pension. This is often presented as the first key welfare state reform in Sweden, a first "universal" social insurance on the road to the Social Democratic model (for example Baldwin, 1990: 83–94), but this interpretation has been questioned by Åmark (2005, 47ff) who points out that the replacement levels were so low that no one could live off the pension alone.
- 1916: almost universal work accident insurance (Edebalk, 1996, Chap. 5).
- 1918: a thorough reform of poor relief. The level of cash income was raised and the poor house model with its mix of physically and mentally ill, old people, the poor, alcoholics, etc., was abolished, and replaced by more care-oriented social policy (Swärd, 2008).
- 1920: the imposition of the eight-hour working day Monday to Friday, a decrease from 10 h, with the same daily wage (Bengtsson & Molinder, 2017).
- 1920: progressive capital taxation (Henrekson & Stenkula, 2015: 21–22).
- 1927: abolition of the Master and Servant law (*Tjänstehjonsstadgan*). The reform strengthened the position of weak groups in the labour markets, especially servants (Moberg, 1978).
- 1933: new counter-cyclical public works policy with market-level wages, unlike the old public works for unemployed (cf. Unga, 1976).

- 1934: support for trade union-run unemployment insurance, which strengthened trade unions (Rothstein, 1990) and guaranteed better living standards for the unemployed (Åmark, 2005: 71–76).
- 1934: maximum inheritance tax raised from 4 to 20%. Further sharpened in 1948 to a maximum of 60% (Henrekson & Stenkula, 2015: 29).
- 1935 and 1937: important improvements to the pension system (Åmark, 2005: 70–71).
- 1938: two weeks of paid vacation (Isaksson, 2000: 355–359).
- 1939: income tax is made substantially progressive (Henrekson & Stenkula, 2015: 18–19, Fig. 1.4). Before 1918 the maximum marginal tax rate was below 15%; in 1918 it was raised to 30%, thereafter it increased gradually, and by the time of WW2 it was around 60% (see Fig. 2).

As this list shows there is certainly a string of important reforms in the 1910s, 1920s, and 1930s. But how important was democratization for the pace and ambition of the reforms? We may note that scholars like Unga (1976) and Edebalk (1996) point to the advances of the labour movement in the first two decades of the 1900s as an important driver of reforms. Edebalk points, for example, to the 1909 general strike in which more than 300,000 workers refused to work for a month or more. The three-day general strike for universal suffrage in 1902, with about 120,000 participants, also seems important in this context. Since the first failed reform attempts in the 1880s the spectre of the socialist movement—in Germany or domestically—had been an important motivation for policymakers. This speaks to an anticipation hypothesis, with reforms ushered in as a pre-emptive strategy of co-optation. This complicates the evaluation of causality: if we accept that the labour movement was one of the drivers of democratization in Sweden (cf. Berins Collier, 1999), and also one of the drivers of social reforms, then there is an identification issue.

From a historical case study point of view, it seems reasonable to see democratization as connected to the growth of redistributive reforms, but as neither a necessary cause—there were reforms before formal democratization, at least before women also got the vote—nor a sufficient cause. If we follow Åmark, Sejersted, and others, then there was a *temporal lag* between the formal democratization of 1921 and the reform wave of the 1930s. In their analyses, democracy is not really seen as a determinant factor. Åmark and Sejersted both view the 1930s as the start of a modern social insurance system and Social Democratic hegemony, after the "Red-Green" alliance with the Farmers' League in 1932–1933 (Sejersted, 2005: 165; cf. Nyman, 1944 on the alliance). The second half of the 1930s, before the outbreak of WW2, and the late 1940s, were also seen as "harvest time" in the labour movement. As the trade union economist Meidner said in 1945: "The labour movement has conquered society. Now it is time to shape society as we want it /…/ harvest time lies before us" (quoted in Ekdahl, 2001: 186). The lag between democratization and the intensified reform pace of the 1930s and 1940s shows that democratization in itself was not enough to pass reforms.

We could complicate the strong focus on the 1930s slightly. Complementing Wetterberg (2010: 82), the biographer of the Liberal Prime Minister Nils Edén who led the government from October 1917 to March 1920, we might say that Edén is underestimated in Swedish history. In fact, the poor relief reform of 1918 as well as the eight-hour working day reform of 1918 were important reforms for equalization, and both were imposed as a package with democratization. If we also consider tax reforms and labour reforms such as the 1927 abolishment of the Master and Servant law, then the 1910s and 1920s appear as equally interesting decades of reform.

The Swedish case shows that very little happened immediately after democratization. There are at least two different temporalities to be considered. First, in the short-run, the wave of public mobilization with democratic and egalitarian demands in 1917–1921 pushed for democracy and equalization and reached three large breakthroughs: universal suffrage, poor relief reform, and the eight-hour working day. This democratic push redistributed income immediately by moving income from capital owners to wage earners (cf. Bengtsson & Molinder, 2017; Bengtsson et al., 2020). This happened because trade unions and worker militancy meant that workers could demand a larger share of the surplus. But more comprehensive reforms demanded a new sort of politics with a much larger degree of public involvement. This did not arise automatically with formal democratization (cf. Lindert, 1994: 21 on Britain in the 1920s). As the Brazilian case also reveals, the reform process is a more complex temporal phenomenon.

3 The Brazilian Case Study

3.1 *Historical Background on Democratization*

Three dates mark Brazil's transition to full democracy. These are (a) the suffrage extension of 1891, which gave all literate male workers the vote no matter their level of income, (b) the introduction of literate women into the franchise in 1932, and (c) full democratization in 1988, implemented for the first time in the presidential and congressional elections in 1989 and 1990, respectively.

Brazil's first independent constitution, in 1824, following three centuries of Portuguese rule, stipulated that only domestically born, literate, rich male Catholics aged 25 and over could vote directly for local councilmen and indirectly for state and national deputies in elections that were rife with fraud. An electoral law of 1881 extended the suffrage to non-Catholics and naturalized citizens, but it still officially excluded poor literates, women, slaves and the illiterate, which in total made up at least 85% of the voting-age population (Love, 1970). Slavery was abolished in 1888, a year before the military revolt against the monarchy, and three years before the new republican constitution. The main democratic reforms of the 1891 Constitution, apart from the abolishment of slavery, were to have direct elections at all levels of government, to expand suffrage by removing the income requirement for voting,[5] to reduce the legal minimum age to 21 for all men, and to decentralize government powers (ibid). Given that most slaves were illiterate, the democratic effect of abolition was fundamentally tied to advances in literacy. Together, the inclusion of more males in the franchise and the increase in literacy appreciably increased voter participation from 2 to 8% between the final parliamentary election of the empire in 1886 and the presidential elections at the beginning of the new century (Fig. 5). Voter participation stagnated at around 5% of the voting-age population until the 1920s, while the literacy rate stagnated at 35%

This oligarchic political system was interrupted during Getúlio Vargas' 1930 Liberal Alliance revolution and his "populist" reign until 1945. An electoral reform in 1932 allowed married women to vote if they had the permission of their husbands, which was stipulated in the 1934 Constitution (Hahner, 1980). The new text also reduced the voting age to 18,

[5] Until 1891 this was defined at 200 *milréis* (Love, 1970).

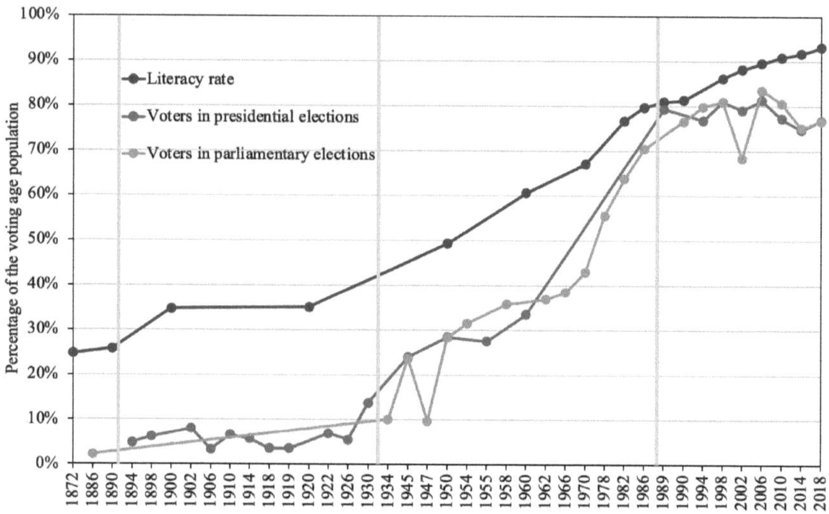

Fig. 5 Literacy and political participation in Brazil, 1872–2018 (*Source* [Gethin and Morgan, 2021]. *Note* Grey bars indicate the years of democratization in 1891 [all literate adult men], 1932 [all literate adult women], and 1988 [all illiterate adults]; the literacy rate refers to the proportion of the voting-age population who can read and write. Voters are the people who actually voted in all presidential and parliamentary elections as a share of the voting-age population defined in Table 2 for the different periods. Between 1886 and 1934 no data was found for parliamentary elections, but a similar evolution as for presidential elections can be expected. Between 1960 and 1989 no direct elections for the president were held)

made voting anonymous and compulsory among eligible male citizens, but maintained the literacy requirement. These changes did not, however, lead to any significant rise in political mobilization in the short term. As Fig. 5 shows, the 1934 congressional elections drew a smaller proportion of the voting-age population than the 1930 presidential contest (10% compared to 14%).

In 1937, Vargas suspended formal democracy by establishing a dictatorship (*Estado Novo*), with the president appointing state governors, who in turn named municipal prefects. The 1934 provisions were preserved in the 1937 Constitution and were again retained in the 1946 Constitution after the overthrow of the Vargas dictatorship by the military in

1945, fearing continued undemocratic "populism" (Skidmore, 1976). A marked increase in voter participation, following the continued expansion of literacy, can be observed during this era of rapid industrialization and urbanization (Fig. 5), with participation doubling from the previous period and fluctuating around 30–35% of the voting-age population. However, despite the democratic progress the proportion of voters remained comparatively low. For example, the 1960 presidential election in Brazil mobilized only 18% of the total population, compared to 44% in Argentina's 1958 presidential election (Love, 1970).

Among the growing number of parties, two pro-Vargas "populist" parties, created in the twilight of his dictatorship, dominated government during the 1945–1964 period—the centrist Social Democratic Party (PSD), and the leftist Brazilian Labour Party (PTB)—while the opposition was led by the anti-Vargas right-wing National Democratic Union (UDN), supported by the dwindling Republican Party (PR). The Congress was also dominated by these two pro-Vargas parties, with the balance of power tilting towards the quickly growing PTB (Table 2). Therefore, for at least the first half of the twentieth century, Brazil seemed to be in a vicious cycle whereby mass political voice to influence public policy was restricted by literacy requirements on voting, which mainly favoured urban inhabitants. The growing division between the urban-orientated "populist" executive—elected via a majoritarian

Table 2 Distribution (%) of congressional seats in Brazil among principal parties, 1945–1962

Year	*Social Progressive Party (PSP) %*	*Brazilian Labour Party (PTB) %*	*Social Democratic Party (PSD) %*	*Republican Party (PR) %*	*National Democratic Union (UDN) %*
1945	–	7.6	52.8	2.8	28.6
1947	15.7	10.5	52.6	15.7	5.2
1950	7.8	16.7	36.8	3.6	26.6
1954	8.8	17.7	36.5	4.9	22.3
1958	7.6	19.0	36.5	4.9	22.3
1962	5.6	25.4	30.0	2.4	22.9

Source Tribunal Superior Eleitoral (2013)
Note Number of parties went from 9 in 1945 to 13 in 1962

voting system by literate citizens—and the rural-dominated "patriarchal" legislature—elected in proportion to the total population of voting constituencies—was the origin of much of the political instability in the early 1960s in Brazil (Furtado, 1965). These divergences, alongside the military not wanting the labour politician João Goulart to assume the presidency after the resignation of Janio Quadros, gave way to a Constitutional Amendment voted by Congress that installed a parliamentary system, abolishing the executive role of the presidency (Loureiro, 2017). This change was reversed when put to referendum in 1963. Alongside a slowdown of economic growth, and the ambitious reforms proposed by the then PTB government (including universal suffrage), these dynamics fuelled the civil-military coup against the executive of Goulart in 1964 (Love, 1970; Morgan & Souza, 2019).

The decisive role of the urban vote in majoritarian elections up to the 1960s helps to explain why the military dictatorship (1964–1985) abolished the elections for the President of the Republic and State Governors for a large part of its reign, banning all previously existing parties, and imposing a two-party system. Direct elections could only be held for federal and state deputies and municipal councillors among approved candidates, either from the military's National Renewal Alliance (ARENA) or from the artificial "catch-all" opposition, the Brazilian Democratic Movement (MDB). The 1979 reforms saw the military government abandon the two-party system in order to split the opposition, which was gaining electoral ground. ARENA was dissolved and replaced by the Democratic Social Party (PDS), and subsequently by the Liberal Front Party (PFL) until 2007, and the Democrats (DEM) from 2007; while the MDB rebranded into the PMDB. New parties were formed including the left-wing Worker's Party (PT) and Democratic Labour Party (PDT), and the right-wing Brazilian Social Democracy Party (PSDB). The 1988 Constitution definitively adopted universal suffrage with the abolishment of the literacy requirement. By then the literacy rate had increased to 80%, from 60% in 1960 (Fig. 5). From there on into the new century, the share of voters stabilized at around 75–80% of adults. In this period, the Presidency was dominated by conservative or liberal candidates until the 2003 election of Lula da Silva of the PT, while Congress was highly fragmented among a larger number of parties (Table 3).

Table 3 Distribution (%) of congressional seats in Brazil among principal parties, 1990–2010

Year	*Democratic Labour Party (PDT) %*	*Workers' Party (PT) %*	*Brazilian Democratic Movement Party (PMDB) %*	*Liberal Front Party/Democrats (PFL/DEM) %*	*Brazilian Social Democratic Party (PSDB) %*
1990	8.9	6.9	21.4	16.5	7.5
1994	6.6	9.7	20.8	17.3	12.2
1998	4.8	11.5	16.1	20.4	19.2
2002	4.0	17.7	14.6	16.3	13.6
2006	4.6	16.1	17.3	12.6	12.8
2010	5.2	16.7	15.2	8.3	10.5

Source Tribunal Superior Eleitoral (2013)
Note Number of parties went from 19 in 1990 to 23 in 2010

3.2 Trends in Taxation, Social Spending, and Inequality

Figure 6 shows how taxation began to increase steadily during the 1940s, doubling from 12% of GDP in 1940 to 25% in 1970, after which it stabilized before increasing again after 1988. Trade-related taxes (import tariffs and export duties) shrank to insignificance by 1950, while consumption taxes grew significantly from 5% of GDP in 1940 to 14% in 1970. Consumption taxes continued to be the largest category for the remainder of the twentieth century, only being overtaken by direct taxation in the 2010s. We should note the regressive nature of Brazil's tax system compared to Sweden's. By the end of the period, after growing for many decades, direct income taxes had still not reached 50% of total tax take, a ratio reached by Sweden 90 years previously. Moreover, until the 1960s the progressiveness of personal income tax, as measured by the top marginal rate, trended upward in similar fashion to Sweden. But since then, and particularly since the 1980s the rate collapsed to less than half the value of preceding decades.

Rising public social spending in Brazil drove much of the increase in taxation, as well as its changing composition. Social security transfers overtook other social spending in 1946 and sharply increased over the following decades, especially from the 1960s onwards in line with social contributions (Fig. 7). Education spending rose much more steadily, without clean breaks after 1946. Healthcare spending was much more

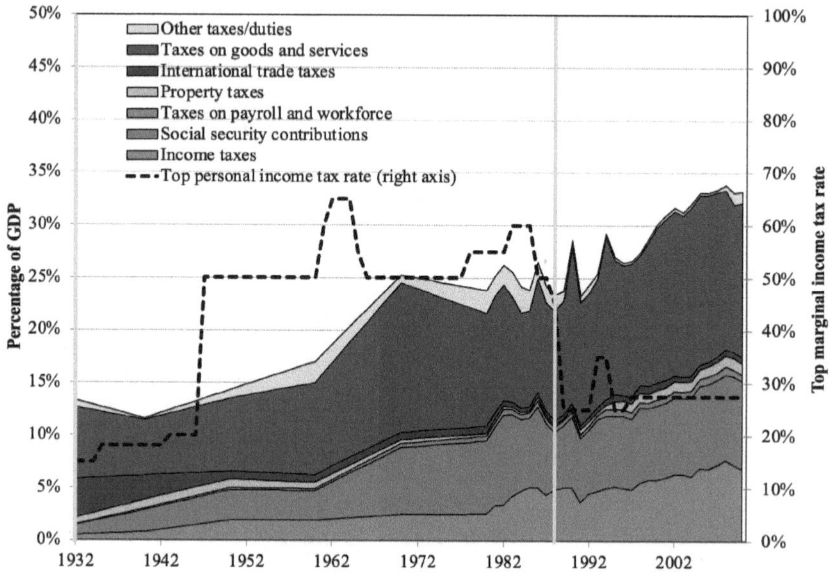

Fig. 6 Taxes in Brazil, 1932–2010 (*Sources* Authors' calculation for 1932–1970 using data from IBGE [2017]; 1980–1989 from Varsano et al. [1998]; 1990–2010 from OECD/ECLAC/CIAT/IDB [2015]. The top personal income tax rate 1932–2010 is from the *Secretaria da Receita Federal*. *Note* Tax decomposition for 1932–1970 is linearly interpolated from point estimates for each decade. Grey bars indicate the years of democratization in 1932 [all literate adult women] and 1988 [all illiterate adults]. All literature adult men were given the vote in 1891)

stagnant until the new provisions in the 1988 Constitution brought it to a level with the trend in education spending. Another break associated with the 1988 Constitution was spending on labour-related items (employment support schemes, worker-training programmes, etc.), and to a lesser extent housing and urban services (utilities and public transportation), which have yet to reach levels of the intense industrialization years of the 1950s. In terms of effecting monetary redistribution, social security transfers have more of a direct effect, especially as they are included in pre-tax incomes in surveys and administrative data, while other types of spending gradually bear their effects over the life cycle.

Pre-tax income inequality (Fig. 8) was extremely high and growing from the final days of the Old Republic, through the booming industrial

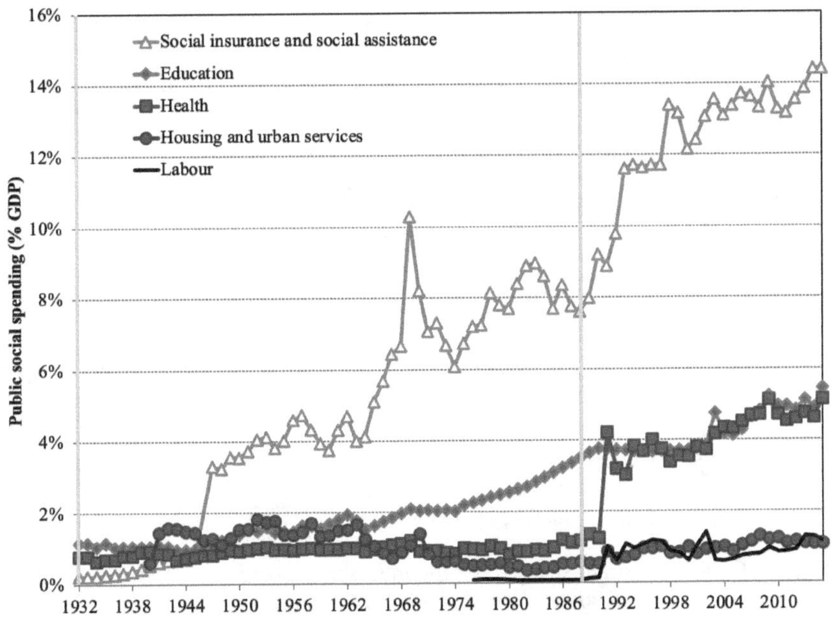

Fig. 7 Public social spending in Brazil, 1932–2015 (*Sources* Author's calculation using data from IBGE [2017] and from the *Ministério de Fazenda* [2014]. *Note* Grey bars indicate the years of democratization in 1932 [all literate adult women] and 1988 [all illiterate adults]. All literature adult men were given the vote in 1891)

economy of the 1930s, and especially during the war-time profiteering until 1943 (Morgan & Souza, 2019). In this period the top percentile went from 20% of total income in 1926 to 29% of total income in 1942 (by comparison, the share of the top percentile in Sweden in the 1920s and 1930s was about 13–14%; see Fig. 4), while the Gini coefficient increased by seven percentage points from 0.50 to 0.57. The top 1% share then plummeted alongside the capital share, until the early 1960s, amid a period of rapidly rising median wages, and falling inequality within occupational groups, but rising inequality between groups (Astorga, 2021; Morgan & Souza, 2019).[6] The trends reverted after the civil-military

[6] Astorga (2021: 7) distinguishes between four occupational groups in his analysis using dynamic distribution tables: "Group 1 (employers, managers, and professionals), Group 2

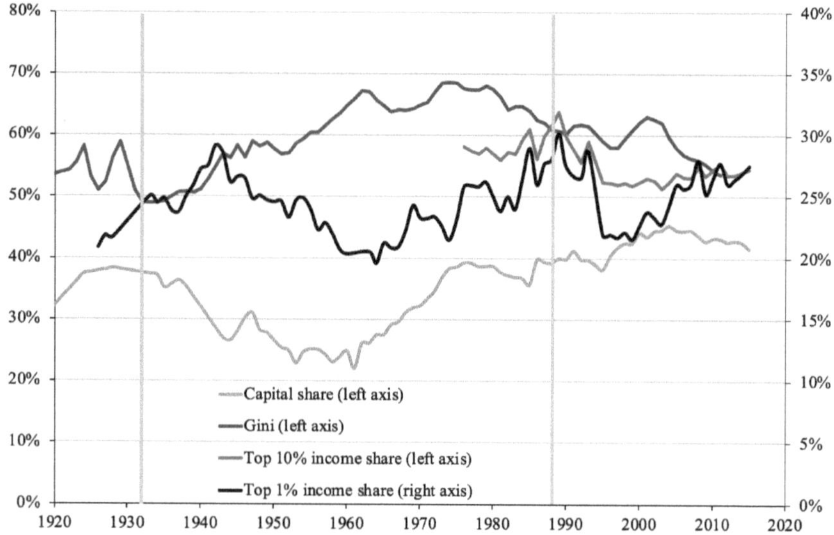

Fig. 8 Capital income share, top income shares, and occupational Gini in Brazil, 1920–2015 (*Sources* Capital share and top income shares from Morgan and Souza [2019]; occupational Gini, representing pre-tax personal income of the economically active population, from Astorga [2021]. *Note* Grey bars indicate the years of democratization in 1932 [all literate adult women] and 1988 [all illiterate adults]. All literature adult men were given the vote in 1891)

coup in 1964. From then on, the capital share and top income shares were in unison until the early 2000s, when the labour share began its secular growth after declining for four decades. The Gini coefficient continued to increase throughout the post-war period until the 1980s, explained principally by rising inequality between occupational groups (Astorga, 2021). Top income concentration grew strongly after the macroeconomic stabilization plan of 1994 ended the hyperinflation that marked the highly inegalitarian transition to full universal suffrage in 1988 (Morgan & Souza, 2019).

(technicians and administrators—white collar workers), Group 3 (semi-skilled blue collars workers, other urban workers in relatively low productivity sectors such as retailing and transport, and artisans), and Group 4 (rural workers and personal services—including domestic servants—plus unskilled urban workers)".

3.3 Democratization and Redistributive Reforms

As portrayed above, the evolution of democracy in Brazil was not a linear, self-sustained evolution, as in Sweden. Despite notable progress in voter participation since the 1891 suffrage extension—in a context of severely limited suffrage (see Fig. 5)—the party system of the Old Republic did not particularly cater to national-level politics (Fritscher & Musacchio, 2010; Love, 1970). A system of national mobilization and welfare state policies commenced in the Vargas era (1930–1945). The 1934 and 1937 Constitutions both emphasized a stronger presence of the federal government in society, as well as the inclusion of women in the franchise. Between the elections of 1926 and 1945 we see the share of voters increase by a factor of five (Fig. 5). At the same time, there was progression in redistributive welfare state measures in direct taxation and social insurance (Figs. 6 and 7), but an ambiguous evolution of income inequality with rising top shares, falling then rising occupational inequality, and a declining capital share (Fig. 8). If anything, these dynamics suggest that rising inequality—through the growing dispersion of earnings between groups in the context of the first large industrialization and urbanization wave—spurred increases in social transfers and direct taxation, especially social security contributions.

A fundamental force in this changing landscape was worker mobilization. Vargas' authoritarian "corporatist" swing from 1937 and "populist" turn from 1943 sought to elevate the status of the (formal) worker and strike a better bargain with capitalists. Progressive new employment laws were passed, including a new wage policy in 1940 and the Consolidation of Labour Laws (CLT) in 1943, which continue to regulate statutory labour rights in Brazil to this day. That these reforms were passed in a non-democratic period (the *Estado Novo* dictatorship), reveals a similar instance of anticipation and co-optation as in the Swedish case. Anticipating the end of war-time conditions, and a new constitutional period with prior suffrage attainments, Vargas sought to win over the (urban) working class with his policies and pronouncements (Skidmore, 1976). For example, in his Labour Day speech in 1944 Vargas recognized that "liberty, in the strict sense of political franchising, is not enough to solve the complex social question...Supporting workers economically is tantamount to giving them the true sense of freedom and security to express their political opinions" (Vargas, 1951: 291). This rhetoric would continue in a more sophisticated fashion into the following decade, as power alternated between the two pro-Vargas parties, who increasingly bet on worker mobilization and strikes to pass reforms.[7]

The political economy strategy of co-opting workers using social benefits gained traction particularly in countries with unelected authoritarian governments or weakly supported executives, where the state apparatus was perceived to lack legitimacy (Cutler & Johnson, 2004). The "political legitimacy theory" of social insurance predicts that such states will be the first to introduce social *insurance* programmes, rather than means-tested or universal benefits, as under an insurance system economically, and thus politically, important workers contribute to a system administered by the state, which gives them an interest in its survival (ibid). Bismarck's social reforms in Germany are the classic examples. But this pattern also emerges in Latin America from the 1930s onwards, with Alessandri's weak executive in Chile, and with the authoritarian regimes of Vargas in Brazil and subsequently Perón in Argentina (Mesa-Lago, 1978). In all three cases, the government disbursed protection paternalistically, often before the insured (i.e. formal urban workers) established themselves as a powerful interest group, so as to co-opt the emerging influence of trade unions for political support (ibid).

With the continuing growth of the urban workforce in Brazil, associated unionization grew by 5.6% per year between 1938 and 1963, with urban union density increasing from about 18 to 40% among workers in industry and the public sector (IBGE, 2006). Earnings dispersion among different categories of workers continued to grow with the intense growth in manufacturing and formal employment (IBGE, 2017), while top shares followed the secular decline in the capital share after 1943, indicating a structural change in the economy. How do these dynamics relate to the timing of redistributive reforms? Here we consider the most notable reforms for our analysis since Brazil became a republic.

- 1891: the inheritance tax (*Imposto sobre Transmissão Causa Mortis e Doação* [ITCMD]) is created, and regulated in 1898 as a state-level tax. Progressive tax rates varied by state from 0.5% to 22%. Between 1932 and 1965 top marginal rates increased in most states to between 32 and 65%. A constitutional amendment in 1965 during

[7] The rhetoric and its accompanying economic strategy was facilitated by the banning of the Brazilian Communist Party (PCB) by Congress in 1948, after the Superior Electoral Tribunal revoked the party's registration in 1947 (Skidmore, 1976).

the military dictatorship made the tax proportional to real estate values at a single rate of 2% (Morgan & Carvalho Junior, 2021).

- 1922: the personal income tax is instituted and first applied to incomes in 1923 at a top marginal tax rate of 8%. This rate would increase steadily to 10% in 1925, 15% in 1930, 18% in 1935, and 20% in 1943 (Nobrega, 2014).
- 1933: the national pension institutes (*Institutos de Aposentadoria e Pensões* [IAPs]) are created to disburse pensions to separate categories of private-sector male urban workers, in addition to the pre-existing company-based retirement funds of the *Caixas de Aponsentadoria e Pensões* (CAPs), created in 1923–1926 (Malloy, 1977a).
- 1940: the first minimum wages are introduced in urban areas at the state-district level. The highest minimum wage (in the Federal District of the city of Rio de Janeiro) was twice as high as the lowest (in the state of Maranhão in the northeast). A federal minimum wage, merging state-level minimum wages, would not come into effect until 1984 (Saboia, 1984).
- 1947: the top marginal personal income tax rate is increased from 20 to 50%. In 1961 it was increased to 60%, and in 1962 to 65% (Nobrega, 2014).
- 1952: The minimum wage is adjusted by 160% on average across all states to recoup all the previous losses due to inflation since 1940. Minimum wages continued to rise sharply in real terms until 1962, faster than the national income per adult (Morgan & Souza, 2019).
- 1963: rural workers are given the right to a minimum wage defined at the state level (Skidmore, 1976).
- 1964: In March, President Goulart announces a congressional bill on universal suffrage, which was never voted through due to the military coup in April, a year before the next presidential election (Skidmore, 1976).

What the timing of these reforms convey is that there was an array of important redistributive legislation passed (and proposed) before the military dictatorship, as partial democratization and labour mobilization made notable gains, especially among the growing urban population. Importantly, this period was characterized by relatively organized social and political movements based on reformist ideas, but also a bureaucracy that was divided between permanent, selectively recruited civil servants, and politically appointed civil servants under the control of labour leaders

(Malloy, 1979). Alongside the rural-conservative faction of the PSD, and the more right-wing parties in Congress, technocratic division made the passing of the more radical reforms increasingly difficult. Furthermore, the "corporatist" model of welfare state exacerbated an "insiders vs outsiders" institutional dynamic—that is, between urban vs. rural, formal vs. informal, and industry/civil service vs. commerce/agriculture—as social rights (pensions, minimum wages, unionization, etc.) were tied to occupational class and status. State bureaucratic agencies, which flourished during the Vargas era and became solidified during the military dictatorship, were historically seen to have more influence than political parties, at least until the return to democracy in the late 1980s. Separate national confederations for industry, commerce, agriculture, and public sector workers were created at the national and state levels during the Vargas administration. Occupational pension plans were set up to supplant the existing company-based funds rather than replace them. Legislative additions to existing norms and structures were adopted, rather than reform overhauls that completely redefined criteria along universalist principles. The period of consolidation and growth of this model between the 1930s and the 1960s coincided with a rise in earnings inequality, driven by inequality between occupational groups (see Fig. 8).

Given the limits on political participation, Brazil had to rely on the enlightened discretion of its governing elite for much of the social policy changes early on. This helps to explain why the military regime retained and expanded on the welfare state institutions created in the Vargas era (1930–1945), increasing social transfers as patronage in a context of local political competition for legitimacy in managing national economic development (Behring & Boschetti, 2011; Weyland, 1996). Hence, for example, the granting of pensions to women in 1967, thirty-five years after they were given the right to vote. These reforms were particularly pertinent in the countryside, where the proportion of illiterate constituents was higher and where votes carried more weight, given that legislative representation was set in proportion to the total population of voting constituencies. Thus, in 1971 the Médici government (1969–1974) enacted the very first social security scheme for agricultural workers (FUNRURAL), which would be administered by rural unions and the National Confederation of Workers in Agriculture (CONTAG). It also guaranteed welfare benefits to the rural poor in 1974, which were subsidized by urban workers (Malloy, 1977b). Furthermore, minimum wages were more stable or fell less sharply in rural districts (Taylor et al., 1980,

Tables 10-8 and 10-9). The aim was to control rural–urban migration and ensure political support for the military alliance in electorally important constituencies (Malloy, 1977b). If we transition to the important fiscal policies implemented after full democratization in 1988, we see a mix of pro-poor spending reforms and pro-rich tax reforms.

- 1988: Pensions are granted for dependents. All social benefits are indexed to inflation and to the minimum wage. The national health service is created, granting universal access to healthcare across the country, and leading to a large hospital construction programme in rural areas in 1991 (Weyland, 1996).
- 1988: a tax reform is passed, which reduces the top marginal personal income tax rate from 50 to 25% (Michelet et al., 2015).
- 1992: the state-level inheritance tax returns to being a progressive tax. The maximum marginal tax rate of 8% is established (Carvalho Junior and Morgan, 2021).
- 1993: non-contributory means-tested pensions for urban informal workers (Weyland, 1996).
- 1995: distributed corporate profits and dividends are exempted from the personal income tax base (Nóbrega, 2014).
- 1996: the minimum wage starts to increase in real terms. Between 1995 and 2010, the real value of the minimum wage doubled, with the fastest increases occurring after 2000.
- 2003: creation of "*Bolsa Familia*", which combined and expanded previous subsidies into a single conditional cash transfer programme, providing financial aid to millions of poor Brazilian families (Zucco & Power, 2013).

As Fig. 7 depicts, the immediate aftermath of democratization coincided with a marked increase in public social spending, which was provisioned in the new constitution. The difference between the early New Republic and the previous democratic period (1945–1964) in terms of policymaking is that organized labour, which was institutionally strong and growing in the earlier period, now played a significantly reduced role due to their exclusion by the military regime from participating in the deliberation process of social policy. The one exception was agricultural labour, which was included (through CONTAG and local unions) in the administrative process of social security during the dictatorship. The concessions to rural workers (lower pension age than urban workers, expansion of universal healthcare to the countryside) were a response to the unmet demands by CONTAG for agrarian reform and the intended equalization of rural and urban formal workers after democratization (Weyland, 1996). Thus, urban informal workers were only granted minimum welfare benefits that were means-tested in 1993, almost 20 years after their rural counterparts. It was not until the late-1990s that urban and rural workers, formal and informal, were integrated into programmes of social assistance for poverty alleviation. However, no government of the period, facing a complicated parliamentary arithmetic, fundamentally changed the corporatist policy structures it inherited (Medeiros & Souza, 2015). When Congress was given renewed power after 1988 it only became a new channel for the articulation of segmented social interests that developed over the previous decades.

The Brazilian case shows that some redistributive reforms did immediately follow full democratization through the new provisions in the 1988 Constitution. However, as shown, not all groups in the population benefited to the same extent by discretionary policy. Moreover, the redistributive outcomes were not a direct product of deliberate policy changes following democratization. Figure 8 illustrates that occupational inequality was already on a downward trend since 1980. Top income shares and the capital share did fall between the late 1980s until the mid-1990s, but these dynamics had more to do with the resolution of the inflationary crisis of the period, which put to an end the regressive income indexation policy of the previous two decades—when financial incomes were fully indexed to inflation, while wages and social benefits were not (Kane & Morisset, 1993; Morgan & Souza, 2019). Further discretionary redistributive reforms lagged formal democratization by at least a decade. The extent of the reforms of the PT governments after 2002, alongside the inequality dynamics, reveal a compromise style of politics. Given its slim congressional representation (see Table 3), it needed specific parliamentary support to implement each component of its redistributive programme until it entered into a fragile, and ultimately unsuccessful, alliance with the "catch-all" PMDB from 2010 (Gethin & Morgan, 2021).

4 Conclusions

In this chapter, we have shown the importance of political participation and social mobilization as crucial causal mechanisms between democratization and redistribution using the case studies of Sweden and Brazil. However, given that social mobilization is related to democratization and to redistributive reforms, the effect of democratization on redistribution is confounded. In both case studies, we found that some redistribution occurred before democratization—via co-opting reforms that sought to anticipate powerful interest groups and enhance government legitimacy—and after democratization—with distinct temporalities interacting with conjunctural factors.

Bismarck's social insurance reforms of the 1880s were conceded by the elite in a context of popular mobilization but without democratic institutions. It is accepted that without the "apparent threat to the established order" from labour movements these reforms would not have occurred (Skocpol & Rueschemeyer, 1996: 6; cf. Paster, 2012: 96). This strategy can also be seen in Sweden in 1880s and 1900s, and in Brazil in 1930s, 1940s, and 1970s. Popular mobilization with a credible threat of disrupting the distribution of power, like a revolution, can in itself be enough to cause redistribution in an otherwise undemocratic society. As the example of Brazil shows, it can also be enough to cause a *coup d'état* and a military dictatorship.

Therefore, formal democratization (i.e. imposition of universal suffrage) does not immediately cause a political culture of widespread participation and a broad, egalitarian representation of interests. This depends on the inherited habits and cultures of political action, as well as on formal organization patterns involving social movements, working-class political parties, and the public bureaucracy interacting with macroeconomic factors. What the crucial and highly distinct case studies of Sweden and Brazil reveal is that the existence of democracy (i.e. universal suffrage) may be a necessary condition for *sustained* redistribution as Lindert (1994) argued, but democratization itself (i.e. regime change) is not a necessary nor sufficient cause of redistributive reforms. Following the neorealist approach to institutional change (cf. Amable & Palombarini, 2008), democratization should itself be seen as a broader phenomenon of demanded and conceded socio-economic redistribution in a state trying to reconcile conflicting social demands for its own legitimacy.

References

Acemoglu, D., & Robinson, J. A. (2000). Why did the West extend the franchise? Democracy, inequality, and growth in historical perspective. *Quarterly Journal of Economics, 115*(4), 1167–1199. https://doi.org/10.1162/003355300555042

Aidt, T. S., Dutta, J., & Loukoianova, E. (2006). Democracy comes to Europe: Franchise extension and fiscal outcomes 1830–1938. *European Economic Review, 50*(2), 249–283. https://doi.org/10.1016/j.euroecorev.2004.07.004

Aidt, T. S., & Franck, R. (2019). What motivates an oligarchic elite to democratize? Evidence from the roll call vote on the Great Reform Act of 1832. *Journal of Economic History, 79*(3), 773–825. https://doi.org/10.1017/S0022050719000342

Albertus, M. (2017). Landowners and democracy: The social origins of democracy reconsidered. *World Politics, 69*(2), 233–276. https://doi.org/10.1017/S0043887116000277

Amable, B., & Palombarini, P. (2008). A neorealist approach to institutional change and the diversity of capitalism. *Socio-Economic Review, 7*(1), 123–143. https://doi.org/10.1093/ser/mwn018

Åmark, K. (2005). *Hundra år av välfärdspolitik*. Boréa.

Amenta, E. (2003). What we know about the development of social policy: Comparative and historical research in comparative and historical perspective. In J. Mahoney & D. Rueschemeyer (Eds.), *Comparative historical analysis in the social sciences* (pp. 91–130). Cambridge: Cambridge University Press.

Andrae, C. G. (1998). *Revolt eller reform: Sverige inför revolutionerna i Europa 1917–1918*. Carlssons.

Astorga, P. (2021). *Revealing the diversity and complexity behind long-term income inequality in Latin America: A new dataset, 1920–2011*. Working papers in economic history 2021-11. Instituto Figuerola de Historia y Ciencias Sociales, Universidad Carlos III de Madrid.

Baldwin, P. (1990). *The politics of social solidarity: Class bases of the European welfare state*. Cambridge University Press.

Behring, E. R., & Boschetti, I. (2011). *Política social: Fundamentos e história*. Cortez.

Bengtsson, E., Rubolino E., & Waldenström, D. (2020). *What determines the capital share over the long run of history*? WID world working paper No 2020/08. World Inequality Lab.

Bengtsson, E., & Molinder, J. (2017). The economic effects of the 1920 eight-hour working day reform in Sweden. *Scandinavian Economic History Review, 65*(2), 149–168. https://doi.org/10.1080/03585522.2017.1290673

Bengtsson, E., & Waldenström, D. (2018). Capital shares and income inequality: Evidence from the long run. *Journal of Economic History, 78*(3), 712–743. https://doi.org/10.1017/S0022050718000347

Bengtsson, E. (2021). *The Evolution of popular politics in Nineteenth Century Sweden and the road from oligarchy to democracy*. Lund working papers in economic history No. 226. Lund University.

Berins Collier, R. (1999). *Paths toward democracy: The working class and elites in Western Europe and South America*. Cambridge University Press.

Blyth, M. (2002). *Great Transformations: Economic Ideas and Institutional Change in the Twentieth Century*. Cambridge University Press.

Brusewitz, A. (1951). K*ungamakt, herremakt, folkmakt: Författningskampen i Sverige 1906–1918*. Tiden.

Cutler, D. M., & Johnson, R. (2004). The birth and growth of the social insurance state: Explaining old age and medical insurance across countries. *Public Choice, 120*(1), 87–121. https://doi.org/10.1023/B:PUCH.0000035859.20258.e0

Eberhardt, M. (2019). *Democracy does cause growth: Comment*. CEPR Discussion Paper 13659. CEPR.

Edebalk, P. G. (1996). *Välfärdsstaten träder fram: svensk socialförsäkring 1884-1955*. Arkiv.

Edgren, H. (2011). Folkskolan och grundskolan In E. Larsson & J. Westberg (Eds.), *Utbildningshistoria—en introduktion* (pp. 103–120). Studentlitteratur.

Ekdahl, L. (2001). *Mot en tredje väg: En biografi över Rudolf Meidner. I: Tysk flykting och svensk modell*. Arkiv.

Fairfield, T. (2013). Going where the money is: Strategies for taxing economic elites in unequal democracies. *World Development, 47*, 42–57. https://doi.org/10.1016/j.worlddev.2013.02.011

Fritscher, A. C. M., & Musacchio, A. (2010). Endowments, fiscal federalism and the cost of capital for states: Evidence from Brazil, 1891–1930. *Financial History Review, 17*(1), 1–38. https://doi.org/10.1017/S0968565010000041

Furtado, C. (1965). Political obstacles to economic growth in Brazil. *International Affairs (Royal Institute of International Affairs), 41*(2), 252–266. https://doi.org/10.2307/2610619

Gethin, A., & Morgan, M. (2021). *Democracy and the politicization of inequality in Brazil, 1989–2018*. World inequality lab working paper No. 2021/07. Harvard University Press.

Hahner, J. E. (1980). Feminism, women's rights, and the suffrage movement in Brazil, 1850–1932. *Latin American Research Review, 15*(1), 65–111. https://www.jstor.org/stable/2503094

Henrekson, M., & Stenkula, M. (2015). *Swedish taxation since 1862*. IFN.

Hurd, M. (2000). *Public spheres, public mores, and democracy: Hamburg and Stockholm, 1870–1914*. University of Michigan Press.

IBGE. (2006). *Estatísticas do Século XX*. Centro de documentação e disseminação de informações.

Instituto Brasileiro de Geografia e Estatística (2017). *Anuários Estatísticos do Brasil*, 1908–2017. Rio de Janeiro. http://biblioteca.ibge.gov.br/index.php/biblioteca-catalogo?view=detalhes&id=720. Also Estatísticas do Século XX for years 1900–1999. http://seculoxx.ibge.gov.br/pt/.

Isaksson, A. (2000). *Per Albin. IV: Landsfadern*. Wahlström & Widstrand.

Jusko, K. L. (2017). *Who speaks for the poor? Electoral geography, party entry, and representation*. Cambridge University Press.

Kane, C. T., & Morisset, J. (1993). *Who would vote for inflation in Brazil?: An integrated framework approach to inflation and income distribution* (Vol. 1183). World Bank Publications.

Lantz, G. (2019). *An indirect route to equality: Taxing consumers to build the Swedish welfare state* [Doctoral dissertation in Economic History], Umeå University.

Lewin, L. (2010). *Lindman*. Bonniers.

Lindert, P. H. (1994). The rise of social spending, 1880–1930. *Explorations in Economic History, 31*(1), 1–37. https://doi.org/10.1006/exeh.1994.1001

Lindert, P. (2004). *Growing public: Social spending and economic growth since the eighteenth century. Vol. 1: The Story*. Cambridge University Press.

Lindgren, M. (2020). *Utan rösträtt—Kvantitativa effekter av olika rösträttsbegränsningar 1866–2018*. Kungliga Biblioteket.

Lindström, U. (1983). *Fascism in Scandinavia* [Doctoral dissertation], Umeå University.

Loureiro, F. P. (2017). *Empresários, trabalhadores e grupos de interesse: A política econômica nos governos Jânio Quadros e João Goulart, 1961–1964*. SciELO-Editora UNESP.

Love, J. L. (1970). Political participation in Brazil, 1881–1969. *Luso-Brazilian Review, 7*(2), 3–24. https://www.jstor.org/stable/3512756

Mahoney, J. (2000). Strategies of causal inference in small-N analysis. *Sociological Methods & Research, 28*(4), 387–424. https://doi.org/10.1177/0049124100028004001

Malloy, J. M. (1977a). Social security policy and the working class in Twentieth-Century Brazil. *Journal of Interamerican Studies and World Affairs, 19*(1), 35–60. https://doi.org/10.2307/174860

Malloy, J. M. (1977b). Authoritarianism and the extension of social security protection to the rural sector in Brazil. *Luso-Brazilian Review, 14*(2), 195–210. https://www.jstor.org/stable/3513059

Malloy, J. M. (1979). *The Politics of social security in Brazil*. University of Pittsburgh Press.

Medeiros, M., & Souza, P. H. G. (2015). State transfers, taxes and income inequality in Brazil. *Brazilian Political Science Review, 9*(2), 3–29. https://doi.org/10.1590/1981-38212014000200009

Mesa-Lago, C. (1978). *Social security in Latin America: Pressure groups, stratification, and inequality*. University of Pittsburgh Press.

Michelet, J. *et al.* (2015). *Tributaçao de lucros e dividendos no Brasil: Uma perspectiva comparada*. Consultoroia Legislativa.

Miller, M. K. (2015). Democratic pieces: Autocratic elections and democratic development since 1815. *British Journal of Political Science, 45*(3), 501–530. https://doi.org/10.1017/S0007123413000446

Ministério de FazendaMinistério de Fazenda. (2014). Consolidação das contas públicas, 2000–2012. Demonstrativo da despesa por função: Brasília, and balanço do setor público nacional exercício 2013. Ministério da Fazenda. http://www.tesouro.fazenda.gov.br/balanco-do-setor-publico-nacional-bspn

Moberg. (1978). *Från tjänstehjon till hembiträde: En kvinnlig låglönegrupp i den fackliga kampen 1903–1946* [Dissertation in history], Uppsala University.

Morgan, M., & Souza, P. H. G. F. (2019). *Distributing growth during late-development: New evidence on long-run inequality in Brazil. CLADHE VI*. Universidad de Santiago.

Morgan, M., & Carvalho Junior, P. (2021). Taxing wealth: General principles, international perspectives and lessons for Brazil. *Brazilian Journal of Political Economy, 41*(1), 44–64. https://doi.org/10.1590/0101-31572021-3131

Nilsson, T. (1994). *Elitens svängrum: Första kammaren, staten och moderniseringen 1867–1886* [Doctoral dissertation in history], Stockholm University.

Nóbrega, C. B. da. (2014). *História do imposto de renda do Brasil: Um enfoque da pessoa física*. Secretaria da Receita Federal.

Nyman, O. (1944). *Krisuppgörelsen mellan Socialdemokraterna och Bondeförbundet 1933*. Almqvist och Wiksell.

OECD/ECLAC/CIAT/IDB. (2015). *Revenue statistics in Latin America and the Caribbean*. OECD Publishing. http://www.oecd.org/tax/tax-policy/tax-database.htm

Orloff, A. S. (1988). The political origins of America's belated welfare state. In M. Weir, A. S. Orloff, & T. Skocpol (Eds.), *The politics of social policy in the United States* (pp. 37–80). Princeton University Press.

Paster, T. (2012). *The role of business in the development of the welfare state and labor markets in Germany: Containing Social Reforms*. Routledge.

Piketty, T. (2014). *Capital in the twenty-first century*. Harvard University Press.

Piketty, T. (2020). *Capital and ideology*. Harvard University Press.

Ragin, C. C. (1997). Turning the tables: How case-oriented research challenges variable-oriented research. *Comparative Social Research, 123*, 27–42.

Rodrik, D. (1999). Democracies pay higher wages. *Quarterly Journal of Economics, 114*(3), 707–738. https://doi.org/10.1162/003355399556115

Roine, J., & Waldenström, D. (2008). The evolution of top incomes in an egalitarian society: Sweden, 1903–2004. *Journal of Public Economics, 92*(1–2), 366–387. https://doi.org/10.1016/j.jpubeco.2007.06.012

Rothstein, B. (1990). Marxism, institutional analysis, and working-class power: The Swedish case. *Politics & Society, 18*(3), 317–345. https://doi.org/10.1177/003232929001800302

Rothstein, B. (1986). *Den socialdemokratiska staten: Reformer och förvaltning inom svensk arbetsmarknads- och skolpolitik*. Arkiv.

Rustow, D. (1969). *The politics of compromise: A study of parties and cabinet government in Sweden*. Greenwood Press. Reprint, originally published in 1951.

Saboia, J. A. (1984). *Evolução histórica do salário mínimo no Brasil: Fixação, valor real e diferenciação regional*. IPEA, Programa Nacional de Pesquisa Econômica.

Sejersted, F. (2005). *Socialdemokratiets tidsalder: Norge og Sverige i det 20. Århundre*. Pax.

Skidmore, T. E. (1976). *Brasil: De Getúlio Vargas a Castelo Branco (1930–1964)*. Paz e Terra.

Skocpol, T., & Rueschemeyer, D. (1996). Introduction. In D. Rueschemeyer & T. Skocpol (Eds.), *States, social knowledge and the origins of modern social policies* (pp. 3–14). Princeton University Press.

Statistics Sweden. (2018). *Historisk statistik över valåren 1910–2018. Procentuell fördelning av giltiga valsedlar efter parti och typ av val*. https://www.scb.se/hitta-statistik/statistik-efter-amne/demokrati/allmanna-val/allmanna-val-valresultat/pong/tabell-och-diagram/historisk-valstatistik/historisk-statistik-over-valaren-19102018.-procentuell-fordelning-av-giltiga-valsedlar-efter-parti-och-typ-av-val/

Steinmo, S. (1989). Political institutions and tax policy in the United States, Sweden, and Britain. *World Politics, 41*(4), 500–535. https://doi.org/10.2307/2010528

Swärd, H. (2008). Att bekämpa fattigdom med lagar för fattiga – en omöjlig ekvation? In H. Swärd & M.-A. Egerö (Eds.), *Villkorandets politik: Fattigdomens premisser och samhällets åtgärder—då och nu* (pp. 17–39). Egalité förlag.

Taylor, L., Bacha, E. L., Cardoso, E. A., & Lysy, F. J. (1980). *Models of growth and distribution for Brazil*. The World Bank.

Tilton, T. A. (1974). The social origins of liberal democracy: The Swedish case. *American Political Science Review, 68*(2), 561–571. https://doi.org/10.1017/S0003055400117393

Tingsten, H. (1967). *Den svenska socialdemokratins idéutveckling 1*, paperback edition. Aldus/Bonniers. Originally published in 1941.

Tribunal Superior Eleitoral. (2013). Portal de Dados Abertos do TSE. https://dadosabertos.tse.jus.br/dataset/

Unga, N. (1976). *Socialdemokartin och arbetslöshetsfrågan 1912–1934. Framväxten av den 'nya' arbetslöshetspolitiken*. Arkiv.

Vallinder, T. (1962). *I kamp för demokratin. Rösträttsrörelsen i Sverige 1866–1902*. Natur och Kultur.

Vargas, G. (1951). *A nova política do Brasil* (Vol. X). José Olímpio.

Varsano, R., Pessoa, E., da Silva, N. L. C., Alfonso, J. R. R., Araujo, E. A., & Ramundo, J. C. M. (1998). *Uma análise da carga tributária do Brasil*.Texto Para Discussão no 583. IPEA.

Wåhlstrand, A. (1936). Andra kammaren under tiden omkring sekelskiftet. In A. Brusewitz (Ed.), *Studier över den svenska riksdagens sociala sammansättning* (pp. 156–183). Almqvist & Wiksell.

Waltz, K. (1979). *Theory of international politics*. McGraw-Hill.

Wetterberg, G. (2010). *Nils Edén*. Bonniers.

Weyland, K. (1996). *Democracy without equity: Failures of reform in Brazil*. University of Pittsburgh Press.

Zennström, P. (1983). *Axel Danielsson: En biografi*. Arkiv. Reprint; originally published in 1967.

Zucco, C. & Power. T. J. (2013). Bolsa Família and the shift in Lula's electoral base, 2002–2006: A reply to Bohn. *Latin American Research Review, 48*(2), 3–24. https://www.jstor.org/stable/43670073

CHAPTER 10

Conclusions: Comparative Developments in Trade, Industrialization, and Inequality Since 1850

Jorge Álvarez and Svante Prado

This final chapter offers a brief reflection on the contributions that the book has made to the previous discussions of why Scandinavia and South America experienced such different trajectories during the twentieth century. While Scandinavia converged with the rich countries, South America fell behind. This bifurcation occurred even though the two regions developed a similar role as suppliers of natural resources as they were drawn into the emerging Atlantic economy of the late nineteenth

J. Álvarez
Universidad de La República, Montevideo, Uruguay
e-mail: jorge.alvarez@cienciassociales.edu.uy

S. Prado (✉)
University of Gothenburg, Gothenburg, Sweden
e-mail: svante.prado@econhist.gu.se

J. Álvarez and S. Prado (eds.), *Scandinavia and South America—A Tale of Two Capitalisms*, Palgrave Studies in Economic History,
https://doi.org/10.1007/978-3-031-09198-8_10

century. Both regions were peripheral to the heartlands of industrialization, i.e., peripheral in the functions they performed in the world market for commodities. As mentioned in Chapter 2, this divergence has intrigued scholars since at least the seminal contribution of Senghaas (1985), who compared the Scandinavian countries and southern settler economies of Australasia and South America. The string of studies in Senghaas' wake, comparing economies that were geographically and culturally very distant from one another, thus preceded and paralleled the emergence and proliferation of the so-called Great Divergence debate (Pomerantz, 2000). The title of our book promises an attempt to examine the roles of trade, industrialization, and inequality in the diverging pathways of the two regions. We owe to the reader of this volume some final reflections on the ways in which our contributions have developed the issues that fascinated Dieter Senghaas and his followers as well as those areas that we consider fruitful for future research. We begin our reflections on the role of trade, followed by industrialization, and finally inequality.

1 Trade

Trade specialization was a critical factor in shaping the historical development patterns of the Scandinavian and South American countries. Both regions have been characterized as peripheral exporters of raw materials and food, as well as being dependent on demand from the industrialized core countries of Western Europe during the first era of globalization in the late nineteenth century. While the Scandinavian countries transformed their productive structure and diversified their export baskets during the twentieth century, the South American economies remained dependent on exporting natural resource-intensive goods. This difference in export performance had significant consequences for the long-term development trajectories of the two regions.

In order to explain the divergent development paths, the previous research focussed on the technological dynamics that determined the pattern of production and trade specialization at different stages of development. It also focussed on the domestic institutional environments to explain the heterogenous outcomes in innovation and technical change between the two regions. Lingarde and Tylecote (1999) argued that the Scandinavian countries responded successfully to the opportunities of the new technological innovations of the late nineteenth and early twentieth centuries. This responsiveness can be exemplified by the quick transition from steam to electricity and by the widespread and early use of Fordist production modes. The South American economies, in contrast, were exposed to intense cyclical fluctuations associated with high commodity price variability for exports in the world economy. Even during cyclical upswings they did not manage to reduce inequality, expand education, reduce the social distance between workers and managers, or broaden the market for domestically produced goods. South America thereby failed to ascend the technological ladder, which is required to achieve sustainable growth rates.

To increase our understanding of the role of trade in economic growth, Chapter 3 compared how the compositions of the export baskets developed in Scandinavia, the Rio de la Plata region, and Australasia from 1870 to 1970. The chapter showed how the Scandinavian countries transformed their export baskets from natural resource-intensive goods to industrialized goods with high technological content. Australasia performed this transformation to a much lesser degree and only in the post-war period, while the Rio de Plata region almost exclusively exported the same types of agricultural products throughout the period. This picture, however, disguises some exceptions in each region: Denmark remained highly dependent on agricultural exports until the 1950s, and New Zealand, like the Rio de la Plata countries, was highly dependent on agricultural exports during the entire period.

Chapter 4 examined at length the impact of trade specialization on long-term economic growth. Drawing on the post-Keynesian approach of Thirlwall's Law, the chapter argued that goods differ in price volatility and long-term growth prospects because of variations in the income elasticity of demand (Thirlwall, 2011). In a nutshell, the long-term growth rate of a country is constrained by the balance of payments. The results show that the export ratios (exports divided by GDP in current prices) of Scandinavia, the River Plate region, and Australasia were relatively high in comparison with the rich countries, but while the Scandinavian countries maintained a high export ratio throughout the period, the share of exports in GDP across the River Plate region and Australasia tended to fall after the 1930s. These trends were related to the evolution of terms of trade and changes in the composition of commodities for export. Terms of trade played a critical role in the pace of economic growth because export earnings and their capacity to finance imports depended on export prices, import prices, and export volumes. While the terms of trade were relatively stable for Scandinavia, they fluctuated wildly for the southern settler economies, which influenced their short-run fluctuations in export earnings. Increased export earnings stimulated the export sector and indirectly production for domestic markets. However, when terms of trade worsened, the business cycle turned downwards. The trade cycles thus translated into cycles of real output affecting the long-term growth rate negatively.

Differing growth rates are not, however, simply a passive reflection of external conditions. The previous research also attached importance to the capacity of a country to adapt its productive forces to changing demand in the world market. The so-called Staple Theory offers an attempt to associate export outcomes with resource endowments (Watkins, 1963). It also brings into focus the backward and forward linkages as well as the dynamics of the productive and technical changes in various export products. A crucial issue concerns the links between staples and income distribution. A flat income distribution may act as a positive stimulus for domestic growth by inducing spending and investments across several sectors. Drawing on the logic of the Staple Theory, Chapter 3 exemplified some staples that arguably had more linkage effects on growth and diversification than others, which might have had consequential effects on production and income distribution. Sweden, for instance, probably benefited from its vast supply of forests and iron ore, which fostered industries such as sawmilling, the paper industry, the iron and steel sectors, and mechanical engineering. However, this logic does not apply to the case of Denmark, which raced ahead of the settler economies of the River Plate regions and Australasia in the twentieth century: Denmark shared with the southern settler societies a similar specialization in agriculture and cattle rearing. The Staple Theory does not offer guidance when cases with similar endowments lead to different development outcomes. This inconsistency should lead us to suspect that resource endowment is neither the recipe for success nor the trigger for underdevelopment. The following sections therefore bring domestic factors to the fore.

2 Industrialization

Industrialization is the primary, but not the only, means by which countries that lag behind escape their dependence on raw materials. In Scandinavia, Sweden and Finland followed the route of industrialization, whereas Denmark chose to develop through agricultural modernization, and Norway relied on services (Jörberg, 1973). Through industrialization, Sweden and Finland managed to diversify the composition of output so that sophisticated products gradually gained more weight at the expense of raw materials; in other words, output moved upwards in the value-added chain. The importance of this upward shift becomes obvious through the accurate prediction of Thirlwall's Law (Chapter 4), according to which economy-wide growth rates are conditioned on export performance. Although this law offers an impeccable logic, it does not penetrate the underlying mechanisms that enable the shift in output. To begin with, we would like to know more about the preconditions for realizing this shift in output in the two regions.

Productivity is a key factor because it also drives structural transformation. Chapter 3 showed that GDP per capita levels between 1870 and 1970 for the Scandinavian countries approached the levels of the core countries, while for the River Plate region they fell behind. Chapter 5 showed that the GDP per capita levels of Brazil failed to catch up with those of Sweden between 1912 and 2014. This failure to accomplish economy-wide convergence is familiar ground in economic history; the theory of unconditional convergence in economy-wide productivity has not fared well since its original formulation in the mid-1980s in the seminal papers of Abramovitz (1986) and Baumol (1986). Historical experiences show that poor countries do not catch up unconditionally to rich ones. Rodrik (2013), however, tweaked this original formulation of convergence so that unconditional convergence in productivity levels across countries should instead be considered feasible only for manufacturing. Johnson and Papageorgiou (2020), in a recent review of the huge research on cross-country convergence, surmised that this reformulation offers the only glimmer of hope for unconditional convergence but admitted that meticulous studies confirming it were still in short supply.

Chapter 5 was therefore devoted to an analysis of productivity levels in manufacturing in Sweden and Brazil. It indicated an abysmal Brazil–Sweden gap in productivity in the early 1910s, which is as far back in time as our data stretch. The Brazilian productivity level by then was only about 20% of the Swedish. Brazil then rapidly caught up by the early 1980s, but equally rapidly fell back thereafter. This boom-and-bust pattern thus extinguished the glimmering hope for unconditional convergence in manufacturing, which augurs badly for less developed countries. Even convergence in manufacturing is conditional on several determinants, at least since the 1980s; until then, the convergence in Brazilian manufacturing was admittedly impressive. Whether the Brazilian experience was reflected across other less developed countries remains to be seen in future research. Using the parlance of the convergence literature, the two countries belonged to two separate convergence clubs (Baumol & Wolff, 1988). They set out from very different levels of productivity and they followed very different convergence trajectories.

The faltering engine of convergence in the late twentieth century suggests that the supply of human capital, broadly defined, set a constraint. The technology imports required to imitate production methods in the textile industry of the nineteenth century was one thing; the know-how necessary to produce say semiconductors in the twenty-first century is another, and much more difficult, thing. If it is true as Goldin and Katz (1998) say that skills have been complementary to technology since the Second Industrial Revolution, it should come as no surprise that underinvestment in education impedes growth prospects and extinguishes convergence hopes. This is where education comes into play, which was the topic of Chapter 6. It documented a steadfast neglect of education in Brazil beginning in the nineteenth century and persisting through the twentieth century. The previous literature on divergence between South America and Scandinavia also considered educational backwardness an important explanation as to why South America had lower capacities to absorb new technologies for domestic innovations (Blomström & Meller, 1991; Maloney, 2007). Investments in education are probably one of the keys to future development in South America.

For many developed countries, tariffs have fostered industrialization (Chang, 2003). At least for consumer goods, industrialization was not a spontaneous outcome of a fortuitous set of endowments. In Sweden, tariffs were erected to temper the impact of international competition in the early 1890s, which entailed a process of import substitution industrialization until World War I (Bohlin, 2005). Since tariffs were mostly specific and not subject to upward adjustments, it is likely that the effective protection rate declined during the galloping inflation of World War I and in the aftermath of World War II. The dismantling of the tariffs did not occur until the General Agreement on Tariff and Trade was reached in the 1950s, but the effective protection rate had by then already declined significantly. Manufacturing industries were gradually exposed to competition but also protected by the breakdown of international trade by the Great Depression and the two great wars. It was a smooth landing into a world of openness and harsh competition.

The South American experience was different. The whole-hearted attempt to diminish dependence on natural resources was inaugurated by the state-led development regime of the post World War II decades. One of the backdrops to this mobilization of resources was the modest levels of industrialization and productivity achieved thus far. The time was ripe for far-reaching state intervention framed to usher in an era of import substitution industrialization. South America was set on a path to escape industrial backwardness through active governmental policies. The most far-reaching such strategy was launched in Brazil. Topik (1987) argued that until the 1930s, the state had failed to develop Brazil because of the unambitious scope of the previous state-led efforts. This conclusion is reminiscent of Alexander Gerschenkron (1962), who argued that the more industrialization was deferred in European countries, the more peculiar was the strategy for rapid development. Some of the examples of European industrialization that he discussed, such as Germany and Italy, had much more favourable conditions for industrialization and catching up than South America in the 1950s. One may presume that South American countries sought extraordinary solutions to address the arduous challenge of modernizing their economies within a very short timeframe (Katz & Kosacoff, 2000). As Gerschenkron (1962: 7) reminds us, the more backward a country is, the more it is inclined to resort to "the application of institutional instruments to which there was little or no counterpart in the established industrial country". The inferior productivity level in manufacturing as well as the great dependence on natural resources that Brazil had achieved by the 1950s explain why import substitution industrialization was implemented with such eagerness and strong belief.

Why did import substitution industrialization not relieve South America of its dependence on natural resources? There is no doubt that state-led development implied enormous advances for the region in economic growth rates, productivity increases, and technological advances. Nevertheless, the industrialization of South America rested on its traditional exports of natural-resource-intensive commodities. Even though exports were a crucial income source employed to trigger the growth of the domestic economy, the traditional trade specialization posed severe limits. It worked very well while terms of trade behaved favourably and demand in the world market was on the rise. But the problems started when world market conditions deteriorated gradually in the 1960s and manifestly in the 1970s. The volatility of commodity prices in the international market imposed limits for industrialization. Moreover, technologies imported from the rich countries were often deployed unsuccessfully in manufacturing processes because workers lacked adequate skills. Heterogeneity in the pace of new capital investments among firms also meant that machines and equipment belonged to separate generations each with different productivity levels. Machines quickly became obsolete because of the slow adoption of new technological paradigms. In addition, without exports of manufacturing products, the limited size of the domestic market made it difficult for the small countries to take advantage of economies of scale and agglomeration effects.

The sequence of booms and busts is a recurring theme in South American economic history. Bértola and Ocampo (2012) have identified several short-lived episodes of prosperity followed by bouts of depressions that have taken place across the South American countries since the early nineteenth century. They argue that this "truncated" growth regime is the main reason behind the failure to achieve income convergence with the rich countries. As Chapter 3 argued, the up-and-down swing in the aggregate is connected to the dependence on natural resources and the volatility in terms of trade, which have thwarted a sustainable path of industrialization despite the massive state-led push for development in the post World War II decades. The sequence of booms and busts is, however, not just a South American challenge. Research has indicated that long-run growth performance of a country is conditional on institutions designed to cushion the economy from recurrent and protracted setbacks (Cuberes & Jerzmanowski, 2009; Easterly et al., 1993). The key to success is to avoid long-term downswings. Our study of Brazilian manufacturing links to this argument. It is better to grow slowly but sustainably than to go through booms and busts.

In sum, South America did not achieve the same degree of industrialization as Scandinavia throughout the twentieth century whether we consider manufacturing share in GDP or the share of technology-intensive manufacturing industries. South America never achieved the standard to compete internationally for exports of manufacturing products. As a result, it stuck to an export basket devoid of manufacturing products but burdened with natural-resource intensive products, despite the massive, state-led effort for industrialization.

3 Inequality

Inequality as a factor affecting economic performance has taken central stage in the previous discussions of divergence between South America and Scandinavia. As Chapter 2 showed, income distribution and inequality featured in that discussion as key concepts connecting learning, technological innovation, and distribution of social capabilities with the extent of structural change and industrialization. This interest in the role of inequality for divergence likely follows from the glaring contrasts in income and wealth distributions between the two regions in the later twentieth century. While Scandinavia has excelled in its attempts to even out income differentials, South America has failed to reduce inequality significantly. Brazil, in particular, is often depicted as the epitome of unfair distribution of incomes and wealth. Sweden, in contrast, is often epitomized as the paragon of equality but has in fact now been overtaken by the other Scandinavian countries, all of which boast lower Gini coefficients. But the recent surge in historical inequality studies has cautioned us against projecting recent levels of inequality backwards. The available evidence stretching across the entire twentieth century indicates that the level of inequality has been subject to large variations, so we have led astray if we assume that the relative magnitudes of today also applied historically. This insight should focus our efforts on assessing inequality levels for Scandinavia and South America for the latter half of the nineteenth century. This is a daunting task provided the scarcity of information on interpersonal incomes for South America but doing so will make it possible to evaluate the mechanisms of inequality that shaped the different trajectories of the two regions.

This volume has presented some ways to fill in the gaps in our knowledge of inequality. Chapter 8 investigated past levels of inequality for Sweden and Brazil. Somewhat surprisingly, perhaps, this investigation indicated that Brazil was not much more unequal than Sweden by the early twentieth century. If we take this indication at face value, an obvious conclusion is that Sweden was much more unequal then, but joined the great levelling of the twentieth century along with other developed countries. Brazil, however, missed out on the great levelling. A caveat applies to the role of slaves. Because of the massive impact of slavery on Brazilian society, it is difficult to compare the levels of inequality in the two countries. Slavery also makes it hazardous to extrapolate the experience of Brazil to the rest of South America. These challenges should not make us wary of further attempts to compare inequality levels. A task for future research is to nail down the extent to which slaves toiling in the regular labour markets could keep their earnings to themselves.

The role of slaves also has a bearing on the divergence in real wages between Sweden and Brazil, which was an additional topic of Chapter 8. The divergence in real wages between Brazil and Sweden started in the 1880s, as did the divergence in GDP per capita between the two. After abolition in 1888, former slaves began to seek employment in the regular labour markets. At the same time, Europeans poured into Brazil. It is tempting to view this twin supply shock of abolition and immigration as the sole determinant of Brazilian real wage stagnation before the 1930s. Nevertheless, it is productivity that determines the long-term trajectory of real wages. If output per worker increases steadily, which is the factor propelling growth in the aggregate, real wages will also increase. It might happen that, intermittently, real wages do not follow the same trajectory as output per worker, which means that workers do not share equally in the rise of incomes split between labour and capital. As a result of such an intermittent pause, we will observe an emerging gap between productivity and real wages. Labour supply, though, does not suffice to explain productivity. Technological change, broadly defined, is the lever of productivity. A country that does not manage to raise productivity consistently will not enjoy the benefits of increasing incomes shared by labour and capital in often rather fixed proportions. The failure to achieve modern economic growth is thus the most important explanation for the stagnation of real wages in Brazil before the 1930s.

A common thread in the literature on land holdings in settler societies is that inequality impeded development. In fact, most of the discussion of inequality in South America have focussed on wealth, and in particular unequal distribution of land holdings, which was a legacy of the colonial past. Inequality played an important part in Senghaas' (1985) comparison of Denmark and Uruguay. He argued that the more egalitarian land holding system in Denmark explained to some extent the superior development of that country relative to Uruguay. Inequality has also played an important role in the neo-institutional literature on Latin American backwardness. According to Engerman and Sokoloff (1997), natural resource endowments determined the level of inequality and this in turn influenced the outcome of several other economic variables. A somewhat different idea was presented by Acemoglu et al. (2005) according to which colonial powers implemented extractive institutions that fuelled income inequality.

But the level of inequality also affected political institutions by effectively deciding who could wield power and configure economic institutions in their own interests.

Chapter 7, which detailed the configuration of land holdings and distribution of incomes, strengthened Senghaas' (1985) argument. It showed that the distribution was more skewed in Uruguay than in Denmark and New Zealand. In Uruguay, the rewards from exports were concentrated in the hands of a few wealthy property owners, which hindered broad-based participation in the markets for agricultural produce. In Denmark, on the other hand, agricultural modernization grew out of a viable and well-established family unit; and in New Zealand, the agricultural sector hosted a broad base of small and medium-sized producers. These differences in landholding patterns were also visible in the functional distribution of income across the three countries: in Uruguay, the land rent received by the landowners represented on average 50% of agricultural GDP during the 1870–1930 period; in New Zealand, about 40%; and in Denmark, about 19%. Using wage-rental ratios, Chapter 3 illustrated that the globalization forces of the late nineteenth century made South America more unequal and Scandinavia more equal. This result is in line with the literature on late nineteenth-century globalization (O'Rourke & Williamson, 1999). Part of this pattern could however be explained by the initial level of land prices used as a proxy for land rents. The wage to land prices ratio indicates the relative movement between two indices, so the actual levels from which each of the indices depart will have an impact on the rate of change of the ratio. The abundance of fertile land relative to labour could have made land prices lower in South America than in Scandinavia. Future research should attempt to establish the real price of land across the two regions.

Politics seem to have played an important part in the levelling of incomes and wealth in the developed countries during the twentieth century. The previous research on the politics of redistribution argued that the introduction of universal suffrage was instrumental in the shift towards the politics of redistribution. The great levelling did not take place spontaneously, instead it was the deliberate outcome of tax rises and increased social spending associated with the welfare state. These strategies of equality, quite paradoxically, were often implemented in countries that already had a relatively even distribution of incomes; as Lindert (2004, p: 15) once concluded, "redistribution from rich to poor is at least present when and where it seems most needed". The politics of redistribution does not require democracy, though, which Chapter 9 showed by juxtaposing the trajectories of Brazil and Sweden. In a South American context, Brazil implemented ambitious welfare state reforms despite switching back and forth from democratic rule to military dictatorship. These reforms have not aimed at reducing inequality by enhancing the progressiveness of the tax system or spending disproportionately much on the poor. Typically, the reforms have given rulers political credibility by distributing patronage at the regional and local levels. In Sweden, democracy seems to have brought some reduction in inequality, if also aided by labour market developments during the interwar years and increased wartime taxation. The actual welfare state in Sweden did not come into being until the 1950s, which was well over 30 years after universal suffrage was put into practice for the first time in the election of 1921.

In contrast to Brazil, Argentina and Uruguay enjoyed a relatively equal income distribution in a South American context in the early twentieth century. There are several possible explanations for this relative equality: early democratization, as universal male suffrage existed in each country from 1914 and 1916, respectively; successful export-led growth; and from the 1930s, redistribution policies implemented during the state-led industrialization period. Nevertheless, the improvement in income distribution depended on incomes from natural resource exports. From the 1970s onwards, declining terms of trade and sluggish growth rates triggered an increase in inequality in both countries. The experience of the River Plate region shows that even though policies in favour of redistribution play important roles, sustainable inequality reductions are conditioned on development strategies allowing productivity improvements to be spread evenly across all sectors of the economy. Uncovering the social and political mechanisms responsible for the divergence in inequality between South America and Scandinavia requires further studies like that of Chapter 9, uncovering differences in the institutional and political environments as well as the trajectories of growth and structural transformations across the two regions.

References

Abramovitz, M. (1986). Catching up, forging ahead, and falling behind. *Journal of Economic History, 46*(2), 385–406. https://doi.org/10.1017/S0022050700046209

Acemoglu, D., Johnson, S., & Robinson, J. A. (2005). Institutions as a fundamental cause of long-run growth. In P. Aghion & S. N. Durlauf (Eds.), *Handbook of economic growth* (Vol. 1A, pp. 385–472). Elsevier. https://doi.org/10.1016/S1574-0684(05)01006-3

Baumol, W. (1986). Productivity growth, convergence and welfare: What the long-run data show. *American Economic Review, 76*(5), 1072–1085.

Baumol, W., & Wolff, E. N. (1988). Productivity growth, convergence and welfare: Reply. *American Economic Review, 78*, 1155–1159.

Bértola, L., & Ocampo, J. A. (2012). *The economic development of Latin America since independence.* Oxford University Press. https://doi.org/10.1093/acprof:oso/9780199662135.001.0001

Blomström, M., & Meller, P. (1991). *Diverging paths: Comparing a century of Scandinavian and Latin American economic development.* Inter-American Development Bank.

Bohlin, J. (2005). Tariff protection in Sweden 1885–1913. *Scandinavian Economic History Review, 53*(2), 7–29.

Chang, H.-J. (2003). *Kicking away the ladder: Development strategy in historical perspective.* Anthem Press.

Cuberes, D., & Jerzmanowski, M. (2009). Democracy, diversification and growth reversals. *Economic Journal, 119*(540), 1270–1302. https://doi.org/10.1111/j.1468-0297.2009.02287.x

Easterly, W., Kremer, M., Pritchett, L., & Summers, L. H. (1993). Good policy or good luck: Country growth performance and temporary shocks. *Journal of Monetary Economics, 32*(3), 459–483. https://doi.org/10.1016/0304-3932(93)90026-C

Engerman, S. L., & Sokoloff, K. L. (1997). Factor endowments, institutions, and differential paths of growth among New World Economies: A view from economic historians of the United States. In S. Haber (Ed.), *How Latin America fell behind* (pp. 260–304). Stanford University Press.

Gerschenkron, A. (1962). *Economic backwardness in historical perspective.* Belknap Press.

Goldin, C., & Katz, L. F. (1998). The origins of technology-skill complementarity. *Quarterly Journal of Economics, 113*(3), 693–732. https://doi.org/10.1162/003355398555720

Johnson, P., & Papageorgiou, C. (2020). What remains of cross-country convergence? *Journal of Economic Literature, 58*(1), 129–175. https://doi.org/10.1257/jel.20181207

Jörberg, L. (1973). The industrial revolution in the Nordic Countries. 1700–1914In C. M. Cipolla (Ed.), *The Fontana economic history of Europe* (Vol. 4, pp. 375–479). Collins/Fontana.

Katz, J., & Kosacoff, B. (2000). Technological learning, institution building and the microeconomics of import substitution. Industrialization and the state in Latin America: The postwar yearsIn E. Cardenas, J. A. Ocampo, & R. Thorp (Eds.), *An economic history of Twentieth-Century Latin America* (Vol. 3, pp. 36–57). Palgrave.

Lindert, P. (2004). *Growing public: Social spending and economic growth since the eighteenth century* (Vol. 1). Cambridge University Press. https://doi.org/10.1017/CBO9780511510717

Lingarde, S., & Tylecote, A. (1999). Resource-rich countries' success and failure in technological ascent, 1870–1970: The Nordic countries versus Argentina, Uruguay and Brazil. *Journal of European Economic History, 28*, 77–112.

Maloney, W. F. (2007). Missed opportunities: Innovation and resource-based growth in Latin America. In D. Lederman and W. F. Maloney (Eds.), *Natural resources: Neither curse nor destiny*. Stanford University Press and the World Bank.

O'Rourke, K. H., & Williamson, J. G. (1999). *Globalization and history: The evolution of a Nineteenth-Century Atlantic Economy*. MIT Press. https://doi.org/10.7551/mitpress/3310.001.0001

Pomeranz, K. (2000). *The great divergence: China, Europe, and the making of the modern world economy*. Princeton University Press.

Rodrik, D. (2013). Unconditional convergence in manufacturing. *Quarterly Journal of Economics, 128*(1), 165–204. https://doi.org/10.1093/qje/qjs047

Senghaas, D. (1985). *The European experience: A historical critique of development theory*. Berg.

Thirlwall, A. P. (2011). Balance of payments constrained growth models: History and overview. *PSL Quarterly Review, 64*(259), 307–351. https://doi.org/10.1057/9781137023957 2

Topik, S. (1987). *The political economy of the Brazilian state, 1889–1930*. University of Texas Press.

Watkins, M. H. (1963). A staple theory of economic growth. *Canadian Journal of Economics and Political Science/revue Canadienne D'economique Et De Science Politique, 26*(2), 141–158.

Index

J. Álvarez and S. Prado (eds.), *Scandinavia and South America—A Tale of Two Capitalisms*, Palgrave Studies in Economic History,
https://doi.org/10.1007/978-3-031-09198-8

P

R

S

FSC
www.fsc.org
MIX
Papier | Fördert
gute Waldnutzung
FSC® C083411

Kolibri 360 GmbH
Ferdinand-Jühlke-Straße 7
99095 Erfurt, Deutschland
produktsicherheit@kolibri360.de